Symmetry in Mathematical Analysis and Functional Analysis II

Symmetry in Mathematical Analysis and Functional Analysis II

Editors

Savin Treanta
Octav Olteanu

Basel • Beijing • Wuhan • Barcelona • Belgrade • Novi Sad • Cluj • Manchester

Editors

Savin Treanta
Faculty of Applied Sciences
National University of
Science and Technology
Politehnica Bucharest
Bucharest
Romania

Octav Olteanu
Mathematics-Informatics
National University of
Science and Technology
Politehnica Bucharest
Bucharest
Romania

Editorial Office
MDPI
St. Alban-Anlage 66
4052 Basel, Switzerland

This is a reprint of articles from the Special Issue published online in the open access journal *Symmetry* (ISSN 2073-8994) (available at: www.mdpi.com/journal/symmetry/special_issues/61KHPV741X).

For citation purposes, cite each article independently as indicated on the article page online and as indicated below:

Lastname, A.A.; Lastname, B.B. Article Title. *Journal Name* **Year**, *Volume Number*, Page Range.

ISBN 978-3-7258-0618-8 (Hbk)
ISBN 978-3-7258-0617-1 (PDF)
doi.org/10.3390/books978-3-7258-0617-1

© 2024 by the authors. Articles in this book are Open Access and distributed under the Creative Commons Attribution (CC BY) license. The book as a whole is distributed by MDPI under the terms and conditions of the Creative Commons Attribution-NonCommercial-NoDerivs (CC BY-NC-ND) license.

Contents

Preface vii

Muhammad Ghaffar Khan, Bilal Khan, Jianhua Gong, Fairouz Tchier and Ferdous M. O. Tawfiq
Applications of First-Order Differential Subordination for Subfamilies of Analytic Functions Related to Symmetric Image Domains
Reprinted from: *Symmetry* 2023, 15, 2004, doi:10.3390/sym15112004 1

Fahd Masood, Osama Moaaz, Ghada AlNemer and Hamdy El-Metwally
New Monotonic Properties for Solutions of a Class of Functional Differential Equations and Their Applications
Reprinted from: *Symmetry* 2023, 15, 1956, doi:10.3390/sym15101956 15

Bingxian Wang, Honghui Yin and Bo Du
On Asymptotic Properties of Stochastic Neutral-Type Inertial Neural Networks with Mixed Delays
Reprinted from: *Symmetry* 2023, 15, 1746, doi:10.3390/sym15091746 41

Luca Di Persio and Matteo Garbelli
From Optimal Control to Mean Field Optimal Transport via Stochastic Neural Networks
Reprinted from: *Symmetry* 2023, 15, 1724, doi:10.3390/sym15091724 52

Famei Zheng, Xiaojing Wang, Xiwang Cheng and Bo Du
Infinitely Many Positive Solutions to Nonlinear First-Order Iterative Systems of Singular BVPs on Time Scales
Reprinted from: *Symmetry* 2023, 15, 1524, doi:10.3390/sym15081524 64

Octav Olteanu
Symmetry and Asymmetry in Moment, Functional Equations, and Optimization Problems
Reprinted from: *Symmetry* 2023, 15, 1471, doi:10.3390/sym15071471 73

Tareq Hamadneh, Mohammad W. Alomari, Isra Al-Shbeil, Hala Alaqad, Raed Hatamleh, Ahmed Salem Heilat and Abdallah Al-Husban
Refinements of the Euclidean Operator Radius and Davis–Wielandt Radius-Type Inequalities
Reprinted from: *Symmetry* 2023, 15, 1061, doi:10.3390/sym15051061 92

Vuk Stojiljković, Rajagopalan Ramaswamy, Ola A. Ashour Abdelnaby and Stojan Radenović
Some Refinements of the Tensorial Inequalities in Hilbert Spaces
Reprinted from: *Symmetry* 2023, 15, 925, doi:10.3390/sym15040925 113

Rasool Shah, Yousuf Alkhezi and Khaled Alhamad
An Analytical Approach to Solve the Fractional Benney Equation Using the q-Homotopy Analysis Transform Method
Reprinted from: *Symmetry* 2023, 15, 669, doi:10.3390/sym15030669 127

Weiwei Kong, Tianmao Cai, Yugong Luo, Xuetong Wang and Fachao Jiang
Cooperative Multi-Objective Control of Heterogeneous Vehicle Platoons on Highway with Varying Slopes
Reprinted from: *Symmetry* 2022, 14, 2647, doi:10.3390/sym14122647 138

Preface

It is well known that the roles and consequences of symmetry in mathematics and related sciences are very important. In this reprint, we aim to establish some theoretical results (and their applications) in the fields of mathematical and functional analyses, in which the concept of symmetry plays an essential role. In particular, we aim to investigate various problems in areas such as optimization problems, polynomial approximation on unbounded subsets, moment problems, variational inequalities, evolutionary problems, dynamical systems, generalized convexity, partial differential equations, and special spaces of self-adjoint operators. Some of these areas of research are strongly intercorrelated.

Savin Treanta and Octav Olteanu
Editors

Applications of First-Order Differential Subordination for Subfamilies of Analytic Functions Related to Symmetric Image Domains

Muhammad Ghaffar Khan [1], Bilal Khan [2], Jianhua Gong [3,*], Fairouz Tchier [4] and Ferdous M. O. Tawfiq [4]

[1] Institute of Numerical Sciences, Kohat University of Science and Technology, Kohat 26000, Pakistan; ghaffarkhan020@gmail.com
[2] School of Mathematical Sciences, East China Normal University, Shanghai 200241, China; bilalmaths789@gmail.com
[3] Department of Mathematical Sciences, United Arab Emirates University, Al Ain 15551, United Arab Emirates
[4] Mathematics Department, College of Science, King Saud University, Riyadh 22452, Saudi Arabia; ftchier@ksu.edu.sa (F.T.); ftoufic@ksu.edu.sa (F.M.O.T.)
* Correspondence: j.gong@uaeu.ac.ae

Abstract: This paper presents a geometric approach to the problems in differential subordination theory. The necessary conditions for a function to be in various subfamilies of the class of starlike functions and the class of Carathéodory functions are studied, respectively. Further, several consequences of the findings are derived.

Keywords: analytic function; differential subordination; starlike function; symmetric image domain

MSC: Primary 30C45; 30C50; 30C80; Secondary 11B65; 47B38

1. Introduction

Let $\mathbb{C}$ be the complex plane and $\mathbb{E} = \{z : z \in \mathbb{C} \text{ and } |z| < 1\}$ be the open unit disk. Let $\mathcal{A}$ represent the collection of all analytic functions, u, defined on $\mathbb{E}$ and fulfill the criteria $u(0) = 0$ and $u'(0) - 1 = 0$. Thus, each function, u, in class $\mathcal{A}$ has the following Taylor series expansion:

$$u(z) = z + \sum_{n=2}^{\infty} a_n z^n, \ z \in \mathbb{E}. \tag{1}$$

The various subclasses of $\mathcal{A}$ have been studied intensively, for instance, Ref. [1]. Further, let $\mathcal{S}$ denote a subfamily of $\mathcal{A}$, whose members are univalent in unit disk $\mathbb{E}$. Let $\mathcal{S}^*(\alpha)$ and $\mathcal{C}(\alpha)$ be the subfamilies of $\mathcal{A}$ for $0 \leq \alpha < 1$, where $\mathcal{S}^*(\alpha)$ represents starlike functions of order α, and $\mathcal{C}(\alpha)$ represents convex functions of order α. Analytically, these families are represented by

$$\mathcal{S}^*(\alpha) = \left\{ u \in \mathcal{A} : \ \text{Re}\left(\frac{zu'(z)}{u(z)}\right) > \alpha \right\},$$

and

$$\mathcal{C}(\alpha) = \left\{ u \in \mathcal{A} : \ \text{Re}\left(\frac{(zu'(z))'}{u(z)}\right) > \alpha \right\}.$$

In particular, if $\alpha = 0$, then we can observe that $\mathcal{S}^*(0) = \mathcal{S}^*$ and $\mathcal{C}(0) = \mathcal{C}$ are well-known families of starlike functions and convex functions, respectively.

Moreover, for two functions, $u_1, u_2 \in \mathcal{A}$, the expression $u_1 \prec u_2$ denotes that the function u_1 is subordinate to the function u_2 if there exists an analytic function, μ, with the following properties:

$$|\mu(z)| \leq |z| \ \text{ and } \ \mu(0) = 0$$

such that
$$u_1(z) = u_2(\mu(z)) \quad \forall z \in \mathbb{E}.$$

In addition, if $u_2 \in \mathcal{S}$, then the aforementioned conditions can be expressed as follows:
$$u_1 \prec u_2 \text{ if and only if } u_1(0) = u_2(0) \text{ and } u_1(\mathbb{E}) \subset u_2(\mathbb{E}).$$

In 1992, Ma and Minda defined [2]
$$\mathcal{S}^*(\phi) = \left\{ u \in \mathcal{A} : \frac{zu'(z)}{u(z)} \prec \phi(z) \right\} \quad (2)$$

with $\text{Re}(\phi) > 0$ in $\mathbb{E}$. Additionally, the function ϕ maps $\mathbb{E}$ onto a star-shaped region, and the image domain is symmetric about the real axis and starlike with respect to $\phi(0) = 1$, with $\phi'(0) > 0$. The set $\mathcal{S}^*(\phi)$ generalizes several subfamilies of the function class $\mathcal{A}$. Here are seven examples.

1. The class $\mathcal{S}^*[L, M]$ of Janowski starlike functions (see [3,4]) can be viewed by
$$\mathcal{S}^*[L, M] = \mathcal{S}^*\left(\frac{1+Lz}{1+Mz}\right),$$
where $-1 \leq M < L \leq 1$ and $\phi(z) = \frac{1+Lz}{1+Mz}$.

2. For $\phi(z) = \sqrt{1+z}$, the family $\mathcal{S}^*_{\mathcal{L}} = \mathcal{S}^*(\sqrt{1+z})$ was established by Sokól et al. [5].

3. For $\phi(z) = 1 + \sin(z)$, the class $\mathcal{S}^*_{\sin} = \mathcal{S}^*(1 + \sin(z))$ was introduced and studied by Cho et al. [6].

4. Considering the function $\phi(z) = 1 + z - \frac{1}{3}z^3$, we get the family $\mathcal{S}^*_{nep} = \mathcal{S}^*\left(1 + z - \frac{1}{3}z^3\right)$, which was introduced and investigated recently by Wani and Swaminathan [7]. The image of $\mathbb{E}$ under the function $\phi(z) = 1 + z - \frac{1}{3}z^3$ is bounded by a nephroid-shaped region.

5. For $\phi(z) = e^z$, the class $\mathcal{S}^*_e = \mathcal{S}^*(e^z)$ has been defined and studied by Mendiratta [8].

6. Taking $\phi(z) = z + \sqrt{1+z^2}$, we then get the family $\mathcal{S}^*_{cres} = \mathcal{S}^*\left(z + \sqrt{1+z^2}\right)$, which maps $\mathbb{E}$ to a crescent-shaped region and was given by Raina et al. [9].

7. The function $\phi(z) = 1 + \sinh^{-1} z$ gives the following class introduced by Kumar and Arora [10]:
$$\mathcal{S}^*_\rho = \mathcal{S}^*\left(1 + \sinh^{-1} z\right).$$

The natural extensions of differential inequalities on the real line into the complex plane are known as differential subordinations. Derivatives are an essential tool for understanding the properties of real-valued functions. Differential implications can be found in the complex plane when a function is described using differential subordinations. For example, Noshiro and Warschawski provided the univalency criteria for the analytical function theorem, which showed such differential implications. The range of the combination of the function's derivatives is frequently used to determine the properties of a function.

Let h be an analytic function defined on $\mathbb{E}$, with $h(0) = 1$. Recently, Ali et al. [11] have investigated some differential subordination results. More specifically, they studied the following differential subordinations for some particular ranges of α.
$$1 + \frac{\alpha z h'(z)}{h^n(z)} \prec \sqrt{1+z},\ n = 0, 1, 2$$

which can ensure that
$$h(z) \prec \sqrt{1+z}.$$

Similar type results have been investigated by various authors. For example, the articles contributed by Kumar et al. [12,13], Paprocki et al. [14], Raza et al. [15] and Shi et al. [16].

In this paper, we consider the following two subfamilies of analytic functions.

$$\mathcal{S}_{car}^* = \left\{ u \in \mathcal{A} : \frac{zu'(z)}{u(z)} \prec 1 + z + \frac{z^2}{2} \right\} \quad z \in \mathbb{E}, \tag{3}$$

and

$$\mathcal{S}_{3\mathcal{L}}^* = \left\{ u \in \mathcal{A} : \frac{zu'(z)}{u(z)} \prec 1 + \frac{4z}{5} + \frac{z^4}{5} \right\} \quad z \in \mathbb{E}, \tag{4}$$

where the family defined in (3) was introduced by Kumar and Kamaljeet [17], and the family defined in (4) was introduced by Gandhi [18].

The lemma below underlies our considerations in the following sections.

Lemma 1. [19] *For the univalent function* $q : \mathbb{E} \to \mathbb{C}$ *and the analytic functions* λ *and* v *in* $q(\mathbb{E}) \subseteq \mathbb{E}$ *with* $\lambda(z) \neq 0$ *for* $z \in q(\mathbb{E})$, *define*

$$\Theta(z) = zq'(z)\lambda(q(z)) \text{ and } g(z) = v(q(z)) + \Theta(z), z \in \mathbb{E}.$$

Suppose that
1. $g(z)$ *is convex, or* $\Theta(z)$ *is starlike.*
2. $\operatorname{Re}\left(\frac{zg'(z)}{\Theta(z)}\right) > 0, z \in \mathbb{E}.$

If $h \in \mathcal{S}$ *with* $h(0) = q(0), h(\mathbb{E}) \subset \mathbb{E}$, *and*

$$v(h(z) + zh'(z)\lambda(h(z))) \prec v(q(z) + zq'(z)\lambda(q(z))),$$

then $h \prec q$, *and* q *is the best dominant.*

2. Subordination Results for the Class $\mathcal{S}_{car}^*$

Theorem 1. *Let* h *be an analytic function with* $h(0) = 1$ *in the unit disc* $\mathbb{E}$ *and satisfy*

$$1 + \beta z h'(z) \prec 1 + z + \frac{z^2}{2} = \phi_{car}(z), \, z \in \mathbb{E}.$$

Then, we have the following.
1. $h \in \mathcal{S}_\mathcal{L}^*$, *for* $\beta \geq \frac{5}{4(\sqrt{2}-1)}$.
2. $h \in \mathcal{S}_{\sin}^*$, *for* $\beta \geq \frac{5}{4\sin(1)}$.
3. $h \in \mathcal{S}_{nep}^*$, *for* $\beta \geq \frac{15}{8}$.
4. $h \in \mathcal{S}_{\exp}^*$, *for* $\beta \geq \frac{3}{4(1-e^{-1})}$.
5. $h \in \mathcal{S}_{cres}^*$, *for* $\beta \geq \frac{3}{4(2-\sqrt{2})}$.
6. $h \in \mathcal{S}_\rho^*$, *for* $\beta \geq \frac{5}{4\sinh^{-1}(1)}$.

Proof. Consider the analytic function

$$a_\beta(z) = 1 + \frac{4z + z^2}{4\beta},$$

which is a solution of the differential subordination equation

$$1 + \beta z h'(z) \prec 1 + z + \frac{z^2}{2}.$$

Let us take $z \in \mathbb{E}$, $q(z) = a_\beta(z)$, $v(z) = 1$, and $\lambda(z) = \beta$ in Lemma 1. Then, the function $\Theta : \mathbb{E} \to \mathbb{C}$ is given by $\Theta(z) = za'_\beta(z)\lambda(a_\beta(z)) = \phi_{car}(z) - 1$, so $h(z) = 1 + \Theta(z) = \phi_{car}(z)$. Since the function $\phi_{car}(z)$ maps $\mathbb{E}$ into a starlike region (with respect to 1), the function h is starlike. Further, h satisfies $\text{Re}\left(\frac{zh'(z)}{\Theta(z)}\right) > 0$. As an application to Lemma 1, we possess the following property:

$$1 + \beta z h'(z) \prec 1 + \beta z a'_\beta(z) \Rightarrow h(z) \prec a_\beta(z).$$

Each subordination of Theorem 1, is similar to

$$h(z) \prec \omega(z),$$

for each subordinate function in the theorem, which is valid if $a_\beta(z) \prec \omega(z)$, $z \in \mathbb{E}$. Then,

$$\omega(-1) \prec a_\beta(-1) \prec a_\beta(1) \prec \omega(1). \tag{5}$$

This yields the necessary condition for which $h(z) \prec \omega(z)$, $z \in \mathbb{E}$. Looking at the geometry of each of these functions $\omega(z)$, it is noticed that the condition is also sufficient.

1. Let $\omega(z) = \sqrt{1+z}$, then

$$a_\beta(-1) \geq 0 \quad \text{and} \quad a_\beta(1) \leq \sqrt{2},$$

and these inequalities can be reduced to $\beta \geq \frac{3}{4} = \beta_1$ and $\beta \geq \frac{5}{4(\sqrt{2}-1)} = \beta_2$. We note that $\beta_1 - \beta_2 < 0$, and hence the following subordination holds.

$$a_\beta(z) \prec \sqrt{1+z}, \quad \text{if } \beta \geq \max\{\beta_1, \beta_2\} = \beta_2.$$

2. Let $\omega(z) = 1 + \sin(z)$, then by (5),

$$a_\beta(-1) \geq 1 - \sin(1), \quad \text{whenever } \beta \geq \frac{3}{4\sin(1)} = \beta_1.$$

$$a_\beta(1) \leq 1 + \sin(1), \quad \text{whenever } \beta \geq \frac{5}{4\sin(1)} = \beta_2.$$

Notice that $\beta_1 - \beta_2 < 0$. Thus, the following subordination holds.

$$a_\beta(z) \prec 1 + \sin(z), \quad \text{if } \beta \geq \max\{\beta_1, \beta_2\} = \beta_2.$$

3. Let $\omega(z) = 1 + z - \frac{z^3}{3}$, then the inequality $a_\beta(-1) \geq \frac{1}{3}$ gives $\beta \geq \beta_1$ for $\beta_1 = \frac{9}{8}$, and $a_\beta(1) \leq \frac{5}{3}$ gives $\beta \geq \beta_2$ for $\beta_2 = \frac{15}{8}$. Moreover, since $\beta_1 - \beta_2 < 0$,

$$a_\beta(z) \prec 1 + z - \frac{z^3}{3}, \quad \text{if } \beta \geq \max\{\beta_1, \beta_2\} = \beta_2.$$

4. Let $\omega(z) = e^z$, then

$$a_\beta(-1) \geq e^{-1} \quad \text{and} \quad a_\beta(1) \leq e,$$

and these two inequalities yield $\beta \geq \frac{3}{4(1-e^{-1})} = \beta_1$ and $\beta \geq \frac{5}{4(e-1)} = \beta_2$. Thus,

$$a_\beta(z) \prec \sqrt{1+z}, \quad \text{if } \beta \geq \max\{\beta_1, \beta_2\} = \beta_1.$$

5. Let $\omega(z) = z + \sqrt{1+z^2}$, then by Equation (5), we have

$$a_\beta(-1) \geq -1 + \sqrt{2}, \quad \text{whenever } \beta \geq \frac{3}{4\left(2-\sqrt{2}\right)} = \beta_1.$$

$$a_\beta(1) \leq 1 + \sqrt{2}, \quad \text{whenever } \beta \geq \frac{5}{4\sqrt{2}} = \beta_2.$$

Therefore, the subordination $a_\beta(z) \prec z + \sqrt{1+z^2}$ holds if $\beta \geq \max\{\beta_1, \beta_2\} = \beta_1$.

6. Let $\omega(z) = 1 + \sinh^{-1}(z)$, then

$$a_\beta(-1) \geq 1 - \sinh^{-1}(1) \quad \text{and} \quad a_\beta(1) \leq 1 + \sinh^{-1}(1).$$

Thus, two inequalities above yield $\beta \geq \frac{3}{4\sinh^{-1}(1)} = \beta_1$ and $\beta \geq \frac{5}{4\sinh^{-1}(1)} = \beta_2$, and hence

$$a_\beta(z) \prec 1 + \sinh^{-1}(z), \quad \text{if } \beta \geq \max\{\beta_1, \beta_2\} = \beta_2.$$

□

Corollary 1. *Let $u \in \mathcal{A}$ that satisfies the following subordination:*

$$\frac{zu'(z)}{u(z)}\left(\frac{(zu'(z))'}{u'(z)} - \frac{zu'(z)}{u(z)}\right) \prec \frac{2z + z^2}{2\beta} = \phi_{car}(z), z \in \mathbb{E}.$$

Then, we have the following results.

1. $u \in \mathcal{S}^*_L$, for $\beta \geq \frac{5}{4(\sqrt{2}-1)} \approx 3.0178$.
2. $u \in \mathcal{S}^*_{\sin}$, for $\beta \geq \frac{5}{4\sin(1)} \approx 1.4855$.
3. $u \in \mathcal{S}^*_{nep}$, for $\beta \geq \frac{15}{8} \approx 1.875$.
4. $u \in \mathcal{S}^*_{\exp}$, for $\beta \geq \frac{3}{4(1-e^{-1})} \approx 1.1865$.
5. $u \in \mathcal{S}^*_{cres}$, for $\beta \geq \frac{3}{4(2-\sqrt{2})} \approx 1.2803$.
6. $u \in \mathcal{S}^*_\rho$, for $\beta \geq \frac{5}{4\sinh^{-1}(1)} \approx 1.4182$.

Theorem 2. *Let h be analytic with $h(0) = 1$ in unit disc $\mathbb{E}$ and assume that*

$$1 + \beta\frac{zh'(z)}{h(z)} \prec 1 + z + \frac{z^2}{2} = \phi_{car}(z), \ z \in \mathbb{E}.$$

Then, we have the following.

1. $h \in \mathcal{S}^*_L$, for $\beta \geq \frac{5}{4\ln(\sqrt{2})}$.
2. $h \in \mathcal{S}^*_{\sin}$, for $\beta \geq \frac{5}{4\ln(1+\sin(1))}$.
3. $h \in \mathcal{S}^*_{nep}$, for $\beta \geq \frac{5}{4\ln(\frac{5}{3})}$.
4. $h \in \mathcal{S}^*_{\exp}$, for $\beta \geq \frac{5}{4}$.
5. $h \in \mathcal{S}^*_{cres}$, for $\beta \geq \frac{5}{4\ln(1+\sqrt{2})}$.
6. $h \in \mathcal{S}^*_\rho$, for $\beta \geq \frac{5}{4\ln(1+\sinh^{-1}(1))}$.

Proof. Consider the analytic function $b_\beta : \mathbb{E} \to \mathbb{C}$, defined by

$$b_\beta(z) = \exp\left(\frac{4z+z^2}{4\beta}\right), \ z \in \mathbb{E}.$$

Then, b_β is a solution of the differential equation

$$1 + \beta\frac{zh'(z)}{h(z)} = 1 + z + \frac{z^2}{2} = \phi_{car}(z), \ z \in \mathbb{E}.$$

If we take $z \in \mathbb{E}$, $q(z) = b_\beta(z)$, $\nu(z) = 1$, and $\lambda(z) = \frac{\beta}{z}$ in Lemma 1, then the function $\Theta : \mathbb{E} \to \mathbb{C}$ is given by $\Theta(z) = zb'_\beta(z)\lambda(b_\beta(z)) = \phi_{car}(z) - 1$, so $h(z) = 1 + \Theta(z) = \phi_{car}(z)$.

Since the function $\phi_{car}(z)$ maps $\mathbb{E}$ into a starlike region (w.r.to 1), the function h is starlike. Further, h satisfies $\text{Re}\left(\frac{zh'(z)}{\Theta(z)}\right) > 0$. Applying this to Lemma 1, we possess that

$$1 + \beta\frac{zh'(z)}{h(z)} \prec 1 + \beta\frac{zb'_\beta(z)}{b_\beta(z)} \Rightarrow h(z) \prec b_\beta(z).$$

Each subordination of Theorem 1 is similar to

$$h(z) \prec \omega(z),$$

for each subordinate function in the theorem, which is valid if $b_\beta(z) \prec \omega(z), z \in \mathbb{E}$. Here, we use the same technique as in Theorem 1, omitting the rest of the proof. □

Corollary 2. *Let $u \in \mathcal{A}$ that satisfies the following subordination:*

$$\left(\frac{(zu'(z))'}{u'(z)} - \frac{zu'(z)}{u(z)}\right) \prec \frac{2z}{2\beta} + \frac{z^2}{2\beta}, \ z \in \mathbb{E}.$$

Then, we have

1. $u \in \mathcal{S}^*_L$, *for $\beta \geq \frac{5}{4\ln(\sqrt{2})} \approx 3.6067$.*
2. $u \in \mathcal{S}^*_{\sin}$, *for $\beta \geq \frac{5}{4\ln(1+\sin(1))} \approx 2.0473$.*
3. $u \in \mathcal{S}^*_{nep}$, *for $\beta \geq \frac{5}{4\ln(\frac{5}{3})} \approx 2.447$.*
4. $u \in \mathcal{S}^*_{\exp}$, *for $\beta \geq \frac{5}{4} \approx 1.25$.*
5. $u \in \mathcal{S}^*_{cres}$, *for $\beta \geq \frac{5}{4\ln(1+\sqrt{2})} \approx 1.4182$.*
6. $u \in \mathcal{S}^*_\rho$, *for $\beta \geq \frac{5}{4\ln(1+\sinh^{-1}(1))} \approx 1.9778$.*

Theorem 3. *Let h be an analytic function with $h(0) = 1$ in unit disc $\mathbb{E}$ and satisfy that*

$$1 + \beta\frac{zh'(z)}{h^2(z)} \prec 1 + z + \frac{z^2}{2} = \phi_{car}(z), \ z \in \mathbb{E}.$$

Then, the following results.

1. $h \in \mathcal{S}^*_L$, *for $\beta \geq \frac{5\sqrt{2}}{4(\sqrt{2}-1)}$.*
2. $h \in \mathcal{S}^*_{\sin}$, *for $\beta \geq \frac{5(1+\sin(1))}{4\sin(1)}$.*
3. $h \in \mathcal{S}^*_{nep}$, *for $\beta \geq \frac{25}{8}$.*
4. $h \in \mathcal{S}^*_{\exp}$, *for $\beta \geq \frac{5e}{4(e-1)}$.*
5. $h \in \mathcal{S}^*_{cres}$, *for $\beta \geq \frac{5(1+\sqrt{2})}{4\sqrt{2}}$.*
6. $h \in \mathcal{S}^*_\rho$, *for $\beta \geq \frac{5(1+\sinh^{-1}(1))}{4\sinh^{-1}(1)}$.*

Proof. Consider the function $c_\beta : \mathbb{E} \to \mathbb{C}$, defined by

$$c_\beta(z) = \left(1 - \frac{4z+z^2}{4\beta}\right)^{-1},$$

which is the solution of the differential equation:

$$1 + \beta\frac{zh'(z)}{h^2(z)} = 1 + z + \frac{z^2}{2} = \phi_{car}(z).$$

In Lemma 1, let $z \in \mathbb{E}$, $q(z) = c_\beta(z)$, $\nu(z) = 1$, and $\lambda(z) = \frac{\beta}{z^2}$. Then, the function $\Theta : \mathbb{E} \to \mathbb{C}$ is given by $\Theta(z) = z c_\beta'(z) \lambda(c_\beta(z)) = \phi_{car}(z) - 1$, so $h(z) = 1 + \Theta(z) = \phi_{car}(z)$. Since the function $\phi_{car}(z)$ maps $\mathbb{E}$ into a starlike region (w.r.to 1), the function h is starlike. Further, h satisfies $\text{Re}(zh'(z)/\Theta(z)) > 0$. Therefore, from Lemma 1, we possess that

$$1 + \beta \frac{zh'(z)}{h(z)} \prec 1 + \beta \frac{zc_\beta'(z)}{c_\beta(z)} \Rightarrow h(z) \prec c_\beta(z).$$

Each subordination of Theorem 2 is similar to

$$h(z) \prec \omega(z),$$

for each subordinate function in the theorem, which is valid if $s_\beta(z) \prec \omega(z), z \in \mathbb{E}$. Here, we use the same technique as we used in Theorem 1, so we omit the rest of the proof. □

Corollary 3. *Let $u \in \mathcal{A}$ that satisfies the following subordination:*

$$\left(\frac{zu'(z)}{u(z)}\right)^{-1}\left(\frac{(zu'(z))'}{u'(z)} - \frac{zu'(z)}{u(z)}\right) \prec \frac{2z}{2\beta} + \frac{z^2}{2\beta}, \; z \in \mathbb{E}.$$

Then, we have

1. $u \in \mathcal{S}_\mathcal{L}^*$, for $\beta \geq \frac{5\sqrt{2}}{4(\sqrt{2}-1)} \approx 4.2678$.
2. $u \in \mathcal{S}_{\sin}^*$, for $\beta \geq \frac{5(1+\sin(1))}{4\sin(1)} \approx 2.7355$.
3. $u \in \mathcal{S}_{nep}^*$, for $\beta \geq \frac{25}{8} \approx 3.125$.
4. $u \in \mathcal{S}_{\exp}^*$, for $\beta \geq \frac{5e}{4(e-1)} \approx 1.9775$.
5. $u \in \mathcal{S}_{cres}^*$, for $\beta \geq \frac{5(1+\sqrt{2})}{4\sqrt{2}} \approx 2.1339$.
6. $u \in \mathcal{S}_\rho^*$, for $\beta \geq \frac{5(1+\sinh^{-1}(1))}{4\sinh^{-1}(1)} \approx 2.6682$.

At the end of Section 2, as a geometric approach to the problems in differential subordination theory, the following figures in Figure 1 graphically represent the results in the section.

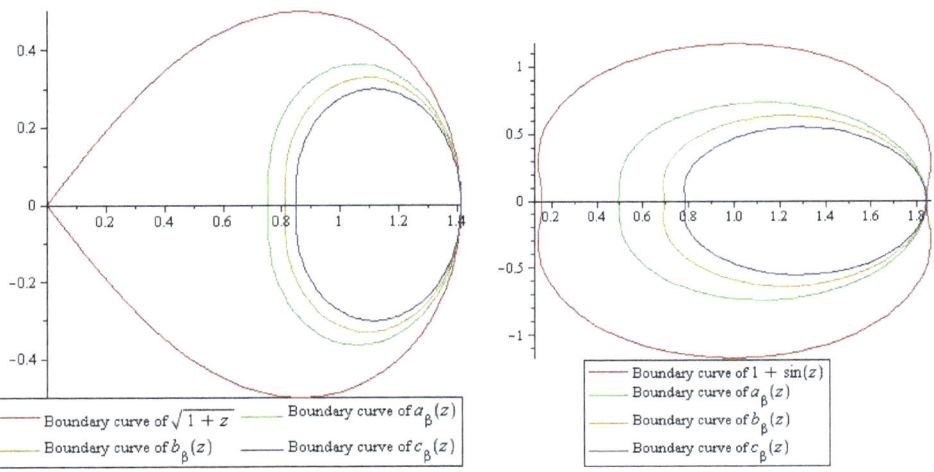

Figure 1. *Cont.*

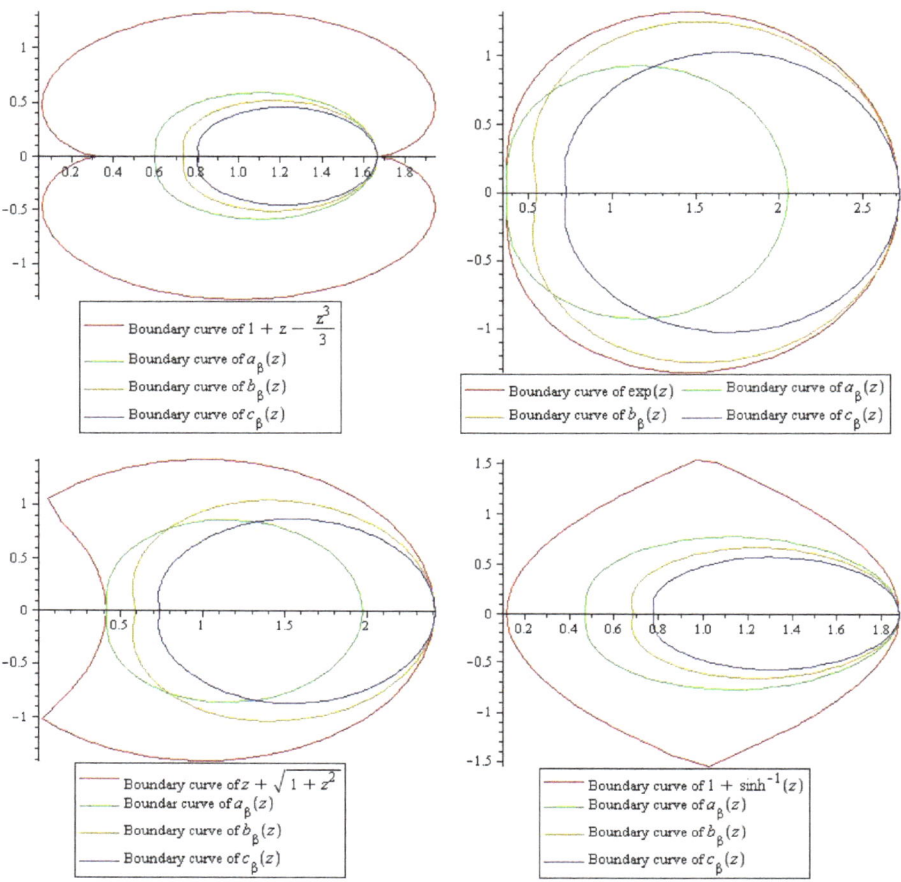

Figure 1. Graphical Representation of Results in Section 2.

3. Subordination Results for Class $\mathcal{S}_{3\mathcal{L}}^*$

Theorem 4. *Let h be an analytic function with $h(0) = 1$ in unit disc $\mathbb{E}$ and satisfy that*

$$1 + \beta z h'(z) \prec 1 + \frac{4z}{5} + \frac{z^4}{5}, \; z \in \mathbb{E}.$$

Then, we have the following.

1. $h \in \mathcal{S}_{\mathcal{L}}^*$, for $\beta \geq \frac{17}{20(\sqrt{2}-1)}$.
2. $h \in \mathcal{S}_{\sin}^*$, for $\beta \geq \frac{17}{20\sin(1)}$.
3. $h \in \mathcal{S}_{nep}^*$, for $\beta \geq \frac{51}{40}$.
4. $h \in \mathcal{S}_{\exp}^*$, for $\beta \geq \frac{15}{20(1-e^{-1})}$.
5. $h \in \mathcal{S}_{cres}^*$, for $\beta \geq \frac{15}{20(2-\sqrt{2})}$.
6. $h \in \mathcal{S}_{\rho}^*$, for $\beta \geq \frac{17}{20\sinh^{-1}(1)}$.

Proof. Consider the differential equation

$$1 + \beta z h'(z) = 1 + \frac{4z}{5} + \frac{z^4}{5}. \tag{6}$$

It is easy to verify that the analytic function $t_\beta : \mathbb{E} \to \mathbb{C}$, defined by

$$t_\beta(z) = 1 + \frac{16z + z^4}{20\beta},$$

is the solution of Equation (6). In Lemma 1, let $z \in \mathbb{E}$, $q(z) = t_\beta(z)$, $\nu(z) = 1$, and $\lambda(z) = \beta$. Then, the function $\Theta : \mathbb{E} \to \mathbb{C}$ is given by $\Theta(z) = z t'_\beta(z) \lambda(t_\beta(z)) = \phi_{car}(z) - 1$, so $h(z) = 1 + \Theta(z) = \phi_{car}(z)$. Since the function $\phi_{car}(z)$ maps $\mathbb{E}$ into a starlike region (w.r.to 1), the function h is starlike. Further, h satisfies $\text{Re}(zh'(z)/\Theta(z)) > 0$. It follows from Lemma 1 that

$$1 + \beta z h'(z) \prec 1 + \beta z t'_\beta(z) \Rightarrow h(z) \prec t_\beta(z).$$

Each subordination of Theorem 1 is similar to

$$h(z) \prec \omega(z),$$

for each subordinate function in the theorem, which is valid if $t_\beta(z) \prec \omega(z)$, $z \in \mathbb{E}$. Then

$$\omega(-1) \prec t_\beta(-1) \prec t_\beta(1) \prec \omega(1). \tag{7}$$

This yields the necessary condition for which $h(z) \prec \omega(z)$, $z \in \mathbb{E}$. Looking at each of these functions' $\omega(z)$ geometry, it can be seen that this condition is also sufficient.

1. Let $\omega(z) = \sqrt{1+z}$, then

$$t_\beta(-1) \geq 0 \quad \text{and} \quad t_\beta(1) \leq \sqrt{2},$$

and the above inequalities reduce to $\beta \geq \frac{15}{20} = \beta_1$ and $\beta \geq \frac{17}{20(\sqrt{2}-1)} = \beta_1$. We note that $\beta_1 - \beta_2 < 0$. Thus,

$$t_\beta(z) \prec \sqrt{1+z}, \quad \text{if } \beta \geq \max\{\beta_1, \beta_2\} = \beta_2.$$

2. Let $\omega(z) = 1 + \sin(z)$, then from Equation (5), we have

$$t_\beta(-1) \geq 1 - \sin(1), \text{ whenever } \beta \geq \frac{15}{20\sin(1)} = \beta_1$$

$$t_\beta(1) \leq 1 + \sin(1), \text{ whenever } \beta \geq \frac{17}{20\sin(1)} = \beta_2.$$

We observe that $\beta_1 - \beta_2 < 0$. Therefore the subordination $t_\beta(z) \prec 1 + \sin(z)$ holds if $\beta \geq \max\{\beta_1, \beta_2\} = \beta_2$.

3. Let $\omega(z) = 1 + z - \frac{z^3}{3}$, then the inequality $t_\beta(-1) \geq \frac{1}{3}$ gives $\beta \geq \beta_1$, where $\beta_1 = \frac{40}{45}$, and $t_\beta(1) \leq \frac{5}{3}$ gives $\beta \geq \beta_2$, where $\beta_2 = \frac{51}{40}$. Further, we note that $\beta_1 - \beta_2 < 0$. Therefore,

$$t_\beta(z) \prec 1 + z - \frac{z^3}{3}, \quad \text{if } \beta \geq \max\{\beta_1, \beta_2\} = \beta_2.$$

4. Let $\omega(z) = e^z$, then

$$t_\beta(-1) \geq e^{-1} \quad \text{and} \quad t_\beta(1) \leq e,$$

and these two inequalities yield to $\beta \geq \frac{15}{20(1-e^{-1})} = \beta_1$ and $\beta \geq \frac{17}{20(e-1)} = \beta_2$. Thus,

$$t_\beta(z) \prec e^z, \quad \text{if } \beta \geq \max\{\beta_1, \beta_2\} = \beta_1.$$

5. Let $\omega(z) = z + \sqrt{1+z^2}$, then from Equation (5),

$$t_\beta(-1) \geq -1 + \sqrt{2}, \text{ whenever } \beta \geq \frac{15}{20(2-\sqrt{2})} = \beta_1.$$

$$t_\beta(1) \leq 1 + \sqrt{2}, \text{ whenever } \beta \geq \frac{17}{20\sqrt{2}} = \beta_2.$$

Therefore, the subordination $t_\beta(z) \prec z + \sqrt{1+z^2}$ holds if $\beta \geq \max\{\beta_1, \beta_2\} = \beta_2$, where $\beta_1 - \beta_2 < 0$.

6. Let $\omega(z) = 1 + \sinh^{-1}(z)$, then

$$t_\beta(-1) \geq 1 - \sinh^{-1}(1) \text{ and } t_\beta(1) \leq 1 + \sinh^{-1}(1),$$

and these two inequalities yield $\beta \geq -\frac{15}{20\sinh^{-1}(1)} = \beta_1$ and $\beta \geq \frac{17}{20\sinh^{-1}(1)} = \beta_2$. Thus,

$$t_\beta(z) \prec 1 + \sinh^{-1}(z), \text{ if } \beta \geq \max\{\beta_1, \beta_2\} = \beta_2.$$

□

Corollary 4. *Let $u \in \mathcal{A}$ that satisfies the following subordination:*

$$\left(\frac{zu'(z)}{u(z)}\right)\left(\frac{(zu'(z))'}{u'(z)} - \frac{zu'(z)}{u(z)}\right) \prec \frac{4z}{5\beta} + \frac{z^4}{5\beta}, \ z \in \mathbb{E}.$$

Then,
1. $u \in \mathcal{S}_\mathcal{L}^*$, for $\beta \geq \frac{17}{20(\sqrt{2}-1)} \approx 2.0521$.
2. $u \in \mathcal{S}_{\sin}^*$, for $\beta \geq \frac{17}{20\sin(1)} \approx 1.0101$.
3. $u \in \mathcal{S}_{nep}^*$, for $\beta \geq \frac{51}{40} \approx 1.275$.
4. $u \in \mathcal{S}_{\exp}^*$, for $\beta \geq \frac{15}{20(1-e^{-1})} \approx 1.1865$.
5. $u \in \mathcal{S}_{cres}^*$, for $\beta \geq \frac{15}{20(2-\sqrt{2})} \approx 1.2803$.
6. $u \in \mathcal{S}_\rho^*$, for $\beta \geq \frac{17}{20\sinh^{-1}(1)} \approx 0.9644$.

Theorem 5. *Let h be an analytic function with $h(0) = 1$ in open unit disc $\mathbb{E}$ and satisfy that*

$$1 + \beta\frac{zh'(z)}{h(z)} \prec 1 + \frac{4z}{5} + \frac{z^4}{5}, \ z \in \mathbb{E}.$$

Then, we have the following results.
1. $h \in \mathcal{S}_\mathcal{L}^*$, for $\beta \geq \frac{17}{20\ln(\sqrt{2})}$.
2. $h \in \mathcal{S}_{\sin}^*$, for $\beta \geq \frac{17}{20\log(1+\sin(1))}$.
3. $h \in \mathcal{S}_{neh}^*$, for $\beta \geq \frac{17}{20\log(\frac{5}{3})}$.
4. $h \in \mathcal{S}_{\exp}^*$, for $\beta \geq \frac{17}{20}$.
5. $h \in \mathcal{S}_{cres}^*$, for $\beta \geq \frac{17}{20\log(1+\sqrt{2})}$.
6. $h \in \mathcal{S}_\rho^*$, for $\beta \geq \frac{17}{20\log(1+\sinh^{-1}(1))}$.

Proof. Consider the analytic function $s_\beta : \mathbb{E} \to \mathbb{C}$, defined by

$$s_\beta(z) = \exp\left(\frac{16z + z^4}{20\beta}\right), \ z \in \mathbb{E}.$$

Then, s_β is a solution of the differential equation:

$$1 + \beta \frac{zh'(z)}{h(z)} = 1 + \frac{4z}{5} + \frac{z^4}{5}, \ z \in \mathbb{E}.$$

Let $z \in \mathbb{E}$, $q(z) = s_\beta(z)$, $\nu(z) = 1$, and $\lambda(z) = \frac{\beta}{z}$. Applying for Lemma 1, the function $\Theta : \mathbb{E} \to \mathbb{C}$ is given by $\Theta(z) = zs'_\beta(z)\lambda(s_\beta(z)) = \phi_{car}(z) - 1$, and so $h(z) = 1 + \Theta(z) = \phi_{car}(z)$. Since the function $\phi_{car}(z)$ maps $\mathbb{E}$ into a starlike region (w.r.to 1), the function h is starlike. Further, h satisfies $\operatorname{Re}(zh'(z)/\Theta(z)) > 0$. Applying Lemma 1, we possess that

$$1 + \beta \frac{zh'(z)}{h(z)} \prec 1 + \beta \frac{zs'_\beta(z)}{s_\beta(z)} \Rightarrow h(z) \prec \widehat{s}_\beta(z).$$

Each subordination of Theorem 1 is similar to

$$h(z) \prec \omega(z),$$

for each subordinate function in the theorem, which is valid if $s_\beta(z) \prec \omega(z), z \in \mathbb{E}$. Here, we use the same technique as in Theorem 1, omitting the rest of the proof. □

Corollary 5. Let $u \in \mathcal{A}$ that satisfies the following subordination.

$$\left(\frac{(zu'(z))'}{u'(z)} - \frac{zu'(z)}{u(z)} \right) \prec \frac{4z}{5\beta} + \frac{z^4}{5\beta}, \ z \in \mathbb{E}.$$

Then, we have
1. $u \in \mathcal{S}^*_L$, for $\beta \geq \frac{17}{20\ln(2)} \approx 1.2263$.
2. $u \in \mathcal{S}^*_{\sin}$, for $\beta \geq \frac{17}{20\log(1+\sin(1))} \approx 1.3922$.
3. $u \in \mathcal{S}^*_{nep}$, for $\beta \geq \frac{17}{20\log(\frac{5}{3})} \approx 1.6640$.
4. $u \in \mathcal{S}^*_{\exp}$, for $\beta \geq \frac{17}{20} \approx 0.85$.
5. $u \in \mathcal{S}^*_{cres}$, for $\beta \geq \frac{17}{20\log(1+\sqrt{2})} \approx 0.9644$.
6. $u \in \mathcal{S}^*_\rho$, for $\beta \geq \frac{17}{20\log(1+\sinh^{-1}(1))} \approx 1.3449$.

Theorem 6. Let h be an analytic function with $h(0) = 1$ in unit disc $\mathbb{E}$ and satisfy that

$$1 + \beta \frac{zh'(z)}{h^2(z)} \prec 1 + \frac{4z}{5} + \frac{z^4}{5}, \ z \in \mathbb{E}.$$

Then, we have the following.
1. $h \in \mathcal{S}^*_L$, for $\beta \geq \frac{17\sqrt{2}}{20(\sqrt{2}-1)}$.
2. $h \in \mathcal{S}^*_{\sin}$, for $\beta \geq \frac{17(1+\sin(1))}{20\sin(1)}$.
3. $h \in \mathcal{S}^*_{nep}$, for $\beta \geq \frac{85}{40}$.
4. $h \in \mathcal{S}^*_{\exp}$, for $\beta \geq \frac{17e}{20(e-1)}$.
5. $h \in \mathcal{S}^*_{cres}$, for $\beta \geq \frac{17(1+\sqrt{2})}{20\sqrt{2}}$.
6. $h \in \mathcal{S}^*_\rho$, for $\beta \geq \frac{17(1+\sinh^{-1}(1))}{20\sinh^{-1}(1)}$.

Proof. Consider the function $d_\beta : \mathbb{E} \to \mathbb{C}$, defined by

$$d_\beta(z) = \left(1 - \frac{16z + z^4}{20\beta}\right)^{-1},$$

which is the solution of the following differential equation.

$$1 + \beta \frac{zh'(z)}{h^2(z)} = 1 + \frac{4z}{5} + \frac{z^4}{5}.$$

Let $z \in \mathbb{E}$, take $q(z) = d_\beta(z)$, $\nu(z) = 1$, and $\lambda(z) = \frac{\beta}{z^2}$ in Lemma 1. Then, the function $\Theta : \mathbb{E} \to \mathbb{C}$ is given by $\Theta(z) = zd'_\beta(z)\lambda(d_\beta(z)) = \phi_{car}(z) - 1$, and so $h(z) = 1 + \Theta(z) = \phi_{car}(z)$. Since the function $\phi_{car}(z)$ maps $\mathbb{E}$ into a starlike region (with respect to 1), the function h is starlike. Further, h satisfies $\text{Re}(zh'(z)/\Theta(z)) > 0$. Applying this to Lemma 1, we find that

$$1 + \beta \frac{zh'(z)}{h(z)} \prec 1 + \beta \frac{zd'_\beta(z)}{d_\beta(z)} \Rightarrow h(z) \prec \widehat{d_\beta}(z).$$

Each subordination of Theorem 2 is similar to

$$h(z) \prec \omega(z),$$

for each subordinate function in the theorem, which is valid if $d_\beta(z) \prec \omega(z), z \in \mathbb{E}$. Here, we use the same technique as in Theorem 1, omitting the rest of the proof. □

Corollary 6. *Let $u \in \mathcal{A}$ that satisfies the following subordination.*

$$\left(\frac{zu'(z)}{u(z)}\right)^{-1}\left(\frac{(zu'(z))'}{u'(z)} - \frac{zu'(z)}{u(z)}\right) \prec \frac{4z}{5\beta} + \frac{z^4}{5\beta}, z \in \mathbb{E}.$$

Then, we have the following results.

1. $u \in \mathcal{S}^*_\mathcal{L}$, for $\beta \geq \frac{17\sqrt{2}}{20(\sqrt{2}-1)} \approx 2.9021$.
2. $u \in \mathcal{S}^*_{\sin}$, for $\beta \geq \frac{17(1+\sin(1))}{20\sin(1)} \approx 1.8601$.
3. $u \in \mathcal{S}^*_{nep}$, for $\beta \geq \frac{85}{40} \approx 2.125$.
4. $u \in \mathcal{S}^*_{\exp}$, for $\beta \geq \frac{17e}{20(e-1)} \approx 1.3447$.
5. $u \in \mathcal{S}^*_{cres}$, for $\beta \geq \frac{17(1+\sqrt{2})}{20\sqrt{2}} \approx 1.451$.
6. $u \in \mathcal{S}^*_\rho$, for $\beta \geq \frac{17(1+\sinh^{-1}(1))}{20\sinh^{-1}(1)} \approx 1.8144$.

We finish Section 3 with the following figures in Figure 2, graphically illustrating the results in this section.

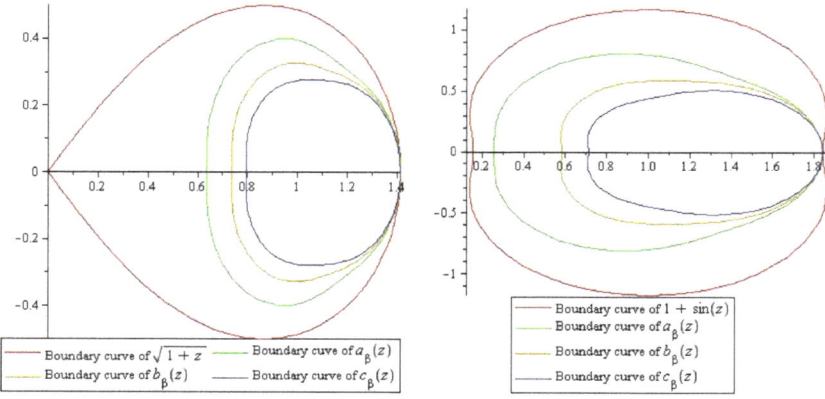

Figure 2. *Cont.*

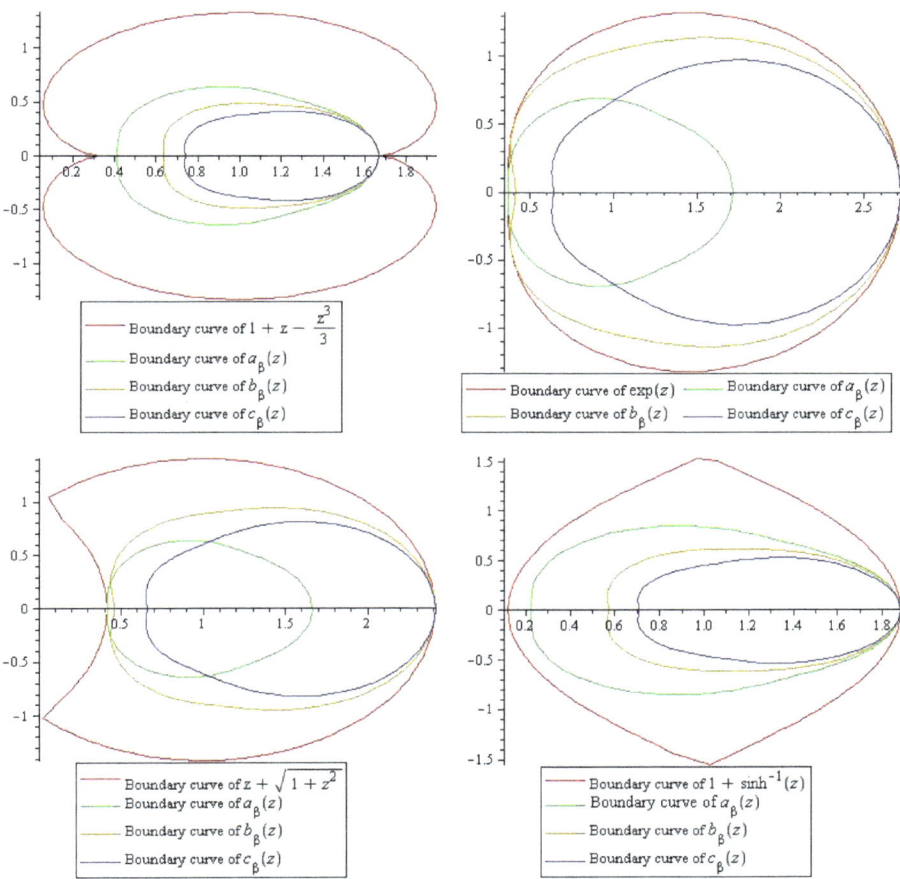

Figure 2. Graphical Representation of Results in Section 3.

4. Conclusions

In this article, we have studied the first-order differential subordination for two symmetric image domains, namely the cardioid domain and the domain bounded by three leaf functions. Further, we examined some graphical interpretations of these results. Moreover, this concept can be extended to meromorphic, multivalent, and quantum calculus functions.

Author Contributions: All authors equally contributed to this article as follows. Conceptualization, M.G.K., B.K., J.G., F.T. and F.M.O.T.; methodology, M.G.K., B.K., J.G., F.T. and F.M.O.T.; formal analysis, M.G.K., B.K., J.G., F.T. and F.M.O.T.; investigation, M.G.K., B.K., J.G., F.T. and F.M.O.T.; resources, M.G.K., B.K., J.G., F.T. and F.M.O.T.; writing—original draft preparation, M.G.K., B.K., J.G., F.T. and F.M.O.T.; writing—review and editing, M.G.K., B.K., J.G., F.T. and F.M.O.T. All authors have read and agreed to the published version of the manuscript.

Funding: The authors acknowledge the funding UAEU Program for Advanced Research (UPAR12S127) from United Arab Emirates University and the Researchers Supporting Project (RSP2023R440) from King Saud University.

Data Availability Statement: Not Applicable.

Conflicts of Interest: The authors declare no conflict of interest.

References

1. Khan, M.F.; Al-shbeil, I.; Khan, S.; Khan, N.; Haq, W.U.; Gong, J. Applications of a q-Differential Operator to a Class of Harmonic Mappings Defined by q-Mittag–Leffler Functions. *Symmetry* **2022**, *14*, 1905. [CrossRef]
2. Ma, W.; Minda, D. A Unified Treatment of Some Special Classes of Univalent Functions. In *Proceeding of Conference on Complex Analytic*; Li, Z., Ren, F., Yang, L., Zhang, S., Eds.; International Press: New York, NY, USA, 1994; pp. 157–169.
3. Janowski, W. Extremal problems for a family of functions with a positive real part and for some related families. *Ann. Polonici Math.* **1971**, *23*, 159–177. [CrossRef]
4. Ur Rehman, M.S.; Ahmad, Q.Z.; Al-Shbeil, I.; Ahmad, S.; Khan, A.; Khan, B.; Gong, J. Coefficient Inequalities for Multivalent Janowski Type q-Starlike Functions Involving Certain Conic Domains. *Axioms* **2022**, *11*, 494. [CrossRef]
5. Sokół, J.; Kanas, S. Radius of convexity of some subclasses of strongly starlike functions. *Zesz. Nauk. Politech. Rzeszowskiej Mat.* **1996**, *19*, 101–105.
6. Cho, N.E.; Kumar, V.; Kumar, S.S.; Ravichandran, V. Radius problems for starlike functions associated with the sine function. *Bull. Iran. Math. Soc.* **2019**, *45*, 213–232. [CrossRef]
7. Wani, L.A.; Swaminathan, A. Starlike and convex functions associated with a Nephroid domain. *Bull. Malays. Math. Sci. Soc.* **2021**, *44*, 79–104. [CrossRef]
8. Mendiratta, R.; Nagpal, S.; Ravichandran, V. On a subclass of strongly starlike functions associated with an exponential function. *Bull. Malays. Math. Sci. Soc.* **2015**, *38*, 365–386. [CrossRef]
9. Raina, R.K.; Sokół, J. On Coefficient estimates for a certain class of starlike functions, Hacettepe. *J. Math. Statist.* **2015**, *44*, 1427–1433.
10. Kumar, S.S.; Arora, K. Starlike functions associated with a petal shaped domain. *arXiv* **2020**, arXiv:2010.10072.
11. Ali, R.M.; Cho, N.E.; Ravichandran, V.; Kumar, S.S. Differential subordination for functions associated with the lemniscate of Bernoulli. *Taiwan. J. Math.* **2012**, *16*, 1017–1026. [CrossRef]
12. Kumar, S.S.; Kumar, V.; Ravichandran, V.; Cho, N.E. Sufficient conditions for starlike functions associated with the lemniscate of Bernoulli. *J. Inequal. Appl.* **2013**, 176. [CrossRef]
13. Kumar, S.; Ravichandran, V. Subordinations for functions with positive real part. *Complex Anal. Oper. Theory* **2018**, *12*, 1179–1191. [CrossRef]
14. Paprocki, E.; Sokół, J. The extremal problems in some subclass of strongly starlike functions. *Zeszyty Nauk. Politech. Rzeszowskiej Mat* **1996**, *20*, 89–94.
15. Raza, M.; Sokół, J.; Mushtaq, S. Differential subordinations for analytic functions. *Iran. J. Sci. Technol. Trans. A Sci.* **2019**, *43*, 883–890. [CrossRef]
16. Shi, L.; Srivastava, H.M.; Khan, M.G.; Khan, N.; Ahmad, B.; Khan, B.; Mashwani, W.K. Certain subclasses of analytic multivalent functions associated with petal-shape domain. *Axioms* **2021**, *10*, 291. [CrossRef]
17. Gupta, P.; Nagpal, S.; Ravichandran, V. Inclusion relations and radius problems for a subclass of starlike functions. *arXiv* **2020**, arXiv:2012.1351v1.
18. Gandhi, S. Radius estimates for three leaf function and convex combination of starlike functions. In *Mathematical. Analysis 1: Approximation Theory. ICRAPAM*; Deo, N., Gupta, V., Acu, A., Agrawal, P., Eds.; Springer: Singapore, 2018; Volume 306.
19. Miller, S.S.; Mocanu, P.T. *Differential Subordinations Theory and Its Applications*; Series of Monographs and Textbooks in Pure and Applied Mathematics; Marcel Dekker Inc.: New York, NY, USA, 2000; Volume 225.

Disclaimer/Publisher's Note: The statements, opinions and data contained in all publications are solely those of the individual author(s) and contributor(s) and not of MDPI and/or the editor(s). MDPI and/or the editor(s) disclaim responsibility for any injury to people or property resulting from any ideas, methods, instructions or products referred to in the content.

Article

New Monotonic Properties for Solutions of a Class of Functional Differential Equations and Their Applications

Fahd Masood [1,*], Osama Moaaz [2,*], Ghada AlNemer [3] and Hamdy El-Metwally [1]

[1] Department of Mathematics, Faculty of Science, Mansoura University, Mansoura 35516, Egypt; helmetwally@mans.edu.eg
[2] Department of Mathematics, College of Science, Qassim University, Buraydah 51452, Saudi Arabia
[3] Department of Mathematical Science, College of Science, Princess Nourah bint Abdulrahman University, P.O. Box 105862, Riyadh 11656, Saudi Arabia; gnnemer@pnu.edu.sa
* Correspondence: fahdmasoud22@std.mans.edu.eg (F.M.); o_moaaz@mans.edu.eg (O.M.)

Abstract: This paper delves into the enhancement of asymptotic and oscillatory behaviors in solutions to even-order neutral differential equations with multiple delays. The main objective is to establish improved inequalities to advance the understanding of oscillation theory for these equations. The paper's approach is centered on improving the understanding of the intricate relationship between solutions and their corresponding functions. This is achieved by harnessing the modified monotonic properties of positive solutions, which provide valuable insights into oscillation behavior. Furthermore, leveraging the symmetry between positive and negative solutions, we derived criteria that ensure oscillation for all solutions, with a specific emphasis on excluding only positive solutions. To illustrate the significance of our findings, we provide an illustrative example.

Keywords: differential equation; oscillatory; non-oscillatory; neutral delay; even order

MSC: 34C10; 34K11

1. Introduction

The central focus of this research revolves around a comprehensive examination of the oscillatory characteristics exhibited by the solutions to an even-order quasilinear differential equation (DE), denoted as

$$\left(r(\ell)\left(y^{(n-1)}(\ell)\right)^{\alpha}\right)' + \sum_{i=1}^{v} q_i(\ell)\chi^{\alpha}(\sigma_i(\ell)) = 0, \; \ell \geq \ell_0, \tag{1}$$

where $y(\ell) = \chi(\ell) + p(\ell)\chi(\mathfrak{y}(\ell))$. In this paper, we assume that

(H_1) $n \geq 4$, α is the ratio of two positive odd integers;

(H_2) $r, \mathfrak{y}, \sigma_i \in C^1([\ell_0, \infty))$, and $q(\ell) \in C([\ell_0, \infty))$;

(H_3) $\mathfrak{y}(\ell) \leq \ell$, $\sigma_i(\ell) \leq \ell$, $\sigma_i'(\ell) > 0$, and $\lim_{\ell \to \infty} \mathfrak{y}(\ell) = \lim_{\ell \to \infty} \sigma_i(\ell) = \infty$;

(H_4) $r(\ell) > 0$, $r'(\ell) \geq 0$, $0 \leq p(\ell) < p_0$ and $q(\ell) \geq 0$;

(H_5) $\pi_0(\ell_0) < \infty$, where

$$\pi_0(\ell) := \int_\ell^\infty \frac{1}{r^{1/\alpha}(s)} ds,$$

and

$$\pi_i(\ell) := \int_\ell^\infty \pi_{i-1}(s) ds, \; i = 1, 2, \ldots, n-2.$$

A function $\chi \in C([\ell_\chi, \infty))$, where $\ell_\chi \geq \ell_0$, is said to be a solution of Equation (1) which has the property $r(y^{(n-1)})^\alpha \in C^1[\ell_\chi, \infty)$, and it satisfies Equation (1) for all

$\chi \in [\ell_\chi, \infty)$. We consider only those solutions χ of Equation (1), which exist on some half-line $[\ell_\chi, \infty)$ and satisfy the condition

$$\sup\{|\chi(\ell)| : \ell \geqslant L\} > 0, \text{ for all } L \geq \ell_\chi.$$

A solution to Equation (1) is termed oscillatory if it does not tend towards either eventual positivity or eventual negativity. Otherwise, it is classified as non-oscillatory. Equation (1) is considered oscillatory when all of its solutions exhibit oscillatory behavior.

A neutral DE is a specialized type of DE in which the rate of change of a function depends not only on its current state but also on past values, introducing a time delay. These equations find significant relevance in various fields such as biology, physics, and engineering, where systems exhibit delayed responses. Neutral DEs provide a crucial mathematical framework for modeling dynamic systems with memory and are instrumental in analyzing real-world phenomena with time-delay effects. Understanding their solutions and behavior is vital for accurately describing and predicting the dynamics of such systems, making them indispensable in scientific and engineering applications, see [1–5].

Oscillation solutions, which refer to the periodic behavior of solutions oscillating around a specific function or value, are commonly observed in physical systems, like mechanical systems, electrical circuits, and biological oscillators. The oscillation theorem is an essential result in the theory of DEs that describes the oscillatory nature of solutions. Its wide-ranging applications span various fields, such as physics, engineering, and economics. The implications of this theorem have a broad range of applications, spanning diverse fields. These include its relevance in analyzing oscillatory systems, like pendulums and vibrating strings, as well as its utility in examining population dynamics and the spread of infectious diseases. Furthermore, the oscillation theorem bears notable importance in the domains of control theory and signal processing. Here, it assumes a pivotal role in evaluating the stability and performance of feedback systems, as demonstrated in [6–8].

Even-order quasilinear DEs represent a significant class of mathematical models that find wide-ranging applications in science and engineering. These equations, often characterized by terms involving the function and its derivatives of the same order, offer a versatile framework for studying complex phenomena. Their utility extends to various fields, including physics, biology, and control theory. Specifically, they are employed to analyze dynamic systems with even-order dynamics, such as mechanical systems, electrical circuits, and heat transfer problems. This versatility makes the study of even-order quasilinear DEs a vital endeavor, as it provides essential insights into the behavior of numerous real-world systems.

In the field of mathematical research, there has been a notable surge in interest in the investigation of delay DEs in unconventional contexts. This keen academic interest is apparent in the body of work such as [9–11]. Similarly, refs. [12–15], have directed their efforts toward understanding neutral DEs. Furthermore, Moaaz et al. extended this analytical exploration to encompass even-order equations in their publications, such as [16,17].

Many investigations have explored the complex topic of oscillations in even-order neutral DEs. These investigations have proposed diverse methodologies aimed at establishing criteria for identifying oscillatory behavior in these equations. It is worth highlighting that this topic has received extensive attention, particularly in the canonical scenario denoted by the integral expression:

$$\int_{\ell_0}^{\infty} \frac{1}{r^{1/\alpha}(s)} ds = \infty, \tag{2}$$

as evidenced by the comprehensive body of prior scholarly works, including references such as [18–20].

We will now discuss several essential findings from previous research papers that have significantly advanced the study of even-order differential equations.

Koplatadze [21], Wei [22], and Koplatadze et al. [23] investigated the oscillation criterion of equation

$$\chi''(\ell) + q(\ell)\chi(\sigma(\ell)) = 0, \ell \geq \ell_0,$$

and obtained sufficient conditions for it to be oscillatory. Similarly, Bai [24] and Karpuz et al. [25] discussed the oscillation criterion for the equation

$$\chi^{(n)}(\ell) + q(\ell)\chi(\sigma(\ell)) = 0, \ell \geq \ell_0,$$

and derived sufficient conditions for all solutions to be oscillatory. Additionally, Baculikova [26] conducted an investigation into the monotonic properties of non-oscillatory solutions concerning the linear equation:

$$(r(\ell)\chi'(\ell))' + q(\ell)\chi(\mathfrak{n}(\ell)) = 0.$$

This investigation considered both delay and advanced scenarios. Furthermore, Ramos et al. [27] introduced a novel oscillation criterion for solutions to the fourth-order quasilinear neutral DE:

$$\left(r(\ell)(z'''(\ell))^\alpha\right)' + q(\ell)\chi^\alpha(\sigma(\ell)) = 0,$$

subject to a non-canonical condition:

$$\int_{\ell_0}^\infty \frac{1}{r^{1/\alpha}(s)} ds < \infty.$$

Furthermore, the research conducted by Han et al. [28], and Li et al. [29] involved an investigation into the asymptotic properties of positive solutions pertaining to the even-order neutral DE, defined as:

$$\left(r(\ell)(\chi(\ell) + p(\ell)\chi(\mathfrak{n}(\ell)))^{(n-1)}\right)' + q(\ell)\chi(\sigma(\ell)) = 0.$$

Lastly, the study carried out by Xing et al. [30] explored various oscillation theorems for the equation:

$$\left(r(\ell)\left((\chi(\ell) + p(\ell)\chi(\mathfrak{n}(\ell)))^{(n-1)}\right)^\alpha\right)' + q(\ell)\chi^\alpha(\sigma(\ell)) = 0,$$

subject Condition (2).

Li and Rogovchenko [31] explored the asymptotic behavior of solutions to higher-order quasilinear neutral DEs, represented as follows

$$\left(r(\ell)\left((\chi(\ell) + p(\ell)\chi(\mathfrak{n}(\ell)))^{(n-1)}\right)^\alpha\right)' + q(\ell)\chi^\beta(\sigma(\ell)) = 0,$$

with a particular focus on both even- and odd-order equations featuring diverse argument patterns, including alternating delayed and advanced characteristics.

The exploration of asymptotic and oscillatory properties in neutral DEs (NDEs) relies on the intricate relationship between the solution χ and its corresponding function y. In the typical context of second-order equations, the standard association is often defined as:

$$\chi(\ell) > (1 - p(\ell))y(\ell).$$

This expression is widely utilized. Conversely, in the case of positive, decreasing solutions within non-canonical settings, the relevant relationship takes the following form:

$$\chi(\ell) > \left(1 - p(\ell)\frac{\pi_0(\mathfrak{n}(\ell))}{\pi_0(\ell)}\right)y(\ell).$$

This relationship has been demonstrated in previous studies, such as [32,33].

Moaaz et al. [34] developed new inequalities that improve the understanding of the asymptotic and oscillatory behaviors of solutions for fourth-order neutral DEs of the form

$$(r(\ell)(z'''(\ell)))' + q(\ell)\chi(\sigma(\ell)) = 0,$$

specifically in the noncanonical case.

Lemma 1 ([34]). *If χ represents an eventually positive solution of Equation (1), then eventually we have*

$$\chi(\ell) > \sum_{r=0}^{\kappa}\left(\prod_{l=0}^{2r} p\left(\mathfrak{y}^{[l]}(\ell)\right)\right)\left[\frac{y\left(\mathfrak{y}^{[2r]}(\ell)\right)}{p\left(\mathfrak{y}^{[2r]}(\ell)\right)} - y\left(\mathfrak{y}^{[2r+1]}(\ell)\right)\right], \qquad (3)$$

for any $\kappa \geq 0$.

In this study, our primary objective is to build upon earlier work [34], which applied a similar approach to fourth-order equations. Our research is primarily motivated by the desire to extend this methodology, pushing the boundaries of our understanding by encompassing higher-order equations in our current investigation. This expansion marks a significant advancement in the scope of our research, opening up new avenues for exploration and discovery in the field.

2. Auxiliary Results

In this section, we will introduce several essential lemmas that serve as the foundational building blocks for establishing our main results. To streamline our notation, we will define the following expressions:

$$U^{[0]}(\ell) = U(\ell) \text{ and } U^{[j]}(\ell) = U\left(U^{[j-1]}(\ell)\right), \text{ for } j = 1, 2, \ldots, \kappa,$$

$$\sigma(\ell) := \min\{\sigma_i(\ell),\ i = 1, 2, \ldots, v\},$$

$$\tilde{\sigma}(\ell) := \max\{\sigma_i(\ell),\ i = 1, 2, \ldots, v\},$$

$$p_1(\ell; \kappa) := \sum_{r=0}^{\kappa}\left(\prod_{l=0}^{2r} p\left(\mathfrak{y}^{[l]}(\ell)\right)\right)\left[\frac{1}{p\left(\mathfrak{y}^{[2r]}(\ell)\right)} - 1\right]\left(\frac{\mathfrak{y}^{[2r]}(\ell)}{\ell}\right)^{(n-2)/\epsilon},$$

$$p_2(\ell; \kappa) := \sum_{r=0}^{\kappa}\left(\prod_{l=0}^{2r} p\left(\mathfrak{y}^{[l]}(\ell)\right)\right)\left[\frac{1}{p\left(\mathfrak{y}^{[2r]}(\ell)\right)} - \frac{\pi_{n-2}\left(\mathfrak{y}^{[2r+1]}(\ell)\right)}{\pi_{n-2}\left(\mathfrak{y}^{[2r]}(\ell)\right)}\right],$$

$$\widehat{p}_2(\ell; \kappa) := \sum_{r=0}^{\kappa}\left(\prod_{l=0}^{2r} p\left(\mathfrak{y}^{[l]}(\ell)\right)\right)\left[\frac{1}{p\left(\mathfrak{y}^{[2r]}(\ell)\right)} - \frac{\pi_{n-2}\left(\mathfrak{y}^{[2r+1]}(\ell)\right)}{\pi_{n-2}\left(\mathfrak{y}^{[2r]}(\ell)\right)}\right]\frac{\pi_{n-2}^{km}\left(\mathfrak{y}^{[2r]}(\ell)\right)}{\pi_{n-2}^{km}(\ell)},$$

$$Q_0(\ell) := \sum_{i=1}^{v} q_i(\ell)(1 - p(\sigma_i(\ell)))^\alpha,$$

$$Q_j(\ell) := \sum_{i=1}^{v} q_i(\ell) p_j^\alpha(\sigma_i(\ell), \kappa),\ j = 1, 2,$$

and

$$\widehat{Q}_2(\ell) := \sum_{i=1}^{v} q_i(\ell)\widehat{p}_2^\alpha(\sigma_i(\ell), \kappa).$$

Lemma 2 ([35]). *Let $w \in C^m([\ell_0, \infty), (0, \infty))$, $w^{(i)}(\ell) > 0$ for $i = 1, 2, \ldots, m$, and $w^{(m+1)}(\ell) \leq 0$, eventually. Then,*

$$\frac{w(\ell)}{w'(\ell)} \geq \frac{\epsilon}{m}\ell,$$

for every $\epsilon \in (0,1)$.

Lemma 3 ([36]). *Let $f \in C^m([\ell_0, \infty), \mathbb{R}^+)$. Assume that $f^{(m)}(\ell)$ has a fixed sign and is not identically zero on $[\ell_0, \infty)$ and that there exists $\ell_1 \geq \ell_0$, such that $f^{(m-1)}(\ell)f^{(m)}(\ell) \leq 0$ for all $\ell_1 \geq \ell_0$. If $\lim_{\ell \to \infty} f(\ell) \neq 0$, then, for every $\epsilon \in (0,1)$, there exists $\ell_\delta \in [\ell_1, \infty)$, such that*

$$f(\ell) \geq \frac{\epsilon}{(m-1)!} \ell^{m-1} \left| f^{(m-1)}(\ell) \right|,$$

for $\ell \in [\ell_\delta, \infty)$.

Lemma 4 ([37]). *Assuming $\chi > 0$ is a solution of Equation (1), we have that $r\left(y^{(n-1)}\right)^\alpha$ is a decreasing function, and y fulfills one of the subsequent scenarios:*

(C_1) $y^{(r)} > 0$ for $r = 0, 1, n-1$ and $y^{(n)} < 0$;
(C_2) $y^{(r)} > 0$ for $r = 0, 1, n-2$ and $y^{(n-1)} < 0$;
(C_3) $(-1)^r y^{(r)} > 0$ for $r = 0, 1, 2, \ldots, n-1$,

eventually.

Notation 1. *The symbol Ω_i is defined as the collection of all solutions that eventually become positivity, with their respective functions satisfying condition (C_i) for $i = 1, 2, 3$.*

3. Properties of Asymptotic and Monotonic Behaviors

We establish asymptotic and monotonic properties for the solutions of the neutral DE (1), in this section.

3.1. Category Ω_2

Lemma 5. *Assume that $\chi \in \Omega_2$. Then, eventually,*

$(Y_{1,1})$ $y \geq \frac{\epsilon}{n-2} \ell y'$;
$(Y_{1,2})$ $y \geq \frac{\epsilon}{(n-2)!} \ell^{n-2} y^{(n-2)}$ for all $\epsilon \in (0,1)$;
$(Y_{1,3})$ $y^{(n-2)} \geq -r^{1/\alpha} \pi_0 y^{(n-1)}$;
$(Y_{1,4})$ $y^{(n-2)} / \pi_0$ is increasing;
$(Y_{1,5})$ $\chi \geq p_1(\ell; \kappa) y$;
$(Y_{1,6})$ $\left(r\left(y^{(n-1)}\right)^\alpha\right)' \leq -y^\alpha(\sigma) Q_1$.

Proof. $(Y_{1,1})$ By employing Lemma 2 with the substitutions $m = n-2$ and $w = y$, the resulting inequality is

$$y \geq \frac{\epsilon}{n-2} \ell y'.$$

$(Y_{1,2})$ By employing Lemma 3 with the substitutions $m = n-1$ and $f = y$, the resulting inequality is

$$y \geq \frac{\epsilon_0}{(n-2)!} \ell^{n-2} y^{(n-2)},$$

for all $\epsilon_0 \in (0,1)$.

$(Y_{1,3})$ Because $r^{1/\alpha} y^{(n-1)}$ is decreasing, we deduce that

$$\begin{aligned} y^{(n-2)}(\ell) &\geq -\int_\ell^\infty r^{1/\alpha}(s) y^{(n-1)}(s) \frac{1}{r^{1/\alpha}(s)} ds \\ &\geq -r^{1/\alpha} \pi_0 y^{(n-1)}. \end{aligned}$$

($Y_{1,4}$) From ($Y_{1,3}$), we obtain

$$\left(\frac{y^{(n-2)}}{\pi_0}\right)' = \frac{1}{r^{1/\alpha}\pi_0^2}\left(r^{1/\alpha}\pi_0 y^{(n-1)} + y^{(n-2)}\right) \geq 0.$$

($Y_{1,5}$) From Lemma 1, Equation (3) holds. After considering the properties of solutions in the class Ω_2, it can be deduced that $y\left(\mathfrak{y}^{[2r]}\right) \geq y\left(\mathfrak{y}^{[2r+1]}\right)$ for $i = 1, 2, \ldots$. Therefore, Equation (3) can betransformed into

$$\chi > \sum_{r=0}^{\kappa}\left(\prod_{l=0}^{2r} P\left(\mathfrak{y}^{[l]}\right)\right)\left[\frac{1}{P(\mathfrak{y}^{[2r]})} - 1\right] y\left(\mathfrak{y}^{[2r]}\right).$$

By utilizing ($Y_{1,1}$), we obtain

$$y\left(\mathfrak{y}^{[2r]}\right) \geq \left(\frac{\mathfrak{y}^{[2r]}}{\ell}\right)^{(n-2)/\epsilon} y,$$

which, with (4), gives

$$\begin{aligned}\chi &> \sum_{r=0}^{\kappa}\left(\prod_{l=0}^{2r} P\left(\mathfrak{y}^{[l]}\right)\right)\left[\frac{1}{P(\mathfrak{y}^{[2r]})} - 1\right]\left(\frac{\mathfrak{y}^{[2r]}}{\ell}\right)^{(n-2)/\epsilon} y \\ &= p_1(\ell;\kappa) y.\end{aligned}$$

($Y_{1,6}$) When combined with ($Y_{1,5}$), Equation (1) can be expressed as follows:

$$\begin{aligned}\left(r\left(y^{(n-1)}\right)^{\alpha}\right)' &= -\sum_{i=1}^{v} q_i \chi^{\alpha}(\sigma_i) \\ &\leq -\sum_{i=1}^{v} q_i p_1^{\alpha}(\sigma_i;\kappa) y^{\alpha}(\sigma_i) \\ &\leq -y^{\alpha}(\sigma) Q_1.\end{aligned}$$

□

Lemma 6. *Assuming that $\chi \in \Omega_2$ and there exist $\delta > 0$ and $\ell_1 \geq \ell_0$, such that*

$$\frac{1}{\alpha}r^{1/\alpha}(\ell)\pi_0^{1+\alpha}(\ell)\left(\sigma^{n-2}(\ell)\right)^{\alpha} Q_1(\ell) \geq ((n-2)!)^{\alpha}\delta, \qquad (4)$$

we can deduce the following for $\ell \geq \ell_1$:

($Y_{2,1}$) $\lim_{\ell \to \infty} y^{(n-2)}(\ell) = 0$;

($Y_{2,2}$) $y^{(n-2)}/\pi_0^{\beta_0}$ *is decreasing;*

($Y_{2,3}$) $\lim_{\ell \to \infty} y^{(n-2)}(\ell)/\pi_0^{\beta_0}(\ell) = 0$;

($Y_{2,4}$) $y^{(n-2)}/\pi_0^{1-\beta_0}$ *is increasing; for $\ell \geq \ell_0$, where $\beta_0 = \epsilon\delta^{1/\alpha}$, $\epsilon \in (0,1)$ and $\alpha \leq 1$.*

Proof. ($Y_{2,1}$) : Since $\chi \in \Omega_2$, we can conclude that ($Y_{1,1}$)—($Y_{1,6}$) in Lemma 5 are satisfied for all $\ell \geq \ell_1$, with ℓ_1 being large enough. When considering $y^{(n-2)}$ as a positive and decreasing function, it can be deduced that $\lim_{\ell \to \infty} y^{(n-2)}(\ell) = c_1 \geq 0$. Our claim is that $c_1 = 0$. To support this claim, suppose that $c_1 \neq 0$. Consequently, there exists a point where

$y^{(n-2)} \geq c_1 > 0$ eventually. Utilizing this information along with $(Y_{1,2})$, we derive the following inequality

$$\begin{aligned} y &\geq \frac{\epsilon}{(n-2)!}\ell^{n-2}y^{(n-2)} \\ &\geq \frac{\epsilon c_1}{(n-2)!}\ell^{n-2}. \end{aligned}$$

Consequently, from $(Y_{1,6})$, we can deduce that

$$\begin{aligned} \left(r\left(y^{(n-1)}\right)^\alpha\right)' &\leq -y^\alpha(\sigma)Q_1 \\ &\leq -\left(\frac{\epsilon c_1}{(n-2)!}\sigma^{n-2}\right)^\alpha Q_1 \\ &\leq -\epsilon^\alpha c_1^\alpha \frac{(\sigma^{n-2})^\alpha}{((n-2)!)^\alpha}Q_1, \end{aligned}$$

which with Equation (4) gives

$$\begin{aligned} \left(r\left(y^{(n-1)}\right)^\alpha\right)' &\leq -\alpha c_1^\alpha \epsilon^\alpha \delta \frac{1}{r^{1/\alpha}\pi_0^{1+\alpha}} \\ &\leq -\alpha c_1^\alpha \beta_0^\alpha \frac{1}{r^{1/\alpha}\pi_0^{1+\alpha}}. \end{aligned}$$

After integrating the preceding inequality from ℓ_2 to ℓ, the result is as follows

$$\begin{aligned} r(\ell)\left(y^{(n-1)}(\ell)\right)^\alpha &\leq r(\ell_2)\left(y^{(n-1)}(\ell_2)\right)^\alpha - \alpha c_1^\alpha \beta_0^\alpha \int_{\ell_2}^\ell \frac{1}{r^{1/\alpha}(s)\pi_0^{1+\alpha}(s)}ds \\ &\leq \beta_0^\alpha c_1^\alpha \left(\frac{1}{\pi_0^\alpha(\ell_2)} - \frac{1}{\pi_0^\alpha(\ell)}\right). \end{aligned} \qquad (5)$$

Since $\pi_0^{-\alpha}(\ell) \to \infty$ as $\ell \to \infty$, there is a $\ell_3 \geq \ell_2$, such that $\pi_0^{-\alpha}(\ell) - \pi_0^{-\alpha}(\ell_2) \geq \mu_0 \pi_0^{-\alpha}(\ell)$ for all $\mu_0 \in (0,1)$. Hence, Equation (5) becomes

$$y^{(n-1)} \leq -c_1 \mu_0^{1/\alpha} \beta_0 \frac{1}{r^{1/\alpha}\pi_0},$$

for all $\ell \geq \ell_3$. Integrating the last inequality from ℓ_3 to ℓ, we find

$$\begin{aligned} y^{(n-2)}(\ell) &\leq y^{(n-2)}(\ell_3) - c_1\mu_0^{1/\alpha}\beta_0 \int_{\ell_3}^\ell \frac{1}{r^{1/\alpha}(s)\pi_0(s)}ds \\ &\leq y^{(n-2)}(\ell_3) - c_1\mu_0^{1/\alpha}\beta_0 \ln\frac{\pi_0(\ell_3)}{\pi_0(\ell)} \to -\infty \text{ as } \ell \to \infty, \end{aligned}$$

which is a contradiction. Then, $c_1 = 0$.

$(Y_{2,2})$ From (4), $(Y_{1,2})$ and $(Y_{1,6})$, we obtain

$$\left(r\left(y^{(n-1)}\right)^\alpha\right)' \leq -\frac{\alpha\beta_0^\alpha}{r^{1/\alpha}\pi_0^{1+\alpha}}\left(y^{(n-2)}(\sigma)\right)^\alpha.$$

After integrating the previous inequality from ℓ_1 to ℓ, and considering the condition $y^{(n-1)} < 0$, we obtain the following result

$$r(\ell)\left(y^{(n-1)}(\ell)\right)^\alpha \leq r(\ell_1)\left(y^{(n-1)}(\ell_1)\right)^\alpha + \frac{\beta_0^\alpha}{\pi_0^\alpha(\ell_1)}\left(y^{(n-2)}(\ell)\right)^\alpha - \frac{\beta_0^\alpha}{\pi_0^\alpha(\ell)}\left(y^{(n-2)}(\ell)\right)^\alpha.$$

Because $y^{(n-2)}(\ell) \to 0$ as $\ell \to \infty$ there is a $\ell_2 \geq \ell_1$, such that

$$r(\ell_1)\left(y^{(n-1)}(\ell_1)\right)^{\alpha} + \frac{\beta_0^{\alpha}}{\pi_0^{\alpha}(\ell_1)}\left(y^{(n-2)}(\ell)\right)^{\alpha} \leq 0,$$

for $\ell \geq \ell_2$. Therefore, we have

$$r\left(y^{(n-1)}\right)^{\alpha} \leq -\frac{\beta_0^{\alpha}}{\pi_0^{\alpha}}\left(y^{(n-2)}\right)^{\alpha},$$

alternatively,

$$r^{1/\alpha}y^{(n-1)}\pi_0 + \beta_0 y^{(n-2)} \leq 0. \qquad (6)$$

Thus,

$$\left(\frac{y^{(n-2)}}{\pi_0^{\beta_0}}\right)' = \frac{r^{1/\alpha}y^{(n-1)}\pi_0 + \beta_0 y^{(n-2)}}{r^{1/\alpha}\pi_0^{1+\beta_0}} \leq 0.$$

($Y_{2,3}$) Given that $y^{(n-2)}/\pi_0^{\beta_0}$ represents a positive and decreasing function,

$$\lim_{\ell \to \infty} y^{(n-2)}(\ell)/\pi_0^{\beta_0}(\ell) = c_2 \geq 0.$$

Our claim asserts that $c_2 = 0$. To support this claim, assume the contrary, where $c_2 \neq 0$. In such a scenario, it follows that $y^{(n-2)}/\pi_0^{\beta_0} \geq c_2 > 0$ eventually. Let us introduce the function

$$w = \frac{y^{(n-2)} + \pi_0 r^{1/\alpha}y^{(n-1)}}{\pi_0^{\beta_0}}.$$

Considering the expression ($Y_{1,3}$), it is observed that $w > 0$ and

$$\begin{aligned}
w' &= \frac{y^{(n-1)} + \pi_0\left(r^{1/\alpha}y^{(n-1)}\right)' - y^{(n-1)}}{\pi_0^{\beta_0}(\ell)} + \beta_0 \frac{y^{(n-2)} + \pi_0 r^{1/\alpha}y^{(n-1)}}{r^{1/\alpha}\pi_0^{1+\beta_0}} \\
&= \frac{\left(r^{1/\alpha}y^{(n-1)}\right)'}{\pi_0^{\beta_0-1}} + \beta_0 \frac{y^{(n-2)}}{r^{1/\alpha}\pi_0^{1+\beta_0}} + \beta_0 \frac{y^{(n-1)}}{\pi_0^{\beta_0}} \\
&= \frac{1}{\alpha}\frac{\left(r\left(y^{(n-1)}\right)^{\alpha}\right)'\left(r^{1/\alpha}y^{(n-1)}\right)^{1-\alpha}}{\pi_0^{\beta_0-1}} \\
&\quad + \beta_0 \frac{y^{(n-2)}}{r^{1/\alpha}\pi_0^{1+\beta_0}} + \beta_0 \frac{y^{(n-1)}}{\pi_0^{\beta_0}}.
\end{aligned}$$

Using ($Y_{1,2}$), ($Y_{1,6}$), and Equation (4), we obtain

$$\left(r\left(y^{(n-1)}\right)^{\alpha}\right)' \leq -\alpha\beta_0^{\alpha}\frac{1}{r^{1/\alpha}\pi_0^{1+\alpha}}\left(y^{(n-2)}(\sigma)\right)^{\alpha}. \qquad (7)$$

From Equation (6), we know that

$$r^{1/\alpha}y^{(n-1)} \leq -\beta_0 \frac{y^{(n-2)}}{\pi_0},$$

and

$$\left(r^{1/\alpha}y^{(n-1)}\right)^{1-\alpha} \geq \left(\beta_0 \frac{y^{(n-2)}}{\pi_0}\right)^{1-\alpha}. \qquad (8)$$

Using (7) and (8), we obtain

$$w' \leq -\frac{\beta_0^\alpha}{\pi_0^{\beta_0-1}} \frac{1}{r^{1/\alpha}\pi_0^{1+\alpha}} \left(y^{(n-2)}(\sigma)\right)^\alpha \left(\beta_0 \frac{y^{(n-2)}}{\pi_0}\right)^{1-\alpha}$$
$$+ \beta_0 \frac{y^{(n-2)}}{r^{1/\alpha}\pi_0^{1+\beta_0}} + \beta_0 \frac{y^{(n-1)}}{\pi_0^{\beta_0}}.$$

Since $y^{(n-1)} < 0$, $\sigma(\ell) \leq \ell$, we obtain $y^{(n-2)}(\sigma(\ell)) \geq y^{(n-2)}(\ell)$, and then

$$w' \leq -\frac{\beta_0^\alpha}{\pi_0^{\beta_0-1}} \frac{1}{r^{1/\alpha}\pi_0^{1+\alpha}} \left(y^{(n-2)}\right)^\alpha \left(\beta_0 \frac{y^{(n-2)}}{\pi_0}\right)^{1-\alpha}$$
$$+ \beta_0 \frac{y^{(n-2)}}{r^{1/\alpha}\pi_0^{1+\beta_0}} + \beta_0 \frac{y^{(n-1)}}{\pi_0^{\beta_0}}$$
$$\leq -\beta_0 \frac{y^{(n-2)}}{r^{1/\alpha}\pi_0^{1+\beta_0}} + \beta_0 \frac{y^{(n-2)}}{r^{1/\alpha}\pi_0^{1+\beta_0}} + \beta_0 \frac{y^{(n-1)}}{\pi_0^{\beta_0}}$$
$$\leq \beta_0 \frac{y^{(n-1)}}{\pi_0^{\beta_0}}.$$

Using the fact that $y^{(n-2)}/\pi_0^{\beta_0} \geq c_2$, and Equation (6), we have

$$w' \leq \beta_0 \frac{y^{(n-1)}}{\pi_0^{\beta_0}} \leq \beta_0 \frac{1}{\pi_0^{\beta_0}} \left(\frac{-\beta_0 y^{(n-2)}}{r^{1/\alpha}\pi_0}\right)$$
$$\leq -\frac{y^{(n-2)}}{\pi_0^{\beta_0}} \frac{\beta_0^2}{r^{1/\alpha}\pi_0} \leq \frac{-c_2\beta_0^2}{r^{1/\alpha}\pi_0} < 0.$$

The function w tends toward a constant non-negative value due to its consistent positive and decreasing nature. After integrating the preceding inequality from ℓ_3 to ∞, the result is as follows

$$-w(\ell_3) \leq -\beta_0^2 c_2 \lim_{\ell \to \infty} \ln \frac{\pi_0(\ell_3)}{\pi_0(\ell)},$$

or equivalently

$$w(\ell_3) \geq \beta_0^2 c_2 \lim_{\ell \to \infty} \ln \frac{\pi_0(\ell_3)}{\pi_0(\ell)} \to \infty,$$

which is a contradiction, and we obtain $c_2 = 0$.

($Y_{2,4}$) Now, we have

$$\left(r^{1/\alpha} y^{(n-1)} \pi_0 + y^{(n-2)}\right)'$$
$$= \left(r^{1/\alpha} y^{(n-1)}\right)' \pi_0 - y^{(n-1)} + y^{(n-1)}$$
$$= \left(r^{1/\alpha} y^{(n-1)}\right)' \pi_0$$
$$= \frac{1}{\alpha} \left(r\left(y^{(n-1)}\right)^\alpha\right)' \left(r^{1/\alpha} y^{(n-1)}\right)^{1-\alpha} \pi_0,$$

which with (7) and (8), we obtain

$$
\begin{aligned}
\left(r^{1/\alpha}y^{(n-1)}\pi_0 + y^{(n-2)}\right)' & \\
\leq -\beta_0^\alpha \frac{1}{r^{1/\alpha}\pi_0^{1+\alpha}}\left(y^{(n-2)}(\sigma)\right)^\alpha &\left(\beta_0\frac{y^{(n-2)}}{\pi_0}\right)^{1-\alpha}\pi_0 \\
\leq -\beta_0^\alpha \frac{1}{r^{1/\alpha}\pi_0^\alpha}\left(y^{(n-2)}\right)^\alpha &\left(\beta_0\frac{y^{(n-2)}}{\pi_0}\right)^{1-\alpha} \\
\leq \frac{-\beta_0}{r^{1/\alpha}\pi_0}y^{(n-2)}.
\end{aligned}
$$

When we integrate the previous inequality from ℓ to ∞, we arrive at

$$-r^{1/\alpha}(\ell)y^{(n-1)}(\ell)\pi_0(\ell) - y^{(n-2)}(\ell) \leq -\beta_0 \int_\ell^\infty \frac{1}{r^{1/\alpha}(s)\pi_0(s)}y^{(n-2)}(s)ds,$$

or equivalently

$$
\begin{aligned}
r^{1/\alpha}(\ell)y^{(n-1)}(\ell)\pi_0(\ell) + y^{(n-2)}(\ell) &\geq \beta_0 \int_\ell^\infty \frac{1}{r^{1/\alpha}(s)\pi_0(s)}y^{(n-2)}(s)ds \\
&\geq \beta_0 \frac{y^{(n-2)}(\ell)}{\pi_0(\ell)}\int_\ell^\infty \frac{1}{r^{1/\alpha}(s)}ds \\
&\geq \beta_0 y^{(n-2)}(\ell).
\end{aligned}
$$

That is,
$$r^{1/\alpha}y^{(n-1)}\pi_0 + (1-\beta_0)y^{(n-2)} \geq 0.$$

Thus,
$$\left(\frac{y^{(n-2)}}{\pi_0^{1-\beta_0}}\right)' = \frac{\pi_0 r^{1/\alpha}y^{(n-1)} + (1-\beta_0)y^{(n-2)}}{r^{1/\alpha}\pi_0^{2-\beta_0}} \geq 0. \qquad (9)$$

□

If the condition $\beta_0 \leq 1/2$ holds, we have the opportunity to improve the characteristics stated in Lemma 6. This improvement is demonstrated in the subsequent lemma.

Lemma 7. *Assuming that $\chi \in \Omega_2$ and Condition (4) is satisfied. If the following limit is satisfied:*

$$\lim_{\ell \to \infty} \frac{\pi_0(\sigma(\ell))}{\pi_0(\ell)} = \lambda < \infty, \qquad (10)$$

and there exists an increasing sequence $\{\beta_j\}_{j=1}^m$ defined as follows:

$$\beta_j := \beta_0 \frac{\lambda^{\beta_{j-1}}}{(1-\beta_{j-1})^{1/\alpha}},$$

where $\alpha \leq 1, \beta_0 = \epsilon\delta^{1/\alpha}, \beta_{m-1} \leq 1/2$ and $\beta_m, \epsilon \in (0,1)$, then eventually,

$(Y_{3,1})$ $y^{(n-2)}/\pi_0^{\beta_m}$ *is decreasing;*

$(Y_{3,2})$ $\lim_{\ell \to \infty} y^{(n-2)}(\ell)/\pi_0^{\beta_m}(\ell) = 0.$

Proof. $(Y_{3,1})$ Since $\chi \in \Omega_2$, we can conclude that $(Y_{1,1})$–$(Y_{1,5})$ in Lemma 5 are satisfied for all $\ell \geq \ell_1$, with ℓ_1 being large enough. Furthermore, from Lemma 6, we have that $(Y_{2,1})$–$(Y_{2,4})$ hold.

Now, assume that $\beta_0 \leq 1/2$, and

$$\beta_1 := \beta_0 \frac{\lambda^{\beta_0}}{(1-\beta_0)^{1/\alpha}}.$$

Next, we will prove $(Y_{3,1})$ and $(Y_{3,2})$ at $m=1$. Following the proof in Lemma 6, we obtain the inequality:

$$\left(r\left(y^{(n-1)}\right)^\alpha\right)' \leq -\alpha\beta_0^\alpha \frac{1}{r^{1/\alpha}\pi_0^{1+\alpha}}\left(y^{(n-2)}(\sigma)\right)^\alpha,$$

By integrating the final inequality from ℓ_1 to ℓ, and employing $(Y_{2,2})$ and condition (10), we can derive the following expression

$$r(\ell)\left(y^{(n-1)}(\ell)\right)^\alpha$$
$$\leq r(\ell_1)\left(y^{(n-1)}(\ell_1)\right)^\alpha - \alpha\beta_0^\alpha \int_{\ell_1}^\ell \frac{1}{r^{1/\alpha}(s)\pi_0^{1+\alpha}(s)}\left(y^{(n-2)}(\sigma(s))\right)^\alpha ds$$
$$\leq r(\ell_1)\left(y^{(n-1)}(\ell_1)\right)^\alpha - \alpha\beta_0^\alpha \int_{\ell_1}^\ell \frac{1}{r^{1/\alpha}(s)\pi_0^{1+\alpha}(s)}\pi_0^{\alpha\beta_0}(\sigma(s))\left(\frac{y^{(n-2)}(s)}{\pi_0^{\beta_0}(s)}\right)^\alpha ds$$
$$\leq r(\ell_1)\left(y^{(n-1)}(\ell_1)\right)^\alpha - \alpha\beta_0^\alpha \left(\frac{y^{(n-2)}(\ell)}{\pi_0^{\beta_0}(\ell)}\right)^\alpha \int_{\ell_1}^\ell \frac{\pi_0^{-1-\alpha+\alpha\beta_0}(s)}{r^{1/\alpha}(s)} \frac{\pi_0^{\alpha\beta_0}(\sigma(s))}{\pi_0^{\alpha\beta_0}(s)} ds$$
$$\leq r(\ell_1)\left(y^{(n-1)}(\ell_1)\right)^\alpha - \alpha\beta_0^\alpha \lambda^{\alpha\beta_0}\left(\frac{y^{(n-2)}(\ell)}{\pi_0^{\beta_0}(\ell)}\right)^\alpha \int_{\ell_1}^\ell \frac{\pi_0^{-1-\alpha+\alpha\beta_0}(s)}{r^{1/\alpha}(s)} ds$$
$$\leq r(\ell_1)\left(y^{(n-1)}(\ell_1)\right)^\alpha - \frac{\beta_0^\alpha \lambda^{\alpha\beta_0}}{1-\beta_0}\left(\frac{y^{(n-2)}(\ell)}{\pi_0^{\beta_0}(\ell)}\right)^\alpha \left(\frac{1}{\pi_0^{\alpha(1-\beta_0)}(\ell)} - \frac{1}{\pi_0^{\alpha(1-\beta_0)}(\ell_1)}\right)$$
$$\leq r(\ell_1)\left(y^{(n-1)}(\ell_1)\right)^\alpha + \beta_1^\alpha \frac{1}{\pi_0^{\alpha(1-\beta_0)}(\ell_1)}\left(\frac{y^{(n-2)}(\ell)}{\pi_0^{\beta_0}(\ell)}\right)^\alpha - \beta_1^\alpha \left(\frac{y^{(n-2)}(\ell)}{\pi_0(\ell)}\right)^\alpha.$$

Using the fact that $y^{(n-2)}(\ell)/\pi_0^{\beta_0}(\ell) \to 0$ as $\ell \to \infty$, we have that

$$r(\ell_1)\left(y^{(n-1)}(\ell_1)\right)^\alpha + \beta_1^\alpha \frac{1}{\pi_0^{\alpha(1-\beta_0)}(\ell_1)}\left(\frac{y^{(n-2)}(\ell)}{\pi_0^{\beta_0}(\ell)}\right)^\alpha \leq 0.$$

Therefore,

$$r\left(y^{(n-1)}\right)^\alpha \leq -\beta_1^\alpha \left(\frac{y^{(n-2)}}{\pi_0}\right)^\alpha,$$

or equivalently

$$r^{1/\alpha}y^{(n-1)}\pi_0 + \beta_1 y^{(n-2)} \leq 0,$$

and then

$$\left(\frac{y^{(n-2)}}{\pi_0^{\beta_1}}\right)' = \frac{\pi_0 r^{1/\alpha}y^{(n-1)} + \beta_1 y^{(n-2)}}{r^{1/\alpha}\pi_0^{1+\beta_1}} \leq 0.$$

By employing the method previously utilized, we can demonstrate that

$$\lim_{\ell \to \infty} \frac{y^{(n-2)}(\ell)}{\pi_0^{\beta_1}(\ell)} = 0,$$

and
$$\left(\frac{y^{(n-2)}}{\pi_0^{1-\beta_1}}\right)' \geq 0.$$

Moreover, if $\beta_{k-1} < \beta_k \leq 1/2$, then we can establish that
$$r^{1/\alpha} y^{(n-1)} \pi_0 + \beta_k y^{(n-2)} \leq 0, \quad (11)$$
and
$$\lim_{\ell \to \infty} \frac{y^{(n-2)}(\ell)}{\pi_0^{\beta_k}(\ell)} = 0,$$
for $k = 2, 3, \ldots, m$. This, in turn, concludes the proof of the Lemma. □

Theorem 1. *Assuming that condition (4) is satisfied. If*
$$\beta_0 > 1/2, \quad (12)$$
then $\Omega_2 = \varnothing$. Here, β_0 is defined according to Lemma 6.

Proof. Assume that $\chi \in \Omega_2$ leads to a contradiction. According to Lemma 6, the functions $y^{(n-2)}/\pi_0^{\beta_0}$ and $y^{(n-2)}/\pi_0^{1-\beta_0}$ are decreasing and increasing for $\ell \geq \ell_1$, respectively. As a result, we can conclude that
$$\beta_0 \leq 1/2.$$

This conclusion contradicts the initial assumption. Hence, the proof is considered complete. □

Theorem 2. *Let us assume that conditions (4) and (10) are satisfied. Suppose there exists a positive integer value m, such that the following inequality holds*
$$\liminf_{\ell \to \infty} \int_{\sigma(\ell)}^{\ell} \pi_0(s) \pi_0^{\alpha-1}(\sigma(s)) \left(\sigma^{n-2}(s)\right)^{\alpha} Q_1(s) ds > \frac{\alpha \beta_m^{\alpha-1}(1-\beta_m)((n-2)!)^{\alpha}}{e}, \quad (13)$$
then $\Omega_2 = \varnothing$, where $\alpha \leq 1$.

Proof. Let us assume the opposite scenario, where $\chi \in \Omega_2$. According to the information provided in Lemma 7, it follows that both $(Y_{3,1})$ and $(Y_{3,2})$ hold.
We can now establish the function in the following manner
$$w = r^{1/\alpha} y^{(n-1)} \pi_0 + y^{(n-2)}.$$

From $(Y_{1,3})$, we can deduce that $w > 0$ when $\ell \geq \ell_1$. Furthermore, according to $(Y_{3,1})$, we can conclude that
$$r^{1/\alpha} y^{(n-1)} \pi_0 \leq -\beta_m y^{(n-2)}.$$

Next, based on the definition of w, we can derive that
$$\begin{aligned} w(\ell) &= r^{1/\alpha} y^{(n-1)} \pi_0 + \beta_m y^{(n-2)} - \beta_m y^{(n-2)} + y^{(n-2)} \\ &\leq (1-\beta_m) y^{(n-2)}. \end{aligned} \quad (14)$$

By employing Lemma 5, we can determine that $(Y_{1,1})$–$(Y_{1,5})$ hold. From $(Y_{1,2})$ and $(Y_{1,6})$, we obtain

$$\begin{aligned}
w' &= \left(r^{1/\alpha} y^{(n-1)}\right)' \pi_0 \\
&\leq \frac{1}{\alpha} \left(r\left(y^{(n-1)}\right)^\alpha\right)' \left(r^{1/\alpha} y^{(n-1)}\right)^{1-\alpha} \pi_0 \\
&\leq -\frac{1}{\alpha} \left(\sum_{i=1}^{v} q_i p_1^\alpha(\sigma_i; \kappa)\right) y^\alpha(\sigma) \left(r^{1/\alpha} y^{(n-1)}\right)^{1-\alpha} \pi_0 \\
&\leq -\frac{1}{\alpha} Q_1 y^\alpha(\sigma) \left(\beta_m \frac{y^{(n-2)}}{\pi_0}\right)^{1-\alpha} \pi_0 \\
&\leq -\frac{1}{\alpha} \beta_m^{1-\alpha} Q_1 \pi_0 y^\alpha(\sigma) \left(\frac{y^{(n-2)}}{\pi_0}\right)^{1-\alpha} \\
&\leq -\frac{1}{\alpha} \beta_m^{1-\alpha} Q_1 \pi_0 \left(\frac{\epsilon}{(n-2)!} \sigma^{n-2}\right)^\alpha \left(y^{(n-2)}(\sigma)\right)^\alpha \left(\frac{y^{(n-2)}}{\pi_0}\right)^{1-\alpha}.
\end{aligned}$$

Using $(Y_{1,4})$ in Lemma 5, we note that $y^{(n-2)}(\ell)/\pi_0(\ell)$ is increasing, then

$$\frac{y^{(n-2)}(\sigma)}{\pi_0(\sigma)} \leq \frac{y^{(n-2)}}{\pi_0},$$

and

$$\left(\frac{y^{(n-2)}(\sigma)}{\pi_0(\sigma)}\right)^{1-\alpha} \leq \left(\frac{y^{(n-2)}}{\pi_0}\right)^{1-\alpha}.$$

Therefore,

$$w' \leq -\frac{1}{\alpha} \frac{\beta_m^{1-\alpha} \epsilon^\alpha}{((n-2)!)^\alpha} Q_1 \frac{\pi_0}{\pi_0^{1-\alpha}(\sigma)} \left(\sigma^{n-2}\right)^\alpha y^{(n-2)}(\sigma).$$

From Equation (14), we obtain the following

$$w' + \frac{1}{\alpha} \frac{\epsilon^\alpha \beta_m^{1-\alpha}}{((n-2)!)^\alpha (1-\beta_m)} \frac{\pi_0}{\pi_0^{1-\alpha}(\sigma)} \left(\sigma^{n-2}\right)^\alpha Q_1 w(\sigma) \leq 0. \tag{15}$$

Therefore, w represents a constructive solution to the differential inequality (15). Nevertheless, according to the findings presented in Theorem 2.1.1 from [8], condition (13) ensures the oscillatory nature of Equation (15). Consequently, this contradiction serves as conclusive evidence for proving the theorem. □

3.2. Category Ω_3

Lemma 8. *Suppose that $\chi \in \Omega_3$. Under this assumption, the following conditions hold for sufficiently large values of ℓ:*

$(Y_{4,1})$ *The expression y/π_{n-2} is monotonically increasing;*

$(Y_{4,2})$ *For all $i = 0, 1, 2, \ldots, n-2$, we have $(-1)^{i+1} y^{(n-i-2)} \leq r^{1/\alpha} y^{(n-1)} \pi_i$.*

Proof. ($Y_{4,1}$) Suppose that $\chi \in \Omega_3$. From Equation (1), we have $r\left(y^{(n-1)}\right)^\alpha$ is decreasing, and, hence,

$$r^{1/\alpha}(\ell)y^{(n-1)}(\ell)\int_\ell^\infty \frac{1}{r^{1/\alpha}(s)}ds \geq \int_\ell^\infty \frac{1}{r^{1/\alpha}(s)}r^{1/\alpha}(s)y^{(n-1)}(s)ds$$
$$= \lim_{\ell\to\infty} y^{(n-2)}(\ell) - y^{(n-2)}(\ell). \qquad (16)$$

Given that $y^{(n-2)}$ represents a positive and decreasing function, it exhibits convergence toward a non-negative constant, as $\ell \to \infty$. Consequently, the Equation (16) can be represented as

$$-y^{(n-2)} \leq r^{1/\alpha}y^{(n-1)}\pi_0,$$

which implies that

$$\left(\frac{y^{(n-2)}}{\pi_0}\right)' = \frac{r^{1/\alpha}\pi_0 y^{(n-1)} + y^{(n-2)}}{r^{1/\alpha}\pi_0^2} \geq 0,$$

which leads to

$$-y^{(n-3)}(\ell) = \int_\ell^\infty \frac{y^{(n-2)}(s)}{\pi_0(s)}\pi_0(s)ds \geq \frac{y^{(n-2)}(\ell)}{\pi_0(\ell)}\pi_1(\ell).$$

This implies

$$\left(\frac{y^{(n-3)}}{\pi_1}\right)' = \frac{\pi_1 y^{(n-2)} + y^{(n-3)}\pi_0}{\pi_1^2} \leq 0.$$

Additionally, we iterate the aforementioned procedure $(n-4)$ times to yield

$$\left(\frac{y'}{\pi_{n-3}}\right)' \leq 0.$$

Now

$$-y(\ell) = \int_\ell^\infty \frac{y'(s)}{\pi_{n-3}(s)}\pi_{n-3}(s)ds \leq \frac{y'(\ell)}{\pi_{n-3}(\ell)}\pi_{n-2}(\ell).$$

This implies

$$\left(\frac{y}{\pi_{n-2}}\right)' = \frac{\pi_{n-2}y' + y\pi_{n-3}}{\pi_{n-2}^2} \geq 0.$$

($Y_{4,1}$) Assume that $\chi \in \Omega_3$. Then, we obtain

$$r^{1/\alpha}(\ell)y^{(n-1)}(\ell)\pi_0(\ell) \geq \int_\ell^\infty \frac{r^{1/\alpha}(s)y^{(n-1)}(s)}{r^{1/\alpha}(s)}ds \geq -y^{(n-2)}(\ell),$$

or equivalently

$$y^{(n-2)} \geq -r^{1/\alpha}y^{(n-1)}\pi_0.$$

After integrating the final inequality from ℓ to ∞, the result is expressed as

$$-y^{(n-3)}(\ell) \geq -\int_\ell^\infty r^{1/\alpha}(s)y^{(n-1)}(s)\pi_0(s)ds$$
$$\geq -r^{1/\alpha}(\ell)y^{(n-1)}(\ell)\int_\ell^\infty \pi_0(s)ds$$
$$\geq -r^{1/\alpha}(\ell)y^{(n-1)}(\ell)\pi_1(s),$$

or equivalently

$$y^{(n-3)} \leq r^{1/\alpha}y^{(n-1)}\pi_1.$$

After integrating the final inequality from ℓ to ∞, the result is expressed as

$$\begin{aligned}
-y^{(n-4)}(\ell) &\leq \int_\ell^\infty r^{1/\alpha}(s)y^{(n-1)}(s)\pi_1(s)ds \\
&\leq r^{1/\alpha}(\ell)y^{(n-1)}(\ell)\int_\ell^\infty \pi_1(s)ds \\
&\leq r^{1/\alpha}(\ell)y^{(n-1)}(\ell)\pi_2(\ell),
\end{aligned}$$

or equivalently

$$y^{(n-4)} \geq -r^{1/\alpha}y^{(n-1)}\pi_2.$$

Through iterative integration of the preceding inequality from ℓ to ∞, we deduce that

$$(-1)^{i+1}y^{(n-i-2)} \leq r^{1/\alpha}y^{(n-1)}\pi_i,$$

for $i = 0, 1, 2, \ldots, n-2$. The lemma's proof is now complete. $\square$

Lemma 9. *If $\chi \in \Omega_3$, then eventually*

$(Y_{5,1})$ $\chi > p_2(\ell,\kappa)y;$

$(Y_{5,2})$ $\left(r\left(y^{(n-1)}\right)^\alpha\right)' \leq -Q_2 y^\alpha(\widetilde{\sigma}).$

Proof. $(Y_{5,1})$ From Lemma 1, we have Equation (3) holds. From $(Y_{4,1})$, we conclude that

$$y\left(\eta^{[2r+1]}\right) \leq \frac{\pi_{n-2}\left(\eta^{[2r+1]}\right)}{\pi_{n-2}\left(\eta^{[2r]}\right)} y\left(\eta^{[2r]}\right),$$

which, with Equation (3), gives

$$\chi > \sum_{r=0}^\kappa \left(\prod_{l=0}^{2r} p\left(\eta^{[l]}\right)\right)\left[\frac{1}{p\left(\eta^{[2r]}\right)} - \frac{\pi_{n-2}\left(\eta^{[2r+1]}\right)}{\pi_{n-2}\left(\eta^{[2r]}\right)}\right] y\left(\eta^{[2r]}\right). \qquad (17)$$

Since y is decreasing, then Equation (17) becomes

$$\begin{aligned}
\chi &> \sum_{r=0}^\kappa \left(\prod_{l=0}^{2r} p\left(\eta^{[l]}\right)\right)\left[\frac{1}{p\left(\eta^{[2r]}\right)} - \frac{\pi_{n-2}\left(\eta^{[2r+1]}\right)}{\pi_{n-2}\left(\eta^{[2r]}\right)}\right] y \\
&= p_2(\ell,\kappa)y(\ell).
\end{aligned}$$

$(Y_{5,2})$ Equation (1) with $(Y_{5,1})$ becomes

$$\begin{aligned}
\left(r\left(y^{(n-1)}\right)^\alpha\right)' &= \sum_{i=1}^v -q_i \chi^\alpha(\sigma_i) \\
&\leq -\sum_{i=1}^v q_i p_2^\alpha(\sigma_i,\kappa) y^\alpha(\sigma_i) \\
&\leq -y^\alpha(\widetilde{\sigma})Q_2.
\end{aligned}$$

Therefore, the Lemma's proof has been successfully concluded. $\square$

Lemma 10. *Assume that $\chi \in \Omega_3$. If*

$$\int_{\ell_0}^\infty \left(\frac{1}{r(u)}\int_{\ell_0}^u Q_2(s)ds\right)^{1/\alpha} du = \infty, \qquad (18)$$

and there exists a $k_0 \in (0,1)$, such that

$$\frac{1}{\alpha}\pi_{n-2}^{\alpha+1}(\ell)\pi_{n-3}^{-1}(\ell)Q_2(\ell) \geq k_0^{\alpha}. \tag{19}$$

Then

$(Y_{6,1})$ $\lim_{\ell \to \infty} y(\ell) = 0$;

$(Y_{6,2})$ $y(\ell)/\pi_{n-2}^{k_0}(\ell)$ is decreasing;

$(Y_{6,3})$ $\lim_{\ell \to \infty} y(\ell)/\pi_{n-2}^{\beta_0}(\ell) = 0$;

Proof. $(Y_{6,1})$ Assume that $\chi \in \Omega_3$. Since y is positive and decreasing, we have that $\lim_{\ell \to \infty} y(\ell) = c_3 \geq 0$. Assume the contrary, that $c_3 > 0$. Then there is a $\ell_2 \geq \ell_1$ with $y \geq c_3$ for $\ell \geq \ell_2$. Then from $(Y_{5,2})$, we obtain

$$\left(r\left(y^{(n-1)}\right)^{\alpha}\right)' \leq -y^{\alpha}(\widetilde{\sigma})Q_2$$
$$\leq -c_3^{\alpha}Q_2.$$

Integrating this inequality twice from ℓ_2 to ℓ, we obtain

$$r(\ell)\left(y^{(n-1)}(\ell)\right)^{\alpha} - r(\ell_2)\left(y^{(n-1)}(\ell_2)\right)^{\alpha} \leq -c_3^{\alpha}\int_{\ell_2}^{\ell}Q_2(s)ds.$$

Using case (C_3), we have $y^{(n-1)} < 0$ for $\ell \geq \ell_1$. Then, $r(\ell_2)\left(y^{(n-1)}(\ell_2)\right)^{\alpha} < 0$, and so

$$y^{(n-1)}(\ell) \leq -\frac{c_3}{r^{1/\alpha}(\ell)}\int_{\ell_2}^{\ell}Q_2(s)ds,$$

and then

$$y^{(n-2)}(\ell) \leq y^{(n-2)}(\ell_2) - c_3\int_{\ell_2}^{\ell}\left(\frac{1}{r(u)}\int_{\ell_2}^{u}Q_2(s)ds\right)^{1/\alpha}du \to -\infty \text{ as } \ell \to \infty.$$

This contradicts the positivity of $y^{(n-2)}$. Therefore, $c_3 = 0$.

$(Y_{6,2})$ Integrating $(Y_{5,2})$ from ℓ_2 to ℓ, and using Equation (19), we obtain

$$r(\ell)\left(y^{(n-1)}(\ell)\right)^{\alpha} \leq r(\ell_2)\left(y^{(n-1)}(\ell_2)\right)^{\alpha} - y^{\alpha}(\widetilde{\sigma}(s))\int_{\ell_2}^{\ell}Q_2(s)ds$$
$$\leq r(\ell_2)\left(y^{(n-1)}(\ell_2)\right)^{\alpha} - y^{\alpha}(\ell)\int_{\ell_2}^{\ell}Q_2(s)ds$$
$$\leq r(\ell_2)\left(y^{(n-1)}(\ell_2)\right)^{\alpha} - y^{\alpha}(\ell)\int_{\ell_2}^{\ell}\alpha k_0^{\alpha}\frac{\pi_{n-3}(s)}{\pi_{n-2}^{\alpha+1}(s)}ds$$
$$\leq r(\ell_2)\left(y^{(n-1)}(\ell_2)\right)^{\alpha} + k_0^{\alpha}\frac{y^{\alpha}(\ell)}{\pi_{n-2}^{\alpha}(\ell_2)} - k_0^{\alpha}\frac{y^{\alpha}(\ell)}{\pi_{n-2}^{\alpha}(\ell)},$$

which, with $(Y_{6,1})$, gives

$$r\left(y^{(n-1)}\right)^{\alpha} \leq -k_0^{\alpha}\frac{y^{\alpha}}{\pi_{n-2}^{\alpha}},$$

or equivalently

$$r^{1/\alpha}y^{(n-1)} \leq -k_0\frac{y}{\pi_{n-2}}. \tag{20}$$

Thus, from (Y$_{4,2}$) at $i = n - 3$, we have
$$\frac{y'}{\pi_{n-3}} \leq -k_0 \frac{y}{\pi_{n-2}},$$
or equivalently
$$\pi_{n-2} y' + k_0 \pi_{n-3} y \leq 0. \tag{21}$$

Consequently,
$$\left(\frac{y}{\pi_{n-2}^{k_0}}\right)' = \frac{\pi_{n-2} y' + k_0 \pi_{n-3} y}{\pi_{n-2}^{k_0+1}} \leq 0.$$

(Y$_{6,3}$) Since $y/\pi_{n-2}^{k_0}$ is both positive and decreasing, we can conclude that $\lim_{\ell \to \infty} y(\ell)/\pi_{n-2}^{k_0}(\ell) = c_4 \geq 0$. Now, let's assume the opposite, that is, $c_4 > 0$. In this case, there exists a $\ell_2 \geq \ell_1$ with $y/\pi_{n-2}^{k_0} \geq c_4$ for $\ell \geq \ell_2$. Next, we define:
$$\varphi := \frac{y + r^{1/\alpha} y^{(n-1)} \pi_{n-2}}{\pi_{n-2}^{k_0}}.$$

Then, from (Y$_{4,2}$), $\varphi \geq 0$ for $\ell \geq \ell_2$. Differentiating φ and (Y$_{4,2}$), we find

$$\begin{aligned}
\varphi'(\ell) &= \frac{1}{\pi_{n-2}^{2k_0}(\ell)} \left[\pi_{n-2}^{k_0}(\ell) \left(y'(\ell) - r^{1/\alpha}(\ell) y^{(n-1)}(\ell) \pi_{n-3}(\ell) + \left(r^{1/\alpha}(\ell) \chi^{(n-1)}(\ell)\right)' \pi_{n-2}(\ell) \right) \right. \\
&\quad \left. + k_0 \pi_{n-2}^{k_0-1}(\ell) \pi_{n-3}(\ell) \left(y(\ell) + r^{1/\alpha}(\ell) y^{(n-1)}(\ell) \pi_{n-2}(\ell) \right) \right] \\
&\leq \frac{1}{\pi_{n-2}^{k_0+1}(\ell)} \left[\left(r^{1/\alpha}(\ell) y^{(n-1)}(\ell)\right)' \pi_{n-2}^2(\ell) + k_0 \pi_{n-3}(\ell) \left(y(\ell) + r^{1/\alpha}(\ell) y^{(n-1)}(\ell) \pi_{n-2}(\ell) \right) \right] \\
&\leq \frac{1}{\pi_{n-2}^{k_0+1}(\ell)} \left[\frac{1}{\alpha} \left(r(\ell) \left(y^{(n-1)}(\ell) \right)^\alpha \right)' \left(r^{1/\alpha}(\ell) y^{(n-1)}(\ell) \right)^{1-\alpha} \pi_{n-2}^2(\ell) \right. \\
&\quad \left. + k_0 \pi_{n-3}(\ell) \left(y(\ell) + r^{1/\alpha}(\ell) y^{(n-1)}(\ell) \pi_{n-2}(\ell) \right) \right].
\end{aligned}$$

Using (Y$_{5,2}$), we find
$$\varphi' \leq \frac{1}{\pi_{n-2}^{k_0+1}} \left[\frac{-1}{\alpha} Q_2 y^\alpha(\widetilde{\sigma}) \left(r^{1/\alpha} y^{(n-1)} \right)^{1-\alpha} \pi_{n-2}^2 \right. \\
\left. + k_0 \pi_{n-3} y + k_0 \pi_{n-3} r^{1/\alpha} y^{(n-1)} \pi_{n-2} \right].$$

Since $\alpha \leq 1$, $y^{(n-1)} \leq 0$, and
$$r^{1/\alpha} y^{(n-1)} \leq -k_0 \frac{y}{\pi_{n-2}},$$
also
$$-r^{1/\alpha} y^{(n-1)} \geq k_0 \frac{y}{\pi_{n-2}},$$
which implies that
$$\left(r^{1/\alpha} y^{(n-1)} \right)^{1-\alpha} \geq \left(k_0 \frac{y}{\pi_{n-2}} \right)^{1-\alpha}.$$

Then
$$\varphi' \leq \frac{1}{\pi_{n-2}^{k_0+1}} \left[\frac{-1}{\alpha} Q_2 y^\alpha \left(k_0 \frac{y}{\pi_{n-2}} \right)^{1-\alpha} \pi_{n-2}^2 \right.$$
$$\left. + k_0 \pi_{n-3} y + k_0 \pi_{n-3} r^{1/\alpha} y^{(n-1)} \pi_{n-2} \right]$$
$$\leq \frac{1}{\pi_{n-2}^{k_0+1}} \left[\frac{-k_0^{1-\alpha}}{\alpha} Q_2 \pi_{n-2}^{\alpha+1} y \right.$$
$$\left. + k_0 \pi_{n-3} y + k_0 \pi_{n-3} r^{1/\alpha} y^{(n-1)} \pi_{n-2} \right].$$

Using Equation (19), we obtain

$$\varphi'(\ell) \leq \frac{1}{\pi_{n-2}^{k_0+1}(\ell)} \left[-k_0 \pi_{n-3}(\ell) y(\ell) + k_0 \pi_{n-3}(\ell) y(\ell) + k_0 \pi_{n-3}(\ell) r^{1/\alpha}(\ell) y^{(n-1)}(\ell) \pi_{n-2}(\ell) \right]$$
$$= \frac{1}{\pi_{n-2}^{k_0}(\ell)} k_0 \pi_{n-3}(\ell) r^{1/\alpha}(\ell) y^{(n-1)}(\ell). \tag{22}$$

Using the fact that $y/\pi_{n-2}^{k_0} \geq c_4$ with (20), we obtain

$$r^{1/\alpha} y^{(n-1)} \leq -k_0 \frac{y}{\pi_{n-2}} \leq -k_0 c_4 \pi_{n-2}^{k_0-1}. \tag{23}$$

Combining (22) and (23), we obtain

$$\varphi' \leq -k_0^2 c_4 \frac{\pi_{n-3}}{\pi_{n-2}} < 0.$$

By integrating the preceding inequality from ℓ_2 to ℓ, we obtain

$$\varphi(\ell_2) \geq k_0^2 c_4 \ln \frac{\pi_{n-2}(\ell_2)}{\pi_{n-2}(\ell)} \to \infty \text{ as } \ell \to \infty,$$

a contradiction, and so, $c_4 = 0$. Consequently, the lemma's proof is now complete. □

Lemma 11. *Let's suppose that $\chi(\ell) \in \Omega_3$ and (18) and (19) are satisfied for a certain value of $k_0 \in (0,1)$. If, for every i from 1 to $m-1$, it holds that $k_{i-1} \leq k_i < 1$, then*
$(Y_{7,1,m})$ $y/\pi_{n-2}^{k_m}$ *is decreasing;*
$(Y_{7,2,m})$ $\lim_{\ell \to \infty} y(\ell)/\pi_{n-2}^{k_m}(\ell) = 0;$
where
$$k_j = k_0 \frac{\lambda_1^{k_{j-1}}}{(1-k_{j-1})^{1/\alpha}}, \ j = 1, 2, \ldots, m, \tag{24}$$
and
$$\frac{\pi_{n-2}(\widetilde{\sigma}(\ell))}{\pi_{n-2}(\ell)} \geq \lambda_1, \text{ for all } \ell \geq \ell_1, \tag{25}$$
for some $\lambda_1 \geq 1$.

Proof. $(Y_{7,1,m})$: Assume that $\chi \in \Omega_3$. Then, from Theorem 10, we obtain that $(Y_{6,1})$–$(Y_{6,3})$ hold. By applying the induction, we establish the validity of $(Y_{7,1,0})$–$(Y_{7,3,0})$ based on Lemma 11. Now, let us assume that $(Y_{7,1,m-1})$–$(Y_{7,3,m-1})$ are true. When we integrate $(Y_{5,2})$ from ℓ_2 to ℓ, we obtain the following expression:

$$r(\ell)\left(y^{(n-1)}(\ell)\right)^\alpha \leq r(\ell_2)\left(y^{(n-1)}(\ell_2)\right)^\alpha - \int_{\ell_2}^\ell y^\alpha(\widetilde{\sigma}(s)) Q_2(s) ds. \tag{26}$$

Using $(Y_{7,1,m-1})$, we obtain

$$y(\widetilde{\sigma}) \geq \pi_{n-2}^{k_{m-1}}(\widetilde{\sigma}) \frac{y}{\pi_{n-2}^{k_{m-1}}}.$$

Then Equation (26) becomes

$$r(\ell)\left(y^{(n-1)}(\ell)\right)^\alpha \leq r(\ell_2)\left(y^{(n-1)}(\ell_2)\right)^\alpha \\ - \int_{\ell_2}^\ell \pi_{n-2}^{\alpha k_{m-1}}(\widetilde{\sigma}(s)) \frac{y^\alpha(s)}{\pi_{n-2}^{\alpha k_{m-1}}(s)} Q_2(s) ds.$$

The fact that $y/\pi_{n-2}^{k_{m-1}}$ is a decreasing function, in conjunction with this, yields

$$r(\ell)\left(y^{(n-1)}(\ell)\right)^\alpha \leq r(\ell_2)\left(y^{(n-1)}(\ell_2)\right)^\alpha \\ - \frac{y^\alpha(\ell)}{\pi_{n-2}^{\alpha k_{m-1}}(\ell)} \int_{\ell_2}^\ell \pi_{n-2}^{\alpha k_{m-1}}(s) \frac{\pi_{n-2}^{\alpha k_{m-1}}(\widetilde{\sigma}(s))}{\pi_{n-2}^{\alpha k_{m-1}}(s)} Q_2(s) ds.$$

Hence, from (19) and (25), we obtain

$$r(\ell)\left(y^{(n-1)}(\ell)\right)^\alpha$$
$$\leq r(\ell_2)\left(y^{(n-1)}(\ell_2)\right)^\alpha - \lambda_1^{\alpha k_{m-1}} \frac{y^\alpha(\ell)}{\pi_{n-2}^{\alpha k_{m-1}}(\ell)} \int_{\ell_2}^\ell \pi_{n-2}^{\alpha k_{m-1}}(s) Q_2(s) ds$$
$$\leq r(\ell_2)\left(y^{(n-1)}(\ell_2)\right)^\alpha - \alpha k_0^\alpha \lambda_1^{\alpha k_{m-1}} \frac{y^\alpha(\ell)}{\pi_{n-2}^{\alpha k_{m-1}}(\ell)} \int_{\ell_2}^\ell \frac{\pi_{n-3}(s)}{\pi_{n-2}^{\alpha(1-k_{m-1})+1}(s)} ds$$
$$= r(\ell_2)\left(y^{(n-1)}(\ell_2)\right)^\alpha - k_0^\alpha \frac{\lambda_1^{\alpha k_{m-1}}}{1-k_{m-1}} \frac{y^\alpha(\ell)}{\pi_{n-2}^{\alpha k_{m-1}}(\ell)} \left(\frac{1}{\pi_{n-2}^{\alpha(1-k_{m-1})}(\ell)} - \frac{1}{\pi_{n-2}^{\alpha(1-k_{m-1})}(\ell_2)}\right)$$
$$= r(\ell_2)\left(y^{(n-1)}(\ell_2)\right)^\alpha + k_m^\alpha \frac{y^\alpha(\ell)}{\pi_{n-2}^{\alpha k_{m-1}}(\ell)} \frac{1}{\pi_{n-2}^{\alpha(1-k_{m-1})}(\ell_2)} - k_m \frac{y^\alpha(\ell)}{\pi_{n-2}^\alpha(\ell)},$$

this, coupled with the observation that $\lim_{\ell \to \infty} y(\ell)/\pi_{n-2}^{k_{m-1}}(\ell) = 0$, yields

$$r\left(y^{(n-1)}\right)^\alpha \leq -k_m^\alpha \frac{y^\alpha}{\pi_{n-2}^\alpha},$$

or equivalently

$$r^{1/\alpha} y^{(n-1)} \leq -k_m \frac{y}{\pi_{n-2}}. \qquad (27)$$

Hence, based on $(Y_{4,2})$ at $i = n-3$, we can deduce that

$$\frac{y'}{\pi_{n-3}} \leq -k_m \frac{y}{\pi_{n-2}},$$

or equivalently

$$\pi_{n-2} y' + k_m \pi_{n-3} y \leq 0. \qquad (28)$$

Consequently,

$$\left(\frac{y}{\pi_{n-2}^{k_m}}\right)' = \frac{1}{\pi_{n-2}^{k_m+1}} (\pi_{n-2} y' + k_m \pi_{n-3} y) \leq 0.$$

Using the same approach employed in demonstrating ($Y_{6,2}$) as shown in Lemma 10, can ascertain that $\lim_{\ell\to\infty} y(\ell)/\pi_{n-2}^{k_m}(\ell) = 0$. This conclusion marks the end of the proof. □

Lemma 12. *Assuming that $\chi(\ell) \in \Omega_3$, and conditions (18), and (19) are satisfied for some $k_0 \in (0,1)$. If $k_{i-1} \leq k_i < 1$ for all $i = 1, 2, \ldots, m-1$, then*

$$\chi > \widehat{p}_2(\ell; \kappa) y.$$

Proof. Similar to the argument presented in the proof of Lemma 9, we obtain the Equation (17). Considering ($Y_{7,1,m}$), we deduce that

$$y\left(\mathfrak{y}^{[2r]}\right) \geq \frac{\pi_{n-2}^{k_m}\left(\mathfrak{y}^{[2r]}\right)}{\pi_{n-2}^{k_m}} y,$$

which with (17) yields

$$\begin{aligned}
\chi &> \sum_{r=0}^{\kappa}\left(\prod_{l=0}^{2r} p\left(\mathfrak{y}^{[l]}\right)\right)\left[\frac{1}{p\left(\mathfrak{y}^{[2r]}\right)} - \frac{\pi_{n-2}\left(\mathfrak{y}^{[2r+1]}\right)}{\pi_{n-2}\left(\mathfrak{y}^{[2r]}\right)}\right] \frac{\pi_{n-2}^{k_m}\left(\mathfrak{y}^{[2r]}\right)}{\pi_{n-2}^{k_m}} y \\
&= \widehat{p}_2(\ell; \kappa) y(\ell).
\end{aligned}$$

□

Theorem 3. *Let's assume that conditions (18) and (19) hold, and that there exists a positive integer m such that*

$$\liminf_{\ell\to\infty} \int_{\sigma(\ell)}^{\ell} \pi_{n-2}(s) \pi_{n-2}^{\alpha-1}(\widetilde{\sigma}(s)) Q_2(s) \, ds > \frac{\alpha k_m^{\alpha-1}(1-k_m)}{e}. \tag{29}$$

Under these conditions, we can conclude that $\Omega_3 = \varnothing$, where $\alpha \leq 1$.

Proof. Let us assume the opposite, i.e., $\chi \in \Omega_3$. According to Lemma 11, both ($Y_{7,1,m}$) and ($Y_{7,2,m}$) are satisfied.

Now, we can define the function as follows

$$w = r^{1/\alpha} y^{(n-1)} \pi_{n-2} + y.$$

Based on ($Y_{4,2}$) at $i = n-2$, we find that $w \geq 0$ for $\ell \geq \ell_2$. Additionally, using (27), we obtain

$$r^{1/\alpha} y^{(n-1)} \pi_{n-2} \leq -k_m y.$$

Hence, from the definition of w, we can deduce that

$$\begin{aligned}
w &= r^{1/\alpha} y^{(n-1)} \pi_{n-2} + k_m y^{(n-2)} - k_m y^{(n-2)} + y^{(n-3)} \\
&\leq (1-k_m) y^{(n-2)}.
\end{aligned} \tag{30}$$

Thus,

$$w' = \left(r^{1/\alpha} y^{(n-1)}\right)' \pi_{n-2} - r^{1/\alpha} y^{(n-1)} \pi_{n-3} + y'.$$

From ($Y_{4,2}$) at $i = n-3$, we find

$$\begin{aligned}
w' &\leq \left(r^{1/\alpha} y^{(n-1)}\right)' \pi_{n-2} \\
&= \frac{1}{\alpha}\left(r\left(y^{(n-1)}\right)^{\alpha}\right)'\left(r^{1/\alpha} y^{(n-1)}\right)^{1-\alpha} \pi_{n-2}.
\end{aligned}$$

Using $(Y_{5,2})$ and $(Y_{4,2})$ at $i = n-2$, we deduce that

$$\begin{aligned} w' &\leq \frac{-1}{\alpha} Q_2 y^\alpha(\widetilde{\sigma}) \left(r^{1/\alpha} y^{(n-1)}\right)^{1-\alpha} \pi_{n-2} \\ &\leq \frac{-1}{\alpha} Q_2 y^\alpha(\widetilde{\sigma}) \left(-k_m \frac{y}{\pi_{n-2}}\right)^{1-\alpha} \pi_{n-2} \\ &= \frac{-k_m^{1-\alpha}}{\alpha} Q_2 y^\alpha(\widetilde{\sigma}) \left(\frac{y}{\pi_{n-2}}\right)^{1-\alpha} \pi_{n-2}. \end{aligned}$$

Using $(Y_{4,1})$ in Lemma 8, we observe that $y(\ell)/\pi_{n-2}(\ell)$ is increasing, then

$$\frac{y(\widetilde{\sigma}(\ell))}{\pi_{n-2}(\widetilde{\sigma}(\ell))} \leq \frac{y(\ell)}{\pi_{n-2}(\ell)},$$

and

$$\left(\frac{y(\widetilde{\sigma})}{\pi_{n-2}(\widetilde{\sigma})}\right)^{1-\alpha} \leq \left(\frac{y}{\pi_{n-2}}\right)^{1-\alpha}.$$

Therefore,

$$\begin{aligned} w' &\leq \frac{-k_m^{1-\alpha}}{\alpha} Q_2 y^\alpha(\widetilde{\sigma}) \left(\frac{y(\widetilde{\sigma})}{\pi_{n-2}(\widetilde{\sigma})}\right)^{1-\alpha} \pi_{n-2} \\ &= \frac{-k_m^{1-\alpha}}{\alpha} \pi_{n-2}^{\alpha-1}(\widetilde{\sigma}) \pi_{n-2} Q_2 y(\widetilde{\sigma}), \end{aligned}$$

which, from Equation (30), gives

$$w' + \frac{1}{\alpha} \frac{k_m^{1-\alpha}}{1-k_m} \pi_{n-2}^{\alpha-1}(\widetilde{\sigma}) \pi_{n-2} Q_2 w(\widetilde{\sigma}) \leq 0. \tag{31}$$

Therefore, the positive solution w to the differential inequality can be deduced from Equation (31). Notably, according to the findings in Theorem 2.1.1 in [8], the condition expressed in Equation (29) ensures that Equation (31). This logical contradiction serves as conclusive evidence for proving the Theorem. □

Theorem 4. *Under the assumption that Equations (18) and (19) are satisfied, we consider a positive integer m, such that*

$$\liminf_{\ell \to \infty} \int_{\sigma(\ell)}^{\ell} \pi_{n-2}(s) \pi_{n-2}^{\alpha-1}(\widetilde{\sigma}(s)) \widehat{Q}_2(s) ds > \frac{\alpha k_m^{\alpha-1}(1-k_m)}{e}. \tag{32}$$

If the above inequality holds, then $\Omega_3 = \varnothing$.

Proof. To demonstrate this, we utilize the relationship

$$\chi > \widehat{p}_2(\ell; \kappa) y,$$

with respect to Equation (1), employing the identical proof technique used in the previous theorem. □

3.3. Category Ω_1

We know that

$$y = \chi + p\chi(\mathfrak{y}),$$

and

$$\chi = y - p\chi(\mathfrak{y}) \geq y - py(\mathfrak{y}).$$

Since $y' > 0$, then
$$\chi \geq (1-p)y.$$

Lemma 13. *If*
$$\liminf_{\ell \to \infty} \int_{\sigma(\ell)}^{\ell} \frac{(\sigma^{n-1}(s))^\alpha}{r(\sigma(s))} Q_0(s) ds > \frac{((n-1)!)^\alpha}{e},\tag{33}$$
then $\Omega_1 = \varnothing$.

Proof. If we consider the contrary scenario where $\chi \in \Omega_1$, it becomes clear from the information provided by (C_1), that
$$\lim_{\ell \to \infty} y(\ell) \neq 0.$$
Therefore, it can be deduced from Lemma 3 that, for any $\epsilon \in (0,1)$,
$$y(\sigma) \geq \frac{\epsilon}{(n-1)!} \frac{\sigma^{n-1}}{r(\sigma)} \left(r(\sigma) y^{(n-1)}(\sigma) \right)\tag{34}$$
eventually. Using Equation (34) in Equation (1), we see that
$$\begin{aligned}\left(r\left(\chi^{(n-1)}\right)^\alpha\right)' &= -\sum_{i=1}^{v} q_i \chi^\alpha(\sigma_i) \\ &\leq -\sum_{i=1}^{v} q_i (1-p(\sigma_i))^\alpha y^\alpha(\sigma_i) \\ &\leq -y^\alpha(\sigma) Q_0 \\ &\leq -Q_0 \left(\frac{\epsilon}{(n-1)!} \frac{\sigma^{n-1}}{r(\sigma)} \right)^\alpha \left(r(\sigma) \left(y^{(n-1)}(\sigma)\right)^\alpha \right).\end{aligned}$$

Consider the function $\theta = r\left(y^{(n-1)}\right)^\alpha$. By observing the last inequality, it becomes clear that $\theta(\ell)$ serves as a positive solution to the delay differential inequality, expressed as:
$$\theta' + \frac{\epsilon^\alpha}{((n-1)!)^\alpha} Q_0 \frac{(\sigma^{n-1})^\alpha}{r(\sigma)} \theta(\sigma) \leq 0.\tag{35}$$

Therefore, the positive solution θ to the differential inequality can be deduced from Equation (35). Notably, according to the findings in Theorem 2.1.1 in [8], the condition expressed in Equation (33) ensures that Equation (35) this logical contradiction serves as conclusive evidence for proving the Theorem. □

4. Criteria for Oscillation

This section extends the groundwork laid in the preceding sections to introduce fresh criteria for confirming the oscillatory nature of all solutions within Equation (1). To be more precise, we have pinpointed particular conditions that conclusively exclude the existence of positive solutions in all three scenarios, denoted as (C_1), (C_2), and (C_3). By amalgamating these conditions, as expounded in the subsequent theorems, we can establish robust criteria for ascertaining oscillation.

Theorem 5. *Assume that Equations (12), (29) and (33) hold. Then Equation (1) is oscillatory.*

Theorem 6. *Assume that Equations (13), (29) and (33) hold. Then Equation (1) is oscillatory.*

Theorem 7. *Assume that Equations (12), (32) and (33) hold. Then Equation (1) is oscillatory.*

Theorem 8. *Assume that Equations (13), (32) and (33) hold. Then Equation (1) is oscillatory.*

Example 1. *Consider the NDE*

$$\left(\ell^{4\alpha}\left(\left(\chi(\ell) + \mathrm{p}_0\chi(\mathfrak{y}_0\ell)\right)'''\right)^{\alpha}\right)' + \sum_{i=1}^{v} q_0\ell^{\alpha-1}\chi^{\alpha}(\sigma_i\ell) = 0,\ \ell \geq 1, \qquad (36)$$

where $0 \leq \mathrm{p}_0 < 1$, $\mathfrak{y}_0, \sigma_i \in (0,1)$, $i = 1,2,\ldots,v$, *and* $q_0 > 0$. *By comparing Equation (1) and Equation (36), we see that* $n = 4$, $r(\ell) = \ell^{4\alpha}$, $q_i(\ell) = q_0\ell^{\alpha-1}$, $\mathrm{p}(\ell) = \mathrm{p}_0$, $\mathfrak{y}(\ell) = \mathfrak{y}_0\ell$, $\sigma_i(\ell) = \sigma_i\ell$. *It is easy to find that*

$$\pi_0(\ell) = \frac{1}{3\ell^3},\ \pi_1(\ell) = \frac{1}{6\ell^2},\ \pi_2(\ell) = \frac{1}{6\ell},$$

$$\sigma(\ell) := \min\{\sigma_i\ell,\ i = 1,2,\ldots,v\} = \sigma_0\ell,$$

$$\widetilde{\sigma}(\ell) := \max\{\sigma_i\ell,\ i = 1,2,\ldots,v\} = \widetilde{\sigma}_0\ell,$$

$$\lambda = \frac{\pi_0(\sigma(\ell))}{\pi_0(\ell)} = \frac{1}{\sigma_0^3},\ \lambda_1 = \frac{\pi_2(\widetilde{\sigma}(\ell))}{\pi_2(\ell)} = \frac{1}{\widetilde{\sigma}_0},$$

$$\mathrm{p}_1(\ell;\kappa) = (1-\mathrm{p}_0)\sum_{r=0}^{\kappa} \mathrm{p}_0^{2r}\mathfrak{y}^{4r/\epsilon},$$

$$\mathrm{p}_2(\ell;\kappa) = \left[\frac{1}{\mathrm{p}_0} - \frac{1}{\mathfrak{y}_0}\right]\sum_{r=0}^{m} \mathrm{p}_0^{2r+1},$$

$$\widehat{\mathrm{p}}_2(\ell;\kappa) = \left[\frac{1}{\mathrm{p}_0} - \frac{1}{\mathfrak{y}_0}\right]\sum_{r=0}^{m} \mathrm{p}_0^{2r+1}\frac{1}{\mathfrak{y}_0^{2rk_m}},$$

$$\delta = \frac{vq_0(1-\mathrm{p}_0)}{2\alpha 3^{\alpha+1}}\sigma_0^{2\alpha}\sum_{r=0}^{\kappa} \mathrm{p}_0^{2r}\mathfrak{y}^{4r/\epsilon},$$

$$\beta_0 = \epsilon\left(\frac{vq_0(1-\mathrm{p}_0)}{2\alpha 3^{\alpha+1}}\sigma_0^{2\alpha}\sum_{r=0}^{\kappa} \mathrm{p}_0^{2r}\mathfrak{y}^{4r/\epsilon}\right)^{1/\alpha},$$

$$\beta_j := \beta_0 \frac{1}{(1-\beta_{j-1})^{1/\alpha}}\left(\frac{1}{\sigma_0^3}\right)^{\beta_{j-1}},\ j=1,2,\ldots,m,$$

$$k_0 = \left(\frac{1}{\alpha}\frac{1}{6^\alpha}vq_0\left[\frac{1}{\mathrm{p}_0} - \frac{1}{\mathfrak{y}_0}\right]\sum_{r=0}^{\kappa} \mathrm{p}_0^{2r+1}\right)^{1/\alpha},$$

$$k_j = k_0 \frac{1}{(1-k_{j-1})^{1/\alpha}}\left(\frac{1}{\widetilde{\sigma}_0}\right)^{k_{j-1}},\ j=1,2,\ldots,m.$$

Condition Equation (12) leads to

$$q_0 > \frac{2^{-\alpha+1}3^{\alpha+1}}{\epsilon^{\alpha}\sigma_0^{2\alpha}(1-\mathrm{p}_0)\sum_{r=0}^{\kappa}\mathrm{p}_0^{2r}\mathfrak{y}^{4r/\epsilon}}, \qquad (37)$$

while condition Equation (13) results in

$$q_0 > \frac{\alpha 6^{\alpha}\sigma_0^{\alpha-3}\beta_m^{\alpha-1}(1-\beta_m)}{v(1-\mathrm{p}_0)^{\alpha}\left(\sum_{r=0}^{\kappa}\mathrm{p}_0^{2r}\mathfrak{y}^{4r/\epsilon}\right)^{\alpha}\ln\frac{1}{\widetilde{\sigma}_0}}\frac{1}{\mathrm{e}}. \qquad (38)$$

Condition Equation (29) gives

$$q_0 > \frac{\alpha 6^\alpha \widetilde{\sigma}_0^{\alpha-1} k_m^{\alpha-1}(1-k_m)}{v\left[\frac{1}{p_0} - \frac{1}{v_0}\right]^\alpha \left(\sum_{r=0}^m p^{2r+1}\right)^\alpha \ln \frac{1}{\sigma_0}} \frac{1}{e}, \qquad (39)$$

while condition Equation (32) yields

$$q_0 > \frac{\alpha 6^\alpha \widetilde{\sigma}_0^{\alpha-1} k_m^{\alpha-1}(1-k_m)}{v\left[\frac{1}{p_0} - \frac{1}{v_0}\right]^\alpha \left(\sum_{r=0}^\kappa p_0^{2r+1} \frac{1}{v_0^{2rk_m}}\right)^\alpha \ln \frac{1}{\sigma_0}} \frac{1}{e}. \qquad (40)$$

Lastly, condition Equation (33) produces

$$q_0 > \frac{\sigma_0^\alpha 6^\alpha}{v(1-p_0)^\alpha \ln \frac{1}{\sigma_0}} \frac{1}{e}. \qquad (41)$$

To determine the oscillation of Equation (36), we can apply various theorems.

Theorems 5–8 provide conditions for the oscillatory behavior of Equation (36). Theorem 5 asserts that the satisfaction of Equations (37), (39) and (41) leads to oscillations in Equation (36). Similarly, Theorem 6 indicates that the fulfillment of Equations (38), (39) and (41) results in oscillations in Equation (36). In the same vein, Theorem 7 establishes that if Equations (37), (40) and (41) are met, then Equation (36) exhibits oscillatory behavior. Lastly, Theorem 8 demonstrates that oscillations in Equation (36) occur when Equations (38), (40) and (41) are satisfied.

5. Conclusions

In this study, we delved into the investigation of the oscillatory behavior and monotonic properties of even-order quasilinear neutral differential equations. Our main focus was on a specific type of such equations. Through our research, we were able to establish improved relationships that connect the solution and its corresponding function for two out of the three categories of positive solutions in the equation under study. By leveraging these newly derived relationships, we were able to develop criteria to ascertain that categories Ω_2 and Ω_3 contained no positive solutions. A significant contribution of this work was the introduction of novel criteria to assess the oscillation of Equation (1). These criteria provide a valuable tool for analyzing the oscillatory nature of the equation. Looking ahead, it would be intriguing to extend our findings to explore the behavior of non-linear odd-order neutral DEs, opening up exciting possibilities for future research directions.

Author Contributions: Conceptualization, F.M., O.M., G.A. and H.E.-M.; methodology, F.M., O.M., G.A. and H.E.-M.; investigation, F.M., O.M., G.A. and H.E.-M.; writing—original draft preparation, G.A. and H.E.-M.; writing—review and editing, F.M. and O.M. All authors have read and agreed to the published version of the manuscript.

Funding: This research was funded by Princess Nourah bint Abdulrahman University Researchers Supporting Project number (PNURSP2023R45), Princess Nourah bint Abdulrahman University, Riyadh, Saudi Arabia.

Acknowledgments: Princess Nourah bint Abdulrahman University Researchers Supporting Project number (PNURSP2023R45), Princess Nourah bint Abdulrahman University, Riyadh, Saudi Arabia.

Conflicts of Interest: The authors declare no conflict of interest.

References

1. Gyori, I.; Ladas, G. *Oscillation Theory of Delay Differential Equations with Applications*; Clarendon Press: Oxford, UK, 1991.
2. Hale, J.K. *Theory of Functional Differential Equations*; Springer: New York, NY, USA, 1977.
3. Agarwal, R.P.; Bohner, M.; Li, T.; Zhang, C. A new approach in the study of oscillatory behavior of even-order neutral delay differential equations. *Appl. Math. Comput.* **2013**, *225*, 787–794. [CrossRef]

4. Zahariev, A.; Kiskinov, H. Asymptotic Stability of the Solutions of Neutral Linear Fractional System with Nonlinear Perturbation. *Mathematics* **2020**, *8*, 390. [CrossRef]
5. Milev, M.; Zlatev, S. A note about the stability of fractional retarded linear systems with distributed delays. *Int. J. Pure Appl. Math.* **2017**, *115*, 873–881. [CrossRef]
6. Zafer, A. Oscillatory and Nonoscillatory Properties of Solutions of Functional Differential Equations and Difference Equations. Ph.D. Thesis, Iowa State University, Ames, IA, USA, 1992.
7. Erbe, L.H.; Kong, Q.; Zhong, B.G. *Oscillation Theory for Functional Differential Equations*; Marcel Dekker: New York, NY, USA, 1995.
8. Ladde, G.S.; Lakshmikantham, V.; Zhang, B.G. *Oscillation Theory of Differential Equations with Deviating Arguments*; Marcel Dekker: New York, NY, USA, 1987.
9. Dzurina, J. Oscillatory behavior of the second order noncanonical differential equations. *Appl. Math. Lett.* **2017**, *73*, 62–68. [CrossRef]
10. Dzurina, J.; Jadlovská, I. A sharp oscillation result for second-order half-linear noncanonical delay differential equations. *Electron. J. Qual. Theory Differ. Equ.* **2020**, *46*, 1–14. [CrossRef]
11. Almarri, B.; Masood, F.; Muhib, A.; Moaaz, O. New Comparison Results for Oscillation of Even-Order Delay Differential Equations. *Symmetry* **2022**, *14*, 946. [CrossRef]
12. Bazighifan, O.; Ruggieri, M.; Santra, S.S.; Scapellato, A. Qualitative Properties of Solutions of Second-Order Neutral Differential Equations. *Symmetry* **2020**, *12*, 1520. [CrossRef]
13. Jadlovská, I. New criteria for sharp oscillation of second-order neutral delay differential equations. *Mathematics* **2021**, *9*, 2089. [CrossRef]
14. Li, T.; Baculikova, B.; Dzurina, J.; Zhang, C. Oscillation of fourth-order neutral differential equations with p-Laplacian like operators. *Bound. Value Probl.* **2014**, *2014*, 56. [CrossRef]
15. Dzurina, J.; Grace, S.R.; Jadlovská, I.; Li, T. Oscillation criteria for second-order Emden–Fowler delay differential equations with a sublinear neutral term. *Math. Nachrichten* **2020**, *293*, 910–922. [CrossRef]
16. Moaaz, O.; Almarri, B.; Masood, F.; Atta, D. Even-Order Neutral Delay Differential Equations with Noncanonical Operator: New Oscillation Criteria. *Fractal Fract.* **2022**, *6*, 313. [CrossRef]
17. Almarri, B.; Masood, F.; Moaaz, O.; Muhib, A. Amended Criteria for Testing the Asymptotic and Oscillatory Behavior of Solutions of Higher-Order Functional Differential Equations. *Axioms* **2022**, *11*, 718. [CrossRef]
18. Agarwal, R.P.; Grace, S.R.; O'Regan, D. The oscillation of certain higher-order functional differential equations. *Math. Comput. Model.* **2003**, *37*, 705–728. [CrossRef]
19. Baculíková, B.; Džurina, J. Oscillation theorems for higher-order neutral differential equations. *Appl. Math. Comput.* **2012**, *219*, 3769–3778. [CrossRef]
20. Baculíková, B.; Dzurina, J. Comparison theorems for higher-order neutral delay differential equations. *J. Appl. Math. Comput.* **2015**, *49*, 107–118. [CrossRef]
21. Koplatadze, R. Oscillation criteria of solutions of second order linear delay differential inequalities with a delayed argument. *Tr. Inst. Prikl. Mat. IN Vekua* **1986**, *17*, 104–120.
22. Wei, J.J. Oscillation of second order delay differential equation. *Ann. Differ. Equ.* **1988**, *4*, 437–478.
23. Koplatadze, R.; Kvinikadze, G.; Stavroulakis, I.P. Oscillation of second order linear delay differential equations. *Funct. Differ. Equ.* **2000**, *7*, 121–145.
24. Bai, S. The oscillation of the solutions of higher order functional differential equation. *Chin. Quart. J. Math.* **2004**, *19*, 407–411.
25. Karpuz, B.; Ocalan, O.; Ozturk, S. Comparison theorems on the oscillation and asymptotic behaviour of higher-order neutral differential equations. *Glasg. Math. J.* **2010**, *52*, 107–114. [CrossRef]
26. Baculikova, B. Oscillatory behavior of the second order noncanonical differential equations. *Electron. J. Qual. Theory Differ. Equ.* **2019**, *89*, 1–11. [CrossRef]
27. Ramos, H.; Moaaz, O.; Muhib, A.; Awrejcewicz, J. More Effective Results for Testing Oscillation of Non-Canonical Neutral Delay Differential Equations. *Mathematics* **2021**, *9*, 1114. [CrossRef]
28. Han, Z.; Li, T.; Sun, S.; Sun, Y. Remarks on the paper. *Appl. Math. Comput.* **2010**, *215*, 3998–4007.
29. Li, T.; Han, Z.; Zhao, P.; Sun, S. Oscillation of even-order neutral delay differential equations. *Adv. Differ. Equ.* **2010**, *2010*, 184180. [CrossRef]
30. Xing, G.; Li, T.; Zhang, C. Oscillation of higher-order quasi-linear neutral differential equations. *Adv. Differ. Equ.* **2011**, *2011*, 45. [CrossRef]
31. Li, T.; Rogovchenko, Y.V. Asymptotic behavior of higher-order quasilinear neutral differential equations. *Abstr. Appl. Anal.* **2014**, *2014*, 395368. [CrossRef]
32. Agarwal, R.P.; Zhang, C.; Li, T. Some remarks on oscillation of second order neutral differential equations. *Appl. Math. Comput.* **2016**, *274*, 178–181. [CrossRef]
33. Bohner, M.; Grace, S.; Jadlovská, I. Oscillation criteria for second-order neutral delay differential equations. *Electron. J. Qual. Theory Differ. Equ.* **2017**, *60*, 1–12. [CrossRef]
34. Moaaz, O.; Cesarano, C.; Almarri, B. An Improved Relationship between the Solution and Its Corresponding Function in Fourth-Order Neutral Differential Equations and Its Applications. *Mathematics* **2023**, *11*, 1708. [CrossRef]

35. Kiguradze, I.T.; Chanturiya, T.A. *Asymptotic Properties of Solutions of Nonautonomous Ordinary Differential Equations*; Kluwer Acad. Publ.: Dordrecht, The Netherlands, 1993.
36. Agarwal, R.P.; Grace, S.R.; O'Regan, D. *Oscillation Theory for Difference and Functional Differential Equations*; Kluwer Academic: Dordrecht, The Netherlands, 2000.
37. Zhang, C.; Agarwal, R.P.; Bohner, M.; Li, T. New results for oscillatory behavior of even-order half-linear delay differential equations. *Appl. Math. Lett.* **2013**, *26*, 179–183. [CrossRef]

Disclaimer/Publisher's Note: The statements, opinions and data contained in all publications are solely those of the individual author(s) and contributor(s) and not of MDPI and/or the editor(s). MDPI and/or the editor(s) disclaim responsibility for any injury to people or property resulting from any ideas, methods, instructions or products referred to in the content.

Article

On Asymptotic Properties of Stochastic Neutral-Type Inertial Neural Networks with Mixed Delays

Bingxian Wang, Honghui Yin and Bo Du *

School of Mathematics and Statistics, Huaiyin Normal University, Huaian 223300, China
* Correspondence: dubo7307@163.com

Abstract: This article studies the stability problem of a class of stochastic neutral-type inertial delay neural networks. By introducing appropriate variable transformations, the second-order differential system is transformed into a first-order differential system. Using homeomorphism mapping, standard stochastic analyzing technology, the Lyapunov functional method and the properties of a neutral operator, we establish new sufficient criteria for the unique existence and stochastically globally asymptotic stability of equilibrium points. An example is also provided, to show the validity of the established results. From our results, we find that, under appropriate conditions, random disturbances have no significant impact on the existence, stability, and symmetry of network systems.

Keywords: neutral-type inertial neural networks; stochastic; stability; delays

Citation: Wang, B.; Yin, H.; Du, B. On Asymptotic Properties of Stochastic Neutral-Type Inertial Neural Networks with Mixed Delays. *Symmetry* **2023**, *15*, 1746. https://doi.org/10.3390/sym15091746

Academic Editors: Savin Treanta and Octav Olteanu

Received: 24 August 2023
Revised: 8 September 2023
Accepted: 11 September 2023
Published: 12 September 2023

Copyright: © 2023 by the authors. Licensee MDPI, Basel, Switzerland. This article is an open access article distributed under the terms and conditions of the Creative Commons Attribution (CC BY) license (https://creativecommons.org/licenses/by/4.0/).

1. Introduction

Inertial neural network systems (INNs) can be understood as damped neural networks. When the damping exceeds a certain critical value, the dynamic properties of each neuron state will also change. Therefore, studying inertial neural networks can help us to understand the complex changes in neural network systems. NNs are second-order systems, which were first introduced by Wheeler and Schieve [1]. Subsequently, INNs have received increasing attention from scholars, whose dynamic behavior research has received considerable attention. In [2–4], the authors studied bifurcation, chaos and the stability of periodic solutions in a single INN. The dynamics of an inertial two-neuron system with delay were studied in [5]. Draye, Winters and Cheron [6] considered self-selected modular recurrent neural networks with postural and inertial subnetworks. For the global exponential stability in the Lagrange sense for INNs, see [7,8]; for the global convergence problem of impulsive inertial neural networks with variable delay and complex neural networks, see [9,10]; for the antiperiodic problem of INNs, see [11]; for inertial Cohen–Grossberg neural networks, see [12–14]; for inertial BAM neural networks, see [15,16].

In practice, neural network systems are not only affected by damping (inertia) factors, but also by random factors. The research on stochastic neural network systems is relatively mature and has achieved many results. Zhang and Kong [17] considered photovoltaic power prediction based on the hybrid modeling of neural networks and stochastic differential equations. Shu et al. [18] studied the stochastic stabilization of Markov jump quaternion-valued neural networks, by using a sampled-data control strategy. Guo [19] investigated globally robust stability analysis for stochastic Cohen–Grossberg neural networks with impulse control and time-varying delays. For the stability of random cellular neural networks, see [20,21]; for mean square exponential stability and periodic solutions of stochastic Hopfield neural networks, see [22,23]; for the stability problem of recurrent neural networks with random delays, see [24].

Neutral-type neural networks are nonlinear systems, which show neutral properties by involving derivatives with delays. Due to extensive applications in ecology, control theory, biology and physics for neutral-type neural networks, many results have been obtained. He et al. [25] addressed the problem of synchronization control of neutral-type neural networks with sampled data. Using an adaptive event-triggered communication scheme, they obtained some weak synchronization conditions for synchronization control. In [26], a new control scheme was studied for exponential synchronization of coupled neutral-type neural networks with mixed delays. Si, Xie and Lie [27] investigated the global exponential stability of recurrent neural networks with piecewise constant arguments and neutral terms subject to uncertain connection weights. For more results of neutral-type neural networks, see, e.g., [28–33].

Stochastic neutral-type INNs provide more useful models in practical applications. In this paper, we will study the stability problem of a class of stochastic neutral-type inertial neural networks with mixed delays via stochastic analyzing technology and by constructing a suitable Lyapunov–Krasovskii functional. A simulation example is used, to demonstrate the usefulness of our theoretical results. The contributions of this paper are threefold:

(1) In this paper, we introduce a new class of stochastic neutral-type INNs with D-operators, which is different from the existing models (see, e.g., [25–27]).
(2) For constructing a suitable Lyapunov–Krasovskii functional, the mixed delays and the neutral terms are taken into consideration.
(3) Unlike the previous papers, we introduce a new unified framework, to deal with mixed delays, inertia terms and D-operators. It is noted that our main results are also valid in cases of non-neutral systems.

The following sections are organized as follows: Section 2 gives preliminaries and model formulation. In Section 3, sufficient conditions are established for the unique existence of equilibrium points of system (3). The stochastically globally asymptotic stability of equilibrium points is given in Section 4. In Section 5, a numerical example is given, to show the feasibility of our results. Finally, some conclusions are given about this paper.

2. Preliminaries and Problem Formulation

Consider a class of neutral-type INNs with mixed delays as follows:

$$\frac{d^2[(A_ix_i)(t)]}{dt^2} = -a_i\frac{d[(A_ix_i)(t)]}{dt} - b_ix_i(t) + \sum_{j=1}^n c_{ij}f_j(x_j(t)) + \sum_{j=1}^n d_{ij}f_j(x_j(t-\tau_j(t)))$$
$$+ \sum_{j=1}^n e_{ij}\int_{t-\gamma_1}^t f_j(x_j(s))ds + I_i, \tag{1}$$

where $t \geq 0$, $i = 1, 2, \cdots, n$, A_i is a difference operator defined by

$$(A_ix_i)(t) = x_i(t) - c_i(t)x_i(t-\gamma_0). \tag{2}$$

If a random disturbance term is added to system (1), we obtain the following stochastic INNs:

$$d[(A_ix_i)'(t)] = -a_i(A_ix_i)'(t)dt - b_ix_i(t)dt + \sum_{j=1}^n c_{ij}f_j(x_j(t))dt + \sum_{j=1}^n d_{ij}f_j(x_j(t-\tau_j(t)))dt$$
$$+ \left(\sum_{j=1}^n e_{ij}\int_{t-\gamma_1}^t f_j(x_j(s))ds\right)dt + I_idt + \sum_{j=1}^n h_{ij}g_j(x_j(t))dB_i(t), \tag{3}$$

where $x_i(t)$ denotes the neuron state, $c_i(t) \in C(\mathbb{R}, \mathbb{R})$ is neutral parameter, $a_i > 0$ is the damping (inertia) coefficient, $b_i > 0$ is a constant, c_{ij}, d_{ij} and e_{ij} represent the output feedback weight values, I_i represents the threshold or bias of the system, $\gamma_0, \gamma_1, \tau_j(t) > 0$ are delays with $\tau'_j(t) < 1$, and where $\sum_{j=1}^n h_{ij}g_j(x_j(t))dB_i(t)$ represents random perturbation and $B(t) = (B_1(t), B_2(t), \cdots, B_n(t))^T$ is defined as an $n-$dimensional Brownian motion with natural filtering $\{\mathcal{F}_t\}_{t\geq 0}$ on a complete probability space $(\Omega, \mathcal{F}, P)$. The initial conditions of system (1) are given by

$$\begin{cases} x_i(s) = \phi_i(s), \ s \in (-\mu, 0], \ i = 1, 2, \cdots, n, \\ x'_i(s)) = \psi_i(s), \ s \in (-\mu, 0], \ i = 1, 2, \cdots, n, \end{cases}$$

where $\mu = \max\{\gamma_0, \gamma_1, \hat{\tau}\}$, $\hat{\tau} = \max_{t \in \mathbb{R}} \tau_j(t)$. Let

$$y_i(t) = \frac{d[A_i x_i(t)]}{dt} + \xi_i(A_i x_i)(t), \ i = 1, 2, \cdots, n,$$

where $\xi_i > 0$ is a constant. Then, system (3) is changed into the following form:

$$\begin{cases} d[(A_i x_i)(t)] = -\xi_i(A_i x_i)(t)dt + y_i(t)dt, \\ y'_i(t) = -(a_i - \xi_i) y_i(t)dt + [(a_i - \xi_i)\xi_i](A_i x_i)(t)dt - b_i x_i(t)dt \\ \quad + \sum_{j=1}^n c_{ij} f_j(x_j(t))dt + \sum_{j=1}^n d_{ij} f_j(x_j(t - \tau_j(t)))dt \\ \quad + \left(\sum_{j=1}^n e_{ij} \int_{t-\gamma_1}^t f_j(x_j(s))ds \right) dt + I_i(t)dt + \sum_{j=1}^n h_{ij} g_j(x_j(t))dB_i(t). \end{cases} \quad (4)$$

Remark 1. *The operator A_i in (2) is called D-operator (see [34]). D-operator has many excellent properties. On the one hand, it can help us better understand the characteristics of neutral equations and, on the other hand, the above properties can be used to study the dynamic behavior of the solution of the system. Recently, the authors [33] studied a class of neutral inertial neural networks. The differences between this article and [33] are mainly reflected in two aspects: firstly, the neutral-type system in this article has the form of D-operator, while the system in [33] does not; secondly, the system in this article is stochastic, while the system in [33] is deterministic.*

Lemma 1 ([35]). *For $t \in \mathbb{R}$, if $\hat{c}_i < 1$, then, for the operator A_i there exists an inverse operator A_i^{-1}, which satisfies*

$$\|A_i^{-1}\| \leq \frac{1}{1 - \hat{c}_i},$$

where $i = 1, 2, \cdots, n$, $\hat{c}_i = \max_{t \in \mathbb{R}} |c_i(t)|$, A_i is defined by (2).

Definition 1. *If $X^* = (x_1^*, x_2^*, \cdots, x_n^*)^T \in \mathbb{R}^n$ satisfies*

$$-b_i x_i^* + \sum_{j=1}^n \left(c_{ij} + d_{ij} + \gamma_1 e_{ij} \right) f_j(x_j^*) + I_i = 0,$$

then X^* is called the equilibrium point of system (1). If $g_j(x_j^*) = 0$, then system (3) reaches equilibrium state and no longer sends noise interference to other units, indicating that the equilibrium point X^* of system (1) is also the equilibrium point of system (3).

Let $C^{1,2}(\mathbb{R}^+ \times S_h, \mathbb{R}^+)$ be the non-negative function $V(t, X)$ on $\mathbb{R}^+ \times S_h$, where $S_h = \{X : \|X\| < h\} \subset \mathbb{R}^n$, $V(t, X)$ has continuous first and second derivatives for (t, X), respectively.

Definition 2 ([36]). *Give the following system:*

$$\begin{cases} dX(t) = f(t, X(t))dt + g(t, X(t))dB(t), \ t \geq t_0, \\ X(t_0) = X_0. \end{cases} \quad (5)$$

Define the operator:

$$\mathcal{L}V(t, X) = V_t(t, X) + V_X(t, X)f(t, X) + \frac{1}{2}\text{trace}\left[g^T(t, X) V_{XX}(t, X) g(t, X)\right],$$

where $V(t,X) \in C^{1,2}(\mathbb{R}^+ \times S_h, \mathbb{R}^+)$, $V_t(t,X) = \frac{\partial V(t,X)}{\partial t}$,

$$V_X(t,X) = \left(\frac{\partial V(t,X)}{\partial x_1}, \frac{\partial V(t,X)}{\partial x_2}, \cdots, \frac{\partial V(t,X)}{\partial x_n}\right), V_{XX}(t,X) = \left(\frac{\partial^2 V(t,X)}{\partial x_i \partial x_j}\right)_{n \times n}.$$

Definition 3 ([37]). *Let $\Omega \subset \mathbb{R}^n$, where Ω is an n-dimensional open field containing the origin. The function $V(t,X)$ has an infinitesimal upper bound, if there exists a positive definite function $W(X)$, such that $|V(t,X)| \leq W(X)$.*

Definition 4 ([37]). *The function $W(X) \in C(\mathbb{R}^n, \mathbb{R})$ is an infinite positive definite function, if $W(X)$ is positive definite and $W(X) \to +\infty$ for $||X|| \to \infty$.*

Lemma 2 ([37]). *If $H(u) \in C^0$ satisfies*
(i) $H(u)$ is injective on $\mathbb{R}^n$;
(ii) $||H(u)|| \to \infty$ for $||u|| \to \infty$, then $H(u)$ is homeomorphic on $\mathbb{R}^n$.

Lemma 3 ([37]). *If there is a radial unbounded positive definite function $V(t,X) \in C^{1,2}([t_0, +\infty] \times S_h, \mathbb{R}^+)$ with an infinitesimal upper bound, such that $\mathcal{L}V(t,X)$ is negative definite, then the zero solution of system (5) is stochastically globally asymptotically stable.*

Throughout the paper, the following assumptions hold:

(H_1) There exist constants $l_j \geq 0$, such that
$$|f_j(x) - f_j(y)| \leq l_j|x-y|, j = 1, 2, \cdots, n, \forall x, y \in \mathbb{R}.$$

(H_2) There exist constants $\tilde{l}_j \geq 0$, such that
$$|g_j(x) - g_j(y)| \leq \tilde{l}_j|x-y|, j = 1, 2, \cdots, n, \forall x, y \in \mathbb{R}.$$

(H_3) There exist constants $N_j \geq 0$, such that
$$|f_j(x)| \leq \frac{1}{2}N_j, j = 1, 2, \cdots, n, \forall x \in \mathbb{R}.$$

3. Existence of Equilibrium Points

Theorem 1. *Suppose that assumption (H_1) holds. Then, system (1) has a unique equilibrium point, provided that*

$$-b_i + \frac{1}{2}\sum_{j=1}^n (|c_{ij}| + |d_{ij}| + \gamma_1|e_{ij}|)l_j + \frac{1}{2}\sum_{j=1}^n (|c_{ji}| + |d_{ji}| + \gamma_1|e_{ji}|)l_i < 0. \quad (6)$$

Proof. For $u = (u_1, u_2, \cdots, u_n)^T$, consider the mapping $H(u) = (H_1(u), H_2(u), \cdots, H_n(u))^T$, where

$$H_i(u) = -b_i u_i + \sum_{j=1}^n \left(c_{ij} + d_{ij} + \gamma_1 e_{ij}\right) f_j(u_j) + I_i.$$

If $H(u)$ is homeomorphic on $\mathbb{R}^n$, there is a unique equilibrium point u^*, such that $H(u^*) = 0$. Now, we show that $H(u)$ is homeomorphic on $\mathbb{R}^n$. We first show that $H(u)$ is injective on $\mathbb{R}^n$. Assume that there exist $u, v \in \mathbb{R}^n$ with $u \neq v$, such that $H(u) = H(v)$. Then, we have

$$-b_i(u_i - v_i) + \sum_{j=1}^n \left(c_{ij} + d_{ij} + \gamma_1 e_{ij}\right)[f_j(u_j) - f_j(v_j)] = 0, i = 1, 2, \cdots, n. \quad (7)$$

Multiplying both sides of system (7) by $u_i - v_i$ yields

$$-b_i(u_i - v_i)^2 + (u_i - v_i) \sum_{j=1}^{n} \left(c_{ij} + d_{ij} + \gamma_1 e_{ij} \right) [f_j(u_j) - f_j(v_j)] = 0. \qquad (8)$$

Using $a^2 + b^2 \geq 2ab$, (H$_1$) and (8), we have

$$-b_i(u_i - v_i)^2 + \frac{1}{2} \sum_{j=1}^{n} \left(|c_{ij}| + |d_{ij}| + \gamma_1 |e_{ij}| \right) l_j [(u_i - v_i)^2 + (u_j - v_j)^2] \geq 0$$

and

$$\sum_{i=1}^{n} \left(-b_i + \frac{1}{2} \sum_{j=1}^{n} (|c_{ij}| + |d_{ij}| + \gamma_1 |e_{ij}|) l_j + \frac{1}{2} \sum_{j=1}^{n} (|c_{ji}| + |d_{ji}| + \gamma_1 |e_{ji}|) l_i \right) (u_i - v_i)^2 \geq 0. \qquad (9)$$

From (6) and (9), we have $u_i = v_i$, which contradicts the assumption $u_i \neq v_i$. Therefore, $H(u)$ is injective on $\mathbb{R}^n$.

Furthermore, let $\tilde{H}(u) = H(u) - H(0)$. We have

$$u^T \tilde{H}(u) = \sum_{i=1}^{n} u_i \tilde{H}_i(u) = \sum_{i=1}^{n} \left(-b_i u_i^2 + u_i \sum_{j=1}^{n} (c_{ij} + d_{ij} + \gamma_1 e_{ij})(f_j(u_j) - f_j(0)) \right)$$

$$\leq \sum_{i=1}^{n} \left(-b_i + \frac{1}{2} \sum_{j=1}^{n} (|c_{ij}| + |d_{ij}| + \gamma_1 |e_{ij}|) l_j + \frac{1}{2} \sum_{j=1}^{n} (|c_{ji}| + |d_{ji}| + \gamma_1 |e_{ji}|) l_i \right) u_i^2$$

$$\leq -\min_{1 \leq i \leq n} \left(b_i - \frac{1}{2} \sum_{j=1}^{n} (|c_{ij}| + |d_{ij}| + \gamma_1 |e_{ij}|) l_j - \frac{1}{2} \sum_{j=1}^{n} (|c_{ji}| + |d_{ji}| + \gamma_1 |e_{ji}|) l_i \right) \|u\|^2.$$

Using inequality $-X^T Y \leq |X^T Y| \leq \|X\| \|Y\|$, we obtain

$$\|\tilde{H}(u)\| \geq \min_{1 \leq i \leq n} \left(b_i - \frac{1}{2} \sum_{j=1}^{n} (|c_{ij}| + |d_{ij}| + \gamma_1 |e_{ij}|) l_j - \frac{1}{2} \sum_{j=1}^{n} (|c_{ji}| + |d_{ji}| + \gamma_1 |e_{ji}|) l_i \right) \|u\|$$

and $\|\tilde{H}(u)\| \to \infty$ for $\|u\| \to \infty$, i.e., $\|H(u)\| \to \infty$ for $\|u\| \to \infty$. Hence, $H(u)$ is homeomorphic on $\mathbb{R}^n$, and there is a unique equilibrium point for system (1). □

Remark 2. *The proof of Theorem 1 is similar to the one in [38]. For the convenience of readers, we have provided detailed proof of Theorem 1.*

Remark 3. *Since system (1) contains neutral-type terms and inertial terms, some research techniques, such as topological degree methods and fixed point theorems, are not easy for studying the existence of the equilibrium point of system (1). However, under the assumptions of this article, we can easily study the existence of the equilibrium point of system (1), by using homeomorphism mapping.*

4. Stochastically Globally Asymptotic Stability

Theorem 2. *Assume that all conditions of Theorem 1 hold and that assumptions (H$_2$) and (H$_3$) hold. Then, the equilibrium point of system (3) is stochastically globally asymptotically stable, provided that*

$$-2\xi_i + 1 + |(a_i - \xi_i)\xi_i| + b_i(1 - |c_i|)^{-2} + \sum_{j=1}^{n} |d_{ij}| \hat{\omega}_j L_j^2 (1 - \hat{c}_i)^{-2}$$
$$+ \sum_{j=1}^{n} |e_{ij}| \gamma_1 L_j^2 (1 - \hat{c}_i)^{-2} + \sum_{k=1}^{n} \sum_{j=1}^{n} h_{kj}^2 \tilde{l}_i^2 (1 - \hat{c}_i)^{-2} < 0 \qquad (10)$$

and
$$-2(a_i - \xi_i) + 1 + |(a_i - \xi_i)\xi_i| + b_i + \sum_{j=1}^{n} \left(|c_{ij}| + |d_{ij}| + |e_{ij}|\right) < 0, \qquad (11)$$

where $\hat{c}_i = \max_{t \in \mathbb{R}} |c_i(t)|$, $\hat{\omega}_j = \max_{t \in \mathbb{R}} \omega_j(t)$, $\omega_j(t) = \frac{1}{1 - \tau'_j(\mu_j(t))}$, $\mu_j(t)$ is an inverse function of $t - \tau_j(t)$.

Proof. From Theorem 1, system (1) exists a unique equilibrium point. When $g_j(x^*_j) = 0$, systems (1) and (3) have the same equilibrium point. Let $X^* = (x^*_1, x^*_2, \cdots, x^*_n)^T \in \mathbb{R}^n$ be the unique equilibrium point for system (3). Let $(A_i \tilde{x}_i)(t) = (A_i x_i)(t) - A_i x^*_i$ and $\tilde{y}_i(t) = y_i(t) - y^*_i$, where $y^*_i = \xi_i A_i x^*_i$. By (4), we have

$$\begin{cases} d\big[(A_i \tilde{x}_i)(t)\big] = -\xi_i (A_i \tilde{x}_i)(t)dt + \tilde{y}_i(t)dt, \\ \tilde{y}'_i(t) = -(a_i - \xi_i)\tilde{y}_i(t)dt + [(a_i - \xi_i)\xi_i](A_i \tilde{x}_i)(t)dt - b_i \tilde{x}_i(t)dt \\ \quad + \sum_{j=1}^n c_{ij} \tilde{f}_j(\tilde{x}_j(t))dt + \sum_{j=1}^n d_{ij} \tilde{f}_j(\tilde{x}_j(t - \tau_j(t)))dt \\ \quad + \left(\sum_{j=1}^n e_{ij} \int_{t-\gamma_1}^t \tilde{f}_j(\tilde{x}_j(s))ds\right)dt + \sum_{j=1}^n h_{ij} \tilde{g}_j(\tilde{x}_j(t))dB_i(t), \end{cases} \qquad (12)$$

where
$$\tilde{f}_j(\tilde{x}_j(t)) = f_j(\tilde{x}_j(t) + x^*_j) - f_j(x^*_j), \quad \tilde{g}_j(\tilde{x}_j(t)) = g_j(\tilde{x}_j(t) + x^*_j) - g_j(x^*_j).$$

Let
$$\tilde{Z} = (A\tilde{X}, \tilde{Y}) = (A_1 \tilde{x}_1, A_2 \tilde{x}_2, \cdots, A_n \tilde{x}_n, \tilde{y}_1, \tilde{y}_2, \cdots, \tilde{y}_n)$$

and
$$V(t, \tilde{Z}) = \sum_{i=1}^n \left((A_i \tilde{x}_i)^2(t) + \tilde{y}_i^2(t)\right) + \sum_{i=1}^n \sum_{j=1}^n |d_{ij}| \int_{t-\tau_j(t)}^t \omega_j(s) \tilde{f}_j^2(\tilde{x}_j(s))ds \\ + \sum_{i=1}^n \sum_{j=1}^n |e_{ij}| \int_0^{\gamma_1} \int_{t-s}^t \tilde{f}_j^2(\tilde{x}_j(\theta))d\theta ds. \qquad (13)$$

By (13), we obtain
$$V_t(t, \tilde{Z}) = \sum_{i=1}^n \sum_{j=1}^n |d_{ij}| \left(\omega_j(t) \tilde{f}_j^2(\tilde{x}_j(t)) - \tilde{f}_j^2(\tilde{x}_j(t - \tau_j(t)))\right) \\ + \sum_{i=1}^n \sum_{j=1}^n |e_{ij}| \left(\gamma_1 \tilde{f}_j^2(\tilde{x}_j(t)) - \int_0^{\gamma_1} \tilde{f}_j^2(\tilde{x}_j(t - s))ds\right) \qquad (14)$$

$$V_{\tilde{Z}}(t, \tilde{Z}) = 2(A_1 \tilde{x}_1, A_2 \tilde{x}_2, \cdots, A_n \tilde{x}_n, \tilde{y}_1, \tilde{y}_2, \cdots, \tilde{y}_n), \quad V_{\tilde{Z}\tilde{Z}}(t, \tilde{Z}) = 2E_{2n \times 2n}, \qquad (15)$$

where $E_{2n \times 2n}$ is a $2n \times 2n$ identity matrix. From Definition 2, (12), (14) and (15), we obtain

$$\begin{aligned}
\mathcal{L}V(t,\tilde{Z}) &= \sum_{i=1}^{n}\sum_{j=1}^{n}|d_{ij}|\left(\omega_j(t)\tilde{f}_j^2(\tilde{x}_j(t)) - \tilde{f}_j^2(\tilde{x}_j(t-\tau_j(t)))\right) \\
&+ \sum_{i=1}^{n}\sum_{j=1}^{n}|e_{ij}|\left(\gamma_1\tilde{f}_j^2(\tilde{x}_j(t)) - \int_0^{\gamma_1}\tilde{f}_j^2(\tilde{x}_j(t-s))ds\right) \\
&+ 2\sum_{i=1}^{n}A_i\tilde{x}_i\left(-\xi_i(A_i\tilde{x}_i)(t) + \tilde{y}_i(t)\right) \\
&+ 2\sum_{i=1}^{n}\tilde{y}_i\bigg(-(a_i-\xi_i)\tilde{y}_i(t) + [(a_i-\xi_i)\xi_i](A_i\tilde{x}_i)(t) - b_i\tilde{x}_i(t) \\
&+ \sum_{j=1}^{n}c_{ij}\tilde{f}_j(\tilde{x}_j(t)) + \sum_{j=1}^{n}d_{ij}\tilde{f}_j(\tilde{x}_j(t-\tau_j(t))) + \sum_{j=1}^{n}e_{ij}\int_{t-\gamma_1}^{t}\tilde{f}_j(\tilde{x}_j(s))ds\bigg) \\
&+ \sum_{i=1}^{n}\bigg(\sum_{j=1}^{n}h_{ij}\tilde{g}_j(\tilde{x}_j(t))\bigg)^2.
\end{aligned} \quad (16)$$

Using inequalities $a^2 + b^2 \geq 2ab$, $\left(\sum_{i=1}^{n}a_ib_i\right)^2 \leq \sum_{i=1}^{n}a_i^2\sum_{i=1}^{n}b_i^2$, (16) and Lemma 1, we obtain

$$\begin{aligned}
\mathcal{L}V(t,\tilde{Z}) &\leq \sum_{i=1}^{n}\sum_{j=1}^{n}|d_{ij}|\left(\omega_j(t)\tilde{f}_j^2(\tilde{x}_j(t)) - \tilde{f}_j^2(\tilde{x}_j(t-\tau_j(t)))\right) \\
&+ \sum_{i=1}^{n}\sum_{j=1}^{n}|e_{ij}|\left(\gamma_1\tilde{f}_j^2(\tilde{x}_j(t)) - \int_0^{\gamma_1}\tilde{f}_j^2(\tilde{x}_j(t-s))ds\right) \\
&+ 2\sum_{i=1}^{n}\left(-\xi_i(A_i\tilde{x}_i)^2(t) + \frac{(A_i\tilde{x}_i)^2(t) + \tilde{y}_i^2(t)}{2}\right) \\
&+ 2\sum_{i=1}^{n}\left(-(a_i-\xi_i)\tilde{y}_i^2(t) + |(a_i-\xi_i)\xi_i|\frac{(A_i\tilde{x}_i)^2(t) + \tilde{y}_i^2(t)}{2} + b_i\frac{\tilde{y}_i^2(t) + (1-\hat{c}_i)^{-2}(A_i\tilde{x}_i)^2(t)}{2}\right) \\
&+ \sum_{j=1}^{n}|c_{ij}|\frac{\tilde{y}_i^2(t) + \tilde{f}_j^2(\tilde{x}_j(t))}{2} + \sum_{j=1}^{n}|d_{ij}|\frac{\tilde{f}_j(\tilde{x}_j^2(t-\tau_j(t))) + \tilde{y}_i^2(t)}{2} \\
&+ \sum_{j=1}^{n}|e_{ij}|\frac{\tilde{y}_i^2(t) + \gamma_1\int_{t-\gamma_1}^{t}\tilde{f}^2(\tilde{x}_j(s))ds}{2}\bigg) + \sum_{i=1}^{n}\sum_{k=1}^{n}\sum_{j=1}^{n}h_{kj}^2\tilde{l}_i^2\tilde{x}_i^2(t) \\
&\leq \sum_{i=1}^{n}\bigg[-2\xi_i + 1 + |(a_i-\xi_i)\xi_i| + b_i(1-\hat{c}_i)^{-2} + \sum_{j=1}^{n}|d_{ij}|\omega_j(t)L_j^2(1-\hat{c}_i)^{-2} \\
&+ \sum_{j=1}^{n}|e_{ij}|\gamma_1L_j^2(1-\hat{c}_i)^{-2} + \sum_{k=1}^{n}\sum_{j=1}^{n}h_{kj}^2\tilde{l}_i^2(1-\hat{c}_i)^{-2}\bigg](A_i\tilde{x}_i)^2(t) \\
&+ \sum_{i=1}^{n}\bigg[-2(a_i-\xi_i) + 1 + |(a_i-\xi_i)\xi_i| + b_i + \sum_{j=1}^{n}\big(|c_{ij}| + |d_{ij}| + |e_{ij}|\big)\bigg]\tilde{y}_i^2(t).
\end{aligned} \quad (17)$$

In view of (10), (11) and (17), we have $\mathcal{L}V(t,\tilde{Z}) < 0$, i.e., $\mathcal{L}V(t,\tilde{Z})$ is a negative definite. Evidently, $V(t,\tilde{Z})$ is a positive definite. Now, we show that $V(t,\tilde{Z})$ has an infinitesimal upper bound. By assumption (H$_3$), we obtain $|\tilde{f}_j(x)| \leq N_j$ for all $x \in \mathbb{R}$, $j = 1, 2, \cdots, n$. Thus,

$$V(t,\tilde{Z}) = \sum_{i=1}^{n}\left((A_i\tilde{x}_i)^2(t) + \tilde{y}_i^2(t)\right) + \sum_{i=1}^{n}\sum_{j=1}^{n}|d_{ij}|\int_{t-\tau_j(t)}^{t}\omega_j(s)\tilde{f}_j^2(\tilde{x}_j(s))ds$$
$$+ \sum_{i=1}^{n}\sum_{j=1}^{n}|e_{ij}|\int_{0}^{\gamma_1}\int_{t-s}^{t}\tilde{f}_j^2(\tilde{x}_j(\theta))d\theta ds$$
$$\leq \sum_{i=1}^{n}\left((A_i\tilde{x}_i)^2(t) + \tilde{y}_i^2(t)\right) + \sum_{i=1}^{n}\sum_{j=1}^{n}|d_{ij}|\hat{\tau}_j\hat{\omega}_j N_j^2 + \sum_{i=1}^{n}\sum_{j=1}^{n}|e_{ij}|\frac{\gamma_1^2}{2}N_j^2.$$

In view of Definition 3, $V(t,X)$ has an infinitesimal upper bound. Furthermore, by (13), we obtain
$$V(t,\tilde{Z}) \geq \sum_{i=1}^{n}\left((A_i\tilde{x}_i)^2(t) + \tilde{y}_i^2(t)\right).$$

Evidently, we have $V(t,\tilde{Z}) \to +\infty$ for $||\tilde{Z}|| \to \infty$. Hence, by Definition 4, $V(t,\tilde{Z})$ is an infinite positive definite function for $\tilde{Z}$. In view of Lemma 3, the equilibrium point of system (4) is stochastically globally asymptotically stable, i.e., the equilibrium point of system (3) is also stochastically globally asymptotically stable. □

Remark 4. *Constructing an appropriate Lyapunov functions is the key to proving Theorem 2. We innovatively construct Lyapunov functions, based on fully considering neutral operators which are different from the corresponding ones of [9–13].*

5. Examples

Consider the following example:

$$d[(A_1x_1)'(t)] = -a_1(A_ix_1)'(t)dt - b_1x_1(t)dt + \sum_{j=1}^{2}c_{1j}f_j(x_j(t))dt + \sum_{j=1}^{2}d_{1j}f_j(x_j(t-\tau_j(t)))dt$$
$$+ \left(\sum_{j=1}^{2}e_{1j}\int_{t-\gamma_1}^{t}f_j(x_j(s))ds\right)dt + I_1dt + \sum_{j=1}^{2}h_{1j}g_j(x_j(t))dB_1(t),$$
$$d[(A_2x_2)'(t)] = -a_2(A_2x_2)'(t)dt - b_2x_2(t)dt + \sum_{j=1}^{2}c_{2j}f_j(x_j(t))dt + \sum_{j=1}^{2}d_{2j}f_j(x_j(t-\tau_j(t)))dt \quad (18)$$
$$+ \left(\sum_{j=1}^{n}e_{2j}\int_{t-\gamma_1}^{t}f_j(x_j(s))ds\right)dt + I_idt + \sum_{j=1}^{2}h_{2j}g_j(x_j(t))dB_2(t),$$

where
$$i,j=1,2,\ c_1(t) = 0.1\sin\frac{t}{10},\ c_2(t) = 0.1\cos\frac{t}{10},\ a_i = 1.425,\ b_1 = b_2 = 0.3,$$
$$c_{ij} = d_{ij} = 0.15,\ e_{ij} = h_{ij} = -0.25,\ \tau_j(t) = \frac{1}{10}\cos 10t,\ f_j(u) = \frac{0.01\sin^2 u}{u^2+1},$$
$$g_j(u) = \frac{2.5}{2\pi}\times 10^{-2}\sin\frac{u\pi}{2.5},\ \gamma_0 = \gamma_1 = 0.02,\ I_1 = 0.25,\ I_2(t) = 0.35.$$

Evidently, we obtain
$$l_j = N_j = 0.01,\ \tilde{l}_j = 0.005,\ \hat{c}_i = 0.1,\ \hat{\omega}_i = 1.$$

Choosing $\xi_i = 0.745$, we obtain
$$-b_i + \frac{1}{2}\sum_{j=1}^{2}\left(|c_{ij}|+|d_{ij}|+\gamma_1|e_{ij}|\right)l_j + \frac{1}{2}\sum_{j=1}^{2}\left(|c_{ji}|+|d_{ji}|+\gamma_1|e_{ji}|\right)l_i \approx -0.2952 < 0,$$

$$-2\xi_i + 1 + |(a_i - \xi_i)\xi_i| + b_i(1 - |c_i|)^{-2} + \sum_{j=1}^{2} |d_{ij}|\hat{\omega}_j L_j^2 (1 - \hat{c}_i)^{-2}$$

$$+ \sum_{j=1}^{2} |e_{ij}|\gamma_1 L_j^2 (1 - \hat{c}_i)^{-2} + \sum_{k=1}^{2}\sum_{j=1}^{2} h_{kj}^2 \tilde{l}_i^2 (1 - \hat{c}_i)^{-2} \approx -0.1032 < 0$$

and

$$-2(a_i - \xi_i) + 1 + |(a_i - \xi_i)\xi_i| + b_i + \sum_{j=1}^{2} \left(|c_{ij}| + |d_{ij}| + |e_{ij}|\right) \approx -0.0175 < 0.$$

Then, all conditions of Theorems 1 and 2 hold, and system (18) has a unique equilibrium point, which is stochastically globally asymptotically stable. Through simple calculations, system (18) has a unique equilibrium point $(2.5, 2.5)$. Give any three sets of initial values:

$$(x_i(0), x_i'(0)) = (3.45, 2.91); (2.46, 1.25); (1.67, 3.53), \quad i = 1, 2.$$

Figures 1 and 2 show that for system (18) there exists a stochastically globally asymptotically stable equilibrium point $(2.5, 2.5)$.

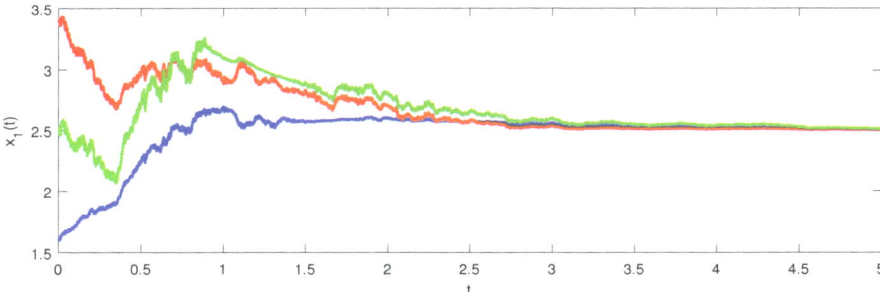

Figure 1. Instantaneous response of state variable $x_1(t)$ in system (18) with different initial conditions.

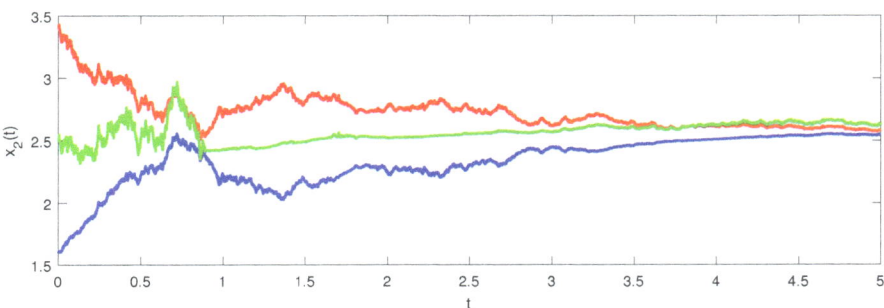

Figure 2. Instantaneous response of state variable $x_2(t)$ in system (18) with different initial conditions.

6. Conclusions

In this article, we studied the stochastically globally asymptotic stability for a class of stochastic inertial delay neural networks, and provided sufficient conditions for determining their existence and stability. This has a certain significance for practical applications and theoretical exploration. The research methods of this article are based on homeomorphism mapping, standard stochastic analyzing technology and the Lyapunov functional method. Using the discussion ideas and methods in this article, the stability problems of other types of stochastic inertial neural networks can be further studied: examples include stochastic inertial neural networks with impulses and stochastic inertial neural networks with a Markov switch.

Author Contributions: Writing—review and editing, B.D. and B.W.; methodology, H.Y. All authors have read and agreed to the published version of the manuscript.

Funding: This research received no external funding.

Data Availability Statement: Not applicable.

Acknowledgments: The authors would like to thank the editor and the anonymous referees for their helpful comments and valuable suggestions regarding this article.

Conflicts of Interest: The authors declare no conflict of interest.

References

1. Wheeler, D.; Schieve, W. Stability and chaos in an inertial two-neuron system. *Phys. D Nonlinear Phenom.* **1997**, *105*, 267–284. [CrossRef]
2. Liu, Q.; Liao, X.; Yang, D.; Guo, S. The research for Hopf bifurcation in a single inertial neuron model with external forcing. *IEEE Int. Conf. Granul. Comput.* **2007**, *85*, 528–833.
3. Liu, Q.; Liao, X.; Guo, S.; Wu, Y. Stability of bifurcating periodic solutions for a single delayed inertial neuron model under periodic excitation. *Nonlinear Anal. Real World Appl.* **2009**, *10*, 2384–2395. [CrossRef]
4. Li, C.; Chen, G.; Liao, X.; Yu, J. Hopf bifurcation and chaos in a single inertial neuron model with time delay. *Eur. Phys. J. B* **2004**, *41*, 337–343. [CrossRef]
5. Liu, Q.; Liao, X.; Liu, Y.; Zhou, S.; Guo, S. Dynamics of an inertial two-neuron system with time delay. *Nonlinear Dyn.* **2009**, *58*, 574–609. [CrossRef]
6. Arik, S. Global robust stability analysis of neural networks with discrete time delays. *Chaos Solitons Fractals* **2005**, *26*, 1407–1414. [CrossRef]
7. Tu, Z.; Cao, J.; Hayat, T. Global exponential stability in Lagrange sense for inertial neural networks with time-varying delays. *Neurocomputing* **2016**, *171*, 524–531. [CrossRef]
8. Wang, J.; Tian, L. Global Lagrange stability for inertial neural networks with mixed time-varying delays. *Neurocomputing* **2017**, *235*, 140–146. [CrossRef]
9. Wan, P.; Jian, J. Global convergence analysis of impulsive inertial neural networks with time-varying delays. *Neurocomputing* **2017**, *245*, 68–76. [CrossRef]
10. Tang, Q.; Jian, J. global exponential convergence for impulsive inertial complex-valued neural networks with time-varying delays. *Math. Comput. Simul.* **2019**, *159*, 39–56. [CrossRef]
11. Ke, Y.; Miao, C. Anti-periodic solutions of inertial neural networks with time delays. *Neural Process. Lett.* **2017**, *45*, 523–538. [CrossRef]
12. Ke, Y.; Miao, C. Stability analysis of inertial Cohen-Grossberg-type neural networks with time delays. *Neurocomputing* **2013**, *117*, 196–205. [CrossRef]
13. Ke, Y.; Miao, C. Exponential stability of periodic solutions for inertial Cohen-Grossberg-type neural networks. *Neural Netw. World* **2014**, *4*, 377–394. [CrossRef]
14. Huang, Q.; Cao, J. Stability analysis of inertial Cohen-Grossberg neural networks with Markovian jumping parameters. *Neurocomputing* **2018**, *282*, 89–97. [CrossRef]
15. Ke, Y.; Miao, C. Stability analysis of BAM neural networks with inertial term and.time delay. *WSEAS Trans. Syst.* **2011**, *10*, 425–438.
16. Ke, Y.; Miao, C. Stability and existence of periodic solutions in inertial BAM neural networks with time delay. *Neural Comput. Appl.* **2013**, *23*, 1089–1099.
17. Zhang, Y.; Kong, L. Photovoltaic power prediction based on hybrid modeling of neural network and stochastic differential equation. *ISA Trans.* **2022**, *128*, 181–206. [CrossRef]
18. Shu, J.; Wu, B.; Xiong, L.; Zhang, H. Stochastic stabilization of Markov jump quaternion-valued neural network using sampled-data control. *Appl. Math. Comput.* **2021**, *400*, 126041. [CrossRef]
19. Guo, Y. Globally robust stability analysis for stochastic Cohen- Grossberg neural networks with impulse control and time-varying delays. *Ukr. Math. J.* **2018**, *69*, 1220–1233. [CrossRef]
20. Hu, J.; Zhong, S.; Liang, L. Exponential stability analysis of stochastic delayed cellular neutral networks. *Chaos Solitons Fractals* **2006**, *27*, 1006–1010. [CrossRef]
21. Xu, J.; Chen, L.; Li, P. On p−th moment exponential stability for stochastic cellular neural networks with distributed delays. *Int. J. Control. Autom. Syst.* **2018**, *16*, 1217–1225. [CrossRef]
22. Liu, L.; Deng, F.; Zhu, Q. Mean square stability of two classes of theta methods for numerical computation and simulation of delayed stochastic Hopfield neural networks. *J. Comput. Appl. Math.* **2018**, *343*, 428–447. [CrossRef]
23. Yang, L.; Fei, Y.; Wu, W. Periodic Solution for del-stochastic high-Order Hopfield neural networks with time delays on time scales. *Neural Process. Lett.* **2019**, *49*, 1681–1696. [CrossRef]

24. Chen, G.; Li, D.; Shi, L.; van Gaans, O.; Lunel, S.V. Stability results for stochastic delayed recurrent neural networks with discrete and distributed delays. *J. Differ. Equ.* **2018**, *264*, 3864–3898. [CrossRef]
25. Zhang, H.; Ma, Q.; Lu, J.; Chu, Y.; Li, Y. Synchronization control of neutral-type neural networks with sampled-data via adaptive event-triggered communication scheme. *J. Frankl. Inst.* **2021**, *358*, 1999–2014. [CrossRef]
26. Yang, X.; Cheng, Z.; Li, X.; Ma, T. xponential synchronization of coupled neutral-type neural networks with mixed delays via quantized output control. *J. Frankl. Inst.* **2019**, *356*, 8138–8153. [CrossRef]
27. Si, W.; Xie, T. Further Results on Exponentially Robust Stability of Uncertain Connection Weights of Neutral-Type Recurrent Neural Networks. *Complexity* **2021**, *2021*, 6941701. [CrossRef]
28. Du, B. Anti-periodic solutions problem for inertial competitive neutral-type neural networks via Wirtinger inequality. *J. Inequalities Appl.* **2019**, *2019*, 187. [CrossRef]
29. Zhang, Z.; Zhou, D. Existence and global exponential stability of a periodic solution for a discrete-time interval general BAM neural networks. *J. Frankl. Inst.* **2010**, *347*, 763–780. [CrossRef]
30. Park, J.; Kwon, O.; Lee, S. LMI optimization approach on stability for delayed neural networks of neutral-type. *Appl. Math. Comput.* **2008**, *196*, 236–244. [CrossRef]
31. Yu, K.; Lien, C. Stability criteria for uncertain neutral systems with interval time-varying delays. *Chaos Solitons Fractals* **2008**, *38*, 650–657. [CrossRef]
32. Zhang, J.; Chang, A.; Yang, G. Periodicity on Neutral-Type Inertial Neural Networks Incorporating Multiple Delays. *Symmetry* **2021**, *13*, 2231. [CrossRef]
33. Wang, C.; Song, Y.; Zhang, F.; Zhao, Y. Exponential Stability of a Class of Neutral Inertial Neural Networks with Multi-Proportional Delays and Leakage Delays. *Mathematics* **2023**, *11*, 2596. [CrossRef]
34. Hale, J. *The Theory of Functional Differential Equations*; Springer: New York, NY, USA, 1977. [CrossRef]
35. Wang, K.; Zhu, Y. Stability of almost periodic solution for a generalized neutral-type neural networks with delays. *Neurocomputing* **2010**, *73*, 3300–3307.
36. Mao, X. *Stochastic Differential Equations and Applications*; Horwood: Chichester, UK, 1997. [CrossRef]
37. Forti, M.; Tesi, A. New conditions for global stability of neural networks with application to linear and quadratic programming problems. *IEEE Trans. Circuits Syst.* **1995**, *42*, 354–366.
38. Zhang, Y.; Liu, W.; Jiang, W. Stability of stochastic and intertial neural networks with time delays. *Appl. Math. J. Chin. Univ.* **2020**, *35*, 83–98. [CrossRef]

Disclaimer/Publisher's Note: The statements, opinions and data contained in all publications are solely those of the individual author(s) and contributor(s) and not of MDPI and/or the editor(s). MDPI and/or the editor(s) disclaim responsibility for any injury to people or property resulting from any ideas, methods, instructions or products referred to in the content.

Perspective

From Optimal Control to Mean Field Optimal Transport via Stochastic Neural Networks

Luca Di Persio [1] and Matteo Garbelli [1,2,*]

[1] Department of Computer Science, University of Verona, Strada le Grazie 15, 37134 Verona, Italy; luca.dipersio@univr.it
[2] Department of Mathematics, University of Trento, Via Sommarive 14, Povo, 38123 Trento, Italy
* Correspondence: matteo.garbelli@unitn.it

Abstract: In this paper, we derive a unified perspective for Optimal Transport (OT) and Mean Field Control (MFC) theories to analyse the learning process for Neural Network algorithms in a high-dimensional framework. We consider a Mean Field Neural Network in the context of MFC theory referring to the mean field formulation of OT theory that may allow the development of efficient algorithms in a high-dimensional framework while providing a powerful tool in the context of explainable Artificial Intelligence.

Keywords: neural network; machine learning; optimal transport; mean field control; mean field optimal transport

Citation: Di Persio, L.; Garbelli, M. From Optimal Control to Mean Field Optimal Transport via Stochastic Neural Networks. *Symmetry* **2023**, *15*, 1724. https://doi.org/10.3390/sym15091724

Academic Editor: Alexander Zaslavski, Savin Treanta, Octav Olteanu and Sergei D. Odintsov

Received: 2 May 2023
Revised: 28 August 2023
Accepted: 31 August 2023
Published: 8 September 2023

Copyright: © 2023 by the authors. Licensee MDPI, Basel, Switzerland. This article is an open access article distributed under the terms and conditions of the Creative Commons Attribution (CC BY) license (https://creativecommons.org/licenses/by/4.0/).

1. Introduction

In recent years, parametric Machine Learning (ML) applications have shown brilliant performance in capturing relevant symmetries and hidden patterns characterizing a specific knowledge base. Specifically, Neural Networks (NNs), i.e., systems of interconnected artificial neurons, constitute a fundamental tool to capture complex patterns and to make accurate predictions for various applications, ranging from computer vision and natural language processing to robotics and reinforcement learning. Their growing popularity has prompted an increasing demand for a deep mathematical description of the underlying training procedures, specifically in high dimensions to tackle the curse of dimensionality.

For this latter research challenge, we consider a novel class of NNs, termed *Mean Field Neural Networks* (MFNNs), which are defined as the limiting object of a *population of NNs* when its number of components tends to infinity. Our aim concerns deriving a unified perspective for this class of models based on existing symmetries between Mean Field Control (MFC) theory and the Optimal Transport (OT) method. Our approach is based on an *infinite dimensional lifting* which allows new insights to be gained into relationships between data in the corresponding finite-dimensional scenario.

We start the analysis by looking at the continuous idealization of a specific class of NNs, namely Residual NNs, also named ResNets, whose training process in a supervised learning scenario is stated as a Mean Field Optimal Control Problem (MFOCP). We consider a deterministic dynamic that evolves in terms of an ordinary differential equation (ODE). Moreover, the training problem of a ResNet is shown to be equivalent to an MFOCP of Bolza type, see [1,2] for further details.

The next passage in our analysis concerns introducing a noisy component into the dynamics of the ODE, moving to a Stochastic Differential Equation (SDE) that allows us to consider the inherent uncertainty connected to the variations in the real-world data, simultaneously allowing for the integration of stochastic aspects into the learning process. Although this second model does not include any mean field terms, it allows the development of a class of algorithms known as Stochastic NNs (SNNs). In [3], the authors develop a sample-wise backpropagation method for SNNs based on backward SDE that models the gradient (with respect to the parameters) process of the loss function, representing a feasible tool for quantifying the uncertainty of the learning process. Another possible approach for probabilistic learning is studied in [4], where the authors develop the so-called Stochastic Deep Network (SDN), namely an NN architecture that can use as input data not only single vectors but also *random vectors* to model the probability distribution of given inputs. Following their analysis, the SDN is considered as an architecture based on the composition of maps between probability measures performing inference tasks and solving ML problems over the space of probability measures.

In the last passage, we merge the stochastic aspect with the mean field one by considering the so-called Mean Field Optimal Transport (MFOT) formulation, recently introduced in [5]. We describe the MFC tools relevant to formalize the training process; hence, we formulate the training problem as MFOT in an infinite-dimensional setting. Considering the collective interactions and distributions of the network's parameters may facilitate the analysis of the network behavior on a macroscopic level, hence improving the interpretability, scalability, and robustness of NNs models, while adding knowledge by highlighting the hidden symmetries and relations between data.

We highlight that the symmetry between mean field models and ML algorithms is also studied in [6], where the authors establish a mathematical relationship between the MFG framework and normalizing flows, a popular method for generative models composed of a sequence of invertible mappings. Similarly, in [7], the authors analyze Generative Adversarial Networks (GANs) from the perspectives of MFGs, providing a theoretical connection between GANs, OT, and MFG and numerical experiments.

This paper is organized as follows: In Section 2, we introduce the mathematical formalism of the supervised learning paradigm while providing the description of the continuous idealization of a Residual NN stated as an MFOCP; in Section 3, we introduce a noisy component into the network dynamic, thus focusing on Stochastic NNs formalized as stochastic optimal control problems; in Section 4, we review the MFG setting in a cooperative scenario defined in terms of MFC theory. Then, we consider recently developed Mean Field Optimal Transport methods that allow MFC problems to be rephrased into OT ones. We also illustrate related approximation schemes and possible connection to an abstract class of NNs that respect the MFOT structure. We conclude by reviewing some methods to *learn*, i.e., approximate, mean field functions that depend on probability distribution, obtained as the limiting object of empirical measures.

2. Residual Neural Networks as a Mean Field Optimal Control Problem

In this section, we present the workflow to treat a feed-forward NN, specifically a Residual NN, as a dynamical system based on the work in [8]. The main reference for this part is the well-known paper in [2], where the authors introduce a continuous idealization of Deep Learning (DL) to study the Supervised Learning (SL) procedure; this is stated as an optimal control problem by considering the associated population risk minimization problem.

2.1. The Supervised Learning Paradigm

Following [9,10], the SL problem aims at estimating the function $\mathcal{F} : \mathcal{X} \to \mathcal{Y}$, commonly known as the Oracle. The space $\mathcal{X}$ can be identified with a subset of $\mathbb{R}^d$ related to input arrays (such as images, string texts, or time series), while $\mathcal{Y}$ is the corresponding target set. Here, for simplicity, we consider $\mathcal{X}$ and $\mathcal{Y}$ Euclidean spaces with different dimensions. Thus, training begins with a set of N input–target pairs $\{x_0^i, y_T^i\}_{i=1}^N$ where:

- $x_0^i \in \mathbb{R}^d$ denotes the inputs of the NN;
- $x_T^i = \mathcal{F}(x_0^i) \in \mathbb{R}^d$ denotes the outputs of the NN;
- $y_T^i \in \mathbb{R}^l$ denotes the corresponding targets.

We assume the same dimension of the Euclidean space for NN inputs and outputs, allowing us to explicitly write a dynamic in terms of a difference equation. Hence, for a ResNet (see [11] for more details) with T layers, the feed-forward propagation is given by

$$x_{t+1} = x_t + f(x_t, \theta_t) \qquad t = 0, \ldots, T-1 \qquad (1)$$

with $f : \mathbb{R}^d \to \mathbb{R}^d$ being a parameterized function and θ_t being the trainable parameters, e.g., bias, weights of the t-th layer that belong to a measurable set $\mathcal{U}$ with values in a subset of the Euclidean space $\mathbb{R}^m$.

Remark 1. *Following [12], we report an example of a domain for parameters of NN with ReLU activation functions. We define the following parameter domain*

$$\Theta = \left\{ (a, w, b) \in \mathbb{R} \times \mathbb{R}^d \times \mathbb{R} : a^2 < ||w|| + b^2 \right\}$$

with activation functions $\phi : \Theta \to \mathbb{R}$ defined as

$$\phi(\theta; x) = a\sigma(w^T x + b), \quad \theta = (a, w, b), \quad \sigma(z) = z^+ = \max\{z, 0\},$$

2.2. Empirical Risk Minimization

We aim at minimizing, over the set of measurable parameters Θ, a *terminal loss function* $\Phi : \mathcal{X} \times \mathcal{Y} \to \mathbb{R}$ plus a regularization term, L, to derive a Supervised Learning problem as an Empirical Risk Minimization (ERP) problem, namely

$$\min_{\theta \in \mathcal{U}} \left[\frac{1}{K} \sum_{i=1}^{N} \Phi(x_T^i, y^i) + \sum_{t=0}^{T-1} L(\theta_t) \right] \qquad (2)$$

over N training data samples indexed by i. We write $\theta = [\theta_0, \ldots \theta_{T-1}]$ to identify the set of all parameters of the network.

If we consider no regularization of the parameters, i.e., $L = 0$, and a quadratic loss function in terms of Φ, then Equation (2) reads

$$J^{ERM}(\theta) = \min_{\theta \in \mathcal{U}} \left[\frac{1}{K} \sum_{i=1}^{N} ||x_T^i - y^i||^2 \right] = \min_{\theta \in \mathcal{U}} \left[\frac{1}{K} \sum_{i=1}^{N} ||f(x^i, \theta) - y^i||^2 \right] \qquad (3)$$

being $x^i = [x_0, \ldots, x_{T_1}]$ the discrete state process defined in Equation (1).

Optimizing J^{ERM} by computing its gradient is computationally expensive, especially if the amount of data K is very large.

To handle the curse of dimensionality, it is usually common to initialize parameters from a θ^0 from a probability distribution, to then optimize their choice inductively according to a Stochastic Gradient Descent scheme

$$\theta^{k+1} = \theta^k - \eta_t \frac{1}{K} \sum_{i=1}^{K} ||f(x^i, \theta) - y^i|| \nabla_\theta f(x^i, \theta) \qquad (4)$$

with learning rate η_t over K optimization steps.

For the sake of completeness, before going to the limit (we pass from a discrete set of training data to the corresponding distribution), we point out in the following remark that it is also possible to associate a measure corresponding to the empirical distribution of the parameters when the number of neurons goes to infinity.

Remark 2. *A different approach, as illustrated, e.g., by Sirignano and Spilipupouls in [13], consists of associating to each layer the corresponding empirical measure and building a measure to describe the whole network, hence working with the empirical measure of controls, rather than states, as presented in Section 4. Following the perspective of mean field term in controls, the SGD*

Equation (4) can be formalized as a minimization method over the set of probability distributions. Moreover, the training of the NN is based on the correspondence between the empirical measure of neurons μ_N and the function f_N that is approximated by the NN. Specifically, it has been proved that training via gradient descent of an over-parametrised one-hidden-layer NN with infinite width is equivalent to gradient flow in Wasserstein space [2,9,14,15]. Conversely, in the small learning rate regime, the training is equivalent to an SDE, see, e.g., [16].

From here on, we deal with empirical distribution and measures associated to the training data.

2.3. Population Risk Minimization as Mean Field Optimal Control Problem

In what follows, we move from the discrete setting to the corresponding continuous idealization by:

- Going from layer index T to continuous parameter t;
- Passing from a discrete set of inputs/output to a distribution μ that represents the joint distribution in $\mathcal{W}_2(\mathbb{R}^d \times \mathbb{R}^l)$, modeling the input label distribution;
- Passing from empirical risk minimization to population risk (i.e., minimization over expectation $\mathbb{E}$).

In particular, we pass to the limit in the number of data samples (number of input-target pairs), also assuming a continuous dynamic in place of layer discretization. The latter limit allows us to describe the dynamic of the state process x with the following Ordinary Differential Equation (ODE)

$$\dot{x}_t = f(x_t, \theta_t), \qquad t \in [0, T], \tag{5}$$

in place of the finite difference Equation (1). We identify the input–target pairs as sampled from a given distribution μ allowing us to write the SL problem as a Population Risk Minimization (PRM) problem.

In summary, we aim at approximating the Oracle function $\mathcal{F}$ using a provided set of training data sampled by a (known) distribution μ_0 by optimizing weights θ_t to achieve maximal proximity between x_T (output) and y_T (target). Thus, we consider a probability space $(\Omega, \mathcal{F}, \mathbb{P})$ and we assume inputs x_0 in $\mathbb{R}^d$ to be sampled from a distribution $\mu_0 \in \mathcal{P}(\mathbb{R}^d)$, with corresponding target y_T in $\mathbb{R}^l$ sampled from a distribution $\nu \in \mathcal{P}(\mathbb{R}^l)$, while the joint probability distribution μ, which models the distribution of the input–target pairs, defined by $\mu := \mathcal{P}(x_0, y_T)$, belongs to the Wasserstein space $\mathcal{W}_2(\mathbb{R}^{(d+l)})$ and has μ_0 and ν as its marginals. We recall that given a metric space (X, d), the p-Wasserstein space $\mathcal{W}_p(X)$ is defined as the set of all Borel probability measures on X with finite p-moments.

The marginal distributions are obtained by projecting the joint probability distribution μ over the subspaces of inputs and output, respectively. We identify the first marginal, i.e., the projection over $\mathbb{R}^l$, with the distribution of inputs

$$\mu_0 = \int_{R^l} \mu(x, y) dy,$$

while the distribution of targets reads

$$\nu = \int_{R^d} \mu(x, y) dx.$$

Moreover, we assume the controls θ_t depend on the whole distribution of input–target pairs capturing the mean field aspect of the training data. We consider a measurable set of admissible controls, i.e., training weights, $\Theta \subseteq \mathbb{R}^m$ and we state a Mean Field Optimal Control Problem (MFOCP) to solve the following PRM problem:

$$\inf_{\theta \in L^\infty([0,T],\Theta)} J^{PRM}(\theta) := \mathbb{E}_\mu \left[\Phi(x_T, y_T) + \int_0^T L(x_t, \theta_t) dt \right] \quad (6)$$

$$\dot{x}_t = f(x_t, \theta_t) \quad 0 \leq t \leq T \quad x_0 \sim \mu_0, \quad (x_0, y_T) \sim \mu$$

We briefly report basic assumptions allowing us to have a solution for (6):
- $f : \mathbb{R}^d \times \Theta \to \mathbb{R}^d$, $L : \mathbb{R}^d \times \Theta \to \mathbb{R}$, $\Phi : \mathbb{R}^d \times \mathbb{R}^l \to \mathbb{R}$ are bounded;
- f, L, Φ are Lipschitz-continuous with respect to x, with the Lipschitz constants of f and L being independent of parameters θ;
- μ has finite support in $\mathcal{W}_2(\mathbb{R}^{(d+l)})$.

Problem (6) can be approached through two different methods: the first one is based on the Hamilton–Jacobi–Bellman (HJB) equation in the Wasserstein space, while the second one is based on a Mean Field Pontryagin Principle. We refer to [17,18] for viscosity solutions to the HJB equation in the Wasserstein space of probability measures, and to [19] for solving the constrained optimal control problems via the Pontryagin Maximum Principle.

For the sake of completeness, let us also cite [20], where the authors introduce a BSDE technique to solve the related Stochastic Maximum Principle, allowing us to consider the uncertainty associated with NN. The authors employ a Stochastic Differential Equation (SDE) in place of the ODE appearing in (6) to continuously approximate a Stochastic Neural Network (SNN). We deepen this approach in the next paragraph.

3. Stochastic Neural Network as a Stochastic Optimal Control Problem

In this paragraph, we generalize the previous setting considering a noisy dynamic, namely adding a stochastic integral to the deterministic setting described by the ODE in Problem (6). The reference model corresponds to Stochastic NN whose discrete state process is described by the following equation

$$X_{n+1} = X_n + hF(X_n, \theta_n) + \sqrt{h}\sigma_n \omega_n, \quad n = 0, 1, \ldots, N-1 \quad (7)$$

with $\{\omega_n\}$ being a sequence of i.i.d. standard Gaussian random variables. We refer to [4] for a theoretical and computational analysis of the SNN.

Equation (7) can be generalized in a continuous setting. To this end, we consider a complete filtered probability space $(\Omega, \mathcal{F}, \mathbb{F}^W, \mathbb{P})$, and we introduce the following SDE

$$X_t = X_0 + \int_0^T F(X_s, \theta_s) + \int_0^T \sigma_s dW_s, \quad (8)$$

with standard Brownian motion $W := (W_t)_{0 \leq t \leq T}$ and diffusion term σ. Analogously to ResNets, the index $T > 0$ represents a continuous parameter modeling the width of the layer, with X_T being the output of the network.

Here, we report the theory developed in [3] to study Equation (8) in the framework of the SOC problem by introducing the control process $u = [\theta, \sigma]$. Thus, we also consider the diffusion σ as a trainable parameter of the model. We start by translating the SDE (8) into the following controlled process, written in differential form

$$dX_t = f(X_t, u_t)dt + g(u_t)dW_t, \quad 0 \leq t \leq T, \quad (9)$$

where $f(X_t, u_t) = F(X_t, \theta_t)$ and $g(u_t) = \sigma_t$. As in classical control theory applied to ML, the aim is to select the control u that minimizes the discrepancy between the SNN output and the data. Accordingly, we define the cost function for our stochastic optimal control problem as

$$J(u) := \mathbb{E}[\Phi(X_T, \Lambda)], \quad (10)$$

with Λ being a random variable that corresponds to the target of a given input, i.e., X_0. Then, the optimal control $u^\star$ is the one that solves

$$J(u^\star) = \inf_{u \in \mathcal{U}[0,T]} J(u)$$

above the class of measurable control $\mathcal{U}$.

At this point, we are able to write the optimization problem that represents the analogue of Equation (6) with stochastic evolution (where the diffusion is also considered as a model parameter) but without reference to the mean field aspect of the learning procedure.

$$\inf_{u \in L^\infty([0,T],\mathcal{U})} J(u) := \mathbb{E}[\Phi(X_T, \Lambda)]$$
$$dX_t = f(X_t, u_t)dt + g(u_t)dW_t, \quad 0 \leq t \leq T \tag{11}$$

Following [3], we address the Stochastic Maximum Principle approach to solve the stochastic optimal control problem stated in (11). Firstly, the functional J is differentiated with respect to the control with a derivative in Gateaux sense over $[0, T]$

$$J'_u(t, u_t) = \mathbb{E}\left[f^i_u(X_t, u_t)^T Y_t + g'_u(u_t)^T Z_t\right]. \tag{12}$$

Then, via the martingale representation of Y_t, the following backward SDE is introduced

$$dY_t = f^i_x(X_t, u_t^\star)^T Y_t + Z_t dW_t, \quad Y_T = \Phi'_x(X_T, \Lambda) \tag{13}$$

to model the back-propagation of the forward state process equation defined in (9) associated with the optimal control $u^\star$.

Finally, the problem is solved via the gradient descent method with step size η_k

$$u_t^{k+1} = u_t^k - \eta_k J'_u(t, u_t^k), \quad k = 0, 1, 2, \ldots, \quad 0 \leq t \leq T. \tag{14}$$

Also in [3], the authors provide a numerical scheme whose main benefit is to derive an estimate of the uncertainty connected to the output of this stochastic class of NNs.

We remark that for Equation (14) it is not possible to write the chain rule as previously performed for Equation (4) due to the presence of the stochastic integral term that, differently from classical ML theory, makes the back-propagation itself a stochastic process, see Equation (13). However, modern programming libraries (e.g., TensorFlow or PyTorch) may perform the computation (14) automatically, reducing the computational cost, hence allowing us to go towards a mean field formulation (in terms of multiple interacting agents) of previous problems.

4. Mean Field Neural Network as a Mean Field Optimal Transport

In this section, we focus on the connection between SOC and OT, highlighting potential symmetries specifically for a class of infinite-dimensional stochastic games.

4.1. Optimal Transport

As seen in Section 3, SOC deals with finding the optimal control policy for a dynamic system in the presence of uncertainty. Conversely, OT theory focuses on finding the optimal map to transport from one distribution to another. More precisely, given two marginal distributions $\mu \in \mathcal{P}(\mathbb{R}^d)$ and $\nu \in \mathcal{P}(\mathbb{R}^d)$, the classical OT problem in the Kantorovich formulation reads

$$\inf_{\pi \in \Pi(\mu,\nu)} \int c(x,y)\pi(dx,dy) \tag{15}$$

where c is a cost function and $\Pi(\mu, \nu)$ corresponds to the set of couplings between μ and ν.

We focus on the setting where μ and ν are distributions computed on $\mathbb{R}^d$, i.e., $\mu \sim (X_1, \ldots, X_d)$ and $\nu \sim (Y_1, \ldots, Y_d)$. The Monge formulation reads

$$\inf_{T:T\#\mu=\nu} \int c(x,T(x))\mu(dx) \tag{16}$$

where the infimum is computed over all measurable maps $T : \mathbb{R}^d \to \mathbb{R}^d$ with the pushforward constraint $T\#\mu = \nu$.

The possibility to link a SOC problem, hence the related mathematical formulation of a specific learning procedure, to the corresponding OT formulation relies on lifting the SOC problem in a proper Wasserstein space. For example, considering the SOC problem introduced in (11), the stochastic process X_t described by Equation (9) can be viewed as a vehicle of mass transportation under an initial measure μ_0.

We mention that there are also specific scenarios where the dynamics of the stochastic control problem can be interpreted as a mass transportation problem, provided that certain assumptions of functionals and cost are guaranteed. For example, in [21,22] and similarly in [23], the authors focus on extending an OT problem into the corresponding SOC formulation for a cost, which depends on the drift and the diffusion coefficients of a continuous semimartingale and the minimization is run among all continuous semimartingales with given initial and terminal distributions.

For example, in [22], the authors consider a special form for the cost function, namely $c(x,y) = L(y-x)$ with $L(u) : \mathbb{R}^d \to [0,+\infty]$ convex in u proving its equivalence to a proper SOC problem based on the so-called graph property. Indeed, we can define an image measure as $\pi_g : \mathbb{R}^d \to \mathbb{R}^d \times \mathbb{R}^d$ mapping x into $(x, g(x))$. Thus, for any measurable map $g : \mathbb{R}^d \to \mathbb{R}^d$, the following equality between the two formulations holds:

$$\int_{\mathbb{R}^d} L(g(x)-x)\mu(dx) = \int_{\mathbb{R}^d \times \mathbb{R}^d} L(y-x)\pi_g(dxdy) \tag{17}$$

Thus, μ_g models a probability measure on $\mathbb{R}^d \times \mathbb{R}^d$ with marginals μ and ν.

For the problem stated in (17), we know from [24] that an optimal measure π^* always exists. Moreover, if the optimal measure π^* is supported by the graph of a measurable map, we say that the graph property holds; that is, if for any π^* optimal for (15), there exists a set Γ satisfying $\pi^*(\Gamma) = 1$ with $\Gamma = (x, \gamma(x))$ for some measurable mapping γ that resembles the NN parameters introduced in Section 2 and analogously $\gamma(x)$ represents the corresponding output according to Equation (1).

4.2. Mean Field Games

In the context of Mean Field Games (MFGs), i.e., stochastic games where a large number of agents interact and influence each other, the link between SOC and OT is particularly explicable, specifically according to the variational formulation of MFGs, which is directly linked to the dynamic formulation of OT by Benamou and Brenier, see, e.g., ref. [25] for an in-depth analysis.

In Section 2, we focus on deterministic evolution by means of Equation (5) with the mean field interactions captured by the loss function as an expectation given a known joint measure μ between the input and target in the corresponding Mean Field Optimal Problem (22). On the other hand, in Section 3, we introduce the stochastic process in Equation (8) and state the learning problem as an SOC as shown in Equation (10) without focusing on the interaction during the evolution but looking at just a single trajectory. Finally, the further natural step relies on extending the previous equation to a McKean–Vlasov setting where the dynamic of a random variable X depends on the other N random variables by the mean of the distribution in order to merge the two scenarios presented in Sections 2 and 3 while extending the problem stated in (10) by allowing the presence of a mean field term.

Indeed, instead of considering a single evolution as in Equation (9), we introduce the following McKean–Vlasov SDE for N particles/agents

$$X_t^i = X_0^i + \int_0^T b\left(X_s^i, m_{X_s}^N, \theta_s\right) + \int_0^T \sigma dW_s, i = 1, \ldots, N \quad (18)$$

with X_0^i being the initial states. We assume a measurable drift $b : [0,T] \times \mathcal{W}_2(\mathbb{R}^d) \times \mathbb{R}^d \to \mathbb{R}$, a constant diffusion σ, and we define the empirical distribution $m_{X_s}^N$ as

$$m_{X_s}^N = \frac{1}{N} \sum_{j=1}^N \delta_{X_s^i}. \quad (19)$$

The main idea would be to model multiple SNNs and generalize the dynamic defined in (9); including the dependence on a mean field term in the drift allows us to model the shared connections between the neurons of different SNNs.

At the limit $N \to \infty$, the *population of SNNs* corresponds to the evolution of a representative SNN, while the empirical measure m^N tends to the probability measure m belonging to the Wasserstein space $\mathcal{W}_2(\mathbb{R}^d)$, i.e., the space of probability measures on $\mathbb{R}^d$ with a finite second-order moment that captures a measure of interactions among SSNs.

More precisely, we introduce the following settings, which we need to define the solution of an MFG.

- A finite time horizon $T > 0$;
- $\mathcal{Q} \subseteq \mathbb{R}^d$ is the state space;
- $\mathcal{W}_2(\mathcal{Q})$ is the space of probability measure over $\mathcal{Q}$;
- $(x, m, \alpha) \in \mathcal{Q} \times \mathcal{W}_2(\mathcal{Q}) \times \mathbb{R}^k$ describes the agent state, the mean field term, and the agent control;
- $f : \mathcal{Q} \times \mathcal{W}_2(\mathcal{Q}) \times \mathbb{R}^k \to \mathbb{R}, (x, m, \alpha) \mapsto f(x, m, \alpha)$ and $g : \mathcal{Q} \times \mathcal{W}_2(\mathcal{Q}) \to \mathbb{R}, (x, m) \mapsto g(x, m)$ provide the running and the terminal cost, respectively;
- $b : \mathcal{Q} \times \mathcal{W}_2(\mathcal{Q}) \times \mathbb{R}^k \to \mathbb{R}^d$ represents the drift function;
- $\sigma > 0$ is the volatility of the state.

Definition 1 (MFG equilibrium). *We consider an MFG problem with a given initial distribution $m_0 \in \mathcal{W}_2(\mathcal{Q})$. A Nash equilibrium is a flow of probability measures $\hat{m} = (\hat{m}(t, \cdot))_{0 \leq t \leq T}$ in $\mathcal{W}_2(\mathcal{Q})$ plus a feedback control $\hat{\alpha} : [0,T] \times \mathcal{Q} \to \mathbb{R}^k$ satisfying the following two conditions:*

1. $\hat{\alpha}$ minimizes J_m^{MFG} over α:

$$\mathbb{E}\left[\int_0^T f(X_t^{m,\alpha}, m(t, \cdot), \alpha(t, X_t^{m,\alpha})) dt + g(X_T^{m,\alpha}, m(T, \cdot))\right]$$

where $(X_t^{m,\alpha})$ solves the SDE

$$dX_t^{m,\alpha} = b(X_t^{m,\alpha}, m(t, \cdot), \alpha(t, X_t^{m,\alpha})) dt + \sigma dW_t$$

with W being a d-dimensional Brownian motion and $X_0^{m,\alpha}$ having distribution m_0;
2. For all $t \in [0,T]$, $\hat{m}$ is the probability distribution of $X_t^{\hat{m}, \hat{\alpha}}$.

4.3. Mean Field Control

Differently from MFG, where players are modeled as competitors, Mean Field Control (MFC) models a framework that considers a large population of agents aiming to cooperate and optimize individual objectives. In the MFC setting, each agent cost depends on a mean field term representing the average behavior of all agents. Accordingly, the solution of an MFC is defined in the following way:

Definition 2 (MFC optimum). *Given $m_0 \in \mathcal{W}_2(\mathcal{Q})$, a feedback control $\alpha^* : [0,T] \times \mathcal{Q} \to \mathbb{R}^k$ is an optimal control for the MFC problem if it minimizes over α J^{MFC} defined by*

$$\mathbb{E}\left[\int_0^T f(X_t^\alpha, m^\alpha(t,\cdot), \alpha(t,X_t^\alpha))dt + g(X_T^\alpha, m^\alpha(T,\cdot))\right] \tag{20}$$

where $m^\alpha(t,\cdot)$ is the probability distribution of the law of X_t^α, under the constraint that the process $(X_t^\alpha)_{t\in[0,T]}$ solves the following McKean–Vlasov-type SDE:

$$dX_t^\alpha = b(X_t^\alpha, m^\alpha(t,\cdot), \alpha(t,X_t^\alpha))dt + \sigma dW_t \tag{21}$$

with X_0^α having distribution m_0.

We refer to [26] for an extensive treatment of McKean–Vlasov control problems (20).

By considering the joint optimization problem of the entire population, MFC enables the analysis of large-scale systems with cooperative agents and provides insights into the emergence of collective behavior. One possibility relies on stating the dynamic in Equation (6) in terms of probability measures. For example, we can consider a continuity equation such as the Fokker–Planck equation to consider the evolution of the density function. Along this setting, we cite the measure theoretical approach for NeurODE developed in [1], where the authors introduced a forward continuity equation in the space of measures with a constrained dynamic in the form of an ODE. Conversely, within the cooperative setting, we can also rely on a novel approach, named Mean Field Optimal Transport, introduced in [5], which we explore in the next paragraph.

4.4. Mean Field Optimal Transport

Mean Field Optimal Transport deals with a framework where all the agents cooperate (such as in MFC) in order to minimize a total cost without terminal cost but with an additional constraint since also the final distribution is prescribed. We notice that the setting with fixed initial and terminal distributions resembles the one introduced in the Population Risk Minimization problem described in Section 2. We follow the numerical scheme introduced in Section 3.1 in [5] to approximate feedback controls, that is, we introduce the following model.

Definition 3 (Mean Field Optimal Transport). *Let $\mathbb{R}^d$, describe the state space and denote by $\mathcal{W}_2(\mathbb{R}^d)$ the set of square-integrable probability measures on $\mathbb{R}^d$. Let $f : \mathbb{R}^d \times \mathcal{W}_2(\mathbb{R}^d) \times \mathbb{R}^k \to \mathbb{R}$ be the running cost, $g : \mathbb{R}^d \times \mathcal{W}_2(\mathbb{R}^d) \to \mathbb{R}$ be the terminal cost, $b : \mathbb{R}^d \times \mathcal{W}_2(\mathbb{R}^d) \times \mathbb{R}^k \to \mathbb{R}^d$ the drift function, and $\sigma \in \mathbb{R}$ the non-negative diffusion. Given two distributions, ρ_0 and $\rho_T \in \mathcal{W}_2(\mathbb{R}^d)$, the aim of MFOT is to compute the optimal feedback control $v : [0,T] \times \mathbb{R}^d \to \mathbb{R}^m$ minimizing*

$$J^{MFOT} : v \mapsto \mathbb{E}\left[\int_0^T f(X_t^v, \mu^v(t), v(t,X_t^v))dt\right] \tag{22}$$

where $\mu^v(t)$ is the distribution of process X_t^v, whose dynamics is given by

$$\begin{cases} X_0^v \sim \rho_0 \quad X_T^v \sim \rho_T \\ dX_t^v = b(X_t^v, \mu^v(t), v(t,X_t^v))dt + \sigma dW_t, \quad t \in [0,T] \end{cases} \tag{23}$$

with ρ_0 and ρ_T the prescribed initial and terminal distributions.

This type of problem incorporates mean field interactions into the drift and the running cost. Furthermore, it encompasses classical OT as a special case by considering $b(x, \mu, a) = a$, $f(x, \mu, a) = \frac{1}{2}a^T a$, and $\sigma = 0$.

The integration of MFC and OT allows us to both tackle the weight optimization problem in NN and to model the flow of information or mass between layers of neurons, while the optimal weights may be computed as the minimizers of the functional with respect to the controls v

$$v^\star = \min_{v \in \mathcal{U}} J^{MFOT}(v) \qquad (24)$$

along all the trajectories X^v, where $\mathcal{U}$ is the set of admissible controls.

Thus, we look at the MFNN as a collection of identical, interchangeable, indistinguishable NNs where the dynamic of the representative agents is a generalization of an SNN (7), allowing a dependence on the term $\mu^{\bar{v}}(t)$ modeling the mean field interactions. By considering the MFNN dynamic as a population of interconnected NNs, we can employ mean field control to analyze the collective behavior and interactions of networks, accounting for their impact on the overall network performance.

To summarize, we are looking at this novel class of NN, i.e., MFNN, as the asymptotic configuration of NNs in a cooperative setting.

We remark that the representative agent does not know the mean field interaction terms, since it depends on the whole population, but an approximated version can be recursively learned. For example, in [5], the authors present a different numerical scheme to solve MFOT:

1. Optimal control via direct approximation of controls v;
2. Deep Galerkin method for solving forward–backward systems of PDEs;
3. Augmented Lagrangian method with Deep Learning exploiting the variational formulation of MFOT and the primal/dual approach.

We briefly review the direct method (1) to approximate feedback-type controls via an optimal control formulation. The controls are assumed to be of feedback form and can be approximated by

$$g(x,\mu) = G(\mathcal{W}_2(\mu, \rho_T)), \qquad \mu \in \mathcal{W}_2(\mathbb{R}^d), \qquad (25)$$

where $G : \mathbb{R}_+ \to \mathbb{R}_+$ is an increasing function. The idea is to use the function in Equation (25) as a penalty for being far from the target distribution ρ_T as the terminal cost to embed the problem into the classical MFG/MFC literature. Intuitively, Equation (25) corresponds to the infinite dimensional analogue of the loss function of the leveraged NN algorithm, where μ is the final distribution that has to be as close as possible in the sense of the Wasserstein metric to the target distribution ρ_T.

In view of obtaining a numerically tractable version of the SDE (23), one may consider a classical discretization Euler–Maruyama scheme, also requiring the set of controls v to be restricted to the ones approximated by NNs v_θ with parameters θ. Moreover, approximating the mean field term m by its finite dimensional counterpart, see Equation (19), allows us to develop a stable numerical algorithm, see Section 3.1 in [5] for further details, particularly with respect to the linked numerical implementation.

4.5. Other Approaches for Learning Mean Field function

For the sake of completeness, we also mention two different methods to deal with the approximation of the mean field function that can be used in parallel with MFOT:

- The first data-driven approach, presented in [27], has been considered to solve a stochastic optimal control problem, where the unknown model parameters were estimated in real time using a *direct filter method*. This method involves transitioning from the Stochastic Maximum Principle to approximate the conditional probability density functions of the parameters given an observation, which is a set of random samples;
- In [28], the authors report a map that by operating over an appropriate classes of neural networks, specifically the *bin-density-based approximation* and *cylindrical approximation*, is able to reconstruct a mapping between the Wasserstein space of probability measures and an infinite dimensional function space on a similar setting to MFG.

5. Conclusions and Further Directions

In the present article, we provided a general overview of methods at the intersection of parametric ML, MFC, and OT. By assuming a dynamical system viewpoint, we considered the deterministic, ODE-based setting of the supervised learning problem, to then incorporate noisy components, allowing for the definition of stochastic NNs, hence introducing the MFOT approach. The latter, derived as the limit in the number of training data, recasts the classical learning process as a Mean Field Optimal Transport one. As a result, we gained a unified perspective on the parameter optimization process, characterizing ML models with a specified learning dynamic, within the framework of OT and MFC, which may allow high-dimensional data sets to be efficiently handled.

We empathise that the major limitation of MFOT (22) concerns the fact that many of its convergence results, such as those related to corresponding forward–backward systems, still need to be verified. Nevertheless, it represents an indubitably fertile and stimulating research ground that should be enhanced since it permits the derivation of techniques that may significantly improve the robustness of algorithms, particularly when dealing with huge sets of training data that are potentially perturbed by random noise components, while also allowing hidden symmetries within data to be highlighted. The latter aspect is particularly interesting when dealing with intrinsically structured problems as, e.g., in the case of NLP tasks, see, e.g., [29,30].

Author Contributions: Conceptualization, M.G.; methodology, M.G.; validation, M.G. and L.D.P.; formal analysis, M.G.; investigation, M.G.; resources, M.G.; writing—original draft preparation, M.G. and L.D.P.; writing—review and editing, M.G. and L.D.P.; supervision, L.D.P. All authors have read and agreed to the published version of the manuscript.

Funding: This research received no external funding.

Institutional Review Board Statement: Not applicable.

Informed Consent Statement: Not applicable.

Data Availability Statement: Not applicable.

Acknowledgments: The authors would like to kindly thank Beatrice Acciaio for her valuable advice.

Conflicts of Interest: The authors declare no conflict of interest.

Abbreviations

The following abbreviations are used in this manuscript:

DL	Deep Learning
HJB	Hamilton–Jacobi–Bellman
MFC	Mean Field Control
MFG	Mean Field Games
MFOCP	Mean Field Optimal Control Problem
ML	Machine Learning
MFOT	Mean Field Optimal Transport
NN	Neural Network
ODE	Ordinary Differential Equation
OT	Optimal Transport
SDE	Stochastic Differential Equation
SNN	Stochastic Neural Network
SGD	Stochastic Gradient Descent

References

1. Bonnet, B.; Cipriani, C.; Fornasier, M.; Huang, H. A measure theoretical approach to the mean-field maximum principle for training NeurODEs. *Nonlinear Anal.* **2023**, *227*, 113161. [CrossRef]
2. E, W.; Han, J.; Li, Q. A mean-field optimal control formulation of deep learning. *Res. Math. Sci.* **2019**, *6*, 10. [CrossRef]

3. Archibald, R.; Bao, F.; Cao, Y.; Zhang, H. A backward SDE method for uncertainty quantification in deep learning. *Discret. Contin. Dyn. Syst.* **2022**, *15*, 2807–2835. [CrossRef]
4. de Bie, G.; Peyré, G.; Cuturi, M. Stochastic Deep Networks. In Proceedings of the 36th International Conference on Machine Learning, PMLR 97, Long Beach, CA, USA, 9–15 June 2019.
5. Baudelet, S.; Frénais, B.; Laurière, M.; Machtalay, A.; Zhu, Y. Deep Learning for Mean Field Optimal Transport. *arXiv* **2023**, arXiv:2302.14739.
6. Huang, H.; Yu, J.; Chen, J.; Lai, R. Bridging mean-field games and normalizing flows with trajectory regularization. *J. Comput. Phys.* **2023**, *487*, 112155. [CrossRef]
7. Cao, H.; Guo, X.; Laurière, M. Connecting GANs, MFGs, and OT. *arXiv* **2020**, arXiv:2002.04112.
8. Li, Q.; Lin, T.; Shen, Z. Deep Learning via Dynamical Systems: An Approximation Perspective. *arXiv* **2019**, arXiv:1912.10382v1.
9. Di Persio, L.; Garbelli, M. Deep Learning and Mean-Field Games: A Stochastic Optimal Control Perspective. *Symmetry* **2021**, *13*, 14. [CrossRef]
10. Li, Q.; Chen, L.; Tai, C.; E, W. Maximum principle based algorithms for deep learning. *J. Mach. Learn. Res.* **2017**, *18*, 5998–6026.
11. He, K.; Zhang, X.; Ren, S.; Sun, J. Deep Residual Learning for Image Recognition. In Proceedings of the 2016 IEEE Conference on Computer Vision and Pattern Recognition (CVPR), Las Vegas, NV, USA, 27–30 June 2016; pp. 770–778. [CrossRef]
12. Wojtowytsch, S. On the Convergence of Gradient Descent Training for Two-layer ReLU-networks in the Mean Field Regime. *arXiv* **2020**, arXiv:2005.13530.
13. Sirignano, J.; Spiliopoulos, K. Mean Field Analysis of Deep Neural Networks. *Math. Oper. Res.* **2021**, *47*, 120–152. [CrossRef]
14. Chizat, L.; Colombo, M.; Fernández-Real, X.; Figalli, A. Infinite-width limit of deep linear neural networks. *arXiv* **2022**, arXiv:2211.16980.
15. Fernández-Real, X.; Figalli, A. The Continuous Formulation of Shallow Neural Networks as Wasserstein-Type Gradient Flows. In *Analysis at Large*; Avila, A., Rassias, M.T., Sinai, Y., Eds.; Springer: Cham, Switzerland, 2022.
16. Chizat, L.; Bach, F. On the global convergence of gradient descent for overparameterized models using optimal transport. In Proceedings of the 32nd Conference on Neural Information Processing Systems (NeurIPS 2018), Montréal, QC, Canada, 3–8 December 2018; pp. 3040–3050.
17. Gangbo, W.; Mayorga, S.; Swiech, A. Finite Dimensional Approximations of Hamilton-Jacobi Bellman Equations in Spaces of Probability Measures. *SIAM J. Math. Anal.* **2021**, *53*, 1320–1356. [CrossRef]
18. Jimenez, C.; Marigonda, A.; Quincampoix, M. Dynamical systems and Hamilton-Jacobi-Bellman equations on the Wasserstein space and their L2 representations. *J. Math. Anal. (SIMA)* **2022**, preprint. Available online: https://cvgmt.sns.it/media/doc/paper/5584/AMCJMQ_HJB_2022-03-30.pdf (accessed on 17 February 2023).
19. Benoît, B. A Pontryagin Maximum Principle in Wasserstein spaces for constrained optimal control problems. *ESAIM Control. Optim. Calc. Var.* **2019**, *25*, 52. [CrossRef]
20. Bao, F.; Cao, Y.; Archibald, R.; Zhang, H. Uncertainty quantification for deep learning through stochastic maximum principle. *arXiv* **2021**, arXiv:3489122.
21. Mikami, T. Two End Points Marginal Problem by Stochastic Optimal Transportation. *SIAM J. Control. Optim.* **2015**, *53*, 2449–2461. [CrossRef]
22. Mikami, T.; Thieullen, M. Optimal transportation problem by stochastic optimal control. *SIAM J. Control Optim.* **2008**, *47*, 1127–1139. [CrossRef]
23. Tan, X.; Nizar Touzi, N. Optimal transportation under controlled stochastic dynamics. *Ann. Probab.* **2013**, *41*, 3201–3240. [CrossRef]
24. Villani, C. *Topics in Optimal Transportation*; Grad. Stud. Math. 58; AMS: Providence, RI, USA, 2003.
25. Benamou, J.D.; Carlier, G.; Santambrogio, F. Variational Mean Field Games. In *Active Particles, Volume 1: Advances in Theory, Models, and Applications*; Bellomo, N., Degond, P., Tadmor, E., Eds.; Springer: Berlin/Heidelberg, Germany, 2017; pp. 141–171.
26. Carmona, R.; Lauriere, M. Deep Learning for Mean Field Games and Mean Field Control with Applications to Finance. In *Machine Learning and Data Sciences for Financial Markets: A Guide to Contemporary Practices*; Capponi, A., Lehalle, C., Eds.; Cambridge University Press: Cambridge, UK, 2023; pp. 369–392. [CrossRef]
27. Archibald, R.; Bao, F.; Yong, J. An Online Method for the Data Driven Stochastic Optimal Control Problem with Unknown Model Parameters. *arXiv* **2022**, arXiv:2208.02241.
28. Pham, H.; Warin, X. Mean-field neural networks: Learning mappings on Wasserstein space. *arXiv* **2022**, arXiv:2210.15179.
29. Mao, K.; Xu, J.; Yao, X.; Qiu, J.; Chi, K.; Dai, G. A text classification model via multi-level semantic features. *Symmetry* **2022**, *14*, 1938. [CrossRef]
30. Yoo, Y.; Heo, T.S.; Park, Y.; Kim, K. A novel hybrid methodology of measuring sentence similarity. *Symmetry* **2021**, *13*, 1442. [CrossRef]

Disclaimer/Publisher's Note: The statements, opinions and data contained in all publications are solely those of the individual author(s) and contributor(s) and not of MDPI and/or the editor(s). MDPI and/or the editor(s) disclaim responsibility for any injury to people or property resulting from any ideas, methods, instructions or products referred to in the content.

Article

Infinitely Many Positive Solutions to Nonlinear First-Order Iterative Systems of Singular BVPs on Time Scales

Famei Zheng, Xiaojing Wang, Xiwang Cheng and Bo Du *

School of Mathematics and Statistics, Huaiyin Normal University, Huaian 223300, China
* Correspondence: dubo7307@163.com

Abstract: Iterative differential equations provide a new idea to study functional differential equations. The study of iterative equations can provide new methods for the study of differential equations with state-dependent delays. In this paper, we are concerned with proving the existence of infinitely many positive solutions to nonlinear first-order iterative systems of singular BVPs on time scales by using Krasnoselskii's cone fixed point theorem in a Banach space. It is worth pointing out that in this paper, we can use the symmetry of the iterative process and Green's function to transform the considered differential equation into an equivalent integral equation, which plays a key role in the proof of the theorem in this paper.

Keywords: positive solution; time scales; existence; iterative system

1. Introduction

In this paper, we consider the following nonlinear first-order iterative system of singular BVPs on time scales:

$$
\begin{cases}
x_i^\Delta(t) + p(t)x_i(\sigma(t)) = \lambda(t)f_i(x_{i+1}(t)), & t \in (0,a]_{\mathbb{T}}, 1 \leq i \leq n, \\
x_{n+1}(t) = x_1(t), \\
x_i(0) = x_i(\sigma(a)),
\end{cases}
\tag{1}
$$

where $i \in \mathbb{N}$, $\lambda(t)$ has a singularity in $(0, \frac{\sigma(a)}{2}]_{\mathbb{T}}$, $f_i : \mathbb{R}^+ \to \mathbb{R}^+$ is continuous, and $p : [0,a]_{\mathbb{T}} \to \mathbb{R}^+$ is right-dense continuous.

Iterative differential equations belong to functional differential equations. In particular, iterative equations can be used to describe functional differential equations with state-dependent delays, see [1–3]. Iterative differential equations provide a new idea to study functional differential equations. Zhao and Liu [4] considered a class of iterative differential equation

$$c_0 x''(t) + c_1 x'(t) + c_2 x(t) = x(p(t) + bx(t)) + h(t) \tag{2}$$

and obtained the existence, uniqueness, and stability of periodic solutions for Equation (2). Eder [5] studied the iterative functional differential equation

$$x'(t) = x^{[2]}(t)$$

and obtained asymptotic properties of solutions. Fečkan [6] further studied the following nonlinear iterative equation

$$x'(t) = f(x^{[2]}(t))$$

with initial condition $x(0) = 0$. In [7], Wang considered the existence of a solution for the following iterative differential equation:

$$x'(t) = f(x(x(t))),$$

where f is a smooth function that maps a closed interval I into itself where this interval contains a fixed point of the unknown function x. Cheng, Si, and Wang [8] studied an iterative functional differential equation

$$x'(t) = f(x(x\cdots(x(t))))$$

and obtained a local existence theorem by means of the Schauder fixed point theorem.

We focus on the study of iterative equations on time scales. The dynamic equations on time scales can unify continuous and discrete systems, so studying them can obtain results with a wider applicability, see [9–11]. Khuddush et al. [12] studied the following second-order iterative system of boundary value problems with singularities on time scales:

$$\begin{cases} x_l^{\Delta\nabla}(t) + \lambda(t)g_l(x_{l+1}(t)) = 0, \ t \in (0, \sigma(a)]_{\mathbb{T}}, 1 \leq l \leq n, \\ x_{n+1}(t) = x_1(t), \\ x_l^{\Delta}(0) = 0, \ x_l(\sigma(a)) = \sum_{k=1}^{n-2} c_k x_l(\xi_k) \end{cases} \quad (3)$$

and some sufficient conditions for the existence of infinitely many positive solutions were obtained by applying Krasnoselskii's cone fixed point theorem in a Banach space. When $p(t) = 0$ in system (1), then Equation (3) is similar to system (1). Therefore, the results of this article generalize the results of article [12]. In [13], the authors studied positive solutions for the iterative system of dynamic equations

$$\begin{cases} u_i^{\Delta^{(n)}}(t) + \lambda_i a_i(t)f_i(u_{i+1}(\sigma(t))) = 0, \ t \in [a, b]_{\mathbb{T}}, 1 \leq i \leq n, \\ u_{n+1}(t) = u_1(t), \\ u_i^{\Delta^{(m)}}(a) = 0, \ u_i(\sigma^n(b)) = 0, \ 0 \leq m \leq n-2. \end{cases}$$

For an iterative system of conformable fractional order dynamic boundary value problems on time scales, see [14]; for nondecreasing and convex C^2 solutions of an iterative functional differential equation, see [15]. In this paper, we will study system (1), which is a singular dynamic system, and obtain the existence of infinitely many positive solutions by applying Krasnoselskii's cone fixed point theorem in a Banach space. To the best of our knowledge, there are few results for the existence of a positive solution to system (1).

The main contributions are summarized in the following two aspects:

(1) We study a class more extensive iterative system with singularity, which generalizes the results of article [12].
(2) We innovatively use Krasnoselskii's cone fixed point theorem on time scales to study the existence of solutions for iterative system (1).

The following sections are organized as follows. Section 2 gives some preliminaries. The existence of positive solutions of system (1) is obtained in Section 3. In Section 4, an example is given to show the feasibility of our results. Section 4 concludes this article with a summary of our results.

2. Preliminaries

The time scales theory, which has received much more attention, was firstly introduced by Hilger [16]. A time scale $\mathbb{T}$ is a nonempty closed subset of $\mathbb{R}$. We give the following notations, and their means can be found in [17]: the forward jump $\sigma(t)$, backward jump operator $\rho(t)$, regressive rd-continuous function $\mathcal{R}$, and the delta derivative $x^{\Delta}(t)$ of $x(t)$. We also give the following notations: $[a, b]_{\mathbb{T}} = \{t \in \mathbb{T}, a \leq t \leq b\}$, the intervals $[a, b)_{\mathbb{T}}, (a, b]_{\mathbb{T}}$ and $[a, b]_{\mathbb{T}}$ are defined similarly. Let $p, q \in \mathcal{R}$. The exponential function is defined by

$$e_p(t, s) = \exp\left(\int_s^t \xi_{\mu(\tau)}(p(\tau))\Delta\tau\right),$$

where $\xi_h(z)$ is the so-called cylinder transformation. If $p, q \in \mathcal{R}$, a circle plus addition is defined by $(p \oplus q) := p + q + \mu pq$. For $p \in \mathcal{R}$, we defined a circle minus p by $(\ominus p) := \frac{-p}{1+\mu p}$.

Lemma 1. [17].

[i] $e_0(t,s) \equiv 1$ and $e_p(t,t) \equiv 1$;
[ii] $e_p(\rho(t),s) = (1 - \mu(t)p(t))e_p(t,s)$;
[iii] $e_p(t,s) = \frac{1}{e_p(s,t)} = e_{\ominus p}(s,t)$;
[iv] $e_p(t,s)e_p(s,r) = e_p(t,r)$;
[v] $e_p(t,s)e_q(t,s) = e_{p \oplus q}(t,s)$.

Lemma 2 (Krasnoselskii's [18]). *Let P be a cone in a Banach space E and Ω_1, Ω_2 are open sets with $0 \in \Omega_1$, $\overline{\Omega}_1 \subset \Omega_2$. Let $\mathcal{L} : E \cap (\overline{\Omega}_2 \setminus \Omega_1) \to E$ be a completely continuous operator such that*
(i) $||\mathcal{L}u|| \leq ||u||$, $u \in E \cap \partial\Omega_1$, and $||\mathcal{L}u|| \geq ||u||$, $u \in E \cap \partial\Omega_2$ or
(ii) $||\mathcal{L}u|| \geq ||u||$, $u \in E \cap \partial\Omega_1$, and $||\mathcal{L}u|| \leq ||u||$, $u \in E \cap \partial\Omega_2$.
Then $\mathcal{L}$ has a fixed point in $E \cap (\overline{\Omega}_2 \setminus \Omega_1)$.

Let $\mathbb{C} = \{u | u : [0, \sigma(a)]_{\mathbb{T}} \to \mathbb{R}$ is continuous$\}$ with the norm $||u|| = \max_{t \in [0,\sigma(a)]_{\mathbb{T}}} |u(t)|$.

Lemma 3. *For any $y \in \mathbb{C}$, the boundary value problem*

$$\begin{cases} x_1^\Delta(t) + p(t)x_1(\sigma(t)) = y(t), \ t \in [0,a]_{\mathbb{T}}, \\ x_1(0) = x_1(\sigma(a)), \end{cases} \quad (4)$$

has a unique solution

$$x_1(t) = \int_0^{\sigma(a)} G(s,t)y(s)ds,$$

where

$$G(s,t) = \begin{cases} (A+1)e_p(s,t), & \text{if } 0 \leq s \leq t \leq \sigma(a) \\ Ae_p(s,t), & \text{if } 0 \leq t < s \leq \sigma(a), \end{cases}$$

$A = \frac{1}{e_p(\sigma(a),0)-1}$.

Proof. Similar to the proof of [19], BVP (4) has a unique solution

$$x_1(t) = \frac{1}{e_p(t,0)}\left[\int_0^t e_p(s,0)y(s)ds + A\int_0^{\sigma(a)} e_p(s,0)y(s)ds\right].$$

Thus,

$$x_1(t) = (A+1)\int_0^t e_p(s,t)y(s)ds + A\int_t^{\sigma(a)} e_p(s,t)y(s)ds$$
$$= \int_0^{\sigma(a)} G(s,t)y(s)ds.$$

□

Lemma 4. *Let $\eta \in (0, \frac{\sigma(a)}{2})_{\mathbb{T}}$. The kernel $G(s,t)$ has the following properties:*
(i) $0 \leq G(s,t) \leq G_L$ for all $t, s \in [0, \sigma(a)]$, where $G_L = \min\{A+1, Ae_p(\sigma(a), 0)\}$;
(ii) $G(s,t) \geq G_l$ for all $s \in [\eta, \sigma(a) - \eta]$, $t \in [0, \sigma(a)]$, where $G_l = \max\{(A+1)e_p(r - \sigma(a), 0), A\}$.

Proof. We first show that case (i) holds. If $0 \leq s \leq t \leq \sigma(a)$, we have

$$G(s,t) \leq A+1. \quad (5)$$

If $0 \leq t < s \leq \sigma(a)$, we have

$$G(s,t) \leq Ae_p(\sigma(a), 0). \quad (6)$$

From (5) and (6), we obtain that

$$G(s,t) \leq \min\{A+1, Ae_p(\sigma(a),0)\} = G_L.$$

Next, we show that case (ii) holds. Let $s \in [\eta, \sigma(a) - \eta]$. If $s \leq t$, we have

$$G(s,t) \geq (A+1)e_p(\eta - \sigma(a), 0). \tag{7}$$

If $s > t$, we have

$$G(s,t) \geq A. \tag{8}$$

From (7) and (8), we obtain that

$$G(s,t) \leq \max\{(A+1)e_p(\eta - \sigma(a), 0), A\} = G_l.$$

□

Obviously, $(x_1(t), x_2(t), \cdots, x_n(t))$ is a solution of the iterative BVP (1) if and only if

$$x_i(t) = \int_0^{\sigma(a)} G(s,t) \lambda(s) f_i(x_{i+1}(s)) \Delta s$$

and

$$x_{n+1}(t) = x_1(t), \ t \in (0,a]_{\mathbb{T}}, \ 1 \leq i \leq n.$$

Then, we have

$$x_1(t) = \int_0^{\sigma(a)} G(s_1,t) \lambda(s_1) f_1 \left[\int_0^{\sigma(a)} G(s_2,s_1) \lambda(s_2) f_2 \left[\int_0^{\sigma(a)} G(s_3,s_2) \cdots \right.\right.$$
$$\left.\left. \times f_{n-1} \left[\int_0^{\sigma(a)} G(s_n, s_{n-1}) \lambda(s_n) f_n(x_1(s_n)) \Delta s_n \right] \cdots \Delta s_3 \right] \Delta s_2 \right] \Delta s_1.$$

For $\eta \in (0, \frac{\sigma(a)}{2})_{\mathbb{T}}$, we define a cone $P_\eta \subset \mathbb{C}$ by

$$P_\eta = \left\{ x \in \mathbb{C} : x(t) \text{ is nonnegative and } \min_{t \in [\eta, \sigma(a) - \eta]_{\mathbb{T}}} x(t) \geq \frac{G_l}{G_L} ||x|| \right\},$$

where G_l and G_L are defined by Lemma 4. For any $x_1 \in P_\eta$, we define an operator $\mathcal{L} : P_\eta \to \mathbb{C}$ by

$$(\mathcal{L}x_1)(t) = \int_0^{\sigma(a)} G(s_1,t) \lambda(s_1) f_1 \left[\int_0^{\sigma(a)} G(s_2,s_1) \lambda(s_2) f_2 \left[\int_0^{\sigma(a)} G(s_3,s_2) \cdots \right.\right.$$
$$\left.\left. \times f_{n-1} \left[\int_0^{\sigma(a)} G(s_n, s_{n-1}) \lambda(s_n) f_n(x_1(s_n)) \Delta s_n \right] \cdots \Delta s_3 \right] \Delta s_2 \right] \Delta s_1.$$

Lemma 5. *For each $\eta \in (0, \frac{\sigma(a)}{2})_{\mathbb{T}}$, $\mathcal{L} : P_\eta \to P_\eta$ is completely continuous.*

Proof. By Lemma 4, we obtain that $G(s,t) \geq 0$ and $(\mathcal{L}x_1)(t)$ for all $s,t \in [0,\sigma(a)]_\mathbb{T}$. Again by Lemma 4, for $x_1 \in P_\eta$, we have

$$||\mathcal{L}x_1|| = \max_{t \in [0,\sigma(a)]_\mathbb{T}} \int_0^{\sigma(a)} G(s_1,t)\lambda(s_1)f_1\left[\int_0^{\sigma(a)} G(s_2,s_1)\lambda(s_2)f_2\left[\int_0^{\sigma(a)} G(s_3,s_2)\cdots\right.\right.$$
$$\left.\left.\times f_{n-1}\left[\int_0^{\sigma(a)} G(s_n,s_{n-1})\lambda(s_n)f_n(x_1(s_n))\Delta s_n\right]\cdots \Delta s_3\right]\Delta s_2\right]\Delta s_1$$
$$\leq G_L \int_0^{\sigma(a)} \lambda(s_1)f_1\left[\int_0^{\sigma(a)} G(s_2,s_1)\lambda(s_2)f_2\left[\int_0^{\sigma(a)} G(s_3,s_2)\cdots\right.\right.$$
$$\left.\left.\times f_{n-1}\left[\int_0^{\sigma(a)} G(s_n,s_{n-1})\lambda(s_n)f_n(x_1(s_n))\Delta s_n\right]\cdots \Delta s_3\right]\Delta s_2\right]\Delta s_1$$

and

$$\min_{t \in [\eta,\sigma(a)-\eta]_\mathbb{T}}\{(\mathcal{L}x_1)(t)\} \geq G_l \int_0^{\sigma(a)} \lambda(s_1)f_1\left[\int_0^{\sigma(a)} G(s_2,s_1)\lambda(s_2)f_2\left[\int_0^{\sigma(a)} G(s_3,s_2)\cdots\right.\right.$$
$$\left.\left.\times f_{n-1}\left[\int_0^{\sigma(a)} G(s_n,s_{n-1})\lambda(s_n)f_n(x_1(s_n))\Delta s_n\right]\cdots \Delta s_3\right]\Delta s_2\right]\Delta s_1$$
$$\geq \frac{G_l}{G_L}||\mathcal{L}x_1||.$$

Hence, $\mathcal{L}x_1 \in P_\eta$ and $\mathcal{L}(P_\eta) \subset P_\eta$. It follows by the Arzela–Ascoli theorem that $\mathcal{L}$ is completely continuous. □

3. Main Results

Theorem 1. *Suppose that the following assumption holds:*

(H_1) *there exists a sequence* $\{t_j\}_{j=1}^\infty$ *such that* $0 < t_{j+1} < t_j < \frac{\sigma(a)}{2}$ *and*

$$\lim_{j \to \infty} t_j = t^* < \frac{\sigma(a)}{2}, \quad \lim_{t \to t_j} \lambda(t) = +\infty.$$

Let $\{\eta_j\}_{j=1}^\infty$ *with* $0 < t_{j+1} < \eta_j < t_j$. *Let* $\{\Gamma_j\}_{j=1}^\infty$ *and* $\{\Lambda_j\}_{j=1}^\infty$ *be such that*

$$\Gamma_{j+1} < \frac{G_l}{G_L}\Lambda_j < \Lambda_j < \theta \Lambda_j < \Gamma_j, \ j \in \mathbb{N},$$

where $\theta \geq \frac{1}{G_l\delta(\sigma(a)-2\eta_1)}$. *Assume that* f_i *statifies*

(H_2) $f_i(u(t)) \leq \Xi\Gamma_j$ *for* $t \in (0,\sigma(a)]_\mathbb{T}$, $0 \leq u \leq \Gamma_j$, *where* $\Xi \leq \frac{1}{G_L \int_0^{\sigma(a)} \lambda(s)\Delta s}$.

(H_3) $f_i(u(t)) \geq \theta \Lambda_j$ *for* $t \in [\eta_j,\sigma(a)-\eta_j]_\mathbb{T}$, $\frac{G_l}{G_L}\Lambda_j \leq u \leq \Lambda_j$.

Then the iterative BVP (1) has infinitely many solutions $\{(x_1^{[j]}, x_2^{[j]}, \cdots, x_n^{[j]})\}_{j=1}^\infty$ *such that* $x_i^{[j]} \geq 0$ *on* $(0,\sigma(a)]_\mathbb{T}$ *for* $i = 1,2,\cdots,n$.

Proof. It follows that by (H_1), there exists $\delta > 0$ such that $\lambda(t) > \delta$. Let

$$\Omega_{1,j} = \{x \in \mathbb{C} : ||x|| < \Gamma_j\}, \Omega_{2,j} = \{x \in \mathbb{C} : ||x|| < \Lambda_j\}.$$

By assumption (H_1), we have

$$0 < t^* < t_{j+1} < \eta_j < t_j < \frac{\sigma(a)}{2} \text{ for } j \in \mathbb{N}.$$

For $j \in \mathbb{N}$, we define the cone P_{η_j} by

$$P_{\eta_j} = \left\{ x \in \mathbb{C} : x(t) \text{ is nonnegative and } \min_{t \in [\eta_j, \sigma(a) - \eta_j]_{\mathbb{T}}} x(t) \geq \frac{G_l}{G_L} ||x|| \right\}.$$

Let $x_1 \in P_{\eta_j} \cap \partial \Omega_{1,j}$. Then, $x_1(s) \leq \Gamma_j$ for all $s \in (0, \sigma(a)]_{\mathbb{T}}$. For $s_{n-1} \in (0, \sigma(a)]_{\mathbb{T}}$, by (H$_2$), we have

$$\int_0^{\sigma(a)} G(s_n, s_{n-1}) \lambda(s_n) f_n(x_1(s_n)) \Delta s_n$$

$$\leq G_L \Xi \Gamma_j \int_0^{\sigma(a)} \lambda(s_n) \Delta s_n$$

$$\leq \Gamma_j.$$

Similar to the above proof, for $s_{n-2} \in (0, \sigma(a)]_{\mathbb{T}}$, by (H$_2$), we also have

$$\int_0^{\sigma(a)} G(s_{n-1}, s_{n-2}) \lambda(s_{n-1}) f_{n-1} \left[\int_0^{\sigma(a)} G(s_n, s_{n-1}) \lambda(s_n) f_n(x_1(s_n)) \Delta s_n \right] \Delta s_{n-1}$$

$$\leq \int_0^{\sigma(a)} G(s_{n-1}, s_{n-2}) \lambda(s_{n-1}) f_{n-1}(\Gamma_j) \Delta s_{n-1}$$

$$\leq G_L \Xi \Gamma_j \int_0^{\sigma(a)} \lambda(s_{n-1}) \Delta s_{n-1}$$

$$\leq \Gamma_j.$$

Thus, we obtain

$$\int_0^{\sigma(a)} G(s_1, t) \lambda(s_1) f_1 \left[\int_0^{\sigma(a)} G(s_2, s_1) \lambda(s_2) f_2 \left[\int_0^{\sigma(a)} G(s_3, s_2) \cdots \right. \right.$$

$$\times f_{n-1} \left[\int_0^{\sigma(a)} G(s_n, s_{n-1}) \lambda(s_n) f_n(x_1(s_n)) \Delta s_n \right] \cdots \Delta s_3 \right] \Delta s_2 \right] \Delta s_1$$

$$\leq \Gamma_j$$

and $(\mathcal{L}x_1)(t) \leq \Gamma_j$. By $\Gamma_j = ||x_1||$ for $x_1 \in P_{\eta_j} \cap \partial \Omega_{1,j}$, we have

$$||\mathcal{L}x_1|| \leq ||x_1||. \tag{9}$$

Next, for $t \in [\eta_j, \sigma(a) - \eta_j]_{\mathbb{T}}$, we have

$$\Lambda_j = ||x_1|| \geq x_1(t) \geq \min_{t \in [\eta_j, \sigma(a) - \eta_j]_{\mathbb{T}}} x_1(t) \geq \frac{G_l}{G_L} ||x_1||.$$

For $s_{n-1} \in [\eta_j, \sigma(a) - \eta_j]_{\mathbb{T}}$, by (H$_3$), we have

$$\int_0^{\sigma(a)} G(s_n, s_{n-1}) \lambda(s_n) f_n(x_1(s_n)) \Delta s_n$$

$$\geq \int_{\eta_j}^{\sigma(a) - \eta_j} G(s_n, s_{n-1}) \lambda(s_n) f_n(x_1(s_n)) \Delta s_n$$

$$\geq G_l \theta \Lambda_j \delta(\sigma(a) - 2\eta_j)$$

$$\geq G_l \theta \Lambda_j \delta(\sigma(a) - 2\eta_1)$$

$$\geq \Lambda_j.$$

Continuing with the bootstrapping argument, we obtain

$$\int_0^{\sigma(a)} G(s_1,t)\lambda(s_1)f_1\left[\int_0^{\sigma(a)} G(s_2,s_1)\lambda(s_2)f_2\left[\int_0^{\sigma(a)} G(s_3,s_2)\cdots\right.\right.$$
$$\left.\left.\times f_{n-1}\left[\int_0^{\sigma(a)} G(s_n,s_{n-1})\lambda(s_n)f_n(x_1(s_n))\Delta s_n\right]\cdots\Delta s_3\right]\Delta s_2\right]\Delta s_1$$
$$\geq \Lambda_j$$

and $(\mathcal{L}x_1)(t) \geq \Lambda_j$. By $\Lambda_j = ||x_1||$ for $x_1 \in P_{\eta_j} \cap \partial\Omega_{2,j}$, we have

$$||\mathcal{L}x_1|| \geq |||x_1||. \tag{10}$$

It is easy to see that $0 \in \Omega_{2,j} \subset \overline{\Omega}_{2,j} \subset \Omega_{1,j}$. In view of (9) and (10), the operator $\mathcal{L}$ has a fixed point $x_1^{[j]} \in P_{\eta_j} \cap (\overline{\Omega}_{1,j}\backslash)\Omega_{2,j}$ such that $x_1^{[j]} \geq 0$ on $(0,a]_\mathbb{T}$. Let $x_{n+1} = x_1$. We obtain infinitely many positive solutions $\{(x_1^{[j]}, x_2^{[j]}, \cdots, x_n^{[j]})\}_{j=1}^\infty$ of BVP (1) given iteratively by

$$x_i(t) = \int_0^{\sigma(a)} G(s,t)\lambda(s)f_i(x_{i+1}(s))\Delta s, \ i = 1,2,\cdots,n.$$

□

Remark 1. *In system (1), the initial conditions are different from the ones in system (2). Obviously, the initial conditions in system (2) are more complicated. In future work, we will study the following iterative system:*

$$\begin{cases} x_l^{\Delta\nabla}(t) + p(t)x_l(\sigma(t)) + \lambda(t)g_l(x_{l+1}(t)) = 0, \ t \in (0,\sigma(a)]_\mathbb{T}, 1 \leq l \leq n, \\ x_{n+1}(t) = x_1(t), \\ x_l^\Delta(0) = 0, \ x_l(\sigma(a)) = \sum_{k=1}^{n-2} c_k x_l(\xi_k), \end{cases}$$

where $l \in \mathbb{N}$, $c_k \in \mathbb{R}^+$ with $\sum_{k=1}^{n-2} c_k < 1$, $0 < \xi_k < \frac{\sigma(a)}{2}$, $\lambda(t) = \Pi_{i=1}^m \lambda_i(t)$ and each $\lambda_i(t) \in L_\nabla^{p_i}\left((0,\sigma(a)]_\mathbb{T}\right)$ ($p_1 \geq 1$) has a singularity in $(0,\frac{\sigma(a)}{2}]_\mathbb{T}$, $g_l : \mathbb{R}^+ \to \mathbb{R}^+$ is continuous, and $p : [0,a]_\mathbb{T} \to \mathbb{R}^+$ is right-dense continuous.

4. Example

Let $\mathbb{T} = \mathbb{R}$, consider the following BVP of model (1):

$$\begin{cases} x_i^\Delta(t) + p(t)x_i(t) = \lambda(t)f_i(x_{i+1}(t)), \ t \in (0,1], 1 \leq i \leq 4, \\ x_5(t) = x_1(t), \\ x_i(0) = x_i(1), \end{cases} \tag{11}$$

Choose

$$p(t) = 2, \ \lambda(t) = \frac{1}{|t - 0.25|^{\frac{1}{2}}}$$

then $\delta = \left(\frac{4}{3}\right)^{\frac{1}{2}}$. For $j \in \mathbb{N}, i = 1,2,3,4$, let

$$f_i(x) = \begin{cases} 0.02 \times 10^{-4j}, \ x \in [10^{-4j}, \infty), \\ \frac{50 \times 10^{-(4j+3)} - 0.02 \times 10^{-4j}}{10^{-(4j+3)} - 10^{-4j}}(x - 10^{-4j}) + 0.02 \times 10^{-6j}, \ x \in [10^{-(4j+3)}, 10^{-4j}], \\ 50 \times 10^{-(4j+3)}, \ x \in [0.01 \times 10^{-(4j+3)}, 10^{-(4j+3)}], \\ \frac{50 \times 10^{-(4j+3)} - 0.02 \times 10^{-6j}}{0.02 \times 10^{-(4j+3)} - 10^{-4j}}(x - 10^{-(4j+4)}) + 0.02 \times 10^{-6j}, \ x \in [10^{-(4j+4)}, 0.02 \times 10^{-(4j+3)}], \\ 0, \ x = 0. \end{cases}$$

Let
$$t_j = \frac{33}{70} - \sum_{k=1}^{j} \frac{1}{4(k+1)^4}, \ \eta_j = 0.5(t_j + t_{j+1}), \ j \in \mathbb{N},$$
then
$$\eta_1 = \frac{493}{1120} - \frac{1}{628} < \frac{493}{1120}$$
and
$$t_{j+1} < \eta_j < t_j.$$
Obviously,
$$t_1 = \frac{493}{1120} < 0.5, \ t_j - t_{j+1} = \frac{1}{4(j+2)^4}.$$
Using $\sum_{j=1}^{\infty} \frac{1}{j^4} = \frac{\pi^4}{90}$, we have
$$t^* = \lim_{j \to \infty} t_j = \frac{33}{70} - \sum_{k=1}^{\infty} \frac{1}{4(k+1)^4} = \frac{33}{70} + \frac{1}{64} - \frac{\pi^4}{360} \approx 0.45.$$
After a simple calculation, we obtain
$$A = 0.18, \ G_L = \min\{A+1, Ae_p(\sigma(a), 0)\} \approx 0.28$$
$$G_l = \max\{(A+1)e_p(\eta - \sigma(a), 0), A\} \approx 0.18, \ \theta \geq \frac{1}{G_l \delta(\sigma(a) - 2\eta_1)} \approx 40,$$
$$\Xi \leq \frac{1}{G_L \int_0^{\sigma(a)} \lambda(s) \Delta s} \approx 1.307.$$
Choose $\Xi = 1.2$. Furthermore, if we take
$$\Gamma_j = 10^{-4j} \text{ and } \Lambda_j = 10^{-(4j+3)},$$
then
$$\Gamma_{j+1} = 10^{-(4j+4)} < \frac{G_l}{G_L} \Lambda_j = 0.64 \times 10^{-(4j+3)}$$
$$< \Lambda_j = 10^{-(4j+3)} < \theta \Lambda_j = 40 \times 10^{-(4j+3)} < \Gamma_j = 10^{-4j}.$$
Obviously, f_i, $(i = 1, 2, 3, 4)$ satisfies the following growth conditions:
(i) $f_i(x) \leq \Xi \Gamma_j = 1.2 \times 10^{-4j}$ for $x \in [0, 10^{-4j}]$,
(ii) $f_i(x) \geq \theta \Lambda_j = 40 \times 10^{-(4j+3)}$ for $x \in [0.64 \times 10^{-(4j+3)}, 10^{-(4j+3)}]$.

Then, all the conditions of Theorem 1 are satisfied. Therefore, by Theorem 1, the BVP (4.1) has infinitely many solutions $\{(x_1^{[j]}, x_2^{[j]}, \cdots, x_n^{[j]})\}_{j=1}^{\infty}$ such that $x_i^{[j]} \geq 0$ on $(0, \sigma(a)]_\mathbb{T}$ for $i = 1, 2, 3, 4$.

5. Discussion and Conclusions

In the past few years, iterative differential equations have received extensive attention. The concept of iterative equations was firstly introduced by Babbage [20] in 1815. Babbage found a function equalling its n−th iterate. The real development of iterative equations began in the twentieth century, for more details, see [21] and related references. Iterative equations are a particular type of delay differential equations that depend on both the time t and the state variable x, which are defined implicitly by the iterates. The theory of time scale calculus unifies the calculus of the theory of continuous equations with that of discrete equations, which gives a new way to study hybrid discrete–continuous dynamical systems and has more applications in any field that requires simultaneous modeling of discrete and continuous data. This paper considers the existence of infinitely many positive solutions of nonlinear first-order iterative systems of singular BVPs on time scales by using

Krasnoselskii's cone fixed point theorem in a Banach space. It should be pointed out that the properties of Green's function are the basis of this study. We believe that the properties of Green's function obtained in this paper can be used to study other types of equations. In future work, we will study the iterative system in Remark 1. Furthermore, we will further investigate iterative systems with impulses and fractional order iterative systems.

Author Contributions: Writing—review and editing, B.D., X.W. and X.C.; Methodology, F.Z. All authors have read and agreed to the published version of the manuscript.

Funding: This work is supported by the National Natural Science Foundation of China (No. 11971197).

Data Availability Statement: Not applicable.

Acknowledgments: The authors would like to thank the editor and the anonymous referees for their helpful comments and valuable suggestions regarding this article.

Conflicts of Interest: The authors declare no conflict of interest.

References

1. Cannon, J. The solution of the heat equation subject to the specifcation of energy. *Q. Appl. Math.* **1963**, *21*, 155–160. [CrossRef]
2. Feckan, M.; Wang, J.; Zhao, H. Maximal and minimal nondecreasing bounded solutions of iterative functional differential equations. *Appl. Math. Lett.* **2021**, *113*, 106886. [CrossRef]
3. Buger, M.; Martin, M. The escaping disaster: A problem related to state-dependent delays. *Z. Angew. Math. Phys.* **2004**, *55*, 547–574.
4. Zhao, H.; Liu, J. Periodic solutions of a second-order functional differential equation with state-dependent argument. *Mediterr. J. Math.* **2018**, *15*, 214 [CrossRef]
5. Eder, E. The functional differential equation $x'(t) = x(x(t))$. *J. Differ. Equ.* **1984**, *54*, 390–400. [CrossRef]
6. Fečkan, M. On a certain type of functional differential equations. *Math. Slovaca* **1993**, *43*, 39–43.
7. Wang, K. On the equation $x'(t) = f(x(x(t)))$. *Funkc. Ekvacioj* **1990**, *33*, 405–425.
8. Cheng, S.; Si, J.; Wang, X. An existence theorem for iterative functional-differential equations. *Acta Math. Hung.* **2002**, *94*, 1–17. [CrossRef]
9. Prasad, K.; Khuddush, M.; Vidyasagar, K. Almost periodic positive solutions for a time-delayed SIR epidemic model with saturated treatment on time scales. *J. Math. Model.* **2021**, *9*, 45–60.
10. Kunkel, C. Positive Solutions to Singular Second-Order Boundary Value Problems on Time Scales. *Adv. Dyn. Syst.* **2019**, *14*, 201–211. [CrossRef]
11. Prasad, K.; Khuddush, M. Existence and global exponential stability of positive almost periodic solutions for a time scales model of Hematopoiesis with multiple time varying variable delays. *Int. J. Differ. Equ.* **2019**, *14*, 149–167. [CrossRef]
12. Khuddush, M.; Prasad, K. Vidyasagar, Infinitely many positive solutions for an iterative system of singular multipoint boundary value problems on time scales. *Rend. Circ. Mat. Palermo Ser. 2* **2022**, *71*, 677–696. [CrossRef]
13. Rao, A.K.; Rao, S.N. Positive solutions for iterative system of nonlinear boundary value problems on time scales. *Asian-Eur. J. Math.* **2011**, *4*, 95–107. [CrossRef]
14. Khuddush, M.; Prasad, K. Infinitely many positive solutions for an iterative system of conformable fractional order dynamic boundary value problems on time scales. *Turk. J. Math.* **2022**, *46*, 338–359.
15. Si, J.; Wang, X.; Cheng, S. Nondecreasing and convex C^2-solutions of an iterative functional differential equation. *Aequationes Math.* **2000**, *60*, 38–56. [CrossRef]
16. Hilger, S. Analysis on measure chains-A unified approach to continuous and discrete calculus. *Results Math.* **1990**, *18*, 18–56. [CrossRef]
17. Bohner, M.; Peterson, A. *Dynamic Equations on Time Scales, An Introduction with Applications*; Birkhäuser: Boston, MA, USA, 2001.
18. Guo, D.; Lakshmikantham, V. *Nonlinear Problems in Abstract Cones*; Academic Press: San Diego, CA, USA, 1988.
19. Sun, J.; Li, W. Existence of solutions to nonlinear first-order PBVPs on time scales. *Nonlinear Anal.* **2007**, *67*, 883–888. [CrossRef]
20. Babbage, C. An essay towards the calculus of functions. *Philos. Trans. R. Soc. Lond.* **1815**, *105*, 389–432.
21. Petuhov, V.R. On a boundary value problem, (Russian. English summary). *Tr. Sem. Teor. Differencial. UravnenilsOtklon. Argum. Univ. Druz. Nar. Patrisa Limumby* **1965**, *3*, 252–262.

Disclaimer/Publisher's Note: The statements, opinions and data contained in all publications are solely those of the individual author(s) and contributor(s) and not of MDPI and/or the editor(s). MDPI and/or the editor(s) disclaim responsibility for any injury to people or property resulting from any ideas, methods, instructions or products referred to in the content.

Article

Symmetry and Asymmetry in Moment, Functional Equations, and Optimization Problems

Octav Olteanu

Department of Mathematics-Informatics, University Politehnica of Bucharest, 060042 Bucharest, Romania; octav.olteanu50@gmail.com

Abstract: The purpose of this work is to provide applications of real, complex, and functional analysis to moment, interpolation, functional equations, and optimization problems. Firstly, the existence of the unique solution for a two-dimensional full Markov moment problem is characterized on the upper half-plane. The issue of the unknown form of nonnegative polynomials on $\mathbb{R} \times \mathbb{R}_+$ in terms of sums of squares is solved using polynomial approximation by special nonnegative polynomials, which are expressible in terms of sums of squares. The main new element is the proof of Theorem 1, based only on measure theory and on a previous approximation-type result. Secondly, the previous construction of a polynomial solution is completed for an interpolation problem with a finite number of moment conditions, pointing out a method of determining the coefficients of the solution in terms of the given moments. Here, one uses methods of symmetric matrix theory. Thirdly, a functional equation having nontrivial solution (defined implicitly) and a consequence are discussed. Inequalities, the implicit function theorem, and elements of holomorphic functions theory are applied. Fourthly, the constrained optimization of the modulus of some elementary functions of one complex variable is studied. The primary aim of this work is to point out the importance of symmetry in the areas mentioned above.

Keywords: polynomial approximation; moment problem; symmetric matrix; self-adjoint operator; implicitly defined function; holomorphic solution

MSC: 41A10; 46A22; 26B10; 47B15; 30A10

Citation: Olteanu, O. Symmetry and Asymmetry in Moment, Functional Equations, and Optimization Problems. *Symmetry* **2023**, *15*, 1471. https://doi.org/10.3390/sym15071471

Academic Editor: Junesang Choi

Received: 26 June 2023
Revised: 10 July 2023
Accepted: 20 July 2023
Published: 24 July 2023

Copyright: © 2023 by the author. Licensee MDPI, Basel, Switzerland. This article is an open access article distributed under the terms and conditions of the Creative Commons Attribution (CC BY) license (https://creativecommons.org/licenses/by/4.0/).

1. Introduction

The classical moment problem is an interpolation problem with the positivity condition on the solution. Namely, given a sequence $(y_j)_{j \geq 0}$ of real numbers, one studies the existence, the uniqueness, and, eventually, the construction of a nondecreasing real-valued function $\sigma(t)$ ($t \geq 0$), which verifies the moment conditions $\int_0^\infty t^j d\sigma = y_j$ ($j = 0, 1, 2, \ldots$). This is the original formulation of the moment problem on $[0, \infty)$, as in the works of T.J. Stieltjes [1], recalled by N.I. Akhiezer in [2]. If such a function σ does exist, the sequence $(y_k)_{k \geq 0}$ is called a Stieltjes moment sequence. In the Markov moment problem, other than the interpolation conditions, a sandwich condition on the solution is imposed as well. Going back to the problem formulated by T.J. Stieltjes, this is a one-dimensional moment problem on an unbounded interval. Specifically, it is an interpolation problem with the condition on the positivity of the measure $d\sigma$. The numbers y_j, $j \in \mathbb{N} = \{0, 1, 2, \ldots\}$ are called the moments of the measure $d\sigma$. The moment problem is an inverse problem: one is looking for an unknown measure, starting from its given moments. The following notations are used:

$$\mathbb{N} = \{0, 1, 2, \ldots\}, \ \mathbb{R}_+ = [0, +\infty).$$

$$\varphi_j(t) := \varphi_j(t) = t^j = t_1^{j_1} \cdots t_n^{j_n}, \ j = (j_1, \ldots, j_n) \in \mathbb{N}^n,$$

$$t = (t_1, \ldots, t_n) \in F, \; n \in \mathbb{N}, \; n \geq 1.$$

For a set $F = F_1 \times \cdots \times F_n \subseteq \mathbb{R}^n$, $n \in \mathbb{N}$, $n \geq 2$, and functions $f_l : F_l \to \mathbb{R}$, $l = 1, \ldots, n$, denote

$$f_1 \otimes \cdots \otimes f_n : F \to \mathbb{R}, \; \left(f_1 \otimes \cdots \otimes f_n\right)(t_1, \ldots, t_n) := f_1(t_1) \cdots f_n(t_n).$$

In general, F is a closed bounded or unbounded subset in $\mathbb{R}^n$, $\mathcal{P} = \mathbb{R}[t_1, \ldots, t_n]$ is the real vector space of all polynomials with real coefficients, and $\mathcal{P}_+(F)$ denotes the convex cone of all polynomials $p \in \mathcal{P}$, taking nonnegative values at all points of F. If X is an ordered vector space, one denotes by X_+ the positive cone of X. The open unit disc in the complex plane is denoted by U, and $\mathbb{T}$ is its boundary, the unit circle. If Y is a Banach lattice and $(y_j)_{j \in \mathbb{N}^n}$ is a given sequence of elements in Y, by a solution for the interpolation problem

$$T(\varphi_j) = y_j, \quad j \in \mathbb{N}^n, \tag{1}$$

One means a linear operator T which verifies (1), mapping a Banach lattice X containing the space of polynomials and the space $C_c(F)$ of all real-valued continuous and compactly supported functions defined on F into the space Y. In most cases, when $Y = \mathbb{R}$, one has a scalar-valued solution. When Y is a function or operator Banach lattice, one requires the order completeness of Y. The reason is to permit application of the Hahn–Banach-type extension results of linear operators having Y as codomain. For general knowledge on the moment problem and related areas, see monographs [2–5]. Basic results in real and complex analysis published in [6] are applied in the present study. Further knowledge in analysis and functional analysis, accompanied by applications, can be found in [7–11]. For more general results than those of Section 3.2 below, related to self-adjoint operators and Hankel moment matrices, see [12]. In the case of the classical moment problem, other than the interpolation conditions (1), the positivity of the solution is imposed: $x \geq 0$ in $X \Longrightarrow T(x) \geq 0$ in Y. If $Y = \mathbb{R}$, this positivity condition implies the representation of the linear positive functional T by means of a positive Borel regular measure [6] on F. A variant of the Markov moment problem appearing in the present article consists of requirements (1) and (2) on the solution, where (2) is as follows:

$$T_1(x) \leq T(x) \leq T_2(x) \quad \forall x \in X_+. \tag{2}$$

Basic earlier results on the classical moment problem have been published in references [13–15]. Articles [16,17] provide solutions to the moment problem on special compact subsets of $\mathbb{R}^n$. The expression of polynomials taking positive values on these compact subsets in terms of special positive polynomials follows as well. In [18], an operator valued moment problem is solved. Article [19] applies extension theorems with two constraints on the linear extension under attention in the Markov moment problem. The codomain space is an order-complete vector lattice. In the articles [20–22], the study of the moment problem on semi-algebraic compact subsets [17] is strongly improved and generalized. Moreover, in [22], the author solves a moment problem on an unbounded semi-algebraic subset. The very recent article [23] applies methods of operator theory to study the stability in some truncated moment problems. Recall that, for $n \geq 2$, there exist nonnegative polynomials on $\mathbb{R}^n$ which are not sums of squares. Hence, in this case, moment problems cannot be solved directly in terms of quadratic forms. An exception is the case pointed out by M. Marshall [24], who found and proved the explicit form of nonnegative polynomials on a strip in terms of sums of squares. This is not a problem in the case $n = 1$, since any nonnegative polynomial on $\mathbb{R}$ is a sum of two squares of polynomials. A similar well-known result is valid for a nonnegative polynomial on the nonnegative semiaxis (see Theorem 2 below). In [25,26], some main results are proven. Namely, in [26], the authors prove that, for $n \geq 2$, there exist moment determinate measures ν on $\mathbb{R}^n$, such that the polynomials are not dense in $L_\nu^2(\mathbb{R}^n)$. New checkable sufficient conditions for determinacy of some usual important measures are proven in [27]. The articles [28,29] solve optimization problems related to the truncated moment problem. In [30], the author constructs a solution for the full moment problem, as a limit of solutions for truncated moment problems. Articles [31,32] provide interesting approximation results, not necessarily referring to the moment problem. References [4,5,18,19,33–37] are devoted to, or contain significant results on, the Markov moment problem. Existence, uniqueness, or construction of the solutions of some Markov moment problems are under attention. Finally, the paper [38] refers to some functional and operatorial equations, whose study is completed in the present article. The unknown function is defined implicitly, and its explicit solution is difficult or impossible to find. The complex case was also considered in [38]. The references illustrate the connection of the moment problem and of functional equations with other research areas, such as operator theory, approximation, optimization, algebra, real and complex analysis, geometric functional analysis, and inverse problems. The first aim of this paper is to apply and give a new proof for the previous polynomial approximation and Markov moment problem results for concrete spaces. The motivation is that that, since the explicit form of nonnegative polynomials is not known, one must approximate any nonnegative function of the positive cone of the space $L^1_\nu(F)$, where ν is a positive moment determinate measure with special nonnegative polynomials. Such polynomials are expressible in terms of sums of squares. Then, passing to the limit, the proof of Theorem 2 from below follows. Namely, in Section 3.1, a two-dimensional full Markov moment problem on $F := \mathbb{R} \times \mathbb{R}_+$ is solved via this method. Unlike the recently reviewed results in [36,37], which refer to the vector-valued moment problem (or to operator-valued moment problems), here, the focus is on the classical scalar Markov moment problem. In this classical case, the linear solution is represented by function $h \in L^\infty_{d\nu}(\mathbb{R} \times \mathbb{R}_+)$, and the inequalities $h_1 \leq h \leq h_2$ hold almost everywhere in $\mathbb{R} \times \mathbb{R}_+$. Therefore, measure theory results for representing the linear form solution are also applied. The existence and the uniqueness of the solutions are derived. This classical case is important since, here, the quadratic forms appearing in Theorem 2, point (b) have real coefficients. Thus, their signature can be determined by means of computational algebraic methods. Theorem 2 follows from Theorem 1, whose proof is new, more complete, and simple, but is omitted in [36,37]. The second purpose is to complete the construction of a polynomial solution for the reduced interpolation problem (1), involving only a finite number of conditions (1) (when $j_l \leq d$, $l = 1, \ldots, n$, for a fixed positive integer d). This is carried out in Section 3.2. Then, in Section 3.3, a concrete functional equation whose solution is defined implicitly is discussed. Special care is accorded to the analyticity of the solutions (see [38] and Theorem 4, discussed in Section 3.3). A related inequality which is valid for a large class of self-adjoint operators is derived in Theorem 5. In Section 3.4, optimization of the modulus of the function

$$\psi(z) = \frac{1}{2}(z + 1/z), \text{ on the circular annulus } \{z \in \mathbb{C}; r \leq |z| \leq R\}, \quad 0 < r < R < \infty,$$

is studied. The points where the extreme values are attained are also determined. All the spaces and linear operators/functionals are considered over the real field unless another specification is mentioned. A connection of the function ψ with the previous section is briefly outlined. In the end, optimization problems of the function $\psi_\alpha(z) := \psi(z^\alpha) = (1/2)(z^\alpha + z^{-\alpha})$, $z \in \mathbb{C} \setminus \{0\}$, $\alpha \in \mathbb{R}$, on the circular annulus

$$\{z \in \mathbb{C}; r \leq |z| \leq R\}, \quad 0 < r < R < 1,$$

are deduced. The rest of the paper is organized as follows. Section 2 summarizes the basic methods applied in this work. Section 3 is devoted to the results and their motivations, while Section 4 (Discussion) and Section 5 (Conclusions) conclude the paper.

2. Methods

The methods applied in this article can be summarized as follows:

(I) Evaluation of the consequences of polynomial approximation on unbounded closed subsets $F \subseteq \mathbb{R}^n$, $n \geq 1$, by means of special polynomials, and their applications to the characterization of the existence and uniqueness of the solution of the full Markov moment problem on $L_\nu^1(F)$, where ν is a moment determinate measure on F. See [27,36,37] and the refences therein for details and general type results. To prove the applied approximation result of Theorem 1 and the related previous results from [36,37], measure theory and a fundamental theorem in functional analysis were applied. Among other results, Fubini's theorem and Haviland theorem [13] were used, as well as an extension of linear positive functionals and operators from a majorizing subspace to the entire domain-ordered vector space [8]. This is a Hahn–Banach-type result. For much more general theorems on the moment problem, deduced from extension of linear operator-type results and giving necessary and sufficient conditions on the existence of the constrained solution, see [19]. Such earlier results do not use any approximation theorem on unbounded subsets of $\mathbb{R}^n$; only polynomial approximation on compact subsets [16] are applied (see also [17]). On the other hand, in references [36,37], polynomial approximation on unbounded subsets is studied as well.

(II) Decomposition of $\mathbb{R}^{d+1}$ ($d \in \mathbb{N} \setminus \{0\}$) as direct sum of orthogonal eigenspaces associated with the symmetric Hankel moment matrix. Such a result also holds true in infinite dimensional separable Hilbert spaces H, for compact self-adjoint operators from H to H (see [7]). This method led to the polynomial solution of the reduced interpolation problem solved in Section 3.2. See [12] for recently published deep results in operator theory, most of them referring to self-adjoint operators defined on proper vector subspaces of a Hilbert space and associated with Hankel moment matrices.

(III) Applying results of analysis over the real field [6,10] and elements of complex analysis [6] for solving functional equations when the unknown holomorphic function is defined implicitly, by means of a given holomorphic function with natural properties. In the present work, this is one of the subjects which is carefully focused on. The analyticity of the involved given or unknown functions plays a significant role. All these analytic functions apply the intersection of their domain with the real axis into the real axis

(IV) Functional calculus for self-adjoint operators [7,8].

(V) Using known inequalities from which new ones are derived. Almost all the results involve this.

(VI) Application of the maximum modulus principle of holomorphic functions for determining the extreme values and the points where they are attained, for the modulus of *Joukowski's* function and for a related elementary function in a closed circular annulus not containing the origin. The corresponding result for fractional powers of the complex variable z is also deduced.

(VII) Measure theory [6,10,27].

3. Results

3.1. Solving Full Scalar-Valued Markov Moment Problems on Unbounded Subsets

These results start with a new detailed proof for one of the previous results on polynomial approximation on unbounded subsets. Here, any Stone–Weierstrass uniform approximation on compact subsets is used. Then, the solution for a full Markov moment problem on $\mathbb{R} \times \mathbb{R}_+$ is derived.

As seen in the Introduction, in the classical moment problem, the positivity of the solution or/and sandwich conditions on the positive cone of the domain space have been studied (see also the Introduction and the references on the moment problem). If a full moment problem on an unbounded subset is under investigation, then the uniqueness of the solution makes sense as well. Next, some consequences of a few results from [37] are proven, where the key point consists of polynomial approximation on unbounded subsets. In the sequel, a two-dimensional Markov moment problem is investigated. Recall the notion of a moment determinate measure ν on a closed subset F of $\mathbb{R}^n$. The positive

Borel measure ν on F is moment-determinate if it is uniquely determinate by its classical moments (which are assumed to be finite). In other words, ν is moment determinate on F if, for any other measure μ, for which

$$\int_F t^j d\mu = \int_F t^j d\nu \quad \forall j \in \mathbb{N}^n,$$

$\mu = \nu$ are present as measures (that is, $\int_F \varphi d\mu = \int_F \varphi d\nu$. for any real-valued continuous compactly supported function φ defined on F) (see [2,4,12,25–27] and many other sources on this subject). This section starts with a new proof for one of the previous polynomial approximation results. Let $d\nu_1 = f_1(t_1)dt_1$, (with $f_1 \in L^1_{dt_1}(\mathbb{R}_+)$) be a positive moment-determinate measure on $\mathbb{R}_+$, with finite moments of all orders, and $d\nu_2 = f_2(t_2)dt_2$, (with $f_2 \in L^1_{dt_2}(\mathbb{R}_+)$) be a positive moment-determinate measure on $\mathbb{R}_+$, with finite moments of all orders. On $\mathbb{R} \times \mathbb{R}_+$, consider the product measure $\nu = \nu_1 \times \nu_2$. Unlike the previous proof of such a result, which used Bernstein polynomials in several variables, measure theory plays the central role in the proof of the next theorem.

Theorem 1. *Any nonnegative function $f \in L^1_\nu(\mathbb{R} \times \mathbb{R}_+)$ can be approximated in $L^1_\nu(\mathbb{R} \times \mathbb{R}_+)$ by a sequence of special nonnegative polynomials $(p_m)_{m \in \mathbb{N}}$, where each p_m is a finite sum of polynomials $p_{m,1} \otimes p_{m,2}$, with $p_{m_1} \in \mathcal{P}_+(\mathbb{R})$, $p_{m_2} \in \mathcal{P}_+(\mathbb{R}_+)$.*

Proof. Any nonnegative function $f \in L^1_\nu(\mathbb{R} \times \mathbb{R}_+)$ can be approximated in $L^1_\nu(\mathbb{R} \times \mathbb{R}_+)$ by a sequence of simple functions, each of which is a finite sum of terms of the form $a\chi_{[a_1,b_1) \times [a_2,b_2)} = a\chi_{[a_1,b_1)} \otimes \chi_{[a_2,b_2)}$, $a \in \mathbb{R}_+$. Consider the cell-decomposition of an open subset of $\mathbb{R} \times \mathbb{R}_+$ as a union of disjoint rectangles $[a_1, b_1) \times [a_2, b_2)$. Since any such rectangle is the union of the compact rectangles of the form $[a_1, b_1 - \varepsilon_k] \times [a_2, b_2 - \varepsilon_k]$, $\varepsilon_k \downarrow 0$, it is sufficient to approximate any function of the form $\chi_{[a_1,c_1] \times [a_2,c_2]}$ by $q_m \otimes r_m$, with $q_m \in \mathcal{P}_+(\mathbb{R})$, $r_m \in \mathcal{P}_+(\mathbb{R}_+)$, in the space $L^1_\nu(\mathbb{R} \times \mathbb{R}_+)$. A simple measure theory argument ensures the existence of a decreasing sequence $(h_m)_m$ of continuous nonnegative functions on $\mathbb{R}$, $h_m \downarrow \chi_{[a_1,c_1]}$, $h_m(t_1) = 1 \, \forall t_1 \in [a_1, c_1]$, $h_m(t_1) = 0 \, \forall t_1 \in \mathbb{R} \setminus [a_1 - \varepsilon_m, c_1 + \varepsilon_m]$, $\varepsilon_m \downarrow 0$. The convergence $h_m \downarrow \chi_{[a_1,c_1]}$ holds pointwise on $\mathbb{R}$. For each $m \in \mathbb{N}$, application of one of the results from [36,37] leads to the existence of a polynomial $q_m \in \mathcal{P}_+(\mathbb{R})$, $q_m(t_1) \geq h_m(t_1) \geq 0$ for all $t_1 \in \mathbb{R}$, such that

$$\int_\mathbb{R} (q_m(t_1) - h_m(t_1)) d\nu_1 \to 0, \quad m \to \infty.$$

This results in $0 \leq q_m(t_1) - \chi_{[a_1,c_1]}(t_1) = (q_m - h_m)(t_1) + \left(h_m - \chi_{[a_1,c_1]}\right)(t_1)$ for all $t_1 \in \mathbb{R}$; hence,

$$\int_\mathbb{R} \left(q_m - \chi_{[a_1,c_1]}\right) d\nu_1 \to 0, \quad m \to \infty.$$

The conclusion is that $q_m \to \chi_{[a_1,c_1]}$ in $L^1_{\nu_1}(\mathbb{R})$, $q_m \geq \chi_{[a_1,c_1]} \geq 0$ on $\mathbb{R}$. Proceeding in the same way, one infers the existence of a sequence of polynomials $r_m \to \chi_{[a_2,c_2]}$, $m \to \infty$, the convergence holding in $L^1_{\nu_2}(\mathbb{R}_+)$. Moreover, $r_m(t_2) \geq \chi_{[a_2,c_2]}(t_2) \geq 0$ for all $t_2 \in \mathbb{R}_+$. The above considerations and Fubini's theorem yield

$$\iint_{\mathbb{R} \times \mathbb{R}_+} q_m \otimes r_m d\nu = \int_\mathbb{R} q_m d\nu_1 \cdot \int_{\mathbb{R}_+} r_m d\nu_2 \to \int_\mathbb{R} \chi_{[a_1,c_1]} d\nu_1 \cdot \int_{\mathbb{R}_+} \chi_{[a_2,c_2]} d\nu_2 =$$
$$\iint_{\mathbb{R} \times \mathbb{R}_+} \left(\chi_{[a_1,\times c_1]} \otimes \chi_{[a_2,c_2]}\right) d\nu = \iint_{\mathbb{R} \times \mathbb{R}_+} \chi_{[a_1,c_1] \times [a_2,c_2]} d\nu, \quad m \to \infty.$$

In other words, also using the fact that $q_m \otimes r_m \geq \chi_{[a_1,c_1]} \otimes \chi_{[a_2,c_2]}$, the preceding convergence can be written as

$$\|q_m \otimes r_m - \chi_{[a_1,c_1]} \otimes \chi_{[a_2,c_2]}\|_{L^1_\nu(\mathbb{R}\times\mathbb{R}_+)} =$$
$$\iint_{\mathbb{R}\times\mathbb{R}_+} \left| q_m \otimes r_m - \chi_{[a_1,c_1]} \otimes \chi_{[a_2,c_2]} \right| d\nu =$$
$$\iint_{\mathbb{R}\times\mathbb{R}_+} \left(q_m \otimes r_m - \chi_{[a_1,c_1]\times[a_2,c_2]} \right) d\nu \to 0, \quad m \to \infty.$$

Thus, $q_m \otimes r_m \to \chi_{[a_1,c_1]} \otimes \chi_{[a_2,c_2]} = \chi_{[a_1,c_1]\times[a_2,c_2]}$, as $m \to \infty$, in $L^1_\nu(\mathbb{R}\times\mathbb{R}_+)$. The conclusion follows. This ends the proof. □

The present proof of Theorem 1 seems to be simpler than using Bernstein polynomials or other uniform approximation results of continuous functions by means of polynomials on compact subsets. On the other hand, Theorem 1 solves only an approximation on the Cartesian product $\mathbb{R} \times \mathbb{R}_+$. One of the reasons for considering this case was that the form of nonnegative polynomials on $\mathbb{R}$ and on $\mathbb{R}_+$, in terms of sums of squares, is simpler compared with that of nonnegative polynomials on any other closed subset of $\mathbb{R}$. As a possible generalization of Theorem 1, it makes sense to consider the following problem. If $F = F_1 \times \cdots \times F_n$, $n \geq 2$, where $F_i \subseteq \mathbb{R}$ is a closed subset, and on F_i a moment-determinate measure ν_i is given, $i = 1, \ldots, n$, considering the product-measure $\nu := \nu_1 \times \cdots \times \nu_n$, the space $L^1_\nu(F)$ and a nonnegative function f from $L^1_\nu(F)$, can one approximate f by finite sums of polynomials $p_1 \otimes \cdots \otimes p_n$, with p_i nonnegative polynomial on F_i, $i = 1, \ldots, n$? In this problem, even in the case when F_i is bounded (i.e., it is compact), it makes sense to also consider the case when F_i is not an interval. For example, this is the case when F_i is the spectrum of a symmetric matrix or of a self-adjoint operator. Clearly, any positive regular Borel measure on a nonempty compact subset of $\mathbb{R}^n$ is moment-determinate, due to the Weierstrass uniform approximation theorem of continuous functions by polynomials on compact subsets.

The purpose of the next result is to show how Theorem 1 can be applied to solve a two-dimensional Markov moment problem in terms of quadratic forms. Namely, such a problem is solved on the upper half-plane $\mathbb{R} \times \mathbb{R}_+$.

Theorem 2. *Let $d\nu_1(t) := e^{-at_1^2} dt_1$, $d\nu_2(t) := e^{-bt_2} dt_2$, $a,b > 0$, $d\nu := d\nu_1 \times d\nu_2$, $t = (t_1,t_2) \in \mathbb{R} \times \mathbb{R}_+$, and $(y_j)_{j \in \mathbb{N}^2}$ be a given sequence of real numbers. Let h_1, h_2 be functions from $L^\infty_{d\nu}(\mathbb{R} \times \mathbb{R}_+)$, such that*

$$0 \leq h_1(t_1,t_2) \leq h_2(t_1,t_2) \text{ almost everywhere in } \mathbb{R} \times \mathbb{R}_+.$$

The following statements are equivalent:

(a) *There exists a unique $h \in L^\infty_{d\nu}(\mathbb{R} \times \mathbb{R}_+)$ which satisfies the conditions $h_1 \leq h \leq h_2$ almost everywhere in $\mathbb{R} \times \mathbb{R}_+$, with*

$$\iint_{\mathbb{R}\times\mathbb{R}_+} t_1^{j_1} t_2^{j_2} h(t_1,t_2) d\nu = y_{(j_1,j_2)}, \quad j := (j_1, j_2) \in \mathbb{N}^2$$

(b) *For any finite subset $J_0 \subset \mathbb{N}^2$, and any $\{\alpha_j ; j \in J_0\} \subset \mathbb{R}$, the following implication holds true:*

$$\sum_{j \in J_0} \alpha_j \varphi_j \in \mathcal{P}_+(\mathbb{R} \times \mathbb{R}_+) \implies \sum_{j \in J_0} \alpha_j \iint_{\mathbb{R}\times\mathbb{R}_+} t^j h_1(t_1,t_2) d\nu \leq \sum_{j \in J_0} \alpha_j y_j, \quad t^j = t_1^{j_1} t_2^{j_2};$$

for any finite subsets $J_k \subset \mathbb{N}$, $k = 1, 2$, and any $\{\alpha_{j_k}\}_{j_k \in J_k} \subset \mathbb{R}$, the following inequalities hold:

$$l \in \{0,1\} := 0 \leq \sum_{i_1, j_1 \in J_1} \left(\left(\sum_{i_2, j_2 \in J_2} \alpha_{i_1} \alpha_{j_1} \alpha_{i_2} \alpha_{j_2} \iint_{\mathbb{R} \times \mathbb{R}_+} t_1^{i_1+j_1} t_2^{i_2+j_2+l} h_1(t_1, t_2) dv \right) \right),$$

$$\sum_{i_1, j_1 \in J_1} \left(\left(\sum_{i_2, j_2 \in J_2} \alpha_{i_1} \alpha_{j_1} \alpha_{i_2} \alpha_{j_2} y_{i_1+j_1,\, i_2+j_2+l} \right) \right)$$

$$\leq \sum_{i_1, j_1 \in J_1} \left(\left(\sum_{i_2, j_2 \in J_2} \alpha_{i_1} \alpha_{j_1} \alpha_{i_2} \alpha_{j_2} \iint_{\mathbb{R} \times \mathbb{R}_+} t_1^{i_1+j_1} t_2^{i_2+j_2+l} h_2(t_1, t_2) dv \right) \right).$$

Proof. The measure $d\nu_1$ is moment-determinate on $\mathbb{R}$ and $d\nu_2$ is moment-determinate on $\mathbb{R}_+$, due to the corresponding results proven in [27]. In the sequel, Theorem 1 is applied. The convex cone of all sums of polynomials of the form $p_1 \otimes p_2$, with p_1 taking nonnegative values on the entire real axis and p_2 taking nonnegative values on $\mathbb{R}_+$, is dense in the positive cone of $L^1_{d\nu}(\mathbb{R} \times \mathbb{R}_+)$, according to Theorem 1 proven above. Condition (b) says that the hypothesis (b) of Theorem 4 from [36] is accomplished. Indeed, any nonnegative polynomial on $\mathbb{R}$ is a sum of two squares of polynomials (with real coefficients) [2], and any nonnegative polynomial on $\mathbb{R}_+$ has the form $p(t) = q^2(t) + tr^2(t)$, $t \in \mathbb{R}_+$, for some polynomials q, r with real coefficients. Next, apply the theorem invoked above, where $\mathcal{P}_{++}(\mathbb{R} \times \mathbb{R}_+)$ stands for the cone of all finite sums of polynomials of the form $p_1 \otimes p_2$, $p_1 \in \mathcal{P}_+(\mathbb{R})$, $p_2 \in \mathcal{P}_+(\mathbb{R}_+)$ (see also the references above for the proofs and details). Since the limit of a finite sum of convergent sequences equals the sum of their limits, the conclusion follows via all these results, passing to the limit as $m \to \infty$. Thus, $(b) \Longrightarrow (a)$ is proven. The converse implication is obvious. This ends the proof. □

Example 1. In Theorem 2, one can take $h_1(t_1, t_2) = t_1^2 t_2 e^{-t_1^2 - t_2}$, $h_2(t_1, t_2) = e^{-2}$, $(t_1, t_2) \in \mathbb{R} \times \mathbb{R}_+$.

The comments following Theorem 1 make sense of the problem of solving full Markov moment problems on Cartesian products of closed intervals endowed with moment-determinate measures in quadratic forms. Thus, Theorem 2 can be generalized as well. On the other hand, in Theorem 2, if conditions mentioned at point (b) are satisfied, then the conclusion (a) follows, without giving any information about explicit expression of the solution h in terms of elementary functions. Only the inequalities for $h_1 \leq h \leq h_2$ are obtained almost everywhere in $\mathbb{R} \times \mathbb{R}_+$ and, of course, the moment interpolation conditions are satisfied by h, although the explicit expressions for h_1 and h_2 in terms of exponential function are known.

3.2. Constructing a Polynomial Solution for a Reduced Interpolation Problem

The next theorem completes and solves results from [36] on the polynomial solution of the interpolation problem (1), formulated for a limited (finite) number of conditions ($j \leq d$).

Theorem 3. *If $[a, b] \subset \mathbb{R}$ is a compact interval, $d \in \mathbb{N}$, $d \geq 1$, $y = (y_0, \ldots, y_d)$ an arbitrary given vector in $\mathbb{R}^{d+1}$, then there exists a polynomial solution p with real coefficients, of degree d, for the interpolation problem*

$$\int_{[a,b]} t^j p(t) dt = y_j, \quad j \in \{0, 1, \ldots, d\}.$$

The coefficients of the solution p with respect to the eigenvectors and eigenvalues of the Hankel matrix $M_d = \left(m_{j+l}\right)_{j,l=0}^{d}$ are given by equality (7) written below, where m_{j+l} is defined by (3), $j, l = 0, 1, \ldots, d$.

Proof. To simplify the notation, consider the case $n = 1$. Condition (1) should be satisfied for all $j \in \{0, 1, \ldots, d\}$. Similar considerations, arguments, and computations can be performed for $n \geq 2$, $j_l \leq d$, $l = 1, \ldots, n$. One looks for a polynomial solution

$$p(t) = \sum_{l=0}^{d} a_l t^l = \sum_{l=0}^{d} a_l \varphi_l(t), \quad a_l \in \mathbb{R}, \quad \sum_{l=0}^{d} a_l^2 > 0, \quad t \in K,$$

such that

$$\int_{[a,b]} t^j p(t) dt = y_j, \quad j \in \{0, 1, \ldots, d\}.$$

The following linear system in the unknowns a_l, $l \in \{0, 1, \ldots, d\}$ should be solved

$$\sum_{l=0}^{d} a_l \int_{[a,b]} t^{j+l} dt = \sum_{l=0}^{d} a_l m_{j+l} = y_j, \quad m_{j+l} := \int_{[a,b]} t^{j+l} dt, \quad j, l = 0, 1, \ldots, d. \quad (3)$$

The square symmetric matrix of this system is

$$M_d := \left(m_{j+l}\right)_{j,l=0}^{d} \quad (4)$$

System (3) may be written as

$$M_d \begin{pmatrix} a_0 \\ \vdots \\ a_d \end{pmatrix} = \begin{pmatrix} y_0 \\ \vdots \\ y_d \end{pmatrix}. \quad (5)$$

The matrix M_d is positive (as a linear symmetric operator) and invertible, since

$$\sum_{j,l=0}^{d} m_{j+l} \lambda_j \lambda_l = \int_{[a,b]} \left(\sum_{j,l=0}^{d} \lambda_j \lambda_l t^{j+l}\right) dt = \int_{[a,b]} \left(\sum_{j=0}^{d} \lambda_j t^j\right)^2 dt > 0,$$

for all $\lambda := (\lambda_0, \ldots, \lambda_d) \neq (0, \ldots, 0)$. The last strict inequality holds, since the square of the polynomial appearing under the integral sign is positive, except for a finite number of the roots of that polynomial. If the polynomial appearing in the last integral would be null, this would contradict the assumption $\lambda \neq 0$. Since the boundary S_d of the unit ball B_{d+1} in $\mathbb{R}^{d+1}$ is closed and bounded (i.e., it is compact), there exists $r > 0$ such that

$$\sum_{j,l=0}^{d} m_{j+l} \lambda_j \lambda_l \geq r,$$

for all vectors $(\lambda_0, \ldots, \lambda_d)$, with $\sum_{l=0}^{d} \lambda_l^2 = 1$. Evaluations (inequalities) for the Euclidean norm $\|a_0, \ldots, a_d\|_2$ of the vector of the unknown coefficients have been also pointed out in [36]. Namely, from (5), one infers that

$$\begin{pmatrix} a_0 \\ \vdots \\ a_d \end{pmatrix} = M_d^{-1} \begin{pmatrix} y_0 \\ \vdots \\ y_d \end{pmatrix} \implies$$

$$\|a_0, \ldots, a_d\|_2 \leq M_d^{-1} \cdot \|y_0, \ldots, y_d\|_2 = \|1/\alpha_{min,d}\| \cdot \|y_0, \ldots, y_d\|_2.$$

Here, $\alpha_{min,d}$ is the smallest (positive) eigenvalue of the positive definite matrix M_d; hence, $1/\alpha_{min,d}$ is the greatest eigenvalue of M_d^{-1}. However, paper [36] does not provide any method for determining all the coefficients $a_0, \ldots, a_d$ of the polynomial solution p regarding the moments y_j, $j \in \{0, 1, \ldots d\}$. In the sequel, this problem is solved without computing (determining) the elements of the matrix M_d^{-1}. As is well known [7], if $\mu_0, \ldots, \mu_d$ are the (note necessarily distinct) positive eigenvalues of the matrix M_d, and $\{f_0, \ldots, f_d\}$ is the orthonormal basis of $\mathbb{R}^{d+1}$ formed by the corresponding eigenvectors, one can write

$$x = \sum_{l=0}^{d} <x, f_l> f_l, \quad M_d x = \sum_{l=0}^{d} \langle x, f_l \rangle \mu_l f_l, \quad x \in \mathbb{R}^{d+1}.$$

Let $\{e_0, \ldots, e_d\}$ be the canonical Hilbert base in $\mathbb{R}^{d+1}$. Then, for $a = (a_0, \ldots, a_d)$, one has

$$a = (a_0, \ldots, a_d) = \sum_{l=0}^{d} a_l e_l = \sum_{l=0}^{d} <a, f_l> f_l \quad (6)$$

The system (5) can be written as

$$\sum_{l=0}^{d} \langle a, f_l \rangle \mu_l f_l = \sum_{l=0}^{d} \langle y, f_l \rangle f_l, \quad y := \sum_{j=0}^{d} y_j e_j$$

Hence, the coefficients $\langle a, f_l \rangle$, $l = 0, 1, \ldots, d$ of the vector

$$a = (a_0, \ldots, a_d) = \sum_{l=0}^{d} a_l e_l \text{ in the base } \{f_0, \ldots, f_d\},$$

are given by the equalities

$$\langle a, f_l \rangle = \mu_l^{-1} \langle y, f_l \rangle, \quad l = 0, 1, \ldots, d. \quad (7)$$

Of note, the right-hand side numbers in (7) can be expressed only in terms of the moments y_l, $l = 0, 1, \ldots, d$. Indeed, μ_l, $l = 0, 1, \ldots, d$ are the (positive) eigenvalues of the Hankel matrix M_d defined by (4), which is known and does not depend on y or on a. The vectors f_l are the eigenvectors of the matrix $M_d = \left(m_{j+l}\right)_{j,l=0}^{d}$. Hence, according to (7) and (6), the unknown vector a can be found starting from the numbers y_l, $l = 0, 1, \ldots, d$. This ends the proof. □

Remark 1. Recall that any sequence $\alpha = (\alpha_n)_{n=0}^{\infty} \in l_2$ defines a holomorphic function f in U, by means of the power series having α_n as coefficients, as was recently recalled in [12]:

$$f(z) := \sum_{n=0}^{\infty} \alpha_n z^n, \quad |z| < 1. \quad (8)$$

The convergence of this power series holds uniformly in any closed disc of radius $r < 1$. Indeed, one can write:

$$|z| \leq r \implies \sum_{n=0}^{\infty} |\alpha_n||z|^n \leq \left(\sum_{n=0}^{\infty} |\alpha_n|^2\right)^{1/2} \cdot \left(\sum_{n=0}^{\infty} |z|^{2n}\right)^{1/2} =$$

$$\|\alpha_2\| \cdot \frac{1}{\sqrt{1-|z|^2}} \leq \|\alpha_2\| \cdot \frac{1}{\sqrt{1-r^2}}.$$

Remark 2. Any sequence $\alpha = (\alpha_n)_{n=0}^{\infty} \in l_1$ defines a holomorphic function as written in (8), which makes sense for $|z| = 1$. The convergence of the power series (8) is absolutely and uniformly on $\overline{U}$; hence, f is also continuous in $\overline{U}$. Conversely, for any holomorphic function f in U, defined and continuous in $\overline{U}$, whose expansion (8) converges absolutely and uniformly on $\overline{U}$, the coefficients of the Taylor expansion (8) form a sequence of the space l_1. Indeed, $|z| = 1 \Longrightarrow \sum_{n=0}^{\infty}|a_n| = \sum_{n=0}^{\infty}|a_n z^n| < \infty$. Such a function is $f(z) := \sum_{n=1}^{\infty} z^n/n^\alpha$, $\alpha > 1$, $|z| \leq 1$.

Theorem 3 provides the coefficients of the polynomial solution only for the truncated moment problem defined by $d+1$ interpolation conditions. An interesting problem might be that of finding the coefficients of the analytic solution $f(z) = \sum_{n=0}^{\infty} \alpha_n z^n$ satisfying the full problem of the interpolation conditions $\int_{[a,b]} t^j f(t) dt = y_j$, $j \in \mathbb{N}$, with $(a_n)_{n=0}^{\infty} \in l_2$, under the assumption $[a,b] \subset (-1,1)$. With the notations from above, a related problem is when the infinite matrix $M := \left(m_{j+l}\right)_{j,l=0}^{\infty}$ defines an invertible operator acting on l_2. Since the operator is self-adjoint and positive, this condition on M is true if and only if $\inf\limits_{\substack{h \in l_2, \\ \|h\|=1}} \langle Mh, h\rangle = \inf\limits_{d \geq 2} \alpha_{min,d} > 0$. Another problem could be, given an interval $[a,b] \subseteq [-1,1]$, look for an analytic function f given by (8), $(a_n)_{n=0}^{\infty} \in l_1$, satisfying the conditions of Remark 2, such that $\int_{[a,b]} t^j f(t) dt = y_j$, $j \in \mathbb{N}$. Such problems seem to belong to operator theory or could be related to optimization problems in the finite dimensional space $\mathbb{R}^{d-1}$, $d \in \mathbb{N}$, $d \geq 2$, passing to the limit as $d \to \infty$.

3.3. On a Class of Analytic Functional Equations

In the sequel, the existence, and properties of the nontrivial holomorphic solution $\widetilde{f}$ of the equation

$$\widetilde{g}(z) = \widetilde{g}\left(\widetilde{f}(z)\right), \tag{9}$$

are studied, where $\widetilde{g}$ is a given holomorphic function defined on a convex domain Ω, such that $\widetilde{g}(\Omega \cap \mathbb{R}) \subseteq \mathbb{R}$ satisfies some conditions, while the nontrivial solution, the function

$$\widetilde{f}, \widetilde{f}(z) \neq z \text{ for all } z \in \Omega \setminus \{x_0\}, \widetilde{f}(x_0) = x_0, \text{ where } x_0 \in \Omega \cap \mathbb{R}$$

is the unique minimum or maximum point for the restriction of $\widetilde{g}$ to an open interval contained in $\Omega \cap \mathbb{R}$ Moreover, the restriction of $\widetilde{f}$ to $\Omega \cap \mathbb{R}$ is decreasing and $\widetilde{f}'(x_0) = -1$. One such concrete functional is Equation (9), whose solution is approximated locally, in the neighborhood of the point $x_0 = 0$.

Remark 3. Define $H(z,w) := \widetilde{g}(z) - \widetilde{g}(w)$, $z, w \in \mathbb{C}$; then, for $w_0 \neq 0$, one has

$$H_w(z_0, w_0) = -\widetilde{g}'(w_0) \neq 0.$$

Thus, the implicit function theorem can be used for the existence of a unique solution h defined in a neighborhood V_0 of z_0, such that $\widetilde{g}(h(z)) = \widetilde{g}(z)$ for all z in V_0. Since $h(z) = z$, $z \in V_0$ is a solution, from the uniqueness of the solution, it follows that the identity mapping is the unique solution. However, this is the trivial solution, which is not of interest. Thus, if g is holomorphic in a region of the complex plane and the other conditions in the statement of Theorem 4 below are satisfied, for finding a nontrivial solution f, the only chance is to look for it in the neighborhood of the point $z_0 = x_0 = 0$ at which the first derivative of g equals zero. For $(z_0, w_0) = (0,0)$, one has $\widetilde{g}'(0) = 0$, so that the implicit function theorem and the uniqueness of the local solution are no longer working. In this case, the proof from [38] works. This last method does not use the implicit function theorem. Only the continuity of f and the properties $f(0) = 0$, f are decreasing, and the analyticity of $\widetilde{g}$ is applied to deduce the complex differentiability of $\widetilde{f}$ at $z_0 = x_0 = 0$.

Theorem 4. *Consider the following functional equation:*

$$h(x) := x - \log(1+x) = h(f(x)) = f(x) - \log(1+f(x)), \quad x \in (-1, \infty).$$

Then, there exists a unique continuous solution f satisfying the equation $h(x) = h(fx))$ for all $x \in (-1, +\infty)$, with the following additional properties:

(i) *f is decreasing on $(-1, \infty)$, and one has*

$$\lim_{x \downarrow -1} f(x) = \infty, \quad \lim_{x \uparrow \infty} f(x) = -1;$$

(ii) *$x_0 = 0$ is the unique fixed point of f;*
(iii) *one has $f^{-1} = f$ on $(-1, \infty)$;*
(iv) *there is a complex neighborhood D of 0 and a holomorphic extension $\widetilde{f}$ of f, $\widetilde{f} : D \to \mathbb{C}$, satisfying the equation*

$$\widetilde{h}\left(\widetilde{f}(z)\right) = \widetilde{h}(z), \ z \in D, \ \widetilde{f}'(0) = -1, \text{ where } \widetilde{h}(z) := z - \log(1+z);$$

(v) *in a disc of sufficiently small radius $\varepsilon > 0$, one has*

$$\widetilde{f}(z) \approx -z(1+2z), \quad |z| < \varepsilon;$$

(vi) *for sufficiently small $\varepsilon > 0$, the following inequality holds:*

$$f(x) > -x(1+2x), \quad \forall x \in [-\varepsilon, 0). \tag{10}$$

Proof. The real-valued function h is continuous on $(-1, +\infty)$, decreasing on $(-1, 0)$ from $+\infty$ to zero, and is increasing on $(0, +\infty)$ from zero to $+\infty$. Applying general-type results from [38], the conclusions stated at points (i)–(iv) follow for a sufficiently small complex neighborhood D of zero contained in the open unit disc U. To prove (v), for sufficiently small $\varepsilon > 0$, $\varepsilon < 1$, one can write the equation $\widetilde{h}\left(\widetilde{f}(z)\right) = \widetilde{h}(z)$, $|z| < \varepsilon$ as

$$\widetilde{f}(z) - z = \log\left(\frac{1+\widetilde{f}(z)}{1+z}\right) = \log\left(1 + \frac{\widetilde{f}(z) - z}{1+z}\right) =$$

$$\int_0^{\frac{\widetilde{f}(z)-z}{1+z}} \frac{1}{1+w} dw = \int_0^{\frac{\widetilde{f}(z)-z}{1+z}} \left(1 - w + w^2 + \cdots + (-1)^n w^n + \cdots\right) dw =$$

$$\frac{\widetilde{f}(z) - z}{1+z} - \frac{1}{2} \cdot \left(\frac{\widetilde{f}(z) - z}{1+z}\right)^2 + \frac{1}{3} \cdot \left(\frac{\widetilde{f}(z) - z}{1+z}\right)^3 - \cdots.$$

Observe that, in the above remarks, for small $\varepsilon > 0$, one has $\left|\frac{\widetilde{f}(z)-z}{1+z}\right| < 1 \ \forall z$ with $|z| \leq \varepsilon$, since $\frac{\widetilde{f}(z)-z}{1+z} \to 0$ as $\varepsilon \to 0$. Hence, if one denotes $w_1 = w_1(z) = \frac{\widetilde{f}(z)-z}{1+z}$, under the above-mentioned conditions, one can write

$$\log(1 + w_1) = \int_0^{w_1} \frac{1}{1+w} dw = \int_0^{w_1} \left(1 - w + w^2 + \cdots + (-1)^n w^n + \cdots\right) dw =$$

$$w_1 - \frac{1}{2} \cdot w_1^2 + \frac{1}{3} \cdot w_1^3 - \cdots.$$

The last integral can be computed on any C^1 path of ends 0 and w_1, whose image is contained in the open unit disc U, according to Cauchy theorem for the holomorphic function $w \mapsto 1/(1+w)$, $|w| < 1$. Such a path is the line segment joining the origin 0 with $w_1 = w_1(z)$. Its parameterization is $w(t) = tw_1$, $t \in [0, 1]$. Integration term by term is allowed due to the uniform convergence of the geometric series $\sum_{n=0}^{\infty}(-w)^n$, for w in the closed disc of radius $|w_1|$, namely, in the disc

$$\{w;\ |w| \leq |w_1| < 1\}.$$

Since $\tilde{f}(z) \neq z$, $\tilde{f}(z) - z \approx 0$ for $|z| < \varepsilon$, $z \neq 0$, dividing by $\tilde{f}(z) - z$ and neglecting the powers $n \geq 2$ of $\tilde{f}(z) - z$, which are very close to zero, one derives that

$$1 \approx \frac{1}{1+z} - \frac{1}{2} \cdot \frac{\tilde{f}(z) - z}{(1+z)^2}.$$

This can be rewritten as

$$2(1+z)^2 - 2(1+z) + \tilde{f}(z) - z \approx 0,$$

which is equivalent to

$$\tilde{f}(z) \approx z - 2z(1+z) = -z(1+2z).$$

Thus, (v) is proven. Next, write the computational result in the proof of point (v) for real

$$z = x \in (-1, 0),$$

x close to zero. For such numbers x, one has

$$f(x) - x > 0,\ 1 + x > 0,\ 1 > \frac{f(x) - x}{1 + x} > 0,$$

and

$$(x) - x = \frac{f(x)-x}{1+x} - \frac{1}{2}\cdot\left(\frac{f(x)-x}{1+x}\right)^2 + \frac{1}{3}\cdot\left(\frac{f(x)-x}{1+x}\right)^3 - \frac{1}{4}\left(\frac{f(x)-x}{1+x}\right)^4 + \cdots =$$
$$\frac{f(x)-x}{1+x} - \frac{1}{2}\cdot\left(\frac{f(x)-x}{1+x}\right)^2 + \left(\frac{f(x)-x}{1+x}\right)^3\left(\frac{1}{3} - \frac{1}{4}\cdot\frac{f(x)-x}{1+x}\right) + r(x).$$

Here, apply the well-known evaluation of the sum of the involved (alternate) Leibniz-type series, whose general term is

$$\frac{(-1)^n}{n+1}\left(\frac{f(x)-x}{1+x}\right)^{n+1}.$$

Namely,

$$\frac{1}{3} - \frac{1}{4}\cdot\frac{f(x)-x}{1+x} > 0,$$

and the rest $r(x)$ is the sum of positive numbers of the form

$$\left(\frac{f(x)-x}{1+x}\right)^{2k+1}\left(\frac{1}{2k+1} - \frac{1}{2k+2}\cdot\frac{f(x)-x}{1+x}\right).$$

The conclusion is $r(x) > 0$, and

$$f(x) - x > \frac{f(x)-x}{1+x} - \frac{1}{2} := \left(\frac{f(x)-x}{1+x}\right)^2.$$

The last inequality is equivalent to

$$1 > \frac{1}{1+x} - \frac{1}{2}\cdot\frac{f(x)-x}{(1+x)^2}, x \in [-\varepsilon, 0).$$

This inequality holds true for sufficiently small $\varepsilon > 0$, $\varepsilon < 1$. Equality occurs in the last inequality if and only if $x = 0$. As seen in the proof of point (v), where the equality sign is replaced by the inequality one, the conclusion is

$$2(1+x)^2 - 2(1+x) > -f(x) + x,$$

$$f(x) > x - 2x(1+x) = -x(1+2x), \quad x \in [-\varepsilon, 0).$$

Thus, (10) is proven. This ends the proof. □

As in the case of Theorem 2, in Theorem 4, there is information on the behavior of the unknown implicitly defined function f, but not on its expression in terms of elementary functions, although the given function h is an elementary analytic function. Only local approximation, inequalities, $f^{-1} = f$, and other main properties of f are available.

Remark 4. Note the following similarity between Sections 3.1 and 3.3. In Theorem 4, the main properties of the function f mentioned above are deduced, but an exact analytic expression for f seems to be impossible to be found. This is a quasi-general remark on the functions defined implicitly. Only the local approximation provided by Theorem 4, and points (v) and (vi), represent a simple way of making an idea in this respect. Similarly, in Theorem 2, a characterization of the existence and uniqueness of the function h with properties mentioned at point (a) is proven. However, a formula for the exact expression of h in terms of the moments is not easily obtained (this is an inverse problem).

Remark 5. From points (i), (ii) of Theorem 4, one already knows that $x \in (-1, 0)$ is equivalent to $f(x) > 0$. Therefore, the assertion (vi) of the same theorem is interesting for $1 + 2x \geq 1 - 2\varepsilon > 0$, that is, for $\varepsilon < 1/2$.

Recall that, if H is an arbitrary real or complex Hilbert space of dimension ≥ 2, and if $\mathcal{A}$ denotes the real vector space of all self-adjoint operators acting on H, then the natural order relation on $\mathcal{A}$ is defined by

$$U, V \in \mathcal{A}, \quad U \leq V \iff \langle Uh, h \rangle \leq \langle Vh, h \rangle \text{ for all } h \in H.$$

Endowed with this order relation and the usual operatorial norm, $\mathcal{A}$ is an ordered Banach space which is not a lattice (if $dim(H) \geq 2$). If f is a continuous real-valued function on the spectrum $\sigma(-A)$, then one can denote by $f(-A)$ the corresponding self-adjoint operator obtained via functional calculus.

Theorem 5. *Let H be an arbitrary real or complex Hilbert space and $\varepsilon \in (0, 1/2]$ be a sufficiently small number, such that the inequality proven at point (vi) of Theorem 4 holds true. Let A be a positive self-adjoint operator from H to itself, such that $\|A\| \leq \varepsilon \leq 1/2$. Then,*

$$f(-A) \geq A(I - 2A). \tag{11}$$

Proof Let t be an arbitrary real number in the spectrum $\sigma(A) \subseteq [0, \varepsilon]$ of the self-adjoint positive operator A, with $\|A\| \leq \varepsilon$. Then, $x := -t \in [-\varepsilon, 0]$. For $-t \in [-\varepsilon, 0)$; according to Theorem 4, point (vi), one has

$$f(-t) > t(1 - 2t).$$

Since $f(0) = 0$, this results in $f(-t) \geq t(1 - 2t)$ for all $-t \in [-\varepsilon, 0]$. By means of functional calculus for continuous functions on the spectrum $\sigma(-A) = -\sigma(A) \subseteq [-\varepsilon, 0]$ of the self-adjoint operator $-A$, one infers that $f(-A) \geq A(I - 2A)$. This ends the proof. □

With the notations and conditions on ε mentioned in Theorems 4 and 5, the following consequence of Theorem 5 follows.

Corollary 1 *If $n \geq 2$ is an integer, then (11) holds for any symmetric $n \times n$ matrix A with real entries, whose eigenvalues are all contained in the interval $[0, \varepsilon]$.*

3.4. On Some Optimization Problems for the Modulus of the Complex Joukowski Function

Let $K_{r,R} := \{z \in \mathbb{C}; r \leq |z| \leq R\}$, where $0 < r < R < \infty$. In any point of $K_{r,R}$, the Joukowski function

$$\psi(z) := \frac{1}{2}(z + 1/z),$$

makes sense. Actually, $\psi \in H(\mathbb{C} \setminus \{0\})$. Next, two optimization-type theorems related to this function are proven, and a consequence is derived.

Theorem 6. *The following inequalities and respective equalities hold:*

$$M := \max_{z \in K_{r,R}} |\psi(z)| = \max_{r \leq |z| \leq R} \left| \frac{1}{2}\left(z + \frac{1}{z}\right) \right| = \frac{1}{2}\max\left\{R + \frac{1}{R}, r + \frac{1}{r}\right\} = \max\{\psi(R), \psi(r)\}. \quad (12)$$

Moreover, one has the following:

(a) $0 < r < R \leq 1 \Longrightarrow M = \frac{1}{2}\left(r + \frac{1}{r}\right) = \psi(r);$

(b) $1 \leq r < R \Longrightarrow M = \frac{1}{2}\left(R + \frac{1}{R}\right) = \psi(R) = |\psi(-R)|;$ and

(c) $0 < r < 1 < R \Longrightarrow$ (12) is the only available information. If $0 < r < 1$ and $R = \frac{1}{r}$, then

$$M = \frac{1}{2}\left(r + \frac{1}{r}\right) = \frac{1}{2}\left(R + \frac{1}{R}\right).$$

Proof. The equality (12) follows from the maximum modulus property [6] for the holomorphic function ψ, followed by the computational conclusion from below. The maximum is attained at a point located on the boundary $\partial K = \{z; |z| = R\} \cup \{z; |z| = r\}$. These lead to

$$M = \max\left\{M_R := \max_{|z|=R} |\psi(z)|, M_r := \max_{|z|=r} |\psi(z)|\right\}.$$

The same computations determine the maximum points on the circles of radiuses R, respective of radius r. Namely, one finds

$$|z| = R \iff z = Re^{i\theta}, \theta \in [0, 2\pi) \Longrightarrow$$

$$\left|z + \frac{1}{z}\right| = \left|z + \frac{\bar{z}}{z\bar{z}}\right| = \left|Re^{i\theta} + \frac{Re^{-i\theta}}{R^2}\right| =$$

$$\left|R(\cos(\theta) + i\sin(\theta)) + \frac{1}{R}(\cos(\theta) - i\sin(\theta))\right| =$$

$$\left|\left(R + \frac{1}{R}\right)\cos(\theta) + i\left(R - \frac{1}{R}\right)\sin(\theta)\right| =$$

$$\left(\left(R + \frac{1}{R}\right)^2 \cos^2(\theta) + \left(R - \frac{1}{R}\right)^2 \sin^2(\theta)\right)^{1/2} =$$

$$\left(R^2 + \frac{1}{R^2} + 2\left(\cos^2(\theta) - \sin^2(\theta)\right)\right)^{1/2} \leq \left(R^2 + \frac{1}{R^2} + 2\right)^{1/2} = R + \frac{1}{R}.$$

Of note, equality occurs in the last inequality if and only if $\sin^2(\theta) = 0$, which means $\cos^2(\theta) = 1$. Thus, the maximum value on $[0, 2\pi)$ is attained at $\theta = 0$ and $\theta = \pi$. The first conclusion is

$$M_R := \max_{|z|=R}\left|\frac{1}{2}\left(z + \frac{1}{z}\right)\right| = \frac{1}{2}\left(R + \frac{1}{R}\right),$$

and this maximum is attained at $z_1 = R$ and at $z_2 = -R$. Repeating the same calculations on the circle $|z| = r$, one obtains:

$$M_r := \max_{|z|=r} \left| \frac{1}{2}\left(z + \frac{1}{z}\right) \right| = \frac{1}{2}\left(r + \frac{1}{r}\right) = \psi(r).$$

Hence, (12) is proven. Next, one must compare M_R with M_r. Namely, to prove (a), assume that $0 < r < R \leq 1$. Then, one computes the difference

$$M_R - M_r = \frac{1}{2}\left(R - r + \left(\frac{1}{R} - \frac{1}{r}\right)\right) = \frac{1}{2}(R - r)\left(1 - \frac{1}{Rr}\right). \tag{13}$$

This results in $M_R - M_r > 0 \iff Rr > 1$, $M_R - M_r < 0 \iff Rr < 1$, $M_R - M_r = 0 \iff Rr = 1$. If $0 < r < R \leq 1$, then $Rr < 1$; hence, $M_R < M_r$, that is, $M = M_r$. Similarly,

$$1 \leq r \langle R \implies Rr \rangle 1 \iff M_R > M_r \implies M = M_R.$$

Clearly, $Rr = 1$ if and only if $M_R = M_r$. According to (13), or simply because $r = 1/R$, this implies

$$\psi(R) = \psi\left(\frac{1}{R}\right) = \psi(r).$$

If $0 < r < 1 < R$ and $R \neq \frac{1}{r}$, then one cannot derive any conclusion regarding the signature of $Rr - 1$, and one has $\psi(R) \neq \psi(r)$. Using (13), this means one cannot decide the signature of $M_R - M_r$. In this case, the conclusion remains the equality written in (12). The proof is complete. □

Corollary 2. *If $0 < r < R < 1$, then $\max\limits_{z \in K_{r,1}} |\psi(z)| = \frac{1}{2}\left(r + \frac{1}{r}\right) = \psi(r)$.*

Proof. One applies Theorem 6 (a) for $R = 1$. □

Next, the minimum value m of the modulus is discussed for the same function ψ, $\psi(z) = \frac{1}{2}\left(z + \frac{1}{z}\right)$, on the subset $K_{R,r}$, also determining the corresponding minimum points.

Theorem 7. *With the above notations, the following statements hold:*

(i) *If $[r, R] \subset (0, 1)$, then $m = \frac{1}{2}\left(\frac{1}{R} - R\right) = \psi(iR) = \psi(-iR)$;*

(ii) *If $[r, R] \subset (1, +\infty)$, then $m = \frac{1}{2}\left(r - \frac{1}{r}\right) = \psi(ir) = \psi(-ir)$;*

(iii) *If $1 \in [r, R]$, then $m = 0 = \psi(i) = \psi(-i)$.*

Proof. For $z = \rho e^{i\theta}$, $\rho > 0$, $\theta \in [0, 2\pi)$, following the computation from the proof of Theorem 6, one finds

$$\left| z + \frac{1}{z} \right| = \left(\rho^2 + \frac{1}{\rho^2} + 2\left(\cos^2(\theta) - \sin^2(\theta)\right)\right)^{1/2} \geq$$

$$\left(\rho^2 + \frac{1}{\rho^2} - 2\right)^{1/2} = \left|\rho - \frac{1}{\rho}\right|, \quad \forall \theta \in [0, 2\pi).$$

Observe that equality occurs in the last inequality if and only if $\cos^2(\theta) = 0$ (that is, $\sin^2(\theta) = 1$), which is equivalent to $\theta \in \{\pi/2, 3\pi/2\}$. Thus,

$$m = \min_{\rho \in [r,R]} \left(\min_{\theta \in [0, 2\pi)} \left| \psi\left(\rho e^{i\theta}\right) \right| \right) = \frac{1}{2} \min_{\rho \in [r,R]} \left| \rho - \frac{1}{\rho} \right|. \tag{14}$$

If $\rho \in [r, R] \subset (0, 1)$, then $\left|\rho - \frac{1}{\rho}\right| = \frac{1}{\rho} - \rho$ and $\min_{\rho \in [r,R]} \left|\rho - \frac{1}{\rho}\right| = \min_{\rho \in [r,R]} \left(\frac{1}{\rho} - \rho\right) = \frac{1}{R} - R$, since the function $g(\rho) = \frac{1}{\rho} - \rho$ is decreasing on $(0, +\infty)$. Hence, $m = \frac{1}{2}\left(\frac{1}{R} - R\right)$ and the minimum value is attained for

$$\rho = R, \quad \theta \in \{\pi/2, 3\pi/2\}.$$

This means the minimum points are iR and $-iR$. Thus, the assertion stated at point (i) is proven. The point (ii) follows via similar reasoning, with the remarks that $\left|\rho - \frac{1}{\rho}\right| = \rho - \frac{1}{\rho} = -g(\rho)$ for $\rho \in [r, R] \subset (1, +\infty)$ and $-g$ is increasing. The minimum points correspond to $\rho = r$, $\theta \in \{\pi/2, 3\pi/2\}$. Thus, (ii) is proven. To prove (iii), observe that the global minimum value zero for m from (14) is attained if and only if $\rho = 1$. The condition $\theta \in \{\pi/2, 3\pi/2\}$ remains from the optimization in the variable θ, so that, in this case, the only minimum points are i and $-i$. This concludes the proof. □

Remark 6. Now, note the connection of the function ψ with the functional equations appearing in the preceding section. As is well-known and easy to prove directly, the unique nontrivial solution f of the functional equation $\psi(f(z)) = \psi(z)$, $z \neq 0$, is

$$f(z) = \frac{1}{z}, \quad z \neq 0.$$

Starting from the function Ψ and an arbitrary sequence $(a_n)_{n \geq 0} \in l_1$, define

$$a_{-n} := a_n, \quad n \in \mathbb{N},$$

$$\psi(z) := \sum_{n \in \mathbb{Z}} a_n z^n, \quad z \in \mathbb{T}.$$

Then, clearly,

$$\psi(z) = a_0 + \sum_{n \geq 1} a_n \left(z^n + \frac{1}{z^n}\right), \quad z \in \mathbb{T},$$

verifies $\psi(z) = \psi\left(\frac{1}{z}\right)$.

From the last two theorems, one derives the following consequence involving fractional power of the variable z.

Corollary 3. *Let $\alpha \in (0, \infty)$ and $\psi_\alpha(z) := \psi(z^\alpha) = (1/2)(z^\alpha + z^{-\alpha})$, $z \in \mathbb{C} \setminus \{0\}$. Then the following hold:*

(i) $0 < r < R \leq 1 \implies \max_{r \leq |z| \leq R} \frac{1}{2}\left|z^\alpha + \frac{1}{z^\alpha}\right| = \frac{1}{2}\left(r^\alpha + \frac{1}{r^\alpha}\right)$;

(ii) $0 < r < R < 1 \implies \min_{r \leq |z| \leq R} \frac{1}{2}\left|z^\alpha + \frac{1}{z^\alpha}\right| = \frac{1}{2}\left(\frac{1}{R^\alpha} - R^\alpha\right)$.

Proof. The following equalities hold:

$$z = \rho e^{i\theta}, \quad w := z^\alpha := e^{\alpha \log(z)} = e^{\alpha(\log(\rho) + i\theta)} = \rho^\alpha := e^{i\alpha\theta}.$$

This implies

$$|w| = |z^\alpha| = \rho^\alpha = |z|^\alpha.$$

This results in

$$r \leq |z| \leq R \iff r^\alpha \leq |w| \leq R^\alpha.$$

Using Theorem 6, assertion (a), these further yield

$$\max_{r \leq |z| \leq R} \frac{1}{2}\left|z^\alpha + \frac{1}{z^\alpha}\right| = \max_{r^\alpha \leq |w| \leq R^\alpha} \frac{1}{2}\left|w + \frac{1}{w}\right| = \frac{1}{2}\left(r^\alpha + \frac{1}{r^\alpha}\right).$$

Thus, the implication (i) is proven. The assertion (ii) follows by means of Theorem 7, point (i). This ends the proof. □

It seems that condition $\alpha \in (0, \infty)$ is not necessary, since $\psi_{-\alpha}(z) = \psi_\alpha(z)$ for all $\alpha \in \mathbb{R}$, $z \neq 0$. An interesting problem could be that of applying the results of Section 3.4 to normal operators having their spectrum in a circular anulus $K_{r,R}$.

4. Discussion

The present article provides new, or improved and completed, versions of previous results on polynomial approximations on unbounded closed subsets, Markov moment problems on such subsets, polynomial solutions for reduced interpolation problems, functional equations, and optimization of the functions ψ and ψ_α in circular annuluses. In the first part, a scalar version of previous theorems on the existence and the uniqueness of the solution for the full Markov moment problem is pointed out (see Theorems 1 and 2). Such theorems use polynomial approximation of any function from $\left(L^1_{dv}\right)_+$ by special nonnegative polynomials, which are expressible in terms of sums of squares, in the space L^1_{dv}. Here, ν is a product $\nu_1 \times \nu_2$, with ν_1 being a moment-determinate measure on $\mathbb{R}$ and ν_2 a moment-determinate measure on $\mathbb{R}_+$. On the other hand, at the end of the paper, it is pointed out that, in the simplest case of the function $\psi(x) = x + 1/x$, $x > 0$, the graph of ψ is not symmetric with respect to the vertical line of equation $x = 1$, passing through the minimum point 1 of ψ located in the interval $(0, \infty)$. However, in the complex analysis framework, considering the meromorphic function

$$\Psi(z) = a_0 + \sum_{n \geq 1} a_n \left(z^n + \frac{1}{z^n}\right), \quad z \in \mathbb{T},$$

note the symmetry of its coefficients (see Remark 6). Additionally, for $z \in \mathbb{T}$, one has $\Psi(z) = \Psi(1/z) = \Psi(\bar{z})$ and $\bar{z}$ is the symmetric of z with respect to the real axis. If all the coefficients a_n, $n \in \mathbb{N}$ are real numbers, $(a_n)_{n \geq 0} \in l_1$, one finds that $\Psi(z) \in \mathbb{R}$ for all $z \in \mathbb{T}$. Part of the previous results is the basis for the new ones. Theorem 3 provides all the Fourier coefficients of the unknown polynomial solution in the orthonormal base defined by the eigenvectors of the Hankel matrix M_d in terms of the given moments, unlike the previous result on this topic [36]. In addition to the results pointed out in the Abstract, in Theorem 5, an inequality valid for any positive self-adjoint operator with sufficiently small norm is deduced from Theorem 4.

5. Conclusions

Sections 3.2–3.4 are directly related to notions and/or results involving symmetry. To name a few of them, in Section 3.2, the matrix M_d is a special symmetric matrix with real entries. In Section 3.3, the graph of the unknown function f is symmetric with respect to the line of equation $y = x$, since f is its own inverse for the operation of composition of functions. In Section 3.4, the symmetry of the coefficients of the meromorphic function Ψ from Remark 6 has already been discussed. As a common aspect of Sections 3.1 and 3.3, in both these sections, one can prove significant properties of the solutions, without knowing their expressions in terms of elementary functions, although the given functions are elementary (see Theorem 2, Example 1, and Theorem 4).

Funding: This research received no external funding.

Data Availability Statement: In this work, no data, except those appearing in the text and in the cited references, are used or generated.

Acknowledgments: The author would like to thank the reviewers for their comments and suggestions, leading to the improvement of the presentation of this paper.

Conflicts of Interest: The author declares no conflict of interest.

References

1. Stieltjes, T.J. Recherche sur les fractions continues. *Ann. Fac. Sci. Univ. Toulouse Math.* **1894**, *8*, J1–J122. [CrossRef]
2. Akhiezer, N.I. *The Classical Moment Problem and Some Related Questions in Analysis*; Oliver and Boyd: Edinburgh, UK, 1965.
3. Berg, C.; Christensen, J.P.R.; Ressel, P. *Harmonic Analysis on Semigroups*; Theory of Positive Definite and Related Functions; Springer: New York, NY, USA, 1984.
4. Schmüdgen, K. The Moment Problem. In *Graduate Texts in Mathematics*; Springer International Publishing AG: Cham, Switzerland, 2017; p. 277. [CrossRef]
5. Krein, M.G.; Nudelman, A.A. *Markov Moment Problem and Extremal Problems*; American Mathematical Society: Providence, RI, USA, 1977.
6. Rudin, W. *Real and Complex Analysis*, 3rd ed.; McGraw-Hill Book Company: Singapore, 1987.
7. Brezis, H. *Functional Analysis, Sobolev Spaces and Partial Differential Equation*; Springer: New York, NY, USA, 2011. [CrossRef]
8. Cristescu, R. *Ordered Vector Spaces and Linear Operators*; Academiei: Bucharest, Romania; Abacus Press: Tunbridge Wells, UK, 1976.
9. Niculescu, C.; Popa, N. *Elements of Theory of Banach Spaces*; Academiei: Bucharest, Romania, 1981. (In Romanian)
10. Choudary, A.D.R.; Niculescu, C.P. *Real Analysis on Intervals*; Springer: New Delhi, India, 2014. [CrossRef]
11. Popescu, S.A.; Jianu, M. *Advanced Mathematics for Engineers and Physicists*; Springer Nature: Cham, Switzerland, 2022. [CrossRef]
12. Berg, C.; Szwark, R. Self-adjoint operators associated with Hankel moment matrices. *J. Funct. Anal.* **2022**, *283*, 109674. [CrossRef]
13. Haviland, E.K. On the momentum problem for distributions in more than one dimension. *Am. J. Math.* **1936**, *58*, 164–168. [CrossRef]
14. Choquet, G. Le problème des moments (The moment problem). In *Séminaire d'Initiation à l'Analise*; Institut H. Poincaré: Paris, France, 1962.
15. Berg, C.; Christensen, J.P.R.; Jensen, C.U. A remark on the multidimensional moment problem. *Math. Ann.* **1979**, *243*, 163–169. [CrossRef]
16. Cassier, G. Problèmes des moments sur un compact de R^n et dôcomposition des polynomes à plusieurs variables (Moment problems on a compact subset of R^n and decomposition of polynomials of several variables). *J. Funct. Anal.* **1984**, *58*, 254–266. [CrossRef]
17. Schmüdgen, K. The K-moment problem for compact semi-algebraic sets. *Math. Ann.* **1991**, *289*, 203–206. [CrossRef]
18. Lemnete, L. An operator-valued moment problem. *Proc. Am. Math. Soc.* **1991**, *112*, 1023–1028. [CrossRef]
19. Olteanu, O. Application de théorèmes de prolongement d'opérateurs linéaires au problème des moments e à une generalization d'un théorème de Mazur-Orlicz, (Applications of theorems on extension of linear operators to the moment problem and to a generalization of Mazur-Orlicz theorem). *Comptes Rendus Acad. Sci. Paris* **1991**, *313*, 739–742.
20. Putinar, M. Positive polynomials on compact semi-algebraic sets. *IU Math J.* **1993**, *42*, 969–984. [CrossRef]
21. Putinar, M.; Vasilescu, F.H. Problème des moments sur les compacts semi-algébriques (The moment problem on semi-algebraic compacts). *Comptes Rendus Acad. Sci. Paris Ser. I* **1996**, *323*, 787–791.
22. Vasilescu, F.H. Spectral measures and moment problems. In *Spectral Analysis and Its Applications (Ion Colojoară Anniversary Volume)*; Theta: Bucharest, Romania, 2003; pp. 173–215.
23. Lemnete-Ninulescu, L. Stability in Truncated Trigonometric Scalar Moment Problems. *Complex Anal. Oper. Theory* **2023**, *17*, 75. [CrossRef]
24. Marshall, M. Polynomials non-negative on a strip. *Proc. Am. Math. Soc.* **2010**, *138*, 1559–1567. [CrossRef]
25. Fuglede, B. The multidimensional moment problem. *Expo. Math.* **1983**, *1*, 47–65.
26. Berg, C.; Thill, M. Rotation invariant moment problems. *Acta Math.* **1991**, *167*, 207–227. [CrossRef]
27. Stoyanov, J.M.; Lin, G.D.; Kopanov, P. New checkable conditions for moment determinacy of probability distributions. *SIAM Theory Probab. Appl.* **2020**, *65*, 497–509. [CrossRef]
28. Tagliani, A. Maximum entropy solutions and moment problem in unbounded domains. *Appl. Math. Lett.* **2003**, *16*, 519–524. [CrossRef]
29. Inverardi, P.L.N.; Tagliani, A. Stieltjies and Hamburger reduced moment problem when MaxEnt solution does not exist. *Mathematics* **2021**, *9*, 309. [CrossRef]
30. Stochel, J. Solving the truncated moment problem solves the full moment problem. *Glasg. Math. J.* **2001**, *43*, 335–341. [CrossRef]
31. Păltineanu, G.; Bucur, I. Some density theorems in the set of continuous functions with values in the unit interval. *Mediterr. J. Math.* **2017**, *14*, 44. [CrossRef]
32. Amato, U.; Della Vecchia, B. New Progressive Iterative Approximation Techniques for Shepard-Type Curves. *Symmetry* **2022**, *14*, 398. [CrossRef]
33. Norris, D.T. Optimal Solutions to the L_∞ Moment Problem with Lattice Bounds. Ph.D. Thesis, Department of Mathematics, College of Arts and Sciences, University Colorado Boulder, Boulder, CO, USA, 2002.

34. Gosse, L.; Runborg, O. Resolution of the finite Markov moment problem. *Comptes Rendus Acad. Sci. Paris* **2005**, *341*, 775–780. [CrossRef]
35. Lemnete-Ninulescu, L.; Zlătescu, A. Some new aspects of the L-moment problem. Rev. Roum. Math. *Pures Appl.* **2010**, *55*, 197–204.
36. Olteanu, O. On Markov moment problem and related results. *Symmetry* **2021**, *13*, 986. [CrossRef]
37. Olteanu, O. Markov moment problems on special closed subsets of R^n. *Symmetry* **2023**, *15*, 76. [CrossRef]
38. Olteanu, O. On a class of functional equations over the real and over the complex fields. *MathLAB J.* **2020**, *7*, 24–33.

Disclaimer/Publisher's Note: The statements, opinions and data contained in all publications are solely those of the individual author(s) and contributor(s) and not of MDPI and/or the editor(s). MDPI and/or the editor(s) disclaim responsibility for any injury to people or property resulting from any ideas, methods, instructions or products referred to in the content.

Article

Refinements of the Euclidean Operator Radius and Davis–Wielandt Radius-Type Inequalities

Tareq Hamadneh [1], Mohammad W. Alomari [2], Isra Al-Shbeil [3], Hala Alaqad [4,*], Raed Hatamleh [5], Ahmed Salem Heilat [5] and Abdallah Al-Husban [2]

[1] Department of Mathematics, Faculty of Science, Al Zaytoonah University of Jordan, Amman 11733, Jordan; t.hamadneh@zuj.edu.jo
[2] Department of Mathematics, Faculty of Science and Information Technology, Irbid National University, Irbid 21110, Jordan; mwomath@gmail.com (M.W.A.)
[3] Department of Mathematics, Faculty of Science, University of Jordan, Amman 11940, Jordan
[4] Department of Mathematical Sciences, United Arab Emirates University, Al Ain 15551, United Arab Emirates
[5] Department of Mathematics, Faculty of Science and Information Technology, Jadara University, Irbid 21110, Jordan
* Correspondence: hala_a@uaeu.ac.ae

Abstract: This paper proves several new inequalities for the Euclidean operator radius, which refine some recent results. It is shown that the new results are much more accurate than the related, recently published results. Moreover, inequalities for both symmetric and non-symmetric Hilbert space operators are studied.

Keywords: Euclidean operator radius; Davis–Wielandt radius; numerical radius

MSC: 47A12; 47A30; 47A63

1. Introduction

Let $\mathscr{A}(\mathscr{M})$ be the Banach algebra of all bounded linear operators defined on a complex Hilbert space $(\mathscr{M}; \langle \cdot, \cdot \rangle)$ with the identity operator $1_{\mathscr{M}}$. For a bounded linear operator M on a Hilbert space $\mathscr{M}$, the numerical range $W(P)$ is the image of the unit sphere of $\mathscr{M}$ under the quadratic form $c \to \langle Mc, c \rangle$ associated with the operator. More precisely,

$$W(M) = \{\langle Mc, c \rangle : c \in \mathscr{M}, \|c\| = 1\}.$$

Moreover, the numerical radius is defined to be

$$w(M) = \sup_{\lambda \in W(T)} |\lambda| = \sup_{\|c\|=1} |\langle Mc, c \rangle|.$$

We recall that the usual operator norm of an operator T is defined to be

$$\|M\| = \sup\{\|Mc\| : c \in \mathscr{M}, \|c\| = 1\},$$

It is well known that $w(\cdot)$ defines an operator norm on $\mathscr{A}(\mathscr{M})$ that is equivalent to the operator norm $\|\cdot\|$. Moreover, we have

$$\frac{1}{2}\|M\| \leq w(M) \leq \|M\| \qquad (1)$$

for any $M \in \mathscr{A}(\mathscr{M})$.

The Euclidean operator radius of an n-tuple $\mathbf{P} = (P_1, \cdots, P_n) \in \mathscr{A}(\mathscr{M})^n := \mathscr{A}(\mathscr{M}) \times \cdots \times \mathscr{A}(\mathscr{M})$ was introduced by Popsecu in [1], where $P_1, \cdots, P_n \in \mathscr{A}(\mathscr{M})$. The Euclidean operator radius of $P_1, \cdots, P_n$ is defined by

$$w_e(P_1, \cdots, P_n) := \sup_{\|c\|=1} \left(\sum_{i=1}^n |\langle P_i c, c \rangle|^2 \right)^{1/2}.$$

Indeed, the Euclidean operator radius was generalized in [2] as follows:

$$w_p(P_1, \cdots, P_n) := \sup_{\|c\|=1} \left(\sum_{i=1}^n |\langle P_i c, c \rangle|^p \right)^{1/p}, \qquad p \geq 1.$$

If $p = 1$, then $w_1(P_1, \cdots, P_n)$ (in addition, it is denoted by $w_R(P_1, \cdots, P_n)$) is called the Rhombic numerical radius, which has been studied in [3]. In particular, if $P_1 = \cdots = P_n = P$, then it is interesting that $w_1(P, \cdots, P) = n\, w(P)$, where $w(P)$ is the numerical radius of P.

We note that the inequality

$$w_\infty(P_1, \cdots, P_n) \leq w_p(P_1, \cdots, P_n) \leq w_R(P_1, \cdots, P_n) \qquad (2)$$

holds for all $p \in (1, \infty)$; see [4].

In addition, Popescu [1] proved that

$$\frac{1}{2\sqrt{n}} \left\| \sum_{k=1}^n P_k P_k^* \right\|^{\frac{1}{2}} \leq w_e(P_1, \cdots, P_n) \leq \left\| \sum_{k=1}^n P_k P_k^* \right\|^{\frac{1}{2}}. \qquad (3)$$

As noted in [5], and as a special case of (3), if $Y = F + iG$ is the Cartesian decomposition of A, then

$$w_e^2(F, G) = \sup_{\|c\|=1} \left\{ |\langle Fc, c \rangle|^2 + |\langle Gc, c \rangle|^2 \right\} = \sup_{\|c\|=1} |\langle Yc, c \rangle|^2 = w^2(Y).$$

Since $Y^*Y + YY^* = 2(F^2 + G^2)$, we have

$$\frac{1}{16} \|Y^*Y + YY^*\| \leq w^2(Y) \leq \frac{1}{2} \|Y^*Y + YY^*\|. \qquad (4)$$

Note that the case of $n = 2$ was studied by Dragomir in [6], and he obtained some interesting results regarding the Euclidean operator radius of two operators $w_e(P_1, P_2)$.

The Euclidean operator radius was generalized in [5] as follows:

$$\omega_p(P_1, \cdots, P_n) := \sup_{\|c\|=1} \left(\sum_{i=1}^n |\langle P_i c, c \rangle|^p \right)^{\frac{1}{p}}, \qquad p \geq 1.$$

In [5], Moslehian, Sattari, and Shebrawi proved several inequalities regarding n-tuple operators $P \in \mathscr{A}(\mathscr{M})^n$. In particular, they proved the following two results:

$$\omega_p(P_1, \cdots, P_n) \leq \frac{1}{2} \left\| \sum_{i=1}^n \left(|P_i|^{2\alpha} + |P_i^*|^{2(1-\alpha)} \right)^p \right\|^{\frac{1}{p}} \qquad (5)$$

and

$$\omega_p(P_1,\cdots,P_n) \le \left\|\sum_{i=1}^n \alpha|P_i|^p + (1-\alpha)|P_i^*|^p\right\|^{\frac{1}{p}} \tag{6}$$

for $\alpha \in [0,1]$ and $p \ge 1$. For the case $p = 2$, (5) and (6) studied upper bounds for the Euclidean operator radius $\omega_e(\cdot)$. It should be noted that in case $n = 1$ and $p = 1$, then (5) reduces to the main result in [7].

An inequality for a product of two Hilbert space operators was also deduced in [3], as follows:

$$\omega_e^{2r}(Q_1^*P_1,\cdots,Q_n^*P_n) \le \frac{1}{2}\left\|\sum_{i=1}^n |P_i|^{4r} + |Q_i|^{4r}\right\| \tag{7}$$

for all $P_i, Q_i \in \mathscr{A}(\mathscr{M})$ and $r \ge 1$. This inequality generalizes and extends the result in [8].

In [2], Sheikhhosseini, Moslehian, and Shebrawi refined the above two inequalities by proving the following two results, respectively,

$$\omega_p(P_1,\cdots,P_n) \le \frac{1}{2}\left\|\sum_{i=1}^n \left(|P_i|^{2\alpha} + |P_i^*|^{2(1-\alpha)}\right)^p\right\|^{\frac{1}{p}} - \inf_{\|c\|=1} \xi(c) \tag{8}$$

where

$$\xi(c) = \frac{1}{2}\sum_{i=1}^n \left(\left\langle|P_i|^{2\alpha p}c,c\right\rangle^{\frac{1}{2}} - \left\langle|P_i^*|^{2(1-\alpha)p}c,c\right\rangle^{\frac{1}{2}}\right)^2$$

and

$$w_p^p(P_1,\cdots,P_n) \le \left\|\sum_{i=1}^n \left(\alpha|P_i|^{\frac{p}{m}} + (1-\alpha)|P_i^*|^{\frac{p}{m}}\right)^m\right\| - \inf_{\|c\|=1} \xi(c) \tag{9}$$

where

$$\xi(c) = \min\{\alpha, 1-\alpha\}\sum_{i=1}^n \left(\left\langle|P_i|^{\frac{p}{m}}c,c\right\rangle^{\frac{m}{2}} - \left\langle|P_i^*|^{\frac{p}{m}}c,c\right\rangle^{\frac{m}{2}}\right)^2.$$

For further inequalities of the Euclidean operator radius combined with several basic properties, the reader may refer to [3,4,6,9,10]. For more generalization, counterparts, and recent related results, the reader may refer to [11–19].

In [19], Alomari proved the following version of the Euclidean operator radius, which generalized the celebrated Kittaneh inequality [20].

$$\frac{1}{2^{p+1}n^{p-1}}\left\|\sum_{k=1}^n P_k^*P_k + P_kP_k^*\right\|^p \le \omega_{2p}^{2p}(P_1,\cdots,P_n) \le \frac{1}{2^p}\left\|\sum_{k=1}^n (P_k^*P_k + P_kP_k^*)^p\right\|$$

for all $P_k \in \mathscr{A}(\mathscr{M})$ ($k = 1,\cdots,n$) and $p \ge 1$. In particular, we have

$$\frac{1}{4}\left\|\sum_{k=1}^n P_k^*P_k + P_kP_k^*\right\| \le \omega_e^2(P_1,\cdots,P_n) \le \frac{1}{2}\left\|\sum_{k=1}^n (P_k^*P_k + P_kP_k^*)\right\|.$$

This article proves several new inequalities for the Euclidean operator radius $\omega(\cdot)$. More precisely, refinement inequalities of some old results are presented. Section 2 recalls some key inequalities used in the following section. Section 3 is focused on the diverse upper bounds for the Euclidean operator radius $\omega(\cdot)$, and this gives an extension and refinements of (5) and (7) when $p = 2$. Our new inequalities are devoted to refining the

Euclidean operator radius $\omega_e(\cdot)$. A similar approach could be used to refine several inequalities for $\omega_p(\cdot)$. Inequalities for symmetric (self-adjoint) and non-symmetric (arbitrary) Hilbert space operators are also covered.

2. Lemmas

To prove our results, we need a sequence of lemmas.

Lemma 1 ([21]). *The Power-Mean inequality states that*

$$t^\alpha s^{1-\alpha} \leq \alpha t + (1-\alpha)s \leq (\alpha t^p + (1-\alpha)s^p)^{\frac{1}{p}} \tag{10}$$

for all $\alpha \in [0,1]$, $s, t \geq 0$ and $p \geq 1$.

Lemma 2 ([22]). *[Theorem 1.4] Let $P \in \mathscr{A}(\mathscr{M})^+$, then*

$$\langle Pc, c\rangle^p \leq \langle P^p c, c\rangle, \qquad p \geq 1 \tag{11}$$

for any vector $c \in \mathscr{M}$. The inequality (11) is reversed if $0 \leq p \leq 1$.

The following result generalizes and refines Kato's inequality or the so-called mixed Schwarz inequality [23].

Lemma 3 ([24]). *[Lemma 5] Let $P \in \mathscr{A}(\mathscr{M})$, $0 \leq \alpha \leq 1$ and $p \geq 1$. Then,*

$$\begin{aligned}|\langle Pc, d\rangle|^{2p} &\leq \beta \left\langle |P|^{2p\alpha} c, c\right\rangle \left\langle |P^*|^{2p(1-\alpha)} d, d\right\rangle \\ &\quad + (1-\beta)|\langle Pc, d\rangle|^p \sqrt{\left\langle |P|^{2p\alpha} c, c\right\rangle \left\langle |P^*|^{2p(1-\alpha)} d, d\right\rangle} \\ &\leq \left\langle |P|^{2p\alpha} c, c\right\rangle \left\langle |P^*|^{2p(1-\alpha)} d, d\right\rangle.\end{aligned} \tag{12}$$

for all $\beta \in [0,1]$.

Corollary 1. *Let $P \in \mathscr{A}(\mathscr{M})$, $0 \leq \alpha, \beta \leq 1$. Then,*

$$\begin{aligned}|\langle Pc, d\rangle|^2 &\leq \beta \left\langle |P|^{2\alpha} c, c\right\rangle \left\langle |P^*|^{2(1-\alpha)} d, d\right\rangle + (1-\beta)|\langle Pc, d\rangle| \sqrt{\left\langle |P|^{2\alpha} c, c\right\rangle \left\langle |P^*|^{2(1-\alpha)} d, d\right\rangle} \\ &\leq \left\langle |P|^{2\alpha} c, c\right\rangle \left\langle |P^*|^{2(1-\alpha)} d, d\right\rangle.\end{aligned} \tag{13}$$

Proof. Setting $p = 1$ in (12). □

Lemma 4 ([24]). *Let $P, Q \in \mathscr{A}(\mathscr{M})$. Then,*

$$\begin{aligned}|\langle Pc, Qd\rangle|^2 &\leq \beta \left\langle |P|^2 c, c\right\rangle \left\langle |Q|^2 d, d\right\rangle + (1-\beta)|\langle Pc, Qd\rangle| \sqrt{\left\langle |P|^2 c, c\right\rangle \left\langle |Q|^2 d, d\right\rangle} \\ &\leq \|Pc\|^2 \|Qd\|^2\end{aligned} \tag{14}$$

for any vectors $c, d \in \mathscr{M}$ and all $\beta \in [0,1]$.

Lemma 5 ([25]). *Let $P \in \mathscr{A}(\mathscr{M})$. Then,*

$$|\langle Pc, c\rangle|^2 \leq \frac{1}{2}\left|\left\langle P^2 c, c\right\rangle\right| + \frac{1}{4}\left\langle \left(|P|^2 + |P^*|^2\right)c, c\right\rangle \tag{15}$$

for any vectors $c \in \mathscr{M}$.

Lemma 6 ([26]). *[Theorem 2.3] Let f be a non-negative convex function on $[0,\infty)$, and let $P, Q \in \mathscr{A}(\mathscr{M})$ be two positive operators. Then,*

$$\left\| f\left(\frac{P+Q}{2}\right) \right\| \leq \left\| \frac{f(P)+f(Q)}{2} \right\|. \tag{16}$$

3. Applications to Numerical Radius Inequalities

We are in a position to state our first main result involving the numerical radius inequalities for a product of two Hilbert space operators.

Theorem 1. *Let $P_k, Q_k \in \mathscr{A}(\mathscr{M})$ ($k = 1, 2, \cdots, n$). Then,*

$$\omega_e^{2r}(Q_1^* P_1, \cdots, Q_n^* P_n)$$
$$\leq \frac{1}{2^r}\beta \left\| \sum_{k=1}^{n} \left(|P_k|^4 + |Q_k|^4\right) \right\|^r + \frac{1}{2^r}(1-\beta)\omega_e^r(Q_1^* P_1, \cdots, Q_n^* P_n) \left\| \sum_{k=1}^{n} \left(|P_k|^2 + |Q_k|^2\right)^2 \right\|^r \tag{17}$$

for all $\beta \in [0,1]$ and $r \geq 1$.

Proof. Let $u \in \mathscr{M}$ be a unit vector. We set $c = P_k u$ and $d = Q_k u$ ($k = 1, \cdots, n$) in the first inequality in (14). Employing the AM–GM inequality, the convexity of t^2 ($t > 0$), and using Lemma 2, we obtain

$$|\langle Q_k^* P_k u, u\rangle|^2$$
$$\leq (1-\beta)|\langle Q_k^* P_k u, u\rangle|\langle |P_k|^2 u, u\rangle^{\frac{1}{2}}\langle |Q_k|^2 u, u\rangle^{\frac{1}{2}} + \beta \langle |P_k|^2 u, u\rangle \langle |Q_k|^2 u, u\rangle.$$
$$\leq (1-\beta)|\langle Q_k^* P_k u, u\rangle|\langle |P_k|^2 u, u\rangle^{\frac{1}{2}}\langle |Q_k|^2 u, u\rangle^{\frac{1}{2}} + \frac{1}{2}\beta\left(\langle |P_k|^2 u, u\rangle^2 + \langle |Q_k|^2 u, u\rangle^2\right)$$
$$\leq \frac{1}{2}(1-\beta)|\langle Q_k^* P_k u, u\rangle|\left(\langle |P_k|^2 u, u\rangle + \langle |Q_k|^2 u, u\rangle\right) + \frac{1}{2}\beta\left(\langle |P_k|^4 u, u\rangle + \langle |Q_k|^4 u, u\rangle\right)$$
$$= \frac{1}{2}(1-\beta)|\langle Q_k^* P_k u, u\rangle|\langle \left(|P_k|^2 + |Q_k|^2\right)u, u\rangle + \frac{1}{2}\beta\langle \left(|P_k|^4 + |Q_k|^4\right)u, u\rangle.$$

Taking the summation over $k = 1$ up to n for both sides, we have

$$\sum_{k=1}^{n} |\langle Q_k^* P_k u, u\rangle|^2$$
$$\leq \frac{1}{2}(1-\beta)\sum_{k=1}^{n}|\langle Q_k^* P_k u, u\rangle|\langle \left(|P_k|^2 + |Q_k|^2\right)u, u\rangle + \frac{1}{2}\beta \sum_{k=1}^{n}\langle \left(|P_k|^4 + |Q_k|^4\right)u, u\rangle$$

Applying the Cauchy–Schwarz inequality to real numbers and then applying Lemma 2, we obtain

$$\sum_{k=1}^{n} |\langle Q_k^* P_k u, u \rangle|^2$$

$$\leq \frac{1}{2}(1-\beta) \sum_{k=1}^{n} |\langle Q_k^* P_k u, u \rangle| \langle \left(|P_k|^2 + |Q_k|^2 \right) u, u \rangle + \frac{1}{2}\beta \sum_{k=1}^{n} \langle \left(|P_k|^4 + |Q_k|^4 \right) u, u \rangle$$

$$\leq \frac{1}{2}(1-\beta) \left(\sum_{k=1}^{n} |\langle Q_k^* P_k u, u \rangle|^2 \right)^{\frac{1}{2}} \left(\sum_{k=1}^{n} \langle \left(|P_k|^2 + |Q_k|^2 \right) u, u \rangle^2 \right)^{\frac{1}{2}}$$
$$+ \frac{1}{2}\beta \langle \sum_{k=1}^{n} \left(|P_k|^4 + |Q_k|^4 \right) u, u \rangle$$

$$\leq \frac{1}{2}(1-\beta) \left(\sum_{k=1}^{n} |\langle Q_k^* P_k u, u \rangle|^2 \right)^{\frac{1}{2}} \left(\sum_{k=1}^{n} \langle \left(|P_k|^2 + |Q_k|^2 \right)^2 u, u \rangle \right)^{\frac{1}{2}}$$
$$+ \frac{1}{2}\beta \langle \left[\sum_{k=1}^{n} \left(|P_k|^4 + |Q_k|^4 \right) \right] u, u \rangle$$

$$= \frac{1}{2}(1-\beta) \left(\sum_{k=1}^{n} |\langle Q_k^* P_k u, u \rangle|^2 \right)^{\frac{1}{2}} \langle \left[\sum_{k=1}^{n} \left(|P_k|^2 + |Q_k|^2 \right)^2 \right] u, u \rangle^{\frac{1}{2}}$$
$$+ \frac{1}{2}\beta \langle \left[\sum_{k=1}^{n} \left(|P_k|^4 + |Q_k|^4 \right) \right] u, u \rangle$$

Again, by applying the convexity of t^r ($r \geq 1$), we obtain

$$\left(\sum_{k=1}^{n} |\langle Q_k^* P_k u, u \rangle|^2 \right)^r$$

$$\leq \left(\frac{1}{2}(1-\beta) \left(\sum_{k=1}^{n} |\langle Q_k^* P_k u, u \rangle|^2 \right)^{\frac{1}{2}} \langle \left[\sum_{k=1}^{n} \left(|P_k|^2 + |Q_k|^2 \right)^2 \right] u, u \rangle^{\frac{1}{2}} \right.$$
$$\left. + \frac{1}{2}\beta \langle \left[\sum_{k=1}^{n} \left(|P_k|^4 + |Q_k|^4 \right) \right] u, u \rangle \right)^r$$

$$\leq \frac{1}{2^r}(1-\beta) \left(\sum_{k=1}^{n} |\langle Q_k^* P_k u, u \rangle|^2 \right)^{\frac{r}{2}} \langle \left[\sum_{k=1}^{n} \left(|P_k|^2 + |Q_k|^2 \right)^2 \right] u, u \rangle^{\frac{r}{2}}$$
$$+ \frac{1}{2^r}\beta \langle \left[\sum_{k=1}^{n} \left(|P_k|^4 + |Q_k|^4 \right) \right] u, u \rangle^r$$

$$\leq \frac{1}{2^r}(1-\beta) \left(\sum_{k=1}^{n} |\langle Q_k^* P_k u, u \rangle|^2 \right)^{\frac{r}{2}} \langle \left[\sum_{k=1}^{n} \left(|P_k|^2 + |Q_k|^2 \right)^2 \right]^r u, u \rangle^{\frac{1}{2}}$$
$$+ \frac{1}{2^r}\beta \langle \left[\sum_{k=1}^{n} \left(|P_k|^4 + |Q_k|^4 \right) \right]^r u, u \rangle$$

Taking the supremum over all unit vectors $u \in \mathcal{M}$, we obtain the desired result in (17). □

Corollary 2. *Let $P_k, Q_k \in \mathcal{A}(\mathcal{M})$ ($k = 1, 2, \cdots, n$). Then,*

$$\omega_e^2(Q_1^* P_1, \cdots, Q_n^* P_n) \leq \frac{1}{2} \left\| \sum_{k=1}^{n} \left(|P_k|^4 + |Q_k|^4 \right) \right\| \tag{18}$$

for all $\beta \in [0, 1]$.

Proof. Setting $\beta = 1$ in (17). □

Theorem 2. *Let $P_k, Q_k \in \mathscr{A}(\mathscr{M})$ ($k = 1, 2, \cdots, n$). Then,*

$$\omega_e^{2r}(Q_1^*P_1, \cdots, Q_n^*P_n) \leq \frac{1}{2^r}(1-\beta)^r \omega_e^r(Q_1^*P_1, \cdots, Q_n^*P_n) \left\| \sum_{k=1}^n \left(|P_k|^2 + |Q_k|^2\right)^2 \right\|^{\frac{r}{2}}$$
$$+ \frac{1}{2^r}\beta^r \left\| \sum_{k=1}^n \left(|P_k|^4 + |Q_k|^4\right) \right\|^r \quad (19)$$

for all $\beta, r \in [0,1]$.

Proof. Form the proof of Theorem 1. Since $t \mapsto t^r$ ($t > 0$)) for subadditive for all $r \in [0,1]$, then we have

$$\left(\sum_{k=1}^n |\langle Q_k^* P_k u, u \rangle|^2\right)^r$$
$$\leq \left(\frac{1}{2}(1-\beta)\left(\sum_{k=1}^n |\langle Q_k^* P_k u, u \rangle|^2\right)^{\frac{1}{2}} \left\langle \left[\sum_{k=1}^n \left(|P_k|^2 + |Q_k|^2\right)^2\right]u, u\right\rangle^{\frac{1}{2}}\right.$$
$$\left. + \frac{1}{2}\beta \left\langle \left[\sum_{k=1}^n \left(|P_k|^4 + |Q_k|^4\right)\right]u, u\right\rangle\right)^r$$
$$\leq \frac{1}{2^r}(1-\beta)^r \left(\sum_{k=1}^n |\langle Q_k^* P_k u, u \rangle|^2\right)^{\frac{r}{2}} \left\langle \left[\sum_{k=1}^n \left(|P_k|^2 + |Q_k|^2\right)^2\right]u, u\right\rangle^{\frac{r}{2}}$$
$$+ \frac{1}{2^r}\beta^r \left\langle \left[\sum_{k=1}^n \left(|P_k|^4 + |Q_k|^4\right)\right]u, u\right\rangle^r$$

Taking the supremum over all unit vectors $u \in \mathscr{M}$, we obtain the desired result. □

Another interesting inequality involving the product of two Hilbert space operators is elaborated in the following result that refines (7).

Theorem 3. *Let $P_k, Q_k \in \mathscr{A}(\mathscr{M})$ ($k = 1, 2, \cdots, n$), $r \geq 1$ and $\beta \in [0,1]$. Then,*

$$\omega_e^{2r}(Q_1^*P_1, \cdots, Q_n^*P_n) \tag{20}$$
$$\leq \frac{1}{2}\beta \left\|\sum_{k=1}^n \left(|P_k|^{4r} + |Q_k|^{4r}\right)\right\| + \frac{1}{\sqrt{2}}(1-\beta)\omega_e^r(Q_1^*P_1, \ldots, Q_n^*P_n)\left\|\sum_{k=1}^n \left(|P_k|^{4r} + |Q_k|^{4r}\right)\right\|^{\frac{1}{2}}$$
$$\leq \frac{1}{2}\left\|\sum_{k=1}^n \left(|P_k|^{4r} + |Q_k|^{4r}\right)\right\|.$$

Proof. Employing (7), then, for all $\beta \in [0,1]$, we have

$$\omega_e^{2r}(Q_1^* P_1, \ldots, S_n^* P_n)$$
$$= \beta \omega_e^{2r}(Q_1^* P_1, \ldots, Q_n^* P_n) + (1-\beta)\omega_e^{2r}(Q_1^* P_1, \ldots, Q_n^* P_n)$$
$$= \beta \omega_e^{2r}(Q_1^* P_1, \ldots, Q_n^* P_n) + (1-\beta)\omega_e^r(Q_1^* P_1, \ldots, Q_n^* P_n)\omega_e^r(Q_1^* P_1, \ldots, S_n^* P_n)$$
$$\leq \frac{1}{2}\beta \left\| \sum_{k=1}^n \left(|P_k|^{4r} + |Q_k|^{4r}\right)\right\| + \frac{1}{\sqrt{2}}(1-\beta)\omega_e^r(Q_1^* P_1, \ldots, Q_n^* P_n)\left\|\sum_{k=1}^n \left(|P_k|^{4r} + |Q_k|^{4r}\right)\right\|^{\frac{1}{2}}$$
$$\leq \frac{1}{2}\left\|\sum_{k=1}^n \left(|P_k|^{4r} + |Q_k|^{4r}\right)\right\|,$$

where the first and second inequalities follow from (7), which proves (20). □

Now, we present some inequalities concerning the numerical radius of Hilbert space operators beginning with generalizing (15).

Theorem 4. *Let $P_k \in \mathscr{A}(\mathscr{M})$ $(k = 1, \cdots, n)$. Then,*

$$w_{2p}^{2p}(P_1, \ldots, P_k) \leq \frac{1}{2}w_p^p\left(P_1^2, \ldots, P_k^2\right) + \frac{1}{2^{p+1}}\left\|\sum_{k=1}^n \left(|P_k|^2 + |P_k^*|^2\right)^p\right\|. \tag{21}$$

for all $p \geq 1$. In particular, we have

$$w_e^2(P_1, \ldots, P_k) \leq \frac{1}{2}w_R\left(P_1^2, \ldots, P_k^2\right) + \frac{1}{4}\left\|\sum_{k=1}^n \left(|P_k|^2 + |P_k^*|^2\right)\right\|. \tag{22}$$

Proof. Replacing P with P_k in (15), we obtain

$$|\langle P_k c, c\rangle|^{2p} \leq \left(\frac{1}{2}\left|\langle P_k^2 c, c\rangle\right| + \frac{1}{2}\left\langle \frac{\left(|P_k|^2 + |P_k^*|^2\right)}{2} c, c\right\rangle\right)^p$$
$$\leq \frac{1}{2}\left[\left|\langle P_k^2 c, c\rangle\right|^p + \frac{1}{2^p}\left\langle \left(|P_k|^2 + |P_k^*|^2\right)c, c\right\rangle^p\right]$$
$$\leq \frac{1}{2}\left[\left|\langle P_k^2 c, c\rangle\right|^p + \frac{1}{2^p}\left\langle \left(|P_k|^2 + |P_k^*|^2\right)^p c, c\right\rangle\right]$$

Summing over k, we obtain

$$\sum_{k=1}^n |\langle P_k c, c\rangle|^{2p} \leq \frac{1}{2}\left[\sum_{k=1}^n \left|\langle P_k^2 c, c\rangle\right|^p + \frac{1}{2^p}\sum_{k=1}^n \left\langle \left(|P_k|^2 + |P_k^*|^2\right)^p c, c\right\rangle\right]$$
$$= \frac{1}{2}\left[\sum_{k=1}^n \left|\langle P_k^2 c, c\rangle\right|^p + \frac{1}{2^p}\left\langle \sum_{k=1}^n \left(|P_k|^2 + |P_k^*|^2\right)^p c, c\right\rangle\right]$$

Taking the supremum over all unit vectors $c \in \mathscr{M}$, we have

$$w_{2p}^{2p}(P_1, \ldots, P_k) \leq \frac{1}{2}w_p^p\left(P_1^2, \ldots, P_k^2\right) + \frac{1}{2^{p+1}}\left\|\sum_{k=1}^n \left(|P_k|^2 + |P_k^*|^2\right)^p\right\|,$$

and this yields (21); the particular case follows by setting $p = 1$ in (21). □

Example 1. Let $P_1 = \begin{bmatrix} 0 & 2 \\ 1 & 0 \end{bmatrix}$ and $P_2 = \begin{bmatrix} 0 & 0 \\ 2 & 0 \end{bmatrix}$ be 2×2-matrices. Employing (20) with $n = 2$, and $p = 1$, we have

$$\omega_e^2(P_1, P_2) = \sup_{\|z\|=1} \left(|\langle P_1 z, z\rangle|^2 + |\langle P_2 z, z\rangle|^2 \right) = 3.25,$$

$$w_R\left(P_1^2, P_2^2\right) = 2$$

$$\left\| \sum_{k=1}^{2} \left(|P_k|^2 + |P_k^*|^2 \right) \right\| = 9.$$

Thus,

$$1.802 = \omega_e(P_1, P_2) \leq \frac{1}{2} w_R(P_1, P_2) + \frac{1}{4} \left\| \sum_{k=1}^{2} \left(|P_k|^2 + |P_k^*|^2 \right) \right\| = 1.802$$

which gives the exact value for $\omega_e(P_1, P_2)$ in this example. In fact, our bound improves both estimates given in (5) and (6).

Corollary 3. Let $P_k, Q_k \in \mathscr{A}(\mathscr{M})$ $(k = 1, \cdots, n)$. Then,

$$w_{2p}^{2p}(Q_1^* P_1, \ldots, Q_k^* P_k)$$
$$\leq \frac{1}{2} w_R^p\left((Q_1^* P_1)^2, \ldots, (Q_1^* P_k)^2\right) + \frac{1}{2^{p+1}} \left\| \sum_{k=1}^{n} \left(|Q_k^* P_k|^2 + |P_k^* Q_k|^2 \right)^p \right\|. \quad (23)$$

for all $p \geq 1$. In particular, we have

$$w_e^2(Q_1^* P_1, \ldots, Q_k^* P_k)$$
$$\leq \frac{1}{2} w_R\left((Q_1^* P_1)^2, \ldots, (Q_1^* P_k)^2\right) + \frac{1}{4} \left\| \sum_{k=1}^{n} \left(|Q_k^* P_k|^2 + |P_k^* Q_k|^2 \right)^p \right\|. \quad (24)$$

Theorem 5. Let $P_k \in \mathscr{A}(\mathscr{M})$ $(k = 1, \cdots, n)$. Then,

$$\omega_e^2(P_1, \cdots, P_n) \leq \beta \left\| \sum_{k=1}^{n} \left(\alpha |P_k|^2 + (1-\alpha)|P_k^*|^2 \right) \right\|$$
$$+ \frac{1}{2}(1-\beta)\omega_e(P_1, \cdots, P_n) \left\| \sum_{k=1}^{n} \left(|P_k|^{2\alpha} + |P_k^*|^{2(1-\alpha)} \right)^2 \right\|^{\frac{1}{2}} \quad (25)$$

for all $0 \leq \alpha, \beta \leq 1$.

Proof. Let $c \in \mathcal{M}$ be a unit vector. Setting $d = c$ in (13), it follows that

$$\begin{aligned}
|\langle P_k c, c \rangle|^2 &\leq \beta \langle |P_k|^{2\alpha} c, c \rangle \langle |P_k^*|^{2(1-\alpha)} c, c \rangle \\
&\quad + (1-\beta) |\langle P_k c, c \rangle| \sqrt{\langle |P_k|^{2\alpha} c, c \rangle \langle |P_k^*|^{2(1-\alpha)} c, c \rangle} \\
&\leq \beta \langle |P_k|^2 c, c \rangle^{\alpha} \langle |P_k^*|^2 c, c \rangle^{(1-\alpha)} \qquad \text{(by (11))} \\
&\quad + (1-\beta) |\langle P_k c, c \rangle| \cdot \frac{1}{2} \left(\langle |P_k|^{2\alpha} c, c \rangle + \langle |P_k^*|^{2(1-\alpha)} c, c \rangle \right) \qquad \text{(by (10))} \\
&\leq \beta \left[\alpha \langle |P_k|^2 c, c \rangle + (1-\alpha) \langle |P_k^*|^2 c, c \rangle \right] \qquad \text{(by (10))} \\
&\quad + \frac{1}{2}(1-\beta) |\langle P_k c, c \rangle| \langle \left(|P_k|^{2\alpha} + |P_k^*|^{2(1-\alpha)} \right) c, c \rangle \\
&= \beta \langle \left(\alpha |P_k|^2 + (1-\alpha) |P_k^*|^2 \right) c, c \rangle \\
&\quad + \frac{1}{2}(1-\beta) |\langle P_k c, c \rangle| \langle \left(|P_k|^{2\alpha} + |P_k^*|^{2(1-\alpha)} \right) c, c \rangle.
\end{aligned}$$

Summing over $k = 1$ up to $k = n$ and then applying the Cauchy–Schwarz inequality for real numbers, we obtain

$$\begin{aligned}
\sum_{k=1}^{n} |\langle P_k c, c \rangle|^2 &\leq \beta \sum_{k=1}^{n} \langle \left(\alpha |P_k|^2 + (1-\alpha) |P_k^*|^2 \right) c, c \rangle \\
&\quad + \frac{1}{2}(1-\beta) \sum_{k=1}^{n} |\langle P_k c, c \rangle| \langle \left(|P_k|^{2\alpha} + |P_k^*|^{2(1-\alpha)} \right) c, c \rangle \\
&\leq \beta \langle \sum_{k=1}^{n} \left(\alpha |P_k|^2 + (1-\alpha) |P_k^*|^2 \right) c, c \rangle \\
&\quad + \frac{1}{2}(1-\beta) \left(\sum_{k=1}^{n} |\langle P_k c, c \rangle|^2 \right)^{\frac{1}{2}} \left(\sum_{k=1}^{n} \langle \left(|P_k|^{2\alpha} + |P_k^*|^{2(1-\alpha)} \right) c, c \rangle^2 \right)^{\frac{1}{2}} \\
&\leq \beta \langle \left[\sum_{k=1}^{n} \left(\alpha |P_k|^2 + (1-\alpha) |P_k^*|^2 \right) \right] c, c \rangle \\
&\quad + \frac{1}{2}(1-\beta) \left(\sum_{k=1}^{n} |\langle P_k c, c \rangle|^2 \right)^{\frac{1}{2}} \left(\langle \left[\sum_{k=1}^{n} \left(|P_k|^{2\alpha} + |P_k^*|^{2(1-\alpha)} \right)^2 \right] c, c \rangle \right)^{\frac{1}{2}}
\end{aligned}$$

Taking the supremum over all unit vectors $c \in \mathcal{M}$, we obtain the required result in (25). □

The following result extends and generalizes the Kittaneh–Moradi inequality [5] for the Euclidean operator radius.

Corollary 4. Let $P_k \in \mathscr{A}(\mathcal{M})$ ($k = 1, 2, \cdots, n$). Then,

$$\omega_e^2(P_1, \cdots, P_n) \leq \frac{1}{6} \left\| \sum_{k=1}^{n} \left(|P_k|^2 + |P_k^*|^2 \right) \right\| + \frac{1}{3} \omega_e(P_1, \cdots, P_n) \left\| \sum_{k=1}^{n} \left(|P_k|^{2\alpha} + |P_k^*|^{2(1-\alpha)} \right)^2 \right\|^{\frac{1}{2}} \qquad (26)$$

for all $0 \leq \alpha, \beta \leq 1$.

Example 2. Let $P_1 = \begin{bmatrix} 0 & 2 \\ 1 & 0 \end{bmatrix}$ and $P_2 = \begin{bmatrix} 0 & 0 \\ 2 & 0 \end{bmatrix}$ be 2×2-matrices. Employing (26) with $n = 2$, $\alpha = \frac{1}{2}$ and $p = 1$, we obtain

$$\omega_e^2(P_1, P_2) = \sup_{\|z\|=1} \left(|\langle P_1 z, z \rangle|^2 + |\langle P_2 z, z \rangle|^2 \right) = 3.25.$$

However,

$$1.8027 = \omega_e(P_1, P_2)$$
$$\leq \left(\frac{1}{6} \left\| |P_1|^2 + |P_1^*|^2 + |P_2|^2 + |P_2^*|^2 \right\| + \frac{1}{3} \omega_e(P_1, P_2) \left\| (|P_1| + |P_1^*|)^2 + (|P_2| + |P_2^*|)^2 \right\|^{1/2} \right)^{1/2}$$
$$= 1.97577$$

However, the upper bound in (5) gives 2.5495 and that in (6) gives 2.1213, and this verifies that our bound in (26) is better than both estimates given in (5) and (6).

A refinement of (6) with $p = 2$ is incorporated in the following result.

Theorem 6. *Let $P_k \in \mathscr{A}(\mathscr{M})$. Then,*

$$\omega_e^2(P_1, \cdots, P_n)$$
$$\leq \beta \left\| \sum_{k=1}^n \left(\alpha |P_k|^2 + (1-\alpha)|P_k^*|^2 \right) \right\| + (1-\beta)\omega_e(P_1, \cdots, P_n) \left\| \sum_{k=1}^n \left(\alpha|P_k|^2 + (1-\alpha)|P_k^*|^2 \right) \right\|^{\frac{1}{2}} \quad (27)$$
$$\leq \left\| \sum_{k=1}^n \left(\alpha|P_k|^2 + (1-\alpha)|P_k^*|^2 \right) \right\|$$

for all $0 \leq \alpha, \beta \leq 1$.

Proof. Let $c \in \mathscr{M}$ be a unit vector. Setting $d = c$ in (13), it follows that

$$|\langle P_k c, c \rangle|^2 \leq \beta \langle |P_k|^{2\alpha} c, c \rangle \langle |P_k^*|^{2(1-\alpha)} c, c \rangle$$
$$+ (1-\beta)|\langle P_k c, c \rangle| \sqrt{\langle |P_k|^{2\alpha} c, c \rangle \langle |P_k^*|^{2(1-\alpha)} c, c \rangle}$$
$$\leq \beta \langle |P_k|^2 c, c \rangle^\alpha \langle |P_k^*|^2 c, c \rangle^{(1-\alpha)} \qquad \text{(by (11))}$$
$$+ (1-\beta)|\langle P_k c, c \rangle| \sqrt{\langle |P_k|^2 c, c \rangle^\alpha \langle |P_k^*|^2 c, c \rangle^{(1-\alpha)}}$$
$$\leq \beta \langle \left(\alpha|P_k|^2 + (1-\alpha)|P_k^*|^2 \right) c, c \rangle$$
$$+ (1-\beta)|\langle P_k c, c \rangle| \sqrt{\langle \left(\alpha|P_k|^2 + (1-\alpha)|P_k^*|^2 \right) c, c \rangle}. \qquad \text{(by (10))}$$

Summing over $k = 1$ up to $k = n$ and then applying the Cauchy–Schwarz inequality for real numbers, we obtain

$$\sum_{k=1}^{n} |\langle P_k c, c \rangle|^2 \leq \beta \sum_{k=1}^{n} \left\langle \left(\alpha |P_k|^2 + (1-\alpha) |P_k^*|^2 \right) c, c \right\rangle$$
$$+ (1-\beta) \sum_{k=1}^{n} |\langle P_k c, c \rangle| \sqrt{\left\langle \left(\alpha |P_k|^2 + (1-\alpha) |P_k^*|^2 \right) c, c \right\rangle}$$
$$\leq \beta \left\langle \left[\sum_{k=1}^{n} \left(\alpha |P_k|^2 + (1-\alpha) |P_k^*|^2 \right) \right] c, c \right\rangle$$
$$+ (1-\beta) \left(\sum_{k=1}^{n} |\langle P_k c, c \rangle|^2 \right)^{\frac{1}{2}} \left(\sum_{k=1}^{n} \left\langle \left(\alpha |P_k|^2 + (1-\alpha) |P_k^*|^2 \right) c, c \right\rangle \right)^{\frac{1}{2}}$$
$$= \beta \left\langle \left[\sum_{k=1}^{n} \left(\alpha |P_k|^2 + (1-\alpha) |P_k^*|^2 \right) \right] c, c \right\rangle$$
$$+ (1-\beta) \left(\sum_{k=1}^{n} |\langle P_k c, c \rangle|^2 \right)^{\frac{1}{2}} \left\langle \left[\sum_{k=1}^{n} \left(\alpha |P_k|^2 + (1-\alpha) |P_k^*|^2 \right) \right] c, c \right\rangle^{\frac{1}{2}}$$

Taking the supremum over all unit vectors $c \in \mathscr{M}$, we obtain the first in (27). To obtain the second inequality from the first inequality, we have

$$\omega_e^2(P_1, \cdots, P_n) \leq \beta \left\| \sum_{k=1}^{n} \left(\alpha |P_k|^2 + (1-\alpha) |P_k^*|^2 \right) \right\|$$
$$+ (1-\beta) \omega_e(P_1, \cdots, P_n) \left\| \sum_{k=1}^{n} \left(\alpha |P_k|^2 + (1-\alpha) |P_k^*|^2 \right) \right\|^{\frac{1}{2}}$$
$$\leq \left\| \sum_{k=1}^{n} \left(\alpha |P_k|^2 + (1-\alpha) |P_k^*|^2 \right) \right\| \quad \text{(by (6) with } p = 2\text{)}$$

which proves the required result. $\square$

A refinement of (5) with $p = 2$ is incorporated in the following result.

Theorem 7. *Let* $P \in \mathscr{A}(\mathscr{M})$. *Then,*

$$\omega_e^2(P_1, \cdots, P_n) \leq \frac{1}{2} \beta \left\| \sum_{k=1}^{n} \left(|P_k|^{4\alpha} + |P_k^*|^{4(1-\alpha)} \right) \right\|$$
$$+ \frac{1}{\sqrt{2}} (1-\beta) \omega_e(P_1, \cdots, P_n) \left\| \sum_{k=1}^{n} \left(|P_k|^{4\alpha} + |P_k^*|^{4(1-\alpha)} \right) \right\|^{\frac{1}{2}} \quad (28)$$

for all $0 \leq \alpha, \beta \leq 1$.

Proof. Let $c \in \mathcal{M}$ be a unit vector. Setting $d = c$ and $p = 2$ in (13), it follows that

$$|\langle P_k c, c \rangle|^2 \leq \beta \langle |P_k|^{4\alpha} c, c \rangle^{\frac{1}{2}} \langle |P_k^*|^{4(1-\alpha)} c, c \rangle^{\frac{1}{2}}$$
$$+ (1-\beta)|\langle P_k c, c \rangle| \sqrt{\langle |P_k|^{4\alpha} c, c \rangle^{\frac{1}{2}} \langle |P_k^*|^{4(1-\alpha)} c, c \rangle^{\frac{1}{2}}}$$
$$\leq \frac{1}{2}\beta \left(\langle |P_k|^{4\alpha} c, c \rangle + \langle |P_k^*|^{4(1-\alpha)} c, c \rangle \right)$$
$$+ \frac{1}{\sqrt{2}}(1-\beta)|\langle P_k c, c \rangle| \sqrt{\left(\langle |P_k|^{4\alpha} c, c \rangle + \langle |P_k^*|^{4(1-\alpha)} c, c \rangle \right)} \quad \text{(by (10))}$$
$$\leq \frac{1}{2}\beta \left\langle \left(|P_k|^{4\alpha} + |P_k^*|^{4(1-\alpha)} \right) c, c \right\rangle$$
$$+ \frac{1}{\sqrt{2}}(1-\beta)|\langle P_k c, c \rangle| \sqrt{\left\langle \left(|P_k|^{4\alpha} + |P_k^*|^{4(1-\alpha)} \right) c, c \right\rangle}.$$

Summing over $k = 1$ up to $k = n$ and then applying the Cauchy–Schwarz inequality for real numbers, we have

$$\sum_{k=1}^n |\langle P_k c, c \rangle|^2 \leq \frac{1}{2}\beta \sum_{k=1}^n \left\langle \left(|P_k|^{4\alpha} + |P_k^*|^{4(1-\alpha)} \right) c, c \right\rangle$$
$$+ \frac{1}{\sqrt{2}}(1-\beta) \sum_{k=1}^n |\langle P_k c, c \rangle| \sqrt{\left\langle \left(|P_k|^{4\alpha} + |P_k^*|^{4(1-\alpha)} \right) c, c \right\rangle}$$
$$\leq \frac{1}{2}\beta \left\langle \left[\sum_{k=1}^n \left(|P_k|^{4\alpha} + |P_k^*|^{4(1-\alpha)} \right) \right] c, c \right\rangle$$
$$+ \frac{1}{\sqrt{2}}(1-\beta) \left(\sum_{k=1}^n |\langle P_k c, c \rangle|^2 \right)^{\frac{1}{2}} \left(\sum_{k=1}^n \left\langle \left(|P_k|^{4\alpha} + |P_k^*|^{4(1-\alpha)} \right) c, c \right\rangle \right)^{\frac{1}{2}}$$
$$= \frac{1}{2}\beta \left\langle \left[\sum_{k=1}^n \left(|P_k|^{4\alpha} + |P_k^*|^{4(1-\alpha)} \right) \right] c, c \right\rangle$$
$$+ \frac{1}{\sqrt{2}}(1-\beta) \left(\sum_{k=1}^n |\langle P_k c, c \rangle|^2 \right)^{\frac{1}{2}} \left\langle \left[\sum_{k=1}^n \left(|P_k|^{4\alpha} + |P_k^*|^{4(1-\alpha)} \right) \right] c, c \right\rangle^{\frac{1}{2}}$$

Taking the supremum over all unit vectors $c \in \mathcal{M}$, we obtain the required result. □

Corollary 5. *Let $P_k \in \mathcal{A}(\mathcal{M})$. Then,*

$$\omega_e^2(P_1, \cdots, P_n) \leq \frac{1}{2}\beta \left\| \sum_{k=1}^n \left(|P_k|^{4\alpha} + |P_k^*|^{4(1-\alpha)} \right) \right\|$$
$$+ \frac{1}{\sqrt{2}}(1-\beta)\omega_e(P_1, \cdots, P_n) \left\| \sum_{k=1}^n \left(|P_k|^{4\alpha} + |P_k^*|^{4(1-\alpha)} \right) \right\|^{\frac{1}{2}}$$
$$\leq \frac{1}{2} \left\| |P_k|^{4\alpha} + |P_k^*|^{4(1-\alpha)} \right\|$$

for all $p \geq 1$ and $0 \leq \alpha, \beta \leq 1$.

Proof. From (28), we have

$$\omega_e^2(P_1, \cdots, P_n) \leq \frac{1}{2}\beta \left\| \sum_{k=1}^n \left(|P_k|^{4\alpha} + |P_k^*|^{4(1-\alpha)} \right) \right\|$$
$$+ \frac{1}{\sqrt{2}}(1-\beta)\omega_e(P_1, \cdots, P_n) \left\| \sum_{k=1}^n \left(|P_k|^{4\alpha} + |P_k^*|^{4(1-\alpha)} \right) \right\|^{\frac{1}{2}}$$
$$\leq \frac{1}{2}\beta \left\| \sum_{k=1}^n \left(|P_k|^{4\alpha} + |P_k^*|^{4(1-\alpha)} \right) \right\|$$
$$+ \frac{1}{2}(1-\beta) \left\| \sum_{k=1}^n \left(|P_k|^{4\alpha} + |P_k^*|^{4(1-\alpha)} \right) \right\| \quad \text{(by (28) with } \beta = 0\text{)}$$
$$= \frac{1}{2} \left\| |P_k|^{4\alpha} + |P_k^*|^{4(1-\alpha)} \right\|,$$

as required. □

The following two results extend the generalized Kittaneh–Moradi inequality (26).

Theorem 8. *Let* $P_k \in \mathscr{A}(\mathscr{M})$ $(k = 1, 2, \cdots, n)$. *Then,*

$$\omega_e^2(P_1, \cdots, P_n) \leq \frac{1}{2}\beta \left\| \sum_{k=1}^n \left(|P_k|^{4\alpha} + |P_k^*|^{4(1-\alpha)} \right) \right\|$$
$$+ \frac{1}{2}(1-\beta)\omega_e(P_1, \cdots, P_n) \left\| \sum_{k=1}^n \left(|P_k|^{2\alpha} + |P_k^*|^{2(1-\alpha)} \right)^2 \right\|^{\frac{1}{2}} \quad (29)$$

for all $0 \leq \alpha, \beta \leq 1$.

Proof. Let $c \in \mathscr{M}$ be a unit vector. Setting $d = c$ in (12) with $p = 1$, it follows that

$$|\langle P_k c, c \rangle|^2 \leq \beta \langle |P_k|^{2\alpha} c, c \rangle \langle |P_k^*|^{2(1-\alpha)} c, c \rangle$$
$$+ (1-\beta)|\langle P_k c, c \rangle| \sqrt{\langle |P_k|^{2\alpha} c, c \rangle \langle |P_k^*|^{2(1-\alpha)} c, c \rangle}$$
$$\leq \frac{1}{2}\beta \left(\langle |P_k|^{2\alpha} c, c \rangle^2 + \langle |P_k^*|^{2(1-\alpha)} c, c \rangle^2 \right) \quad \text{(by (10))}$$
$$+ \frac{1}{2}(1-\beta)|\langle P_k c, c \rangle| \left\langle \left(|P_k|^{2\alpha} + |P_k^*|^{2(1-\alpha)} \right) c, c \right\rangle \quad \text{(by (10))}$$
$$\leq \frac{1}{2}\beta \left\langle |P_k|^{4\alpha} c, c \right\rangle + \left\langle |P_k^*|^{4(1-\alpha)} c, c \right\rangle \quad \text{(by (11))}$$
$$+ \frac{1}{2}(1-\beta)|\langle P_k c, c \rangle| \left\langle \left(|P_k|^{2\alpha} + |P_k^*|^{2(1-\alpha)} \right) c, c \right\rangle$$
$$= \frac{1}{2}\beta \left\langle \left(|P_k|^{4\alpha} + |P_k^*|^{4(1-\alpha)} \right) c, c \right\rangle$$
$$+ \frac{1}{2}(1-\beta)|\langle P_k c, c \rangle| \left\langle \left(|P_k|^{2\alpha} + |P_k^*|^{2(1-\alpha)} \right) c, c \right\rangle$$

Summing over $k = 1$ up to $k = n$, and then applying the Cauchy–Schwarz inequality for real numbers, we obtain

$$\sum_{k=1}^{n}|\langle P_k c, c\rangle|^2 \leq \frac{1}{2}\beta \sum_{k=1}^{n}\left\langle \left(|P_k|^{4\alpha} + |P_k^*|^{4(1-\alpha)}\right)c, c\right\rangle$$
$$+ \frac{1}{2}(1-\beta) \sum_{k=1}^{n}\left(|\langle P_k c, c\rangle|\left\langle \left(|P_k|^{2\alpha} + |P_k^*|^{2(1-\alpha)}\right)c, c\right\rangle\right)$$
$$\leq \frac{1}{2}\beta \left\langle \left[\sum_{k=1}^{n}\left(|P_k|^{4\alpha} + |P_k^*|^{4(1-\alpha)}\right)\right]c, c\right\rangle$$
$$+ \frac{1}{2}(1-\beta)\left(\sum_{k=1}^{n}|\langle P_k c, c\rangle|^2\right)^{\frac{1}{2}}\left(\sum_{k=1}^{n}\left\langle \left(|P_k|^{2\alpha} + |P_k^*|^{2(1-\alpha)}\right)c, c\right\rangle^2\right)^{\frac{1}{2}}$$
$$\leq \frac{1}{2}\beta \left\langle \left[\sum_{k=1}^{n}\left(|P_k|^{4\alpha} + |P_k^*|^{4(1-\alpha)}\right)\right]c, c\right\rangle$$
$$+ \frac{1}{2}(1-\beta)\left(\sum_{k=1}^{n}|\langle P_k c, c\rangle|^2\right)^{\frac{1}{2}}\left(\sum_{k=1}^{n}\left\langle \left(|P_k|^{2\alpha} + |P_k^*|^{2(1-\alpha)}\right)^2 c, c\right\rangle\right)^{\frac{1}{2}}$$
$$= \frac{1}{2}\beta\left\langle \left[\sum_{k=1}^{n}\left(|P_k|^{4\alpha} + |P_k^*|^{4(1-\alpha)}\right)\right]c, c\right\rangle$$
$$+ \frac{1}{2}(1-\beta)\left(\sum_{k=1}^{n}|\langle P_k c, c\rangle|^2\right)^{\frac{1}{2}}\left\langle \left[\sum_{k=1}^{n}\left(|P_k|^{2\alpha} + |P_k^*|^{2(1-\alpha)}\right)^2\right]c, c\right\rangle^{\frac{1}{2}}.$$

We obtain the required result by taking the supremum over all unit vectors $c \in \mathscr{M}$. □

Alomari [24] proved a refinement of Kittaneh–Moradi [27], which is better than the result of Kittaneh and Moradi. An extension of Alomari's inequality (3.9, Ref. [24]) to the Euclidean operator radius is considered in the following result.

Theorem 9. Let $P_k \in \mathscr{A}(\mathscr{M})$ $(k = 1, 2, \cdots, n)$. Then,

$$\omega_e^2(P_1, \cdots, P_n) \leq \frac{1}{4}\lambda \left\|\sum_{i=1}^{n}\left(|P_i|^{2\alpha} + |P_i^*|^{2(1-\alpha)}\right)^2\right\|$$
$$+ \frac{1}{2}(1-\lambda)\omega_e(P_1, \cdots, P_n)\left\|\sum_{k=1}^{n}\left(|P_k|^{2\alpha} + |P_k^*|^{2(1-\alpha)}\right)^2\right\|^{\frac{1}{2}} \quad (30)$$

for all $\lambda \in [0, 1]$. In particular, we have

$$\omega_e^2(P_1, \cdots, P_n) \leq \frac{1}{12}\left\|\sum_{i=1}^{n}\left(|P_i|^{2\alpha} + |P_i^*|^{2(1-\alpha)}\right)^2\right\|$$
$$+ \frac{1}{3}\omega_e(P_1, \cdots, P_n)\left\|\sum_{k=1}^{n}\left(|P_k|^{2\alpha} + |P_k^*|^{2(1-\alpha)}\right)^2\right\|^{\frac{1}{2}} \quad (31)$$
$$\leq \frac{1}{2}\left\|\sum_{k=1}^{n}\left(|P_k|^{2\alpha} + |P_k^*|^{2(1-\alpha)}\right)^2\right\|.$$

Proof. Form (29) and (5), and for all $\lambda \in [0,1]$, we have

$$\omega_e^2(P_1, \cdots, P_n)$$
$$= (1-\lambda)\omega_e^2(P_1, \ldots, P_n) + \lambda \omega_e^2(P_1, \ldots, P_n)$$
$$\leq \frac{1}{2}(1-\lambda)\beta \left\| \sum_{k=1}^{n} \left(|P_k|^{4\alpha} + |P_k^*|^{4(1-\alpha)} \right) \right\|$$
$$+ \frac{1}{2}(1-\lambda)(1-\beta)\omega_e(P_1, \cdots, P_n) \left\| \sum_{k=1}^{n} \left(|P_k|^{2\alpha} + |P_k^*|^{2(1-\alpha)} \right)^2 \right\|^{\frac{1}{2}}$$
$$+ \frac{1}{4}\lambda \left\| \sum_{i=1}^{n} \left(|P_i|^{2\alpha} + |P_i^*|^{2(1-\alpha)} \right)^2 \right\| \qquad \text{(by (5) with } p=2\text{)}$$

Setting $\beta = 0$, we obtain

$$\omega_e^2(P_1, \cdots, P_n)$$
$$\leq \frac{1}{4}\lambda \left\| \sum_{i=1}^{n} \left(|P_i|^{2\alpha} + |P_i^*|^{2(1-\alpha)} \right)^2 \right\| + \frac{1}{2}(1-\lambda)\omega_e(P_1, \cdots, P_n) \left\| \sum_{k=1}^{n} \left(|P_k|^{2\alpha} + |P_k^*|^{2(1-\alpha)} \right)^2 \right\|^{\frac{1}{2}}$$

which gives the required result. The particular case follows by choosing $\lambda = \frac{1}{3}$. The second inequality in (31) follows directly from (5). □

Hence, as pointed out above, (31) is stronger than (26), as well as (31) is much better than the inequalities (5) and (29).

Example 3. Let $C_1 = \begin{bmatrix} 0 & 2 \\ 1 & 0 \end{bmatrix}$ and $C_2 = \begin{bmatrix} 0 & 0 \\ 2 & 0 \end{bmatrix}$ be 2×2-matrices. Employing (31) with $n = 2$, $\alpha = \frac{1}{2}$ and $p = 2$, we obtain

$$\omega_e^2(C_1, C_2) = \sup_{\|z\|=1} \left(|\langle C_1 z, z \rangle|^2 + |\langle C_2 z, z \rangle|^2 \right) = 3.25,$$

$$1.802775638 = \omega_e(C_1, C_2) \leq \sqrt{\frac{1}{12} \left\| \sum_{i=1}^{2} (|C_i| + |C_i^*|)^2 \right\| + \frac{1}{3}\omega_e(C_1, C_2) \left\| \sum_{k=1}^{2} (|C_k| + |C_k^*|)^2 \right\|^{\frac{1}{2}}}$$
$$= 1.802775638$$
$$\leq \sqrt{\frac{1}{2} \left\| \sum_{k=1}^{2} (|C_k| + |C_k^*|)^2 \right\|} = 2.549509757.$$

Fortunately, our bound in (31) gives the exact value of $\omega_e(C_1, C_2)$, which, as shown, is better than both estimates given by (5) and (6) (see Example 2). Moreover, this example proves that our inequality in (31) is better than (26).

Remark 1. All obtained results of Section 3 are valid for the generalized Euclidean operator radius $\omega_p(\cdot)$ ($p \geq 1$) by using (12) instead of (13). We leave the rest of the generalizations to the interested reader.

4. The Davis–Wielandt Radius-Type Inequalities

One of the most recent and interesting generalizations of the numerical range of Hilbert space operators is the Davis–Wielandt shell, which is well known as

$$DW(Q) = \{(\langle Qc, c\rangle, \langle Qc, Qc\rangle), c \in \mathcal{M}, \|c\| = 1\}$$

for any $Q \in \mathscr{A}(\mathcal{M})$. Clearly, the projection of the set $DW(Q)$ on the first coordinate is $W(Q)$.

The Davis–Wielandt shell and its radius were introduced and described firstly by Davis in [28,29] and Wielandt [30]. The Davis–Wielandt radius of $Q \in \mathscr{A}(\mathcal{M})$ is defined as

$$dw(Q) = \sup_{\substack{c \in \mathcal{M} \\ \|c\|=1}} \left\{ \sqrt{|\langle Qc, c\rangle|^2 + \|Qc\|^4} \right\}.$$

One can easily check that $dw(Q)$ is unitarily invariant, but it does not define a norm on $\mathscr{A}(\mathcal{M})$.

It is shown that [25]

$$\max\left\{\omega(Q), \|Q\|^2\right\} \leq dw(Q) \leq \sqrt{\omega^2(Q) + \|Q\|^4} \qquad (32)$$

for all $Q \in \mathscr{A}(\mathcal{M})$. The inequalities are sharp. For further results concerning Davis–Wielandt radius inequalities, the reader may refer to [12,13,15,18,31–40].

The Euclidean Davis–Wielandt radius has been introduced in [19]. In fact, for an n-tuple $\mathbf{M} = (M_1, \cdots, M_n) \in \mathscr{A}(\mathcal{M})^n := \mathscr{A}(\mathcal{M}) \times \cdots \times \mathscr{A}(\mathcal{M})$, i.e., for $M_1, \cdots, M_r \in \mathscr{A}(\mathcal{M})$, one of the most interesting generalizations of the Davis–Wielandt radius $dw(\cdot)$ is the Euclidean Davis–Wielandt radius, which is defined as

$$dw_e(M_1, \cdots, M_n) = \sup_{\substack{c \in \mathcal{M} \\ \|c\|=1}} \left(\sum_{i=1}^{n} \left(|\langle M_i c, c\rangle|^2 + \|M_i c\|^4 \right) \right)^{1/2}. \qquad (33)$$

Indeed, a suitable relation between the Euclidean operator radius and the Euclidean Davis–Wielandt radius (33) can be constructed as follows.

For any positive integer n, let $G_i \in \mathscr{A}(\mathcal{M})$ ($i = 1, \cdots, 2n$). Therefore, we have

$$w_e(G_1, \cdots, G_{2n}) := \sup_{\|c\|=1} \left(\sum_{i=1}^{2n} |\langle G_i c, c\rangle|^2 \right)^{1/2} \quad \text{for all } c \in \mathcal{M}.$$

Let $M_i \in \mathscr{A}(\mathcal{M})$ ($i = 1, \cdots, n$). Define the sequence of operators M_i in terms of G_i, such that

$$\begin{aligned}
G_1 &= M_1, & \text{and} && G_2 &= M_1^* M_1; \\
G_3 &= M_2, & \text{and} && G_4 &= M_2^* M_2; \\
G_5 &= M_3, & \text{and} && G_6 &= M_3^* M_3; \\
&\vdots \\
G_{2n-1} &= M_n, & \text{and} && G_{2n} &= M_n^* M_n.
\end{aligned}$$

Now, we have

$$w_e(G_1,\cdots,G_{2n}) := \sup_{\|c\|=1} \left(\sum_{i=1}^{2n} |\langle G_i c,c\rangle|^2\right)^{1/2}$$
$$= \sup_{\|c\|=1} \left(\sum_{i=1}^{n} \left(|\langle M_i c,c\rangle|^2 + |\langle M_i^* M_i c,c\rangle|^2\right)\right)^{1/2}$$
$$= dw_e(M_1,\cdots,M_n).$$

which gives a very elegant relation between the Euclidean operator radius and the Euclidean Davis–Wielandt radius.

In light of the above construction, we have

Theorem 10 ([19]). *[Theorem 3.4] Let $Q_i \in \mathscr{A}(\mathscr{M})$ ($i=1,\cdots,n$). Then,*

$$\max\left\{w_e(Q_1,\cdots,Q_n), w_e\left(|Q_1|^2,\cdots,|Q_n|^2\right)\right\} \leq dw_e(Q_1,\cdots,Q_n)$$
$$\leq w_e(Q_1,\cdots,Q_n) + w_e\left(|Q_1|^2,\cdots,|Q_n|^2\right).$$

One can generalize the results in Section 3 by following the same procedure above. A very powerful inequality has been proven recently by Alomari [19], as follows:

$$\frac{1}{4}\left\|\sum_{k=1}^{n}\left(|Q_k|^2 + |Q_k^*|^2 + 2|Q_k|^4\right)\right\| \leq dw_e^2(Q_1,\cdots,Q_n) \qquad (34)$$
$$\leq \frac{1}{2}\left\|\sum_{k=1}^{n}\left(|Q_k|^2 + |Q_k^*|^2 + 2|Q_k|^4\right)\right\|.$$

We finish our results by obtaining a new bound for the Davis–Wielandt radius $dw(\cdot)$. To do so, we need the following observation.

Lemma 7 ([19]). *[Lemma 2] Let $Q \in \mathscr{A}(\mathscr{M})$. Then,*

$$w_e(Q,Q^*Q) = dw(Q). \qquad (35)$$

Theorem 11. *Let $Q \in \mathscr{A}(\mathscr{M})$. Then,*

$$dw(Q) \leq \sqrt{\frac{w(Q^2) + \|Q\|^4}{2} + \frac{1}{4}\left\||Q|^2 + |Q^*|^2 + 2|Q|^4\right\|}. \qquad (36)$$

Proof. Replacing P with P_k ($k=1,\cdots,n$) in Lemma 5, we obtain

$$|\langle P_k c,c\rangle|^2 \leq \frac{1}{2}\left|\langle P_k^2 c,c\rangle\right| + \frac{1}{4}\left\langle\left(|P_k|^2 + |P_k^*|^2\right)c,c\right\rangle.$$

Summing over k, we obtain

$$\sum_{k=1}^{n}|\langle P_k c,c\rangle|^2 \leq \frac{1}{2}\sum_{k=1}^{n}\left|\langle P_k^2 c,c\rangle\right| + \frac{1}{4}\sum_{k=1}^{n}\left\langle\left(|P_k|^2 + |P_k^*|^2\right)c,c\right\rangle$$
$$= \frac{1}{2}\sum_{k=1}^{n}\left|\langle P_k^2 c,c\rangle\right| + \frac{1}{4}\left\langle\sum_{k=1}^{n}\left(|P_k|^2 + |P_k^*|^2\right)c,c\right\rangle$$

Taking the supremum over all unit vectors $c \in \mathcal{M}$, we have

$$w_e^2(P_1,\ldots,P_k) \leq \frac{1}{2} w_R\left(P_1^2,\ldots,P_k^2\right) + \frac{1}{4}\left\|\sum_{k=1}^n \left(|P_k|^2 + |P_k^*|^2\right)\right\|. \tag{37}$$

For $n = 2$, we have

$$w_e^2(P_1,P_2) \leq \frac{1}{2} w_R\left(P_1^2, P_2^2\right) + \frac{1}{4}\left\|\left(|P_1|^2 + |P_1^*|^2\right) + \left(|P_2|^2 + |P_2^*|^2\right)\right\|. \tag{38}$$

Now, setting $P_1 = Q$ and $P_2 = Q^*Q$ in (38), by Lemma 7, we have

$$dw^2(Q) = w_e^2\left(Q, |Q|^2\right) \leq \frac{1}{2} w_R\left(Q^2, |Q|^4\right) + \frac{1}{4}\left\||Q|^2 + |Q^*|^2 + 2|Q|^4\right\|.$$

However, since

$$w_R\left(Q^2, |Q|^4\right) = \sup_{\|c\|=1}\left\{\left|\langle Q^2 c, c\rangle\right| + \left|\langle |Q|^4 c, c\rangle\right|\right\} \leq w\left(Q^2\right) + \|Q\|^4,$$

Then, the inequality (36) follows from the previous inequality. □

Example 4. *Let* $Q = \begin{bmatrix} 0 & 2 \\ 0 & 0 \end{bmatrix}$ *be 2×2-matrix. Employing (31), we have*

$$dw(Q) \leq \sqrt{\frac{w(Q^2) + \|Q\|^4}{2} + \frac{1}{4}\left\||Q|^2 + |Q^*|^2 + 2|Q|^4\right\|} = 4.123105626,$$

which is better than both estimates given in (32) (=4.472135954) and in (34) (=4.242640686). It is convenient to note that, according to (32), the lower bound of $dw(Q) \geq 4$. Fortunately, the definition of the Davis–Wielandt radius gives

$$dw(Q) = \sup_{\substack{c \in \mathcal{M} \\ \|c\|=1}} \left\{\sqrt{|\langle Qc, c\rangle|^2 + \|Qc\|^4}\right\} = 4.123105626$$

which is exactly our estimate. This implies that our estimate in (36) is very close to the exact value, in general.

Remark 2. *All obtained results of Section 3 are valid for the generalized Euclidean Davis–Wielandt radius by noting that the number of operators should be $2n$ instead of n and the previously mentioned sequence of operators. We leave the rest of the generalizations to the interested reader.*

5. Conclusions

This work brings together, with several refinements, inequalities for the Eculadeain operator radius $\omega_e(\cdot)$. Namely, it is shown that the inequalities (17)–(31) are much better than (5)–(7). This is shown mathematically and supported with several examples. In fact, some of the obtained results are sharper than other inequalities. Among others, (26), (31), (34), and (36) are the most interesting improved refinements of the obtained inequalities. Nevertheless, the other presented inequalities are still better than (5) and (6) and all amplify their inequalities. Supporting our assertions with various examples, we show that our results are much better than all older and earlier inequalities. Finally, an interesting new bound for the Davis–Wielandt radius (36) is established. We note that our result could be generalized for the generalized operator radius $\omega_p(\cdot)$; we leave the details to the interested reader.

Author Contributions: Conceptualization, T.H., M.W.A.; methodology, M.W.A.; software, I.A.-S., A.S.H.; validation, T.H., I.A.-S., H.A., R.H. and A.S.H.; formal analysis, T.H., M.W.A., H.A.; investigation, M.W.A., H.A., R.H.; resources, M.W.A.; data curation, I.A.-S., H.A., R.H., A.S.H.; writing—original draft preparation, T.H., M.W.A., H.A.; writing—review and editing, T.H., I.A.-S., H.A., R.H., A.A.-H.; visualization, I.A.-S., H.A.; supervision, M.W.A., H.A., R.H.; project administration, H.A.; funding acquisition, H.A., A.A.-H. All authors have read and agreed to the published version of the manuscript.

Funding: This research received no external funding.

Data Availability Statement: Not applicable.

Conflicts of Interest: The authors declare no conflict of interest.

References

1. Popescu, G. Unitary invariants in multivariable operator theory. *Mem. Am. Math. Soc.* **2009**, *200*, 941. [CrossRef]
2. Sheikhhosseini, A.; Moslehian, M.S.; Shebrawi, K. Inequalities for generalized Euclidean operator radius via Young's inequality. *J. Math. Anal. Appl.* **2017**, *445*, 1516–1529. [CrossRef]
3. Bajmaeh A.B.; Omidvar, M.E. Some Inequalities for the numerical radius and Rhombic numerical radius. *Kragujev. J. Math.* **2018**, *42*, 569–577.
4. Alomari, M.W.; Shebrawi, K.; Chesneau, C. Some generalized Euclidean operator radius inequalities. *Axioms* **2022**, *11*, 285. [CrossRef]
5. Moslehian, M.S.; Sattari, M.; Shebrawi, K. Extension of Euclidean operator radius inequalities. *Math. Scand.* **2017**, *120*, 129–144. [CrossRef]
6. Dragomir, S.S. Some inequalities for the Euclidean operator radius of two operators in Hilbert spaces. *Linear Algebra Appl.* **2006**, *419*, 256–264. [CrossRef]
7. Kittaneh, F. Numerical radius inequalities for Hilbert space operators. *Studia Math.* **2005**, *168*, 73–80. [CrossRef]
8. Dragomir, S.S. Power inequalities for the numerical radius of a product of two operators in Hilbert spaces. *Sarajevo J. Math.* **2009**, *5*, 269–278.
9. Sattari, M.; Moslehian, M.S.; Yamazaki, T. Some generalized numerical radius inequalities for Hilbert space operators. *Linear Algebra Appl.* **2015**, *470*, 216–227. [CrossRef]
10. Altwaijry, N.; Feki, K.; Minculete, N. On some generalizations of Cauchy–Schwarz inequalities and their applications. *Symmetry* **2023**, *15*, 304. [CrossRef]
11. Altwaijry, N.; Feki, K. Minculete, Further inequalities for the weighted numerical radius of operators. *Mathematics* **2022**, *10*, 3576. [CrossRef]
12. Bhunia, P.; Bhanja, A.; Bag, S.; Paul, K. Bounds for the Davis–Wielandt radius of bounded linear operators. *Ann. Funct. Anal.* **2021**, *12*, 18. [CrossRef]
13. Bhunia, P.; Sain, D.; Paul, K. On the Davis–Wielandt shell of an operator and the Davis–Wielandt index of a normed linear space. *arXiv* **2020**, arXiv:2006.1532.
14. Bhunia, P.; Paul, K. Some improvements of numerical radius inequalities of operators and operator matrices. *Linear Multilinear Algebra* **2020** . [CrossRef]
15. Feki, K.; Mahmoud, S.A.O.A. Davis–Wielandt shells of semi-Hilbertian space operators and its applications. *Banach J. Math. Anal.* **2020**, *14*, 1281–1304. [CrossRef]
16. Hajmohamadi, M.; Lashkaripour, R.; Bakherad, M. Some generalizations of numerical radius on off-diagonal part of 2×2 operator matrices. *J. Math. Inequalities* **2018**, *12*, 447–457. [CrossRef]
17. Hajmohamadi, M.; Lashkaripour, R.; Bakherad, M. Further refinements of generalized numerical radius inequalities for Hilbert space operators. *Georgian Math. J.* **2021**, *28*, 83–92. [CrossRef]
18. Moghaddam, S.F.; Mirmostafaee, A.K.; Janfada, M. Some Sharp Estimations for Davis–Wielandt Radius in $B(H)$. *Mediterr. J. Math.* **2022**, *19*, 283. [CrossRef]
19. Alomari, M.W. On the Davis–Wielandt radius inequalities of Hilbert space operators. *Linear Multilinear Algebra* **2022**, 1–25. . [CrossRef]
20. Kittaneh, F. A numerical radius inequality and an estimate for the numerical radius of the Frobenius companion matrix. *Studia Math.* **2003**, *158*, 11–17. [CrossRef]
21. Mitrinović, D.S.; Pečarić, J.; Fink, A.M. *Classical and New Inequalities in Analysis*; Kluwer Academic Publishers: Dordrecht, The Netherlands, 1993.
22. Furuta, T.; Mićić, J.; Pečarić, J.; Seo, Y. *Mond–Pečarić Method in Operator Inequalities*, 1st ed.; Ele-Math, Publishing House Element: Zagreb, Croatia, 2005.
23. Kato, T. Notes on some inequalities for linear operators. *Math. Ann.* **1952**, *125*, 208–212. [CrossRef]
24. Alomari, M.W. On Cauchy–Schwarz type inequalities and applications to numerical radius inequalities. *Ricerche Mat.* **2022**, 1–18. [CrossRef]

25. Zamani, A.; Shebrawi, K. Some upper bounds for the Davis–Wielandt radius of Hilbert space operators. *Mediterr. J. Math.* **2020**, *17*, 25. [CrossRef]
26. Aujla, J.; Silva, F. Weak majorization inequalities and convex functions. *Linear Algebra Appl.* **2003**, *369*, 217–233. [CrossRef]
27. Kittaneh, F.; Moradi, H.R. Cauchy–Schwarz type inequalities and applications to numerical radius inequalities. *Math. Ineq. Appl.* **2020**, *23*, 1117–1125. [CrossRef]
28. Davis, C. The shell of a Hilbert-space operator. *Acta Sci. Math.* **1968**, *29*, 69–86.
29. Davis, C. The shell of a Hilbert-space operator. II. *Acta Sci. Math.* **1970**, *31*, 301–318.
30. Wielandt, H. On eigenvalues of sums of normal matrices. *Pacific J. Math.* **1955**, *5*, 633–638. [CrossRef]
31. Al-Zoubi, H.; Abdel-Fattah, F.; Al-Sabbagh, M. Surfaces of finite III-type in the Eculidean 3-space. *WSEAS Trans. Math.* **2021**, *20*, 729–735.
32. Alomari, M.W. Numerical radius inequalities for Hilbert space operators. *Complex Anal. Oper. Theory* **2021**, *15*, 1–19. [CrossRef]
33. Hatamleh, R. On the form of correlation function for a class of nonstationary field with a zero spectrum. *Rocky Mt. J. Math.* **2003**, *33*, 159–173. [CrossRef]
34. Hatamleh, R.; Zolotarev, V.A. Triangular Models of Commutative Systems of Linear Operators Close to Unitary Ones. *Ukr. Math. J.* **2016**, *68*, 791–811. [CrossRef]
35. Li, C.K.; Poon, Y.T. Davis–Wielandt shells of normal operators. *Acta Sci. Math.* **2009**, *75*, 289–297.
36. Li, C.K.; Poon, Y.T. Spectrum, numerical range and Davis–Wielandt shells of normal operator. *Glasgow Math. J.* **2009**, *51*, 91–100. [CrossRef]
37. Li, C.K.; Poon, Y.T.; Sze, N.S. Davis–Wielandt, Shells of operators. *Oper. Matrices* **2008**, *2*, 341–355. [CrossRef]
38. Li, C.K.; Poon, Y.T.; Sze, N.S. Elliptical range theorems for generalized numerical ranges of quadratic operators. *Rocky Mountain J. Math.* **2011**, *41*, 813–832. [CrossRef]
39. Li, C.K.; Poon, Y.T.; Tominaga, M. Spectra, norms and numerical ranges of generalized. *Linear Multilinear Algebra* **2011**, *59*, 1077–1104. [CrossRef]
40. Lins, B.; Spitkovsky, I.M.; Zhong, S. The normalized numerical range and the Davis–Wielandt shell. *Linear Algebra Its Appl.* **2018**, *546*, 187–209. [CrossRef]

Disclaimer/Publisher's Note: The statements, opinions and data contained in all publications are solely those of the individual author(s) and contributor(s) and not of MDPI and/or the editor(s). MDPI and/or the editor(s) disclaim responsibility for any injury to people or property resulting from any ideas, methods, instructions or products referred to in the content.

Article

Some Refinements of the Tensorial Inequalities in Hilbert Spaces

Vuk Stojiljković [1,†], Rajagopalan Ramaswamy [2,*,†], Ola A. Ashour Abdelnaby [2,†] and Stojan Radenović [3]

1. Faculty of Science, University of Novi Sad, Trg Dositeja Obradovića 3, 21000 Novi Sad, Serbia
2. Department of Mathematics, College of Science and Humanities, Prince Sattam bin Abdulaziz Univeristy, Al-Kharj 16278, Saudi Arabia
3. Faculty of Mechanical Engineering, University of Belgrade, Kraljice Marije 16, 11120 Beograd, Serbia
* Correspondence: r.gopalan@psau.edu.sa
† These authors contributed equally to this work.

Abstract: Hermite–Hadamard inequalities and their refinements have been investigated for a long period of time. In this paper, we obtained refinements of the Hermite–Hadamard inequality of tensorial type for the convex functions of self-adjoint operators in Hilbert spaces. The obtained inequalities generalize the previously obtained inequalities by Dragomir. We also provide useful Lemmas which enabled us to obtain the results. The examples of the obtained inequalities for specific convex functions have been given in the example and consequences section. Symmetry in the upper and lower bounds can be seen in the last Theorem of the paper given, as the upper and lower bounds differ by a constant.

Keywords: tensorial product; self-adjoint operators; convex functions

MSC: 26D05; 26D07; 26D20

1. Introduction

The notion of a tensor has its origin in the 19th century, where it was formulated by Gibbs, although he did not formally use the word 'tensor' but 'dyadic'. In modern language, it can be seen as the origin of the tensor definition and its introduction to mathematics. The interplay of inequalities in mathematics is vast, and as such, it has applications in tensors as well. Mathematics and other fields of science are strongly affected by inequalities. There are many types of inequality, but those that involve Jensen, Ostrowski, Hermite–Hadamard and Minkowski inequalities are of particular importance. More about inequalities and their history can be found in the books [1,2]. One of the most celebrated inequalities is the Hermite–Hadamard (HH) inequality, which states the following: If $f^\star : \mathbb{I} \to \mathbb{R}$ is a convex function on an interval $\mathbb{I} \subset \mathbb{R}$ and $r_1, r_2 \in \mathbb{I}$ are such that $r_1 < r_2$, then

$$f^\star\left(\frac{r_1 + r_2}{2}\right) \leqslant \frac{1}{r_2 - r_1} \int_{r_1}^{r_2} f^\star(\lambda) d\lambda \leqslant \frac{f^\star(r_1) + f^\star(r_2)}{2}.$$

Concerning the generalization of this inequality, see the following and references therein for more information [3–14]. Inequalities in Hilbert space were intensively worked on in the 20th century, but a special expansion occurred with the proof of Jensen-type inequality in Hilbert space, the so-called Mond–Pecaric inequality [15]. Let $f : [m, M] \to \mathbb{R}$ be a continuous convex function. If $x \in H$, $(x, x) = 1$, then for every operator C such that $mI \leqslant C \leqslant MI$, where I is identity operator and C is self-adjoint, holds,

$$f((Cx, x)) \leqslant (f(C)x, x).$$

After its introduction, there followed an expansion of a special type of inequalities of the MD (Mond–Pecaric) type in the Hilbert space [16,17]. The recent further development of inequalities in Hilbert space was followed by the definition of an operator convex function by Dragomir in 2011 [18], which is given by the following.

A real valued continuous function f on an interval $\mathbb{I}$ is said to be operator convex (resp. operator concave) if

$$f((1-\lambda)A + \lambda B) \leqslant (resp. \geqslant)(1-\lambda)f(A) + \lambda f(B)$$

in the operator order, for all $\lambda \in [0,1]$ and for every self-adjoint operator A and B on a Hilbert space H whose spectra are contained in I. By introducing the given definition of operator convexity the expansion of another branch of Hilbert inequalities began. You can find more about the class of operator convex functions in the following references [19,20]. For more information on inequalities in Hilbert spaces, see the references [21,22]. Recent advances concerning the theory of inequalities in Hilbert spaces will be shown to supplement the presentation of this work. Alomari [23] gave the following numerical radius inequality.

Let $A, B, C, D \in B(H)$. Let f be a positive, increasing and convex function on $\mathbb{R}$. If f is twice differentiable such that $f'' \geqslant \lambda > 0$, then

$$f(w(DCBA)) \leqslant \frac{1}{2}||f(A^*|B|^2 A) + f(D|C^*|^2 D^*)|| - \inf_{||x||=1} \eta(x),$$

where $\eta(x) := \frac{1}{8}\lambda \langle [A^*|B|^2 A - D|C^*|^2 D^*]x, x\rangle^2$.

The recent generalization of the Cauchy–Schwartz inequality and related inequalities has been given by Altwaijry et al. [24], one of the results given is the following.

If $T, S \in B(H), r \geqslant 1$ and $\lambda \in [0,1]$, then the inequality

$$w^{2r}(S^*T) \leqslant \frac{1}{2}|||T|^{4r} + |S|^{4r}|| - \frac{\lambda(1-\lambda)}{1+\lambda-\lambda^2}\left(|||T|^{4r} + |S|^{4r}|| - w(S^*T)|||T|^{2r} + |S|^{2r}||\right)$$

holds.

Recent research on the tensorial inequalities was carried out by Wang et al. [25], who gave the following inequality.

Let $A = (a_{i_1 i_2 \ldots i_m}) \in \mathbb{C}^{[m,n]}$. If

$$(i)\ |a_{i\ldots i}| > r_i^{[i]}(A), \text{ for all } i \in \langle n \rangle,$$

$$(ii)\ \left(|a_{i\ldots i}| - r_i^{[i]}(A)\right)\left(|a_{j\ldots j}| - \overline{r_j^{[i]}}(A)\right) > \overline{r_i^{[i]}}(A) r_j^{[i]}(A), \text{ for all } i, j \in \langle n \rangle, i \neq j,$$

then A is nonsingular; that is, $0 \notin \sigma(A)$. In this paper, various inequalities of tensorial type will be obtained. The concept of symmetry can be seen in Theorem 4, which gives a generalization of the inequality obtained by Dragomir. Now, we begin with the introduction related to the tensorial product and Hilbert space topic of the paper.

Let $I_1^\star, \ldots, I_k^\star$ be intervals from $\mathbb{R}$ and let $f^\star : I_1^\star \times \ldots \times I_k^\star \to \mathbb{R}$ be an essentially bounded real function defined on the product of the intervals. Let $Q_\star = (Q_{1\star}, \ldots, Q_{k\star})$ be a k-tuple of bounded self-adjoint operators on Hilbert spaces $H_1^\star, \ldots, H_k^\star$ such that the spectrum of $Q_{i\star}$ is contained in $I_i^\star$ for $i = 1, \ldots, k$. We say that such a k-tuple is in the domain of $f^\star$. If

$$Q_{i\star} = \int_{I_i} \lambda_i dE_i(\lambda_i)$$

is the spectral resolution of $Q_{i\star}$ for $i = 1, \ldots, k$ by following [26], we define

$$f^\star(Q_{1\star}, \ldots, Q_{k\star}) := \int_{I_1^\star} \cdots \int_{I_k^\star} f^\star(\lambda_1, \ldots, \lambda_k) dE_1(\lambda_1) \otimes^\star \ldots \otimes^\star dE_k(\lambda_k)$$

as a bounded self-adjoint operator on the tensorial product $H_1^\star \otimes^{\tilde{\star}} \ldots \otimes^{\tilde{\star}} H_k^\star$.

If the Hilbert spaces are of finite dimension, then the above integrals become finite sums, and we may consider the functional calculus for arbitrary real functions. Construction of this type extends the definition of Kornyi [27] for functions of two variables and has the property that

$$f^\star(Q_{1\star}, \ldots, Q_{k\star}) = f_1^\star(Q_{1\star}) \otimes^{\tilde{\star}} \ldots \otimes^{\tilde{\star}} f_k^\star(Q_{k\star}),$$

whenever $f^\star$ can be separated as a product $f^\star(t_1^\star, \ldots, t_k^\star) = f_1^\star(t_1^\star) \ldots f_k^\star(t_k^\star)$ of k functions each depending on only one variable.

2. Preliminaries

We begin this section with certain basic concepts and lemmas, which will be needed in the sequel.

Since we will be using tensorial products, we will define in the following what tensors and tensorial products are in short; for more, consult the following book [28].

Definition 1. *Let $\tilde{U}, \tilde{V}$ and $\tilde{W}$ be vector spaces over the same field $\tilde{F}$. A mapping $\Phi : \tilde{U} \times \tilde{V} \to \tilde{W}$ is called a bilinear mapping if it is linear in each variable separately. Namely, for all $u, u_1, u_2 \in \tilde{U}$, $v, v_1, v_2 \in \tilde{V}$ and $a, b \in \tilde{F}$,*

$\Phi(au_1 + bu_2, v) = a\Phi(u_1, v) + b\Phi(u_2, v)$,
$\Phi(u, av_1 + bv_2) = a\Phi(u, v_1) + b\Phi(u, v_2)$. *If $\tilde{W} = \tilde{F}$, a bilinear mapping $\Phi : \tilde{U} \times \tilde{V} \to \tilde{F}$ is called a bilinear function.*

Definition 2. *Let $\otimes^{\tilde{\star}} : \tilde{U} \times \tilde{V} \to \tilde{W}$ be a bilinear mapping. The pair $(\tilde{W}, \otimes^{\tilde{\star}})$ is called a tensor product space of $\tilde{U}$ and $\tilde{V}$ if it satisfies the following conditions:*

1. $< Im \otimes^{\tilde{\star}} > = \tilde{W}$ *(Generating property)*;
2. $dim < Im \otimes^{\tilde{\star}} > = dim \tilde{U} \cdot dim \tilde{V}$ *(Maximal span property). If $\tilde{W} = \tilde{F}$, a bilinear mapping $\Phi : \tilde{U} \times \tilde{V} \to \tilde{F}$ is called a bilinear function.*

The member $w \in \tilde{W}$ is called a tensor, but not all tensors in $\tilde{W}$ are products of two vectors of the form $u \otimes^{\tilde{\star}} v$. The notation $< Im \otimes^{\tilde{\star}} >$ denotes the span.

Example 1. *Let $u = (x_1, \ldots, x_m) \in \mathbb{R}^m$ and $v = (y_1, \ldots, y_n) \in \mathbb{R}^n$. We can view u and v as column vectors. Namely,*

$$u = \begin{bmatrix} x_1 \\ \vdots \\ x_m \end{bmatrix}, v = \begin{bmatrix} y_1 \\ \vdots \\ y_n \end{bmatrix}$$

*are $m \times 1$ and $n \times 1$ matrices, respectively.
We define $\otimes^{\tilde{\star}} : \mathbb{R}^m \times \mathbb{R}^n \to M_{m,n}$,*

$$u \otimes^{\tilde{\star}} v = uv^t = \begin{bmatrix} x_1y_1 & \cdots & x_1y_n \\ & \vdots & \\ x_my_1 & \cdots & x_my_n \end{bmatrix},$$

an $m \times n$ matrix with entries $A_{ij} = x_iy_j$. $(M_{m,n}, \otimes^{\tilde{\star}})$ is a tensor product space of $\mathbb{R}^m$ and $\mathbb{R}^n$.

Tensors do not need to be matrices. This is just one model given. For more, consult the following book [28].

Remember the following properties of the tensorial product:

$$(Q_\star L_\star) \otimes^{\tilde{\star}} (W_\star R_\star) = (Q_\star \otimes^{\tilde{\star}} W_\star)(L_\star \otimes^{\tilde{\star}} R_\star)$$

that holds for any $Q_\star, W_\star, L_\star, R_\star \in B(H)$.

From the property, we can easily deduce the following consequences:

$$Q_\star^n \otimes^{\tilde{}} W_\star^n = (Q_\star \otimes^{\tilde{}} W_\star)^n, n \geqslant 0,$$

$$(Q_\star \otimes^{\tilde{}} 1)(1 \otimes^{\tilde{}} W_\star) = (1 \otimes^{\tilde{}} W_\star)(Q_\star \otimes^{\tilde{}} 1) = Q_\star \otimes^{\tilde{}} W_\star,$$

which can be extended; for two natural numbers r, s, we have

$$(Q_\star \otimes^{\tilde{}} 1)^s (1 \otimes^{\tilde{}} W_\star)^r = (1 \otimes^{\tilde{}} W_\star)^r (Q_\star \otimes^{\tilde{}} 1)^s = Q_\star^s \otimes^{\tilde{}} W_\star^r.$$

The current research concerning tensorial inequalities in Hilbert space can be seen in the following papers [29–33].

Lemma 1 ([34], p. 4). *Assume that $Q_\star$ and $W_\star$ are self-adjoint operators with $Sp(Q_\star) \subset I$ and $Sp(W_\star) \subset J$. Let f, h be continuous on I, g, k continuous on J and ψ continuous on an interval K that contains the sum of the intervals $h(I) + k(J)$; then*

$$(f^\star(Q_\star) \otimes^{\tilde{}} 1 + 1 \otimes^{\tilde{}} g^\star(W_\star))\psi(h(Q_\star) \otimes^{\tilde{}} 1 + 1 \otimes^{\tilde{}} k(W_\star))$$
$$= \int_I \int_J (f(t) + g(s))\psi(h(t) + k(s))dE_t \otimes^{\tilde{}} dF(s),$$

where $Q_\star$ and $W_\star$ have the spectral resolutions,

$$Q_\star = \int_I t \, dE_t \text{ and } W_\star = \int_J s \, dF_s.$$

Theorem 1 ([35], p. 4). *Assume that $Q_\star$ and $W_\star$ are self-adjoint operators with $Sp(Q_\star) \subset I$ and $Sp(W_\star) \subset J$. Let f be continuous on I; g continuous on J and continuous on an interval K that contains the product of the intervals $f(I)g(J)$, then*

$$\psi(f^\star(Q_\star) \otimes^{\tilde{}} g^\star(W_\star)) = \int_I \int_J \psi(f(t)g(s))dE_t \otimes^{\tilde{}} dF(s),$$

where $Q_\star$ and $W_\star$ have the spectral resolutions

$$Q_\star = \int_I t \, dE_t, W_\star = \int_J s \, dF_s.$$

Theorem 2 ([35], p. 4). *Assume that $Q_\star$ and $W_\star$ are self-adjoint operators with $Sp(Q_\star) \subset I$ and $Sp(W_\star) \subset J$. Let h be continuous on I, k continuous on J and ψ modulus on an interval U that contains the sum of the intervals $h(I) + k(J)$, then*

$$\psi(h(Q_\star) \otimes^{\tilde{}} 1 + 1 \otimes^{\tilde{}} k(W_\star)) = \int_I \int_J \psi(h(t) + k(s))dE_t \otimes^{\tilde{}} dF(s),$$

where $Q_\star$ and $W_\star$ have the spectral resolutions

$$Q_\star = \int_I t \, dE_t, W_\star = \int_J s \, dF_s.$$

In the following, we will obtain theorems that generalize the ones from Dragomir's paper [35]. In recent times, emphasis has been placed on inequalities in Hilbert space, which can be seen from the references to books on inequalities in Hilbert spaces given in the introduction. Motivation for this paper stems from the cited references and from the fact that the Hilbert space inequalities have many applications as indicated in the conclusion section.

Now we begin with the main results of this paper.

3. Main Results

The following Lemma generalizes the Lemma given by Dragomir in the paper ([35], p. 7) which will be instrumental in the obtained results.

Lemma 2. *Let $\psi : I \to \mathbb{R}$ be a convex function on the interval I, $q, w \in I^0$, the interior of I, with $q < w, 0 < \tau \leqslant 1$ and $\xi \in [0,1]$. Then,*

$$\left(\psi'_+\left((1-\xi)\frac{q}{\tau}+\xi w\right)-\psi'_-\left((1-\xi)\frac{q}{\tau}+\xi w\right)\right)\xi\left(w\left(\frac{1}{\tau}-\xi\right)-\frac{q}{\tau}(1-\xi)\right)$$

$$\leqslant (1-\xi)\psi\left(\frac{q}{\tau}\right)+\xi\psi\left(\frac{w}{\tau}\right)-\psi\left((1-\xi)\frac{q}{\tau}+\xi w\right)$$

$$+w\xi\left(1-\frac{1}{\tau}\right)\int_0^1 \psi'\left((1-t)\frac{q}{\tau}+t((1-\xi)\frac{q}{\tau}+\xi w)\right)dt$$

$$\leqslant \left(\psi'_-\left(\frac{w}{\tau}\right)-\psi'_+\left(\frac{q}{\tau}\right)\right)\xi\left(w\left(\frac{1}{\tau}-\xi\right)-\frac{q}{\tau}(1-\xi)\right).$$

Proof. Since ψ is convex on I, it follows that the function is differentiable on I^0 except at a countable number of points; the lateral derivatives ψ' exist in each point of I^0—they are increasing on I^0 and $\psi'_- \leqslant \psi'_+$ on I^0. For any $x, y \in I^0$, we have the following relation:

$$\psi(x) = \psi\left(\frac{y}{\tau}\right) + \int_{\frac{y}{\tau}}^x \psi'(s)ds = \psi\left(\frac{y}{\tau}\right) + \left(x-\frac{y}{\tau}\right)\int_0^1 \psi'\left((1-t)\frac{y}{\tau}+tx\right)dt$$

Assume that $q < w$ and $\xi \in [0,1]$. Then we have

$$\psi\left((1-\xi)\frac{q}{\tau}+\xi w\right)$$

$$= \psi\left(\frac{q}{\tau}\right) + \xi\left(w-\frac{q}{\tau}\right)\int_0^1 \psi'\left((1-t)\frac{q}{\tau}+t((1-\xi)\frac{q}{\tau}+\xi w)\right)dt$$

and

$$\psi\left((1-\xi)\frac{q}{\tau}+\xi w\right)$$

$$= \psi\left(\frac{w}{\tau}\right) + \left(\frac{q}{\tau}(1-\xi)-w\left(\frac{1}{\tau}-1\right)\right)\int_0^1 \psi'\left((1-t)\frac{w}{\tau}+t((1-\xi)\frac{q}{\tau}+\xi w)\right)dt.$$

If we multiply the first top inequality with $(1-\xi)$ and the second by ξ, and add the resulting equalities, we get

$$\psi\left((1-\xi)\frac{q}{\tau}+\xi w\right) = \psi(1-\xi)\left(\frac{q}{\tau}\right)+\xi\psi\left(\frac{w}{\tau}\right)$$

$$+\xi(1-\xi)\left(w-\frac{q}{\tau}\right)\int_0^1 \psi'\left((1-t)\frac{q}{\tau}+t((1-\xi)\frac{q}{\tau}+\xi w)\right)dt$$

$$+\xi\left(\frac{q}{\tau}(1-\xi)-w\left(\frac{1}{\tau}-1\right)\right)\int_0^1 \psi'\left((1-t)\frac{w}{\tau}+t((1-\xi)\frac{q}{\tau}+\xi w)\right)dt.$$

From which we get

$$\psi(1-\xi)\left(\frac{q}{\tau}\right)+\xi\psi\left(\frac{w}{\tau}\right)-\psi\left((1-\xi)\frac{q}{\tau}+\xi w\right)$$

$$+w\xi\left(1-\frac{1}{\tau}\right)\int_0^1 \psi'\left((1-t)\frac{q}{\tau}+t((1-\xi)\frac{q}{\tau}+\xi w)\right)dt$$

$$= \xi\left(-\frac{q}{\tau}(1-\xi)+w\left(\frac{1}{\tau}-1\right)\right)\int_0^1 \psi'\left((1-t)\frac{w}{\tau}+t((1-\xi)\frac{q}{\tau}+\xi w)\right)dt$$

$$-\xi\left(-\frac{q}{\tau}(1-\xi)+w\left(\frac{1}{\tau}-1\right)\right)\int_0^1 \psi'\left((1-t)\frac{q}{\tau}+t((1-\xi)\frac{q}{\tau}+\xi w)\right)dt;$$

an interesting equality in and of itself.

Since $q < w$ and $\xi \in [0,1]$, then $(1-\xi)\frac{q}{\tau}+\xi w \in (\frac{q}{\tau}, w)$ and

$$(1-t)\frac{q}{\tau}+t\left((1-\xi)\frac{q}{\tau}+\xi w\right) \in \left[\frac{q}{\tau}, (1-\xi)\frac{q}{\tau}+\xi w\right],$$

$$(1-t)\frac{w}{\tau}+t\left((1-\xi)\frac{q}{\tau}+\xi w\right) \in \left[(1-\xi)\frac{q}{\tau}+\xi w, \frac{w}{\tau}\right].$$

By the monotonicity of the derivative we have

$$\psi'_+\left((1-\xi)\frac{q}{\tau}+\xi w\right) \leqslant \psi'\left((1-t)\frac{w}{\tau}+t((1-\xi)\frac{q}{\tau}+\xi w)\right) \leqslant \psi'_-\left(\frac{w}{\tau}\right),$$

$$\psi'_+\left(\frac{q}{\tau}\right) \leqslant \psi'\left((1-t)\frac{q}{\tau}+t((1-\xi)\frac{q}{\tau}+\xi w)\right) \leqslant \psi'_-\left((1-\xi)\frac{q}{\tau}+\xi w\right)$$

for any $t \in [0,1]$.

By integrating the inequalities and subtracting them and making use of the identity developed before, we obtain the following inequality:

$$\left(\psi'_+\left((1-\xi)\frac{q}{\tau}+\xi w\right) - \psi'_-\left((1-\xi)\frac{q}{\tau}+\xi w\right)\right)\xi\left(w\left(\frac{1}{\tau}-\xi\right)-\frac{q}{\tau}(1-\xi)\right)$$

$$\leqslant (1-\xi)\psi\left(\frac{q}{\tau}\right)+\xi\psi\left(\frac{w}{\tau}\right)-\psi\left((1-\xi)\frac{q}{\tau}+\xi w\right)$$

$$+w\xi\left(1-\frac{1}{\tau}\right)\int_0^1 \psi'\left((1-t)\frac{q}{\tau}+t((1-\xi)\frac{q}{\tau}+\xi w)\right)dt$$

$$\leqslant \left(\psi'_-\left(\frac{w}{\tau}\right)-\psi'_+\left(\frac{q}{\tau}\right)\right)\xi\left(w\left(\frac{1}{\tau}-\xi\right)-\frac{q}{\tau}(1-\xi)\right).$$

□

Corollary 1. *Letting $\tau \to 1$ in the obtained Lemma, we obtain Lemma 1 given by Dragomir ([35], p. 7).*

$$\left(\psi'_+((1-\xi)q+\xi w) - \psi'_-((1-\xi)q+\xi w)\right)\xi(w-q)(1-\xi)$$

$$\leqslant (1-\xi)\psi(q)+\xi\psi(w)-\psi((1-\xi)q+\xi w)$$

$$\leqslant \left(\psi'_-(w)-\psi'_+(q)\right)\xi(w-q)(1-\xi).$$

Corollary 2. *Considering the convex function $\psi : \mathbb{R} \to (0, +\infty)$, $\psi(x) = e^x$, then we have*

$$(1-\xi)e^{\frac{q}{\tau}}+\xi e^{\frac{w}{\tau}} - e^{(1-\xi)\frac{q}{\tau}+\xi w} + \xi w\left(1-\frac{1}{\tau}\right)\int_0^1 e^{(1-t)\frac{q}{\tau}+t((1-\xi)\frac{q}{\tau}+\xi w)}dt$$

$$\leqslant (e^{\frac{w}{\tau}} - e^{\frac{q}{\tau}})\xi\left(w\left(\frac{1}{\tau}-\xi\right)-\frac{q}{\tau}(1-\xi)\right).$$

Corollary 3. *From Lemma 2, we can observe that the term in the beginning of the chain of inequalities is positive if we assume ψ to be differentiable; therefore, we can observe the following:*

$$0 \leqslant (1-\xi)\psi\left(\frac{q}{\tau}\right)+\xi\psi\left(\frac{w}{\tau}\right)-\psi\left((1-\xi)\frac{q}{\tau}+\xi w\right)$$

$$+ w\xi\left(1 - \frac{1}{\tau}\right)\int_0^1 \psi'\left((1-t)\frac{q}{\tau} + t((1-\xi)\frac{q}{\tau} + \xi w)\right)dt$$

$$\leq \left(\psi'\left(\frac{w}{\tau}\right) - \psi'\left(\frac{q}{\tau}\right)\right)\xi\left(w\left(\frac{1}{\tau} - \xi\right) - \frac{q}{\tau}(1-\xi)\right).$$

In the following theorem, we generalize the result given by Dragomir.

Theorem 3. *Assume that ψ is a differentiable convex function on the interval I, and $Q_\star$ and $W_\star$ are self-adjoint operators with $Sp(Q_\star), Sp(W_\star) \subset I$; then, for all $\tau \in (0,1]$, we have*

$$0 \leq (1-\xi)\psi\left(\frac{Q_\star}{\tau}\right) \otimes^\star 1 + \xi 1 \otimes^\star \psi\left(\frac{W_\star}{\tau}\right) - \psi\left(\frac{1-\xi}{\tau}Q_\star \otimes^\star 1 + \xi 1 \otimes^\star W_\star\right)$$

$$+ \xi\left(1 - \frac{1}{\tau}\right)\int_0^1 (1 \otimes^\star W_\star)\psi'\left(\frac{1-\xi u}{\tau}Q_\star \otimes^\star 1 + u\xi 1 \otimes^\star W_\star\right)du$$

$$\leq \left(\frac{\xi(1-\xi)}{\tau}Q_\star \otimes^\star 1 - \xi \cdot \left(\frac{1}{\tau} - \xi\right)1 \otimes^\star W_\star\right)(\psi'(Q_\star) \otimes^\star 1 - 1 \otimes^\star \psi'(W_\star)).$$

In particular,

$$0 \leq \frac{\psi(2Q_\star) \otimes^\star 1 + 1 \otimes^\star \psi(2W_\star)}{2} - \psi\left(Q_\star \otimes^\star 1 + \frac{1 \otimes^\star W_\star}{2}\right)$$

$$- \frac{1}{2}\int_0^1 (1 \otimes^\star W_\star)\psi'\left((2-t)Q_\star \otimes^\star 1 + \frac{t}{2}1 \otimes^\star W_\star\right)dt$$

$$\leq \left(\frac{Q_\star \otimes^\star 1}{2} - \frac{3}{4}1 \otimes^\star W_\star\right)(\psi'(Q_\star) \otimes^\star 1 - 1 \otimes^\star \psi'(W_\star)).$$

Proof. Assume that $Q_\star$ and $W_\star$ have the spectral resolutions

$$Q_\star = \int_I t\, dE_t \text{ and } W_\star = \int_I s\, dF_s.$$

If we take the double integral $\int_I \int_I$ over $dE_t \otimes^\star dF(s)$ in the inequality we obtained in Corollary 3, then we get

$$0 \leq \int_I \int_I \left((1-\xi)\psi\left(\frac{t}{\tau}\right) + \xi\psi\left(\frac{s}{\tau}\right) - \psi\left((1-\xi)\frac{t}{\tau} + \xi s\right)\right)dE(t) \otimes^\star dF(s)$$

$$+ \int_I \int_I \left(s\xi\left(1 - \frac{1}{\tau}\right)\int_0^1 \psi'\left((1-u)\frac{t}{\tau} + u((1-\xi)\frac{t}{\tau} + \xi s)\right)du\right)dE(t) \otimes^\star dF(s)$$

$$\leq \int_I \int_I \left((\psi'(s) - \psi'(t))\xi\left(s\left(\frac{1}{\tau} - \xi\right) - \frac{t}{\tau}(1-\xi)\right)\right)dE(t) \otimes^\star dF(s).$$

Using the properties given in preliminaries, we obtain the following, where for the part that has the composite function we use Theorem 2, setting $h(t) = (1-\xi)t$, and $k(s) = \xi s$. We apply the Fubini's Theorem to the second term on the left hand side, and therefore all together we obtain

$$\int_I \int_I \psi\left((1-\xi)\frac{t}{\tau} + \xi s\right)dE(t) \otimes^\star dF(s) = \psi\left(\frac{1-\xi}{\tau}Q_\star \otimes^\star 1 + \xi 1 \otimes^\star W_\star\right)$$

$$0 \leq (1-\xi)\psi\left(\frac{Q_\star}{\tau}\right) \otimes^\star 1 + \xi 1 \otimes^\star \psi\left(\frac{W_\star}{\tau}\right) - \psi\left(\frac{1-\xi}{\tau}Q_\star \otimes^\star 1 + \xi 1 \otimes^\star W_\star\right)$$

$$+ \xi\left(1 - \frac{1}{\tau}\right)\int_0^1 (1 \otimes^\star W_\star)\psi'\left[\frac{1-u\xi}{\tau}Q_\star \otimes^\star 1 + u\xi 1 \otimes^\star W_\star\right]du.$$

$$\leqslant \xi\left(\frac{1}{\tau} - \xi\right) 1 \otimes^* \psi'(W_\star) B - \xi\left(\frac{1}{\tau} - \xi\right) \psi'(Q_\star) \otimes^* W_\star$$
$$- \frac{\xi(1-\xi)}{\tau} Q_\star \otimes^* \psi'(W_\star) + \frac{\xi(1-\xi)}{\tau} \psi'(Q_\star) Q_\star \otimes^* 1.$$

By rewriting the terms using the tensorial properties in the following way,

$$(1 \otimes^* W_\star)(1 \otimes^* \psi'(W_\star)) = 1 \otimes^* \psi'(W_\star) W_\star, \quad \psi'(Q_\star) \otimes^* W_\star = (\psi'(Q_\star) \otimes^* 1)(1 \otimes^* W_\star).$$

and regrouping, we obtain the original inequality,

$$0 \leqslant (1-\xi)\psi\left(\frac{Q_\star}{\tau}\right) \otimes^* 1 + \xi 1 \otimes^* \psi\left(\frac{W_\star}{\tau}\right) - \psi\left(\frac{1-\xi}{\tau} Q_\star \otimes^* 1 + \xi 1 \otimes^* W_\star\right)$$
$$+ \xi\left(1 - \frac{1}{\tau}\right) \int_0^1 (1 \otimes^* W_\star) \psi'\left(\frac{1-\xi u}{\tau} Q_\star \otimes^* 1 + u\xi 1 \otimes^* W_\star\right) du$$
$$\leqslant \left(\frac{\xi(1-\xi)}{\tau} Q_\star \otimes^* 1 - \xi \cdot \left(\frac{1}{\tau} - \xi\right) 1 \otimes^* W_\star\right)(\psi'(Q_\star) \otimes^* 1 - 1 \otimes^* \psi'(W_\star)).$$

For the particular value, let $\tau, \xi = \frac{1}{2}$. □

Corollary 4. *Setting $\tau = 1$, we obtain the inequality given by Dragomir ([35], p. 9):*

$$0 \leqslant (1-\xi)\psi(Q_\star) \otimes^* 1 + \xi 1 \otimes^* \psi(W_\star) - \psi((1-\xi)Q_\star \otimes^* 1 + \xi 1 \otimes^* W_\star)$$
$$\leqslant \xi(1-\xi)(Q_\star \otimes^* 1 - 1 \otimes^* W_\star)(\psi'(Q_\star) \otimes^* 1 - 1 \otimes^* \psi'(W_\star)).$$

Lemma 3. *Let $\psi : I \subset \mathbb{R} \to \mathbb{R}$ be a twice-differentiable function on the interval I^0 the interior of I. If there exist the constants c, C such that*

$$c \leqslant \psi''(t) \leqslant C \text{ for any } t \in I^0,$$

then

$$\frac{1}{2} c \xi(1-\xi)\left(w - \frac{q}{\tau}\right)^2 \leqslant (1-\xi)\psi\left(\frac{q}{\tau}\right) + \xi\psi\left(\frac{w}{\tau}\right) - \psi\left((1-\xi)\frac{q}{\tau} + \xi w\right)$$
$$- w\xi\left(1 - \frac{1}{\tau}\right) \int_0^1 \left(c\left((1-t)\frac{q}{\tau} + t((1-\xi)\frac{q}{\tau} + \xi w)\right) - \psi'\left((1-t)\frac{q}{\tau} + t((1-\xi)\frac{q}{\tau} + \xi w)\right)\right) dt$$
$$\leqslant (1-\xi)\psi\left(\frac{q}{\tau}\right) + \xi\psi\left(\frac{w}{\tau}\right) - \psi\left((1-\xi)\frac{q}{\tau} + \xi w\right)$$
$$- w\xi\left(1 - \frac{1}{\tau}\right) \int_0^1 \left(C\left((1-t)\frac{q}{\tau} + t((1-\xi)\frac{q}{\tau} + \xi w)\right) - \psi'\left((1-t)\frac{q}{\tau} + t((1-\xi)\frac{q}{\tau} + \xi w)\right)\right) dt$$
$$\leqslant \frac{1}{2} C \xi(1-\xi)\left(w - \frac{q}{\tau}\right)^2.$$

Proof. We consider the auxiliary function $\psi_C : I \subset \mathbb{R} \to \mathbb{R}$ defined by $\psi_C(x) = \frac{1}{2} x^2 C - \psi(x)$. The function ψ_C is differentiable on I^0 and $\psi_C''(x) = C - \psi''(x) \geqslant 0$, showing that ψ_C is a convex function on I^0. By the convexity of ψ_C, we have for any $q, w \in I^0$ and $\xi \in [0, 1]$ that

$$0 \leqslant (1-\xi)\psi_C\left(\frac{q}{\tau}\right) + \xi\psi_C\left(\frac{w}{\tau}\right) - \psi_C\left((1-\xi)\frac{q}{\tau} + \xi w\right)$$
$$+ w\xi\left(1 - \frac{1}{\tau}\right) \int_0^1 \psi_C'\left((1-t)\frac{q}{\tau} + t((1-\xi)\frac{q}{\tau} + \xi w)\right) dt,$$

which, when rearranged, gives us the right hand side inequality. The left hand side inequality follows in a similar way by considering the auxiliary function $\psi_C(x) = \psi(x) - \frac{1}{2}cx^2$, which is twice-differentiable and convex on I^0. The middle inequality follows by comparing the integral parts of the left hand part of the right inequality and the right hand side of the left hand side inequality. If we take $\psi(x) = x^2$, then the inequality reduces to an equality $c = C = 2$. □

Corollary 5. *Setting $\tau = 1$ in the Lemma, it reduces to the Lemma 2 given by Dragomir ([35], p. 11)*

$$\frac{1}{2}c\xi(1-\xi)(w-q)^2 \leqslant (1-\xi)\psi(q) + \xi\psi(w) - \psi((1-\xi)q + \xi w) \leqslant \frac{1}{2}C\xi(1-\xi)(w-q)^2.$$

Theorem 4. *Let $\psi : I \subset \to \mathbb{R}$ be a twice-differentiable function on the interval I^0, the interior of I. If there exist the constants c, C such that the condition holds, then for any self-adjoint operators $Q_\star, W_\star$ with $SP(Q_\star), SP(W_\star) \subset I$,*

$$\frac{c}{2}\xi(1-\xi)\left(\frac{1}{\tau}Q_\star \otimes^{\tilde{}} 1 - 1 \otimes^{\tilde{}} W_\star\right)^2 \leqslant (1-\xi)\psi\left(\frac{Q_\star}{\tau}\right) \otimes^{\tilde{}} 1 + \xi 1 \otimes^{\tilde{}} \psi\left(\frac{W_\star}{\tau}\right)$$

$$- \psi\left(\frac{1-\xi}{\tau}Q_\star \otimes^{\tilde{}} 1 + \xi 1 \otimes^{\tilde{}} W_\star\right)$$

$$- \xi\left(1 - \frac{1}{\tau}\right)\int_0^1 \left[c\left(\frac{1-u\xi}{\tau}Q_\star \otimes^{\tilde{}} W_\star + u\xi(1 \otimes^{\tilde{}} W_\star)^2\right)\right.$$

$$\left. - (1 \otimes^{\tilde{}} W_\star)\psi'\left(\frac{(1-u\xi)}{\tau}Q_\star \otimes^{\tilde{}} 1 + u\xi 1 \otimes^{\tilde{}} W_\star\right)\right]du$$

$$\leqslant (1-\xi)\psi\left(\frac{Q_\star}{\tau}\right) \otimes^{\tilde{}} 1 + \xi 1 \otimes^{\tilde{}} \psi\left(\frac{W_\star}{\tau}\right) - \psi\left(\frac{1-\xi}{\tau}Q_\star \otimes^{\tilde{}} 1 + \xi 1 \otimes^{\tilde{}} W_\star\right)$$

$$- \xi\left(1 - \frac{1}{\tau}\right)\int_0^1 \left[C\left(\frac{1-u\xi}{\tau}Q_\star \otimes^{\tilde{}} W_\star + u\xi(1 \otimes^{\tilde{}} W_\star)^2\right)\right.$$

$$\left. - (1 \otimes^{\tilde{}} W_\star)\psi'\left(\frac{1-u\xi}{\tau}Q_\star \otimes^{\tilde{}} 1 + u\xi 1 \otimes^{\tilde{}} W_\star\right)\right]du$$

$$\leqslant \frac{C}{2}\xi(1-\xi)\left(\frac{1}{\tau}Q_\star \otimes^{\tilde{}} 1 - 1 \otimes^{\tilde{}} W_\star\right)^2.$$

Proof. Assume that Q and W have spectral resolutions

$$Q = \int_I t\,dE_t \text{ and } W = \int_I s\,dF_s.$$

If we take the double integral $\int_I \int_I$ over $dE(t) \otimes^{\tilde{}} dF(s)$ in the inequality which we obtained in Lemma 3, then we get

$$\frac{1}{2}c\xi(1-\xi)\int_I\int_I \left(-s + \frac{t}{\tau}\right)^2 dE(t) \otimes^{\tilde{}} dF(s)$$

$$\leqslant (1-\xi)\int_I\int_I \psi\left(\frac{t}{\tau}\right)dE(t) \otimes^{\tilde{}} dF(s) + \int_I\int_I \xi\psi\left(\frac{s}{\tau}\right)dE(t) \otimes^{\tilde{}} dF(s)$$

$$- \int_I\int_I \psi\left((1-\xi)\frac{t}{\tau} + \xi s\right)dE(t) \otimes^{\tilde{}} dF(s)$$

$$- \int_I\int_I w\xi\left(1 - \frac{1}{\tau}\right)\int_0^1 d\left((1-u)\frac{t}{\tau} + u((1-\xi)\frac{t}{\tau} + \xi w)\right)du\,dE(t) \otimes^{\tilde{}} dF(s)$$

$$+ \int_I \int_I w\xi\left(1 - \frac{1}{\tau}\right) \int_0^1 \psi'\left((1-u)\frac{t}{\tau} + u((1-\xi)\frac{t}{\tau} + \xi w)\right) du\, dE(t) \otimes^* dF(s)$$

$$\leqslant (1-\xi) \int_I \int_I \psi\left(\frac{t}{\tau}\right) dE(t) \otimes^* dF(s) + \int_I \int_I \xi\psi\left(\frac{s}{\tau}\right) dE(t) \otimes^* dF(s)$$

$$- \int_I \int_I \psi\left((1-\xi)\frac{t}{\tau} + \xi s\right) dE(t) \otimes^* dF(s)$$

$$- \int_I \int_I w\xi\left(1 - \frac{1}{\tau}\right) \int_0^1 C\left((1-u)\frac{t}{\tau} + u((1-\xi)\frac{t}{\tau} + \xi w)\right) du\, dE(t) \otimes^* dF(s)$$

$$+ \int_I \int_I w\xi\left(1 - \frac{1}{\tau}\right) \int_0^1 \psi'\left((1-u)\frac{t}{\tau} + u((1-\xi)\frac{t}{\tau} + \xi w)\right) du\, dE(t) \otimes^* dF(s)$$

$$\leqslant \frac{1}{2} C\xi(1-\xi) \int_I \int_I \left(-s + \frac{t}{\tau}\right)^2 dE(t) \otimes^* dF(s),$$

since

$$\int_I \int_I \left(-s + \frac{t}{\tau}\right)^2 dE(t) \otimes^* dF(s) = \int_I \int_I \left(\frac{t^2}{\tau^2} - \frac{2}{\tau}ts + s^2\right) dE(t) \otimes^* dF(s)$$

$$= \int_I \int_I \frac{t^2}{\tau^2} dE(t) \otimes^* dF(s) - \frac{2}{\tau} \int_I \int_I ts\, dE(t) \otimes^* dF(s) + \int_I \int_I s^2 dE(t) \otimes^* dF(s)$$

$$= \frac{1}{\tau^2} Q_\star^2 \otimes^* 1 - \frac{2}{\tau} Q_\star \otimes^* W_\star + 1 \otimes^* W_\star^2.$$

Using the tensorial properties we get

$$\int_I \int_I \left(-s + \frac{t}{\tau}\right)^2 dE(t) \otimes^* dF(s) = \left(\frac{1}{\tau} Q_\star \otimes^* 1 - 1 \otimes^* W_\star\right)^2.$$

Using Fubini's Theorem on the term with the integral under the spectral resolution, we obtain the original inequality,

$$\frac{c}{2}\xi(1-\xi) \left(\frac{1}{\tau} Q_\star \otimes^* 1 - 1 \otimes^* W_\star\right)^2$$

$$\leqslant (1-\xi)\psi\left(\frac{Q_\star}{\tau}\right) \otimes^* 1 + \xi 1 \otimes^* \psi\left(\frac{W_\star}{\tau}\right) - \psi\left(\frac{1-\xi}{\tau} Q_\star \otimes^* 1 + \xi 1 \otimes^* W_\star\right)$$

$$- \xi\left(1 - \frac{1}{\tau}\right) \int_0^1 \left[c\left(\frac{1-u\xi}{\tau} Q_\star \otimes^* W_\star + u\xi(1 \otimes^* W_\star)^2\right)\right.$$

$$\left. - (1 \otimes^* W_\star)\psi'\left(\frac{(1-u\xi)}{\tau} Q_\star \otimes^* 1 + u\xi 1 \otimes^* W_\star\right)\right] du$$

$$\leqslant (1-\xi)\psi\left(\frac{Q_\star}{\tau}\right) \otimes^* 1 + \xi 1 \otimes^* \psi\left(\frac{W_\star}{\tau}\right) - \psi\left(\frac{1-\xi}{\tau} Q_\star \otimes^* 1 + \xi 1 \otimes^* W_\star\right)$$

$$- \xi\left(1 - \frac{1}{\tau}\right) \int_0^1 \left[C\left(\frac{1-u\xi}{\tau} Q_\star \otimes^* W_\star + u\xi(1 \otimes^* W_\star)^2\right)\right.$$

$$\left. - (1 \otimes^* W_\star)\psi'\left(\frac{1-u\xi}{\tau} Q_\star \otimes^* 1 + u\xi 1 \otimes^* W_\star\right)\right] du$$

$$\leqslant \frac{C}{2}\xi(1-\xi)\left(\frac{1}{\tau} Q_\star \otimes^* 1 - 1 \otimes^* W_\star\right)^2.$$

□

4. Some Examples and Consequences

In the following sequel we give examples which demonstrate the obtained Theorems.

Example 2. *We consider the power function, $f(t) = t^z$, $t > 0$, which is convex for $z \in (-\infty, 0) \cup [1, +\infty)$. From Theorem 3 for $A, B > 0$, we obtain the following:*

$$0 \leqslant \frac{1}{\tau^z}((1-\xi)Q_\star^z \otimes^* 1 + \xi 1 \otimes^* W_\star^z) - \left(\frac{1-\xi}{\tau} Q_\star \otimes^* 1 + \xi 1 \otimes^* W_\star\right)^z$$

$$+ z\xi\left(1 - \frac{1}{\tau}\right) \int_0^1 (1 \otimes^* W_\star) \left(\frac{1-\xi u}{\tau} Q_\star \otimes^* 1 + u\xi 1 \otimes^* W_\star\right)^{z-1} du$$

$$\leqslant z\left(\frac{\xi(1-\xi)}{\tau} Q_\star \otimes^* 1 - \xi \cdot \left(\frac{1}{\tau} - \xi\right) 1 \otimes^* W_\star\right) \left(Q_\star^{z-1} \otimes^* 1 - 1 \otimes^* W_\star^{z-1}\right).$$

Corollary 6. *Letting $\tau = 1$, we obtain the example given by Dragomir ([35], p. 15):*

$$0 \leqslant (1-\xi)Q_\star^z \otimes^* 1 + \xi 1 \otimes^* W_\star^z - ((1-\xi)Q_\star \otimes^* 1 + \xi 1 \otimes^* W_\star)^z$$

$$\leqslant z\xi(1-\xi)(Q_\star \otimes^* 1 - 1 \otimes^* W_\star)\left(Q_\star^{z-1} \otimes^* 1 - 1 \otimes^* W_\star^{z-1}\right).$$

Setting $\xi, \tau = \frac{1}{2}$, we get

$$0 \leqslant 2^{z-1}(Q_\star^z \otimes^* 1 + 1 \otimes^* W_\star^z) - \left(Q_\star \otimes^* 1 + \frac{1}{2} 1 \otimes^* W_\star\right)^z$$

$$- \frac{z}{2} \int_0^1 (1 \otimes^* W_\star)\left((2-u)Q_\star \otimes^* 1 + \frac{u}{2} 1 \otimes^* W_\star\right)^{z-1} du$$

$$\leqslant z\left(\frac{1}{2} Q_\star \otimes^* 1 - \frac{3}{4} 1 \otimes^* W_\star\right)\left(Q_\star^{z-1} \otimes^* 1 - 1 \otimes^* W_\star^{z-1}\right).$$

Using the inequality obtained in Theorem 4, we obtain

$$\frac{c}{2}\xi(1-\xi)\left(\frac{1}{\tau}Q_\star \otimes^* 1 - 1 \otimes^* W_\star\right)^2$$

$$\leqslant \frac{1}{\tau^z}((1-\xi)Q_\star^z \otimes^* 1 + \xi 1 \otimes^* W_\star^z) - \left(\frac{1-\xi}{\tau} Q_\star \otimes^* 1 + \xi 1 \otimes^* W_\star\right)^z$$

$$- \xi\left(1 - \frac{1}{\tau}\right) \int_0^1 \left[c\left(\frac{1-u\xi}{\tau} Q_\star \otimes^* W_\star + u\xi(1 \otimes^* W_\star)^2\right)\right.$$

$$\left. - z(1 \otimes^* W_\star)\left(\frac{(1-u\xi)}{\tau} Q_\star \otimes^* 1 + u\xi 1 \otimes^* W_\star\right)^{z-1}\right] du$$

$$\leqslant \frac{1}{\tau^z}((1-\xi)Q_\star^z \otimes^* 1 + \xi 1 \otimes^* W_\star^z) - \left(\frac{1-\xi}{\tau} Q_\star \otimes^* 1 + \xi 1 \otimes^* W_\star\right)^z$$

$$- \xi\left(1 - \frac{1}{\tau}\right) \int_0^1 \left[C\left(\frac{1-u\xi}{\tau} Q_\star \otimes^* W_\star + u\xi(1 \otimes^* W_\star)^2\right)\right.$$

$$\left. - z(1 \otimes^* W_\star)\left(\frac{(1-u\xi)}{\tau} Q_\star \otimes^* 1 + u\xi 1 \otimes^* W_\star\right)^{z-1}\right] du$$

$$\leqslant \frac{C}{2}\xi(1-\xi)\left(\frac{1}{\tau}Q_\star \otimes^* 1 - 1 \otimes^* W_\star\right)^2.$$

Example 3. Let us consider now the convex function $f(t) = e^{\alpha t}, t, \alpha \in \mathbb{R}$ and $\alpha \neq 0$. From Theorem 3, we get the following for self-adjoint operators $Q_\star$ and $W_\star$:

$$(1-\xi)e^{\frac{\alpha}{\tau}Q_\star} \otimes^{\tilde{}} 1 + \xi 1 \otimes^{\tilde{}} e^{\frac{\alpha}{\tau}W_\star} - e^{\alpha(\frac{1-\xi}{\tau}Q_\star \otimes^{\tilde{}} 1 + \xi 1 \otimes^{\tilde{}} W_\star)}$$

$$+\alpha\xi\left(1 - \frac{1}{\tau}\right)\int_0^1 (1 \otimes^{\tilde{}} W_\star) e^{\alpha(\frac{1-\xi u}{\tau}Q_\star \otimes^{\tilde{}} 1 + u\xi 1 \otimes^{\tilde{}} W_\star)} du$$

$$\leqslant \alpha\left(\frac{\xi(1-\xi)}{\tau}Q_\star \otimes^{\tilde{}} 1 - \xi \cdot \left(\frac{1}{\tau} - \xi\right) 1 \otimes^{\tilde{}} W_\star\right)(e^{\alpha Q_\star} \otimes^{\tilde{}} 1 - 1 \otimes^{\tilde{}} e^{\alpha W_\star}).$$

Corollary 7. Setting $\tau = 1$ in the obtained inequality, we recover the example given by Dragomir ([35], p. 15)

$$0 \leqslant (1-\xi)e^{\alpha Q_\star} \otimes^{\tilde{}} 1 + u1 \otimes^{\tilde{}} e^{\alpha W_\star} - e^{\alpha((1-\xi)Q_\star \otimes^{\tilde{}} 1 + \xi 1 \otimes^{\tilde{}} W_\star)}$$

$$\leqslant \alpha\xi(1-\xi)(Q_\star \otimes^{\tilde{}} 1 - 1 \otimes^{\tilde{}} W_\star)(e^{\alpha Q_\star} \otimes^{\tilde{}} 1 - 1 \otimes^{\tilde{}} e^{\alpha W_\star}).$$

Setting $\xi, \tau = \frac{1}{2}$, we obtain

$$\frac{1}{2}\left(e^{2\alpha Q_\star} \otimes^{\tilde{}} 1 + 1 \otimes^{\tilde{}} e^{2\alpha W_\star}\right) - e^{\alpha(Q_\star \otimes^{\tilde{}} 1 + \frac{1}{2}1 \otimes^{\tilde{}} W_\star)} - \frac{\alpha}{2}\int_0^1 (1 \otimes^{\tilde{}} W_\star)e^{\alpha((2-u)Q_\star \otimes^{\tilde{}} 1 + \frac{u}{2}1 \otimes^{\tilde{}} W_\star)} du$$

$$\leqslant z\left(\frac{1}{2}Q_\star \otimes^{\tilde{}} 1 - \frac{3}{4}1 \otimes^{\tilde{}} W_\star\right)(e^{\alpha Q_\star} \otimes^{\tilde{}} 1 - 1 \otimes^{\tilde{}} e^{\alpha W_\star}).$$

Using the inequality obtained in Theorem 4, we obtain

$$\frac{c}{2}\xi(1-\xi)\left(\frac{1}{\tau}Q_\star \otimes^{\tilde{}} 1 - 1 \otimes^{\tilde{}} W_\star\right)^2 \leqslant (1-\xi)e^{\frac{\alpha}{\tau}Q_\star} \otimes^{\tilde{}} 1 + \xi 1 \otimes^{\tilde{}} e^{\frac{\alpha}{\tau}W_\star} - e^{\alpha(\frac{1-\xi}{\tau}Q_\star \otimes^{\tilde{}} 1 + \xi 1 \otimes^{\tilde{}} W_\star)}$$

$$-\xi\left(1 - \frac{1}{\tau}\right)\int_0^1 \left[c\left(\frac{1-u\xi}{\tau}Q_\star \otimes^{\tilde{}} W_\star + u\xi(1 \otimes^{\tilde{}} W_\star)^2\right) - z(1 \otimes^{\tilde{}} W_\star)e^{\left(\frac{1-u\xi}{\tau}Q_\star \otimes^{\tilde{}} 1 + u\xi 1 \otimes^{\tilde{}} W_\star\right)}\right] du$$

$$\leqslant (1-\xi)e^{\frac{\alpha}{\tau}Q_\star} \otimes^{\tilde{}} 1 + \xi 1 \otimes^{\tilde{}} e^{\frac{\alpha}{\tau}W_\star} - e^{\alpha(\frac{1-\xi}{\tau}Q_\star \otimes^{\tilde{}} 1 + \xi 1 \otimes^{\tilde{}} W_\star)}$$

$$-\xi\left(1 - \frac{1}{\tau}\right)\int_0^1 \left[C\left(\frac{1-u\xi}{\tau}Q_\star \otimes^{\tilde{}} W_\star + u\xi(1 \otimes^{\tilde{}} W_\star)^2\right) - z(1 \otimes^{\tilde{}} W_\star)e^{\left(\frac{(1-u\xi)}{\tau}Q_\star \otimes^{\tilde{}} 1 + u\xi 1 \otimes^{\tilde{}} W_\star\right)}\right] du$$

$$\leqslant \frac{C}{2}\xi(1-\xi)\left(\frac{1}{\tau}Q_\star \otimes^{\tilde{}} 1 - 1 \otimes^{\tilde{}} W_\star\right)^2.$$

5. Conclusions

Tensors have become important in various fields, for example in physics, because they provide a concise mathematical framework for formulating and solving physical problems in fields such as mechanics, electromagnetism, quantum mechanics, and many others. As such, inequalities are crucial in numerical aspects. Reflected in this work is the generalized Dragomir's lemma, which, as a consequence, has new inequalities of the classical type. Using that lemma enabled us to generalize the results from Dragomir [35]. New HH inequalities are given, as well as the consequences showing our generalization. Examples of specific convex functions and their inequalities using our results are given in the section on examples and consequences. Plans for future research can be reflected in the fact that the obtained inequalities in this work can be sharpened or generalized by using other methods. An interesting perspective can be seen in incorporating other techniques for Hilbert space inequalities with the techniques shown in this paper. One direction is the technique of the Mond–Pecaric inequality, which we will work on.

Author Contributions: Investigation: V.S. and R.R.; Methodology: V.S., R.R. and S.R.; Project administration: R.R. and S.R.; Software: V.S. and O.A.A.A.; Supervision: R.R. and S.R.; Writing original draft: V.S. and R.R.; Writing review and editing: V.S., R.R., O.A.A.A. and S.R. All authors have read and agreed to the published version of the manuscript.

Funding: This study is supported via funding from Prince sattam bin Abdulaziz University project number (PSAU/2023/R/1444).

Acknowledgments: This study is supported via funding from Prince sattam bin Abdulaziz University project number (PSAU/2023/R/1444).

Conflicts of Interest: The authors declare no conflict of interest.

References

1. Mitrinovic, D.S. *Analytic Inequalities*; Springer: Berlin/Heidelberg, Germany, 1970.
2. Pečarić, J.; Proschan, F.; Tong, Y. *Convex Functions, Partial Orderings, and Statistical Applications*; Academic Press, Inc.: Cambridge, MA, USA, 1992.
3. Stojiljković, V.; Ramaswamy, R.; Abdelnaby, O.A.A.; Radenović, S. Some Novel Inequalities for LR-(k,h-m)-p Convex Interval Valued Functions by Means of Pseudo Order Relation. *Fractal Fract.* **2022**, *6*, 726. [CrossRef]
4. Stojiljković, V.; Ramaswamy, R.; Alshammari, F.; Ashour, O.A.; Alghazwani, M.L.H.; Radenović, S. Hermite–Hadamard Type Inequalities Involving (k-p) Fractional Operator for Various Types of Convex Functions. *Fractal Fract.* **2022**, *6*, 376. [CrossRef]
5. Stojiljković, V.; Ramaswamy, R.; Ashour Abdelnaby, O.A.; Radenović, S. RiemannLiouville Fractional Inclusions for Convex Functions Using Interval Valued Setting. *Mathematics* **2022**, *10*, 3491. [CrossRef]
6. Stojiljkovic, V. Hermite Hadamard Type Inequalities Involving (k-p) Fractional Operator with $(\alpha, h\text{-}m)\text{-}p$ convexity. *Eur. J. Pure Appl. Math.* **2023**, *16*, 503–522. [CrossRef]
7. Afzal, W.; Abbas, M.; Macías-Díaz, J.E.; Treanţă, S. Some H-Godunova-Levin Function Inequalities Using Center Radius (Cr) Order Relation. *Fractal Fract.* **2022**, *6*, 518. [CrossRef]
8. Afzal, W.; Alb Lupaş, A.; Shabbir, K. Hermite–Hadamard and Jensen-Type Inequalities for Harmonical (h1, h2)-Godunova-Levin Interval-Valued Functions. *Mathematics* **2022**, *10*, 2970. [CrossRef]
9. Afzal, W.; Shabbir, K.; Treanta, S.; Nonlaopon, K. Jensen and Hermite–Hadamard type inclusions for harmonical h-Godunova-Levin functions. *AIMS Math.* **2023**, *8*, 3303–3321. [CrossRef]
10. Afzal, W.; Shabbir, K.; Botmart, T. Generalized version of Jensen and Hermite–Hadamard inequalities for interval-valued (h_1, h_2)-Godunova-Levin functions. *AIMS Math.* **2022**, *7*, 19372–19387. [CrossRef]
11. Afzal, W.; Nazeer, W.; Botmart, T.; Treanta, S. Some properties and inequalities for generalized class of harmonical Godunova-Levin function via center radius order relation. *AIMS Math.* **2023**, *8*, 1696–1712. [CrossRef]
12. Butt, S.I.; Tariq, M.; Aslam, A.; Ahmad, H.; Nofal, T.A. Hermite–Hadamard type inequalities via generalized harmonic exponential convexity and applications. *J. Funct. Spaces* **2021**, *2021*, 5533491. [CrossRef]
13. Chandola, A.; Agarwal, R.; Pandey, M.R. Some New Hermite–Hadamard, Hermite–Hadamard Fejer and Weighted Hardy Type Inequalities Involving (k-p) Riemann- Liouville Fractional Integral Operator. *Appl. Math. Inf. Sci.* **2022**, *16*, 287–297.
14. Chen, H.; Katugampola, U.N. Hermite–Hadamard and Hermite–Hadamard-Fejr type inequalities for generalized fractional integrals. *J. Math. Anal. Appl.* **2017**, *446*, 1274–1291. [CrossRef]
15. Mond, B.; Pečarić, J.E. Convex inequalities in Hilbert spaces. *Houst. J. Math.* **1993**, *19*, 405–420.
16. Mond, B.; Pečarić, J.E. Bounds for Jensen's inequality for several operators. *Houst. J. Math.* **1994**, *20*, 645–651.
17. Mičič, J.; Seo, Y.; Takahasi, S.-E.; Tominaga, M. Inequalities of Furuta and Mond-Pecaric. *Math. Ineq. Appl.* **1999**, *2*, 83–112.
18. Dragomir, S.S. Hermite–Hadamard's type inequalities for operator convex functions. *Appl. Math. Comput.* **2011**, *218*, 766–772. [CrossRef]
19. Ghazanfari, A.G. Some new Hermite–Hadamard type inequalities for two operator convex function. *arXiv* **2012**, arXiv:1207.0928v1.
20. Bakherad, M.; Abbas, H.; Mourad, B.; Sal Moslehian, M. Operator P-class functions. *J. Inequalities Appl.* **2014**, *2014*, 451. [CrossRef]
21. Pečarić, J.; Furuta, T.; Hot, J.M.; Seo, Y. *Inequalities for Bounded Selfadjoint Operators on a Hilbert Space*; Element: Zagreb, Croatia, 2005.
22. Dragomir S.S. *Inequalities for the Numerical Radius of Linear Operators in Hilbert Spaces*; Springer: Cham, Switzerland, 2013. [CrossRef]
23. Alomari, M.W.; Bercu, G.; Chesneau, C. On the Dragomir Extension of Furuta's Inequality and Numerical Radius Inequalities. *Symmetry* **2022**, *14*, 1432. [CrossRef]
24. Altwaijry, N.; Feki, K.; Minculete, N. On Some Generalizations of Cauchy-Schwarz Inequalities and Their Applications. *Symmetry* **2023**, *15*, 304. [CrossRef]
25. Wang, X.; Lv, H. Quasi-Double Diagonally Dominant H-Tensors and the Estimation Inequalities for the Spectral Radius of Nonnegative Tensors. *Symmetry* **2023**, *15*, 439. [CrossRef]
26. Araki, H.; Hansen, F. Jensen's operator inequality for functions of several variables. *Proc. Am. Math. Soc.* **2000**, *128*, 20. [CrossRef]
27. Koranyi, A. On some classes of analytic functions of several variables. *Trans. Am. Math. Soc.* **1961**, *101*, 520–554. [CrossRef]
28. Guo, H. *What Are Tensors Exactly?* World Scientific: Singapore, 2021. [CrossRef]

29. Dragomir, S.S. An Inequality Improving the first Hermite–Hadamard inequality for convex-functions defined on linear spaces and applications for semi-inner products. *J. Inequal. Pure Appl. Math.* **2002**, *3*, 31.
30. Dragomir, S.S. An inequality improving the second Hermite–Hadamard inequality for convex functions defined on linear spaces and applications for semi-inner products. *J. Inequal. Pure Appl. Math.* **2002**, *3*, 35.
31. Dragomir, S.S. Bounds for the normalized Jensen functional. *Bull. Austral. Math. Soc.* **2006**, *74*, 417–478. [CrossRef]
32. Dragomir, S.S. A note on Youngís inequality, Revista de la Real Academia de Ciencias Exactas, Físicas y Naturales. *Ser. A Mat.* **2017**, *11*, 349–354.
33. Dragomir, S.S.; Cerone, P.; Sofo, A. Some remarks on the trapezoid rule in numerical integration. *Indian J. Pure Appl. Math.* **2000**, *3*. Available online: https://core.ac.uk/download/pdf/10835036.pdf (accessed on 2 January 2023).
34. Dragomir, S.S. An Ostrowski Type Tensorial Norm Inequality for Continuous Functions of Selfadjoint Operators in Hilbert Spaces, ResearchGate. November 2022. ResearchGate Preprint. Available online: https://www.researchgate.net/profile/S-Dragomir/publication/365656709_AN_OSTROWSKI_TYPE_TENSORIAL_NORM_INEQUALITY_FOR_CONTINUOUS_FUNCTIONS_OF_SELFADJOINT_OPERATORS_IN_HILBERT_SPACES/links/637d6dc41766b34c5449fc52/AN-OSTROWSKI-TYPE-TENSORIAL-NORM-INEQUALITY-FOR-CONTINUOUS-FUNCTIONS-OF-SELFADJOINT-OPERATORS-IN-HILBERT-SPACES.pdf (accessed on 2 January 2023).
35. Dragomir, S.S. Refinements and Reverses Of Tensorial Hermite–Hadamard Inequalities for Convex Functions of Self-adjoint Operators in Hilbert Spaces, ResearchGate, November 2022, ResearchGate Preprint. Available online: https://www.researchgate.net/profile/S-Dragomir/publication/363737336_REFINEMENTS_AND_REVERSES_OF_TENSORIAL_HERMITE-HADAMARD_INEQUALITIES_FOR_CONVEX_FUNCTIONS_OF_SELFADJOINT_OPERATORS_IN_HILBERT_SPACES/links/632bdbc670cc936cd327b539/REFINEMENTS-AND-REVERSES-OF-TENSORIAL-HERMITE-HADAMARD-INEQUALITIES-FOR-CONVEX-FUNCTIONS-OF-SELFADJOINT-OPERATORS-IN-HILBERT-SPACES.pdf (acessed on 2 January 2023).

Disclaimer/Publisher's Note: The statements, opinions and data contained in all publications are solely those of the individual author(s) and contributor(s) and not of MDPI and/or the editor(s). MDPI and/or the editor(s) disclaim responsibility for any injury to people or property resulting from any ideas, methods, instructions or products referred to in the content.

Article

An Analytical Approach to Solve the Fractional Benney Equation Using the q-Homotopy Analysis Transform Method

Rasool Shah [1,*], Yousuf Alkhezi [2,*] and Khaled Alhamad [3]

[1] Department of Mathematics, Abdul Wali Khan University Mardan, Mardan 23200, Pakistan
[2] Mathematics Department, College of Basic Education, Public Authority for Applied Education and Training (PAAET), Shuwaikh 70654, Kuwait
[3] College of Technological Studies, The Public Authority for Applied Education and Training (PAAET), Shuwaikh 70654, Kuwait
* Correspondence: shahrasool26@gmail.com (R.S.); ya.alkhezi@paaet.edu.kw (Y.A.)

Abstract: This paper introduces an analytical approach for solving the Benney equation using the q-homotopy analysis transform method. The Benney equation is a nonlinear partial differential equation that has applications in diverse areas of physics and engineering. The q-homotopy analysis transform method is a numerical technique that has been successfully employed to solve a broad range of nonlinear problems. By utilizing this method, we derive approximate analytical solutions for the Benney equation. The results demonstrate that this method is a powerful and effective tool for obtaining accurate solutions for the equation. The proposed method offers a valuable contribution to the existing literature on the behavior of the Benney equation and provides researchers with a useful tool for solving this equation in various applications.

Keywords: q-homotopy analysis transform method; Benney equation; Atangana–Baleanu derivative; Laplace transform

1. Introduction

Fractional nonlinear partial differential equations (PDEs) are a type of mathematical model that describes the behavior of systems with complex dynamics. These equations involve fractional derivatives, which generalize the classical concept of differentiation to non-integer orders. Nonlinearity, on the other hand, refers to the property that the solutions of the equation are not proportional to the input, making it difficult to predict the behavior of the system [1–4].

Fractional derivatives appear naturally in many physical phenomena, such as diffusion, wave propagation, and viscoelasticity, which exhibit memory effects and long-range interactions. These effects are captured by fractional derivatives, which account for the history of the system and its nonlocal interactions. Nonlinearity, on the other hand, arises from the coupling of multiple variables and the nonlinear response of the system to external forces [5,6]. Examples of fractional nonlinear PDEs include the fractional diffusion equation, the fractional wave equation, the fractional Burgers equation, and the fractional KdV equation. These equations have been studied extensively in recent years, both analytically and numerically, to understand their properties and to develop efficient methods for solving them [7–9].

One of the main challenges in dealing with fractional nonlinear PDEs is their complexity and the lack of closed-form solutions. Analytical methods are limited to specific cases and often rely on approximation techniques or numerical simulations. Numerical methods, on the other hand, are more general but require high computational resources and careful validation to ensure accuracy and stability [10–12]. Despite these challenges, fractional nonlinear PDEs have numerous applications in science and engineering, such as in the modeling of transport phenomena, fluid dynamics, materials science, and biological systems. They provide a powerful tool for understanding the behavior of complex systems and for designing control strategies to optimize their performance [13–15].

Fractional partial differential equations (FPDEs) and symmetry are closely related concepts in mathematical physics. In particular, symmetry plays a crucial role in the study of fractional differential equations. Symmetry is the invariance of a mathematical object under certain transformations [16–18]. In the case of differential equations, it refers to the invariance of the equation under certain transformations of its solutions. Symmetry can be used to simplify the problem and to identify solutions that satisfy certain boundary conditions [19,20].

The investigation of nonlinear physical issues is of paramount importance in acquiring meaningful insights. Numerous scholars have employed diverse techniques to articulate nonlinear fractional differential equations (FDEs) in order to derive the necessary outcomes.

The Benney equation general form, as in [21], is given by

$$\psi_\omega(\eta,\omega) + (\psi^n(\eta,\omega))_\eta + \psi_{\eta\eta}(\eta,\omega) + \beta\psi_{\eta\eta\eta}(\eta,\omega) + \psi_{\eta\eta\eta\eta}(\eta,\omega) = 0, \qquad (1)$$

where β is the positive constant called the characterizing dispersion and n is a positive integer.

The Benney equation has several applications in various practical domains such as solitons theory, dynamics, physics, and fluid mechanics. The long waves on a viscous fluid traveling down an inclined plane and the unstable drift waves are described by the Benney equation in plasma; to learn more about the Benney equation's applications, see [21,22].

We are particularly interested in the fractional-order Benney equation for our analysis:

$$^{ABC}D_\omega^\kappa \psi_\omega(\eta,\omega) + \left(\psi^3(\eta,\omega)\right)_\eta + \psi_{\eta\eta}(\eta,\omega) + \beta\psi_{\eta\eta\eta}(\eta,\omega) + \psi_{\eta\eta\eta\eta}(\eta,\omega) = 0. \qquad (2)$$

There are several well-established techniques and algorithms that have gained prominence in providing analytical or numerical solutions for the fractional-order Benney problem in recent times. Akinlar et al. proposed a hybrid approach that effectively combined the advantages of both wavelets and fractional calculus to obtain an approximate solution to the Benney equation in fractional order [21]. Similarly, the extended homotopy perturbation approach was employed to investigate the Benney equation [23]. Furthermore, Kamal Shah et al. developed a novel technique known as LADM, which was well-suited for studying the Benney equation in the context of Caputo–Febrizio fractional derivatives [24]. These techniques have proven to be robust and effective in solving the fractional-order Benney problem, thereby contributing significantly to the field of fractional calculus.

Liao [25] introduced the homotopy analysis technique (HAM), in which, after choosing an auxiliary linear operator, an endless mapping was created from an initial hunch to a precise answer. The auxiliary parameter confirmed the convergence of the solution. Determining solutions to nonlinear issues representing real-world applications takes less time when semianalytical approaches are combined with an appropriate transform. The Laplace transform and the q-homotopy analysis transform technique (q-HATM) [26–28] have been combined. Its capacity to modify two potent computational approaches for investigating FDEs gives it an advantage. We may regulate the convergence area of the solution series in a sizable allowable domain by selecting the appropriate $\hbar$.

2. Preliminaries

The Laplace transform and several fundamental definitions of fractional derivatives are explained here.

Definition 1. *The fractional order Atangana–Baleanu (AB) derivative for a function $\psi \in \mathbb{H}^1(u,\epsilon)$ ($\epsilon > \mu$), $\kappa \in [0,1]$ in the Riemann–Liouville sense is presented as follows*

$$^{ABC}_\mu D_\omega^\kappa(\psi(\omega)) = \frac{\mathcal{N}[\kappa]}{1-\kappa}\frac{d}{d\omega}\int_\mu^\omega \psi'(\rho) E_\kappa\left[\kappa\frac{(\omega-\rho)^\kappa}{\kappa-1}\right]d\rho. \qquad (3)$$

Definition 2. *The AB fractional integral is defined by*

$$_{\mu}^{AB}I_{\omega}^{\kappa}(\psi(\omega)) = \frac{1-\kappa}{\mathcal{N}[\kappa]}\psi(\omega) + \frac{\kappa}{B[\kappa]\Gamma(\kappa)}\int_{\mu}^{\omega}\psi(\rho)(\omega-\rho)^{\kappa-1}d\rho. \quad (4)$$

Definition 3. *The fractional-derivative Laplace transform (LT) is given by*

$$\mathcal{L}_{\omega}[_{\mu}^{AB}D_{\omega}^{\kappa}(\psi(\omega))] = \frac{\mathcal{N}[\kappa]}{1-\kappa}\frac{s^{\kappa}\mathcal{L}_{\omega}[\psi(\omega)] - s^{\kappa-1}\psi(0)}{s^{\kappa}+\kappa(1-\kappa)},\ 0<\kappa\leq 1. \quad (5)$$

3. Methodology

We provide the general methodology of the q-HATM [29–32] for the fractional order Benney equation

$$^{ABC}D_{\omega}^{\kappa}\psi(\eta,\omega) + (\psi^{n}(\eta,\omega))_{\eta} + \psi_{\eta\eta}(\eta,\omega) + \beta\psi_{\eta\eta\eta}(\eta,\omega) + \psi_{\eta\eta\eta\eta}(\eta,\omega) = 0, \quad (6)$$

with the initial condition

$$\psi(\eta,0) = f(\eta), \quad (7)$$

where $^{ABC}D_{\omega}^{\kappa}\psi(\eta,\omega)$ is the AB derivative of $\psi(\eta,\omega)$.

On using the LT on Equation (6), after simplification, we have

$$\mathcal{L}[\psi(\eta,\omega)] - \frac{f(\eta)}{s} + \frac{1}{\mathcal{N}[\kappa]}\left(1-\kappa+\frac{\kappa}{s^{\kappa}}\right)\mathcal{L}\left[(\psi^{n}(\eta,\omega))_{\eta} + \psi_{\eta\eta}(\eta,\omega) + \beta\psi_{\eta\eta\eta}(\eta,\omega) + \psi_{\eta\eta\eta\eta}(\eta,\omega)\right] = 0. \quad (8)$$

The nonlinear operator is defined as follows

$$N[\phi(\eta,\omega;q)] = \mathcal{L}[\phi(\eta,\omega;q)] - \frac{f(\eta)}{s} + \frac{1}{\mathcal{N}[\kappa]}\left(1-\kappa+\frac{\kappa}{s^{\kappa}}\right)\mathcal{L}\left[(\phi^{n}(\eta,\omega;q))_{\eta} + \phi_{\eta\eta}(\eta,\omega;q)\right.$$

$$\left. + \beta\phi_{\eta\eta\eta}(\eta,\omega;q) + \phi_{\eta\eta\eta\eta}(\eta,\omega;q)\right]. \quad (9)$$

Here, $\phi(\eta,\omega;q)$ is the real-valued function with respect to η, ω, and $q \in [0,\frac{1}{n}]$. Now, we define a homotopy as follows

$$(1-nq)\mathcal{L}[\phi(\eta,\omega;q) - \psi_0(\eta,\omega)] = \hbar q N[\phi(\eta,\omega;q)], \quad (10)$$

where $\hbar$ is an auxiliary parameter, $\mathcal{L}$ is the LT, and $q \in [0,\frac{1}{n}]$ ($n \geq 1$) is the embedding parameter. For $q = 0$ and $q = \frac{1}{B}$, the following hold true

$$\phi(\eta,\omega;0) = \psi_0(\eta,\omega),\ \phi(\eta,\omega;\frac{1}{n}) = \psi(\eta,\omega). \quad (11)$$

Thus, by intensifying q from 0 to $\frac{1}{n}$, the solution $\phi(\eta,\omega;q)$ varies from the initial guess $\psi_0(\eta,\omega)$ to $\psi(\eta,\omega)$. Defining $\phi(\eta,\omega;q)$ with respect to q by using the Taylor theorem, we obtain

$$\phi(\eta,\omega;q) = \psi_0(\eta,\omega) + \sum_{m=1}^{\infty}\psi_m(\eta,\omega)q^m, \quad (12)$$

where

$$\psi_m = \frac{1}{m!}\frac{\partial^m \phi(\eta,\omega;q)}{\partial q^m}|_{q=0}. \quad (13)$$

The series (10) converges at $q = \frac{1}{n}$ for the proper choice of $\psi_0(\eta,\xi,\omega)$, n, and $\hbar$. Then,

$$\psi(\eta,\omega) = \psi_0(\eta,\omega) + \sum_{m=1}^{\infty}\psi_m(\eta,\omega)\left(\frac{1}{n}\right)^m. \quad (14)$$

Taking the derivative of Equation (10) with respect to the embedding parameter q, setting $q = 0$, and dividing by $m!$, we obtain

$$\mathcal{L}[\psi(\eta,\omega) - k_m \psi_{m-1}(\eta,\omega)] = \hbar \mathcal{R}_m(\vec{\psi}_{m-1}), \tag{15}$$

where $h \neq 0$ is an auxiliary parameter, and the vectors are defined as

$$\vec{\psi}_m = [\psi_0(\eta,\omega), \psi_1(\eta,\omega), \cdots, \psi_m(\eta,\omega)]. \tag{16}$$

On applying the inverse LT on Equation (15), one obtains

$$\psi_m(\eta,\omega) = k_m \psi_{m-1}(\eta,\omega) + \hbar \mathcal{L}^{-1}[\mathcal{R}_m(\vec{\psi}_{m-1})], \tag{17}$$

$$\mathcal{R}_m(\vec{\psi}_{m-1}) = \frac{1}{(m-1)!} \frac{\partial^{m-1} N[\phi(x,t;q)]}{\partial q^{m-1}}\bigg|_{q=0},$$

where

$$\mathfrak{R}_m(\vec{\psi}_{m-1}) = \mathcal{L}[\psi_{m-1}(\eta,\omega)] - \left(1 - \frac{k_m}{n}\right)\left(\frac{f(\eta)}{s}\right) + \frac{1}{\mathcal{N}[\kappa]}\left(1 - \kappa + \frac{\kappa}{s^\kappa}\right)\mathcal{L}\left[(\psi^n(\eta,\omega))_\eta\right.$$

$$\left. + \psi_{\eta\eta}(\eta,\omega) + \beta \psi_{\eta\eta\eta}(\eta,\omega) + \psi_{\eta\eta\eta\eta}(\eta,\omega)\right], \tag{18}$$

and

$$k_m = \begin{cases} 0, & m \leq 1, \\ n, & m > 1. \end{cases} \tag{19}$$

Using Equations (17) and (18), one can obtain the series of $\psi_m(\eta,\omega)$. Lastly, the series q-HATM solution is defined as

$$\psi(\eta,\omega) = \sum_{m=0}^{\infty} \psi_m(\eta,\omega). \tag{20}$$

Theorem 1. *If $\exists$ a constant $0 < \varepsilon < 1$ in such a way that $\|u_{m+1}(x,t)\| \leq \varepsilon \|u_m(x,t)\|$ for each value of m, and if the truncated series $\sum_{m=0}^{r} u_m(x,t)\left(\frac{1}{n}\right)^m$ is an approximate solution $u(x,t)$, then the maximum absolute truncated error is determined by [26]*

$$\left\| u(x,t) - \sum_{m=0}^{r} u_m(x,t)\left(\frac{1}{n}\right)^m \right\| \leq \frac{\varepsilon^{r+1}}{n^r(n-\varepsilon)} \|u_0(x,t)\|.$$

4. Numerical Problems

Problem 1. *Consider the fractional order Benney equation with the ABR derivative given by*

$$^{ABR}D_\omega^\kappa \psi(\eta,\omega) + 3\psi^2(\eta,\omega)\psi_\eta(\eta,\omega) + \psi_{\eta\eta}(\eta,\omega) + \beta \psi_{\eta\eta\eta}(\eta,\omega) + \psi_{\eta\eta\eta\eta}(\eta,\omega) = 0, \ 0 < \kappa \leq 1,$$
$$\psi(\eta,0) = \eta^2. \tag{21}$$

Using the Laplace transform on Equation (21) and the initial condition, we obtain

$$\mathcal{L}[\psi(\eta,\omega)] = \frac{\eta^2}{s} - \frac{1}{\mathcal{N}[\kappa]}((1-\kappa+\frac{\kappa}{s^\kappa}))\mathcal{L}\left[3\psi^2(\eta,\omega)\psi_\eta(\eta,\omega) + \psi_{\eta\eta}(\eta,\omega) + \beta \psi_{\eta\eta\eta}(\eta,\omega) + \psi_{\eta\eta\eta\eta}(\eta,\omega)\right]. \tag{22}$$

Here, we define the nonlinear operator as

$$N[\phi(\eta,\omega;q)] = \mathcal{L}[\phi(\eta,\omega;q)] - \frac{\eta^2}{s} + \frac{1}{\mathcal{N}[\kappa]}((1-\kappa+\frac{\kappa}{s^\kappa}))\mathcal{L}\left[3\phi^2(\eta,\omega;q)\phi_\eta(\eta,\omega;q) + \phi_{\eta\eta}(\eta,\omega;q)\right.$$
$$\left. + \beta\phi_{\eta\eta\eta}(\eta,\omega;q) + \phi_{\eta\eta\eta\eta}(\eta,\omega;q)\right]. \tag{23}$$

The $m-$th order deformation is given by

$$\mathcal{L}[\psi_m(\eta,\omega) - k_m\psi_{m-1}(\eta,\omega)] = \hbar\mathcal{R}_m(\vec{\psi}_{m-1}), \tag{24}$$

where

$$\mathcal{R}_m(\vec{\psi}_m) = \mathcal{L}[\psi(\eta,\omega)] - \frac{\eta^2}{s} + \frac{1}{\mathcal{N}[\kappa]}((1-\kappa+\frac{\kappa}{s^\kappa}))\mathcal{L}\left[3\sum_{i=0}^{m-1}\left(\sum_{j=0}^{i}\psi_j(\eta,\omega)\psi_{i-j}(\eta,\omega)\right)\frac{\partial}{\partial\eta}\psi_{m-i-1}(\eta,\omega)\right.$$
$$\left. + \psi_{\eta\eta}(\eta,\omega) + \beta\psi_{\eta\eta\eta}(\eta,\omega) + \psi_{\eta\eta\eta\eta}(\eta,\omega)\right]. \tag{25}$$

Taking the inverse Laplace transform on Equation (24), we have

$$\psi_m(\eta,\omega) = k_m\psi_{m-1}(\eta,\omega) + \hbar\mathcal{L}^{-1}\left(\mathcal{R}_m(\vec{\psi}_{m-1})\right). \tag{26}$$

Solving the above equation, we find the following terms

$$\psi_0(\eta,\omega) = \eta^2,$$
$$\psi_1(\eta,\omega) = \frac{2\hbar\left(-1+3\eta^5(-1+\kappa)+(-\frac{(3\eta^5+1)\omega^\kappa}{\Gamma(\kappa+1)}+1)\kappa\right)}{\mathcal{N}[\kappa]},$$
$$\psi_2(\eta,\omega) = \frac{2n\hbar\left(-1+3\eta^5(-1+\kappa)+(-\frac{(3\eta^5+1)\omega^\kappa}{\Gamma(\kappa+1)}+1)\kappa\right)}{\mathcal{N}[\kappa]} + \hbar\left(\frac{1}{\Gamma(1+\kappa)^2\mathcal{N}[\kappa]^3}\left(24\left(\Gamma(1+\kappa)^2\right.\right.\right.$$
$$\times (-1+\kappa)\left(1+\kappa^2\left(1+\frac{2\omega^{2\kappa}}{\Gamma(2\kappa+1)}\right)-\kappa\left(\frac{3(-1+\kappa)\omega^\kappa}{\Gamma(\kappa+1)}+2\right)\right) + \left(-\frac{\omega^{3\kappa}\kappa}{\Gamma(3\kappa+1)}\right.$$
$$+ \frac{\omega^{2\kappa}(-1+\kappa)}{\Gamma(2\kappa+1)}\right)\Gamma(2\alpha+1)\kappa^2\left(3\eta^5+1\right)^2\hbar^2\eta\right) + \frac{1}{\mathcal{N}[\kappa]^2}\left(2\left(\mathcal{N}[\kappa](3\eta^5+1)(-1+\kappa)\right.\right.$$
$$+ 3(-1+\kappa)^2\eta^2(21\eta^6+60\beta+22\eta) + \left(-720\eta+\frac{1}{\Gamma(\kappa+1)}\left(126\eta^8+360\beta\eta^2+132\eta^3\right.\right.$$
$$- \mathcal{N}[\alpha](3\eta^5+1) + 6(-(21\eta^7+60\beta\eta+22\eta^2+120)\kappa+120)\eta\big)\omega^\kappa\big)\kappa + 3\eta\big(\kappa^2$$
$$\times \left(\frac{\omega^{2\kappa}}{\Gamma(2\kappa+1)}\left(21\eta^7+60\beta\eta+22\eta^2+120\right)+120\right)+120\big)\big)\hbar\big)\bigg), \tag{27}$$

$\vdots$

In Figure 1, two-dimensional plots of approximate solutions at different fractional orders for the problem in 1. In Figure 2, three-dimensional plots of approximate solutions at different fractional orders for the problem 1. In Table 1, The numerical values of approximate solutions at various fractional values for the problem 1 with $\beta = 1$.

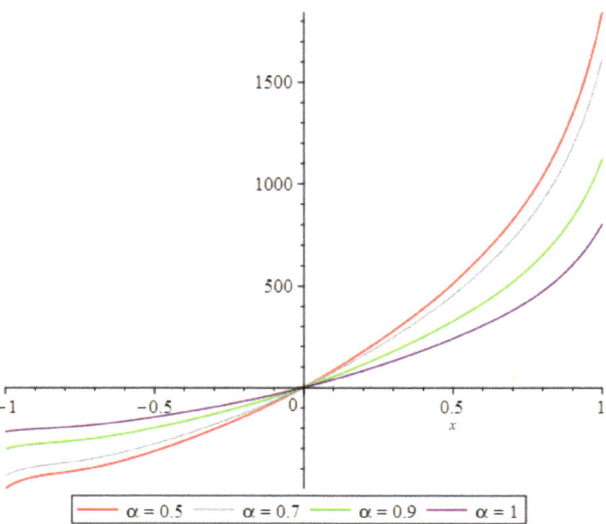

Figure 1. Two-dimensional plots of approximate solutions at different fractional orders for the problem in 1.

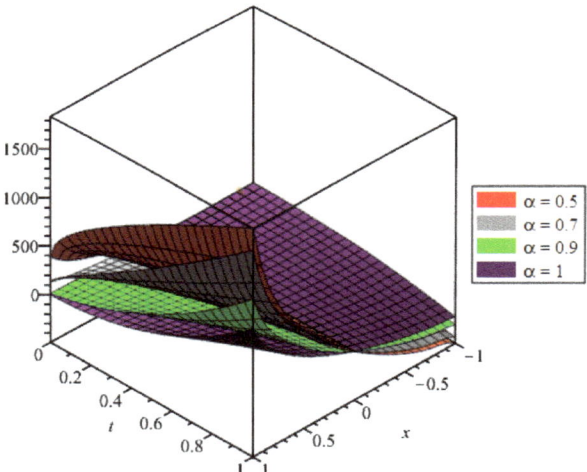

Figure 2. Three-dimensional plots of approximate solutions at different fractional orders for the problem 1.

Table 1. The numerical values of approximate solutions at various fractional values for the problem 1 with $\beta = 1$.

ω	η	$\kappa = 0.5$	$\kappa = 0.7$	$\kappa = 0.9$	$\kappa = 1$
1	0	2.128379167	2.140766367	2.071557441	2
	0.1	85.31665749	75.96945949	54.8749427	40.6761086
	0.2	177.0418155	157.3943186	113.1421651	83.3731548
	0.3	278.2481880	247.2507879	177.4677326	130.5258330
	0.4	390.2002534	346.6438118	248.6191438	182.6863557
	0.5	515.0072901	457.3916866	327.8236424	240.7187498
	0.6	656.8171393	583.0369874	417.4220704	306.2414199
	0.7	824.6185442	731.2090832	522.3800063	382.6390723
	0.8	1038.759922	919.0860269	653.7294243	477.335391
	0.9	1345.435884	1185.467730	836.0769337	606.689905
	1	1846.975581	1615.918535	1123.085975	806.000000

Problem 2. *Consider the fractional order Benney equation with the ABR derivative given by*

$$^{ABR}D_\omega^\kappa \psi(\eta,\omega) + 3\psi^2(\eta,\omega)\psi_\eta(\eta,\omega) + \psi_{\eta\eta}(\eta,\omega) + \beta\psi_{\eta\eta\eta}(\eta,\omega) + \psi_{\eta\eta\eta\eta}(\eta,\omega) = 0, \ 0 < \kappa \leq 1, \quad (28)$$
$$\psi(\eta,0) = \cos\eta.$$

Using the Laplace transform on Equation (28) and the initial condition, we obtain

$$\mathcal{L}[\psi(\eta,\omega)] = \frac{\cos\eta}{s} - \frac{1}{\mathcal{N}[\kappa]}((1-\kappa+\frac{\kappa}{s^\kappa}))\mathcal{L}\left[3\psi^2(\eta,\omega)\psi_\eta(\eta,\omega) + \psi_{\eta\eta}(\eta,\omega) + \beta\psi_{\eta\eta\eta}(\eta,\omega) + \psi_{\eta\eta\eta\eta}(\eta,\omega)\right]. \quad (29)$$

Here, we define the nonlinear operator as

$$N[\phi(\eta,\omega;q)] = \mathcal{L}[\phi(\eta,\omega;q)] - \frac{\cos\eta}{s} + \frac{1}{\mathcal{N}[\kappa]}((1-\kappa+\frac{\kappa}{s^\kappa}))\mathcal{L}\left[3\phi^2(\eta,\omega;q)\phi_\eta(\eta,\omega;q) + \phi_{\eta\eta}(\eta,\omega;q)\right.$$
$$\left. + \beta\phi_{\eta\eta\eta}(\eta,\omega;q) + \phi_{\eta\eta\eta\eta}(\eta,\omega;q)\right]. \quad (30)$$

The $m-$th order deformation is given by

$$\mathcal{L}[\psi_m(\eta,\omega) - k_m\psi_{m-1}(\eta,\omega)] = \hbar\mathcal{R}_m(\vec{\psi}_{m-1}), \quad (31)$$

where

$$\mathcal{R}_m(\vec{\psi}_m) = \mathcal{L}[\psi(\eta,\omega)] - \frac{\cos\eta}{s} + \frac{1}{\mathcal{N}[\kappa]}((1-\kappa+\frac{\kappa}{s^\kappa}))\mathcal{L}\left[3\sum_{i=0}^{m-1}\left(\sum_{j=0}^{i}\psi_j(\eta,\omega)\psi_{i-j}(\eta,\omega)\right)\frac{\partial}{\partial\eta}\psi_{m-i-1}(\eta,\omega)\right.$$
$$\left. + \psi_{\eta\eta}(\eta,\omega) + \beta\psi_{\eta\eta\eta}(\eta,\omega) + \psi_{\eta\eta\eta\eta}(\eta,\omega)\right]. \quad (32)$$

Taking the inverse Laplace transform on Equation (31), we have

$$\psi_m(\eta,\omega) = k_m\psi_{m-1}(\eta,\omega) + \hbar\mathcal{L}^{-1}\left(\mathcal{R}_m(\vec{\psi}_{m-1})\right), \quad (33)$$

Solving the above equation, we find the following terms

$$\psi_0(\eta,\omega) = \cos\eta,$$

$$\psi_1(\eta,\omega) = \frac{\hbar\left(1 + \kappa\left(-1 + \frac{\omega^\kappa}{\Gamma(\kappa+1)}\right)\right)(3\cos(\eta)^2 - \beta)\sin(\eta)}{\mathcal{N}[\kappa]},$$

$$\psi_2(\eta,\omega) = \frac{n\hbar\left(1 + \kappa\left(-1 + \frac{\omega^\kappa}{\Gamma(\kappa+1)}\right)\right)(3\cos(\eta)^2 - \beta)\sin(\eta)}{\mathcal{N}[\kappa]} + \hbar\left(\frac{1}{\Gamma(\kappa+1)^2\mathcal{N}[\kappa]}\right.$$

$$\left(3(3\cos(\eta)^2 - \beta)^2\sin(\eta)^3\hbar^2\left(\left(-1 - \kappa^2\left(1 + \frac{2\omega^{2\kappa}}{\Gamma(2\kappa+1)}\right) + \kappa\left(\frac{3(-1+\kappa)\omega^\kappa}{\Gamma(\kappa+1)} + 2\right)\right)\right.\right.$$

$$\left.\left.\times\Gamma(\kappa+1)^2(-1+\kappa) + \kappa^2\left(\frac{\kappa\omega^{3\kappa}}{\Gamma()3\kappa+1} - \frac{\omega^{2\kappa(-1+\kappa)}}{\Gamma(2\kappa+1)}\right)\Gamma(2\kappa+1)\right)\right)$$

$$+ \frac{1}{\mathcal{N}[\kappa]^2}\left(\hbar\left(\frac{1}{\Gamma(2\kappa+1)}\left(-9\cos(\eta)^5 + 24\beta\cos(\eta)^3 + 54\sin(\eta)(1 - 4\cos(\eta)^2)\right.\right.\right. \quad (34)$$

$$+ \cos(\eta)(9\sin(\eta)^2(3\cos(\eta)^2 - 7\beta) - \beta^2))\omega^{2\kappa}\kappa^2 + \frac{1}{\Gamma(\kappa+1)}(\kappa((54 - 54\kappa$$

$$- \beta\mathcal{N}[\kappa] + 3\cos(\eta)^2(-126 + \mathcal{N}[\kappa] + 126\kappa))\sin(\eta) + 2(-24\beta\cos(\eta)^3 + 9\cos(\eta)^5$$

$$- 27\sin(\eta)^3 + (9(-3\cos(\eta)^2 + 7\beta)\sin(\eta)^2 + \beta^2)\cos(\eta))(-1+\kappa))\omega^\kappa)$$

$$+ (-54 + \beta\mathcal{N}[\kappa] + 54\kappa + 3(72 - \mathcal{N}[\kappa] - 72\kappa)\cos(\eta)^2)\sin(\eta)(-1+\kappa)$$

$$+ (-1+\kappa)^2\cos(\eta)(24\cos(\eta)^2\beta - 9\cos(\eta)^4 + 9\sin(\eta)^2(3\cos(\eta)^2 - 7\beta) - \beta^2)))\bigg),$$

⋮

In Figure 3, Two-dimensional plots of approximate solutions at different fractional orders for the problem 2. In Figure 4, Three-dimensional plots of approximate solutions at different fractional orders for the problem 2. In Table 2, Numerical values of approximate solutions at various fractional values for the problem 2 with $\beta = 1$.

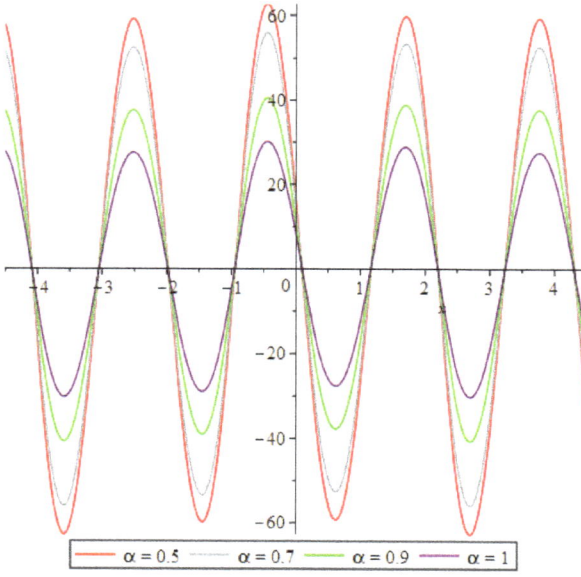

Figure 3. Two-dimensional plots of approximate solutions at different fractional orders for the problem 2.

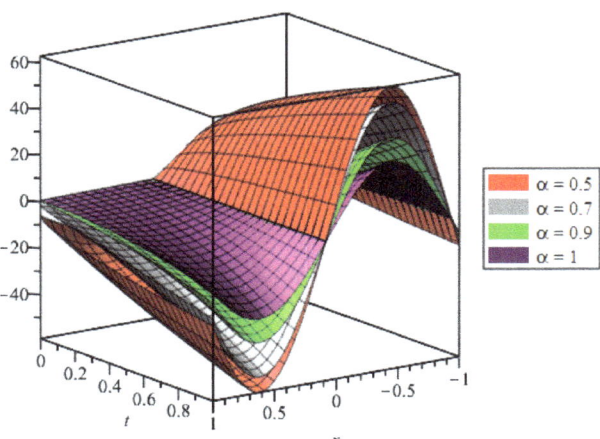

Figure 4. Three-dimensional plots of approximate solutions at different fractional orders for the problem 2.

Table 2. Numerical values of approximate solutions at various fractional values for the problem 2 with $\beta = 1$.

ω	η	$\kappa = 0.5$	$\kappa = 0.7$	$\kappa = 0.9$	q-HATM $\kappa = 1$	LADM $\kappa = 1$
1	0	15.89865417	14.25381518	10.52430944	8	8
	0.1	−1.832024984	−1.543389489	−0.8803186628	−0.4295903926	−0.4295903926
	0.2	−19.14110255	−16.95979593	−12.00254110	−8.646209940	−8.646209940
	0.3	−34.63295823	−30.75026556	−21.94082484	−15.98192520	−15.98192520
	0.4	−47.06736293	−41.81265793	−29.90352005	−21.85367303	−21.85367303
	0.5	−55.44182498	−49.26000190	−35.25928442	−25.79968055	−25.79968055
	0.6	−59.07713582	−52.49340697	−37.58497881	−27.51235592	−27.51235592
	0.7	−57.68973832	−51.26276939	−36.70405550	−26.86375081	−26.86375081
	0.8	−51.42898240	−45.69773137	−32.70565981	−23.91791002	−23.91791002
	0.9	−40.86344304	−36.29615175	−25.93720850	−18.92581335	−18.92581335
	1	−26.91555476	−23.86942018	−16.96996307	−12.30256052	−12.30256052

5. Conclusions

In conclusion, the q-homotopy analysis transform method is a highly promising approach for solving the Benney equation and other nonlinear differential equations. The method's ability to break down complex equations into simpler parts, coupled with its accuracy and consistency with other numerical methods, make it a valuable tool in the field of mathematics. Moreover, the q-homotopy analysis transform method offers several advantages over traditional numerical methods, making it easier to implement and providing greater accuracy. Given its potential, this method is expected to play an increasingly important role in solving nonlinear differential equations in the future, and researchers are encouraged to explore its applications further.

Author Contributions: Conceptualization, R.S.; methodology, R.S. and Y.A.; software, K.A.; validation, Y.A.; formal analysis, R.S.; investigation, K.A.; resources, Y.A.; data curation K.A.; writing—original draft preparation, R.S.; writing—review and editing, Y.A.; visualization, K.A.; supervision, Y.A. All authors have read and agreed to the published version of the manuscript.

Funding: This research received no external funding.

Data Availability Statement: The numerical data used to support the findings of this study are included within the article.

Conflicts of Interest: The authors declare no conflict of interest.

References

1. Gunerhan, H. Optical soliton solutions of nonlinear Davey-Stewartson equation using an efficient method. *Rev. Mex. Fis.* **2021**, 67. [CrossRef]
2. Gunerhan, H.; Dutta, H.; Dokuyucu, M.A.; Adel, W. Analysis of a fractional HIV model with Caputo and constant proportional Caputo operators. *Chaos Solitons Fractals* **2020**, *139*, 110053. [CrossRef]
3. Lacroix, S.F. Trait du calcul differentiel et du calcul integral. *Paris* **1819**, *3*, 409–410.
4. Machado, J.T.; Kiryakova, V.; Mainard, F. Recent history of fractional calculus. *Commun. Non. Sci. Numer. Simul.* **2011**, *16*, 140–1153. [CrossRef]
5. Miller, K.S.; Ross, B. *An Introduction to the Fractional Calculus and Fractional Differential Equations*; John Wiley and Sons: New York, NY, USA, 1993.
6. Podlubny, I. *Fractional Differential Equations, Mathematics in Science and Engineering*; Academic Press: New York, NY, USA, 1999.
7. Naeem, M.; Yasmin, H.; Shah, R.; Shah, N.A.; Chung, J.D. A Comparative Study of Fractional Partial Differential Equations with the Help of Yang Transform. *Symmetry* **2023**, *15*, 146. [CrossRef]
8. Alyobi, S.; Khan, A.; Shah, N.A.; Nonlaopon, K. Fractional Analysis of Nonlinear Boussinesq Equation under Atangana-Baleanu-Caputo Operator. *Symmetry* **2022**, *14*, 2417. [CrossRef]
9. Alshehry, A.S.; Shah, R.; Dassios, I. A reliable technique for solving fractional partial differential equation. *Axioms* **2022**, *11*, 574. [CrossRef]
10. Wang, K.J. The fractal active low-pass filter within the local fractional derivative on the Cantor set. *COMPEL-Int. J. Comput. Math. Electr. Electron. Eng.* **2023**. [CrossRef]
11. Wang, K. Fractal Traveling Wave Solutions For The Fractal-Fractional Ablowitz-Kaup-Newell-Segur Model. *Fractals* **2022**, *30*, 1–9. [CrossRef]
12. Chang, C.H. The stability of traveling wave solutions for a diffusive competition system of three species. *J. Math. Anal. Appl.* **2018**, *459*, 564–576. [CrossRef]
13. Alderremy, A.A.; Shah, R.; Shah, N.A.; Aly, S.; Nonlaopon, K. Comparison of two modified analytical approaches for the systems of time fractional partial differential equations. *AIMS Math.* **2023**, *8*, 7142–7162. [CrossRef]
14. Naeem, M.; Yasmin, H.; Shah, N.A.; Nonlaopon, K. Investigation of Fractional Nonlinear Regularized Long-Wave Models via Novel Techniques. *Symmetry* **2023**, *15*, 220. [CrossRef]
15. Mofarreh, F.; Khan, A.; Abdeljabbar, A. A Comparative Analysis of Fractional-Order Fokker-Planck Equation. *Symmetry* **2023**, *15*, 430. [CrossRef]
16. Wang, L.; Liu, G.; Xue, J.; Wong, K. Channel Prediction Using Ordinary Differential Equations for MIMO systems. *IEEE Trans. Veh. Technol.* **2022**, 1–9. [CrossRef]
17. Liu, Y.; Xu, K.; Li, J.; Guo, Y.; Zhang, A.; Chen, Q. Millimeter-Wave E-Plane Waveguide Bandpass Filters Based on Spoof Surface Plasmon Paritons. *IEEE Trans. Microw. Theory Tech.* **2022**, *70*, 4399–4409. [CrossRef]
18. Xu, K.; Guo, Y.; Liu, Y.; Deng, X.; Chen, Q.; Ma, Z. 60-GHz Compact Dual-Mode On-Chip Bandpass Filter Using GaAs Technology. *IEEE Electron Device Lett.* **2021**, *42*, 1120–1123. [CrossRef]
19. Fedorov, V.E.; Du, W.S.; Turov, M.M. On the unique solvability of incomplete Cauchy type problems for a class of multi-term equations with the Riemann-Liouville derivatives. *Symmetry* **2022**, *14*, 75. [CrossRef]
20. Yamaguchi, R. Analysis of electro-optical behavior in liquid crystal cells with asymmetric anchoring strength. *Symmetry* **2022**, *14*, 85. [CrossRef]
21. Akinlar, M.A.; Secer, A.; Bayram, M. Numerical solution of fractional Benney equation. *Appl. Math. Inf. Sci.* **2014**, *8*, 1633–1637. [CrossRef]
22. Konno, H.; Lomdahl, P.S. The birth-death stochastic processes of solitons in the 1D Benney equation. *J. Phys. Soc. Jpn.* **2000**, *69*, 1629–1641. [CrossRef]
23. Wang, F.; Li, W.; Zhang, H. A new extended homotopy perturbation method for nonlinear differential equations. *Math. Comput. Modell.* **2012**, *55*, 1471–1477. [CrossRef]
24. Shah, K; Seadawy, A.R.; Mahmoud, A.B. On theoretical analysis of nonlinear fractional order partial Benney equations under nonsingular kernel. *Open Phys.* **2022**, *20*, 587–595. [CrossRef]
25. Wan, Z.; Zhang, T.; Liu, Y.; Liu, P.; Zhang, J.; Fang, L.; Sun, D. Enhancement of desulfurization by hydroxyl ammonium ionic liquid supported on active carbon. *Environ. Res.* **2022**, *213*, 113637. [CrossRef]
26. Prakash, A.; Kaur, H. q-homotopy analysis transform method for space and time-fractional KdV-Burgers equation. *Nonlinear Sci. Lett. A* **2018**, *9*, 44–61.
27. El-Tawil, M.A.; Huseen, S.N. The q-homotopy analysis method (q-HAM). *Int. J. Appl. Math. Mech.* **2012**, *8*, 51–75.
28. Liu, K.; Yang, Z.; Wei, W.; Gao, B.; Xin, D.; Sun, C.; Wu, G. Novel detection approach for thermal defects: Study on its feasibility and application to vehicle cables. *High Volt.* **2022**, 1–10.. [CrossRef]
29. Liao, S.J. The Proposed Homotopy Analysis Technique for the Solution of Nonlinear Problems, Ph.D. Thesis. Shanghai Jiao Tong University, Shanghai, China, 1992.
30. Liao, S.J. Homotopy analysis method and its applications in mathematics. *J. Basic Sci. Eng.* **1997**, *5*, 111–125.

31. Liao, S. *Beyond Perturbation: Introduction to Homotopy Analysis Method*; CRC Press: Boca Raton, FL, USA, 2000.
32. Liao, S.J. Notes on the homotopy analysis method: Some definitions and theorems. *Commun. Nonlinear Sci. Numer. Simul.* **2009**, *14*, 83–97. [CrossRef]

Disclaimer/Publisher's Note: The statements, opinions and data contained in all publications are solely those of the individual author(s) and contributor(s) and not of MDPI and/or the editor(s). MDPI and/or the editor(s) disclaim responsibility for any injury to people or property resulting from any ideas, methods, instructions or products referred to in the content.

Article

Cooperative Multi-Objective Control of Heterogeneous Vehicle Platoons on Highway with Varying Slopes

Weiwei Kong [1,*], Tianmao Cai [1], Yugong Luo [2], Xuetong Wang [3] and Fachao Jiang [1]

1. College of Engineering, China Agricultural University, Beijing 100083, China
2. School of Vehicle and Mobility, Tsinghua University, Beijing 100084, China
3. Intelligent System and Software Engineering Center, Pan Asia Technical Automotive Center Co., Ltd., Shanghai 200120, China
* Correspondence: kongweiwei@cau.edu.cn

Abstract: Stability, vehicle safety, energy saving, and passenger comfort are the major objectives of vehicle platooning control. These objectives are coupled, interrelated, and even conflicting, so integrated optimization of multiple objectives is quite challenging. Particularly for heterogeneous platoons, the difficulties are intensified for the differences in vehicle dynamics. In this paper, the concept of symmetry is utilized in the platooning control, that is, the design method of each vehicle's controller is the same. For each controller, it is to solve the optimal solution of multi-objective collaborative optimization. The concept of asymmetry is meanwhile embodied in the parameter setting of each controller, for the vehicle heterogeneity. The contents of this study are as follows. First, a mathematical model is established, in which the differences in vehicle dynamic characteristics of heterogeneous platoon, road slope, and aerodynamics are all taken into account. Then, based on distributed nonlinear model predictive control (DNMPC) method, multi-objective control strategies are proposed for the leader and followers, cooperatively. Furthermore, a weight coefficient optimization method is presented, to further improve the platoon's multi-objective synthesis performance. Finally, comparative experiments are carried out. Results demonstrate that, compared with the classic cruise control method of vehicle platoons, the proposed approach can reduce energy consumption by more than 5% and improve tracking performance on the premise of passenger comfort. Real-road experiments verify that the proposed control system can function effectively and satisfy the computational requirements in real applications.

Keywords: heterogeneous vehicle platoon; multi-objective control; nonlinear model predictive control; distributed control; energy saving

Citation: Kong, W.; Cai, T.; Luo, Y.; Wang, X.; Jiang, F. Cooperative Multi-Objective Control of Heterogeneous Vehicle Platoons on Highway with Varying Slopes. *Symmetry* **2022**, *14*, 2647. https://doi.org/10.3390/sym14122647

Academic Editors: Savin Treanta and Octav Olteanu

Received: 20 November 2022
Accepted: 5 December 2022
Published: 14 December 2022

Publisher's Note: MDPI stays neutral with regard to jurisdictional claims in published maps and institutional affiliations.

Copyright: © 2022 by the authors. Licensee MDPI, Basel, Switzerland. This article is an open access article distributed under the terms and conditions of the Creative Commons Attribution (CC BY) license (https://creativecommons.org/licenses/by/4.0/).

1. Introduction

Currently, there is a widespread concern over vehicle platoon studies due to their considerable potential to enhance road safety, reduce energy consumption and improve traffic efficiency. Early research mainly focused on homogenous platoons. In recent years, more and more studies on heterogeneous platoons have been carried out. Stability, vehicle safety, energy saving, and passenger comfort are the major objectives in the control of autonomous vehicles. Previous studies on heterogeneous platoons have probably focused on one or two objectives, especially stability control. It is of great significance to study the multi-objective control method of heterogeneous platoons, taking all the four objectives into account.

The study on vehicle platoons can trace back to the California PATH project in the 1980s, which proposed the concept of "Platoon" for the first time [1,2]. Since then, vehicle platooning control has been a topic of wide concern. The existing studies on platooning control could be classified according to different control objectives, as shown in Table 1.

The early studies mainly focused on tracking control and stability control [3–10], which are the basis of vehicle platoons. Tracking control is usually achieved by the cruise control system. A Swedish scholar, Alam, proposed a control structure for the truck platoon, in which the leader was controlled by cruise control and the followers were controlled by adaptive cruise control (ACC) [11]. With the development of vehicle-to-vehicle (V2V) communication technology, the cooperative adaptive cruise control (CACC) system gradually attracted more and more attention [12]. Chiedu, N.M. and Keyvan, H.Z. studied a stability analysis of CACC-based platoons [13]. Rakkesh et al. studied a homogenous platoon composed of eight vehicles to compare CACC and ACC systems, and it was proven that the CACC system had better vehicle tracking and energy saving performance [14]. Zegers et al. designed a multi-layer control architecture based on CACC, in order to achieve the stability of and the expected spacing between vehicles of the platoon [15].

Most of the above research was conducted on homogenous platoons. The studies on heterogeneous platoons are more meaningful in practical applications, and, in the meanwhile, more difficult due to the significant differences in dynamic characteristics between vehicles [16,17]. In recent years, many scholars have been committed to studies on heterogeneous platoons, mainly on stability control. Reference [18] analyzed the stability control of a heterogeneous platoon with switched interaction topology, time-varying communication delay, and lag of actuators. Delft University of Technology proposed a novel CACC method for heterogeneous platoons, which effectively achieved stability control [19]. Scholars at the University of Manchester proposed a two-layer distributed control scheme to maintain the stability of a heterogeneous vehicle platoon moving with a constant spacing policy assuming constant velocity of the leading vehicle [20]. In reference [21], stability control for a heterogeneous vehicle platoon was studied, subject to external bounded unknown acceleration disturbances. Reference [22] presented an integrated platoon control framework for heterogeneous vehicles on curved roads with varying slopes and wireless communication delays, in order to guarantee that the perturbations did not grow unbounded as they propagated through the platoon. Zheng et al. at Tsinghua University introduced a distributed model predictive control algorithm for heterogeneous vehicle platoons, which could guarantee internal stability for any unidirectional topology [23]. In 2019, Li et al. further studied the distributed platoon control with more generic topologies [24]. All of these studies aim at the stability control of heterogeneous platoons.

In addition to stability control, studies on energy-saving control of platoons have attracted much attention from scholars. The existing research on energy-saving control of platoons can be categorized into three approaches, shown as follows:

(1) Energy-saving control based on decreasing the air resistance of vehicles: References [25,26] analyzed the aerodynamics of vehicle platoons, and studies in reference [26] have shown that vehicles in different positions of a platoon faced different air resistance. Swedish scholars have designed a small distance between vehicles of a platoon in order to increase the fuel efficiency [27]. Chalmers University of Technology utilized a stochastic optimization method to optimize the speed curve of the leading vehicle, and this method was proven to be more energy efficient than cruise control [28].

(2) Energy-saving control by avoiding unnecessary rapid accelerations or decelerations of platoons based on road information and predicted information of the surrounding vehicles [5]: Turri et al. at the Royal Swedish Institute of Technology proposed a two-layer control architecture for heavy-duty truck platoons [29]. The upper layer obtained and predicted the road geometry information, and utilized a dynamic programming method to calculate the optimal speed curve of platoons. The lower layer achieved vehicle safety and energy saving control based on the MPC method. Assad Alam et al. studied the influence of different road slopes on the fuel consumption of heavy-duty truck platoons, and proposed a method to calculate the optimal energy-saving speed curve by predicting the information of the road ahead [30]. Zhang et al. at Tsinghua University designed an energy management strategy based on predicting the behavior of the preceding vehicles [31].

(3) Energy-saving control based on reducing frequent gear shifts: Valerio Turri et al. discussed a control architecture that could calculate the optimal sequence of gear shifts for a given reference speed profile, and this could realize energy saving and smooth tracking [32].

In the above studies, the majority focused on one single performance factor as the experimental objective, and only a few concerned two objectives, mainly for homogeneous platoons, such as refs. [5,6,11,14]. Recently, some scholars have gradually become concerned about the multi-objective control of heterogeneous platoons. Zhai et al. [33] proposed a switched control strategy of heterogeneous vehicle platoons for multiple objectives with state constraints. In this study, although multiple objectives were taken into account, only fuel economy was designed as an objective function, while vehicle safety and passenger comfort were designed as state constraints. In other words, this method could optimize the single performance of energy saving, and did not actually achieve the integrated optimization of energy saving, safety, and passenger comfort.

Table 1. Classification of existing vehicle platooning control studies.

Tracking/Safety Performance	Stability Performace	Energy-Saving Performance	Comfort Performance
[3–7,11–14,16,33]	[8–10,15,17–24]	[5,11,14,17,25–33]	[6,33]

In summary, fruitful results have been achieved on the stability control or energy-saving control of vehicle platoons. However, the existing studies mainly focus on one or two objectives, and mostly for homogeneous platoons. There still lack systematic studies on multi-objective control of heterogeneous platoons. The major challenge is to achieve the integrated optimization of the four major objectives, for the reason that these objectives are coupled, interrelated, and sometimes even conflicting and contradictory. Furthermore, the vehicle dynamics differences for heterogeneous platoons exacerbate the difficulty. The motivation of this work is to solve this problem. The main work and contributions are as follows:

(1) **A two-layer architecture of the heterogeneous platoon control system is presented**, consisting of a control layer and a dynamic layer, with a distributed controller for each vehicle. This hierarchical and distributed structure is especially suitable for heterogeneous platoon. For dynamic layer, a nonlinear dynamic model of a heterogeneous platoon is presented, characterizing the differences in dynamic properties between vehicles and the influence of the road slope and wind resistance. For the control layer, a wealth of information is utilized for multi-objective solving, including not only the current states of the vehicles, but also their predicted states over a period of time, as well as the expected control signals.

(2) **A cooperative multi-objective control strategy of a heterogeneous platoon is proposed, based on distributed nonlinear model predictive control (DNMPC) method.** Multi-objective DNMPC controllers are designed for the leading vehicle and the following vehicles, cooperatively. For each controller, objective function integrates multiple sub-objective functions, each of which depicts one targeted performance. With this method, the optimization of multiple targets of heterogeneous platoons can be achieved.

(3) **A weight coefficient optimization method based on a non-dominated sorting genetic algorithm (NSGA-II) is presented**, to obtain the optimal weight coefficient set of multiple targets. Instead of the common empirical method in the existing studies, this proposed method is able to achieve coordinated adjustment between multiple targets, which can effectively improve the multi-objective collaborative optimization capability of the heterogeneous platoons.

The remainder of this paper is organized as follows. Section 2 describes the multi-objective control system architecture, and demonstrates the dynamic model of the heterogeneous platoon. In Section 3, the cooperative multi-objective control strategy based on the DNMPC method is presented. The stability analysis based on the Lyapunov theory is introduced as well. Section 4 elaborates on the NSGA-II-based weight coefficient optimization method. Section 5 describes the simulation experiments and real-road tests. Section 6 presents the main conclusions of this investigation.

2. Cooperative Multi-Objective Control System of a Heterogeneous Platoon

2.1. Architecture of the Multi-Objective Control System of a Heterogeneous Platoon

The architecture of the multi-objective control system of a heterogeneous platoon is shown in Figure 1, where α represents the road slope, and $u_i^*(:|t)$ ($i = 1, \ldots, n$) is the optimal control variable of vehicle i, calculated by its controller at time t. $u_i^*(:|t)$ is a sequence, composed of N_p control variables during a predicted time domain $[t, t + N_p\Delta t]$, and there are N_p time steps in one predicted time domain. $u_i^*(1|t)$ is the optimal control variable for the present moment, and y_i refers to the state information of vehicle i, specifically including vehicle position, speed, and the torque.

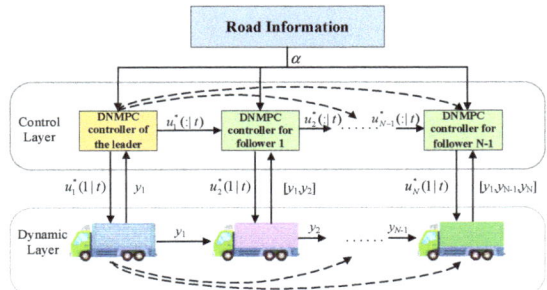

Figure 1. Architecture of the multi-objective control system of a heterogeneous platoon.

As shown in Figure 1, the architecture is a two-layer one. The control layer is composed of the DNMPC controllers of each vehicle. In this study, the concept of symmetry is utilized in the platooning control, that is, the design method of each vehicle's controller is the same. Each controller obtains road information, and sends the optimal control signal to the dynamic layer, from which the state information of each vehicle can be acquired. Dynamic layer is the dynamic model of the heterogeneous platoon.

The proposed architecture and control method in this paper are applicable for various types of communication topologies. In this paper, a predecessor-following leader (PFL) type of communication topology is selected for illustration, which has been reflected by the dashed lines in Figure 1.

The architecture possesses the following advantages:

(1) With a distributed control method for the control layer, each controller is designed with full consideration of the differences in dynamic characteristics between the vehicles. This makes it possible to achieve the best overall performance of the heterogeneous platoon. Moreover, compared with centralized control, it better computational real-time performance, which is more conducive to practical application.

(2) Rich information is supplied to the controller for the calculation of the optimal control variables. The predicted information is fully utilized, which can effectively improve the stability and energy-saving performance of the platoon. As shown in Figure 1, for vehicle i, its controller could obtain the vehicle's current state y_i, control signals $u_i^*(:|t)$, the leading vehicle's state and control signals, y_1 and $u_1^*(:|t)$, and the neighboring vehicles' state and control signals, y_{i-1} and $u_{i-1}^*(:|t)$. It is important to note that these signals include not only the current signal, but also the expected one during a predicted time domain.

(3) Based on the vehicle state from dynamic layer, each controller uses a feedforward–feedback control structure, which is beneficial to improve the control effect.

(4) In the dynamic layer, road information and wind resistance are taken into account in the dynamic model of the platoon, which could further improve the platoon's energy-saving performance.

2.2. Dynamic Model of a Heterogeneous Platoon

Force analysis of one vehicle on the ramp is shown in Figure 2, where α represents road slope, F_T for driving force, F_W for air resistance, F_g for slope resistance, and F_f for rolling resistance.

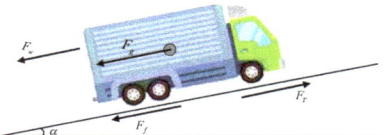

Figure 2. Force analysis of a vehicle on the ramp.

F_T, F_W, F_g, and F_f can be calculated according to Equations (1)–(4), described as follows:

$$F_T = \frac{4i_0\eta_m}{r_w}T_q(t) \quad (1)$$

$$F_w = \frac{1}{2}C_d A \rho v^2(t) \quad (2)$$

$$F_f = fmg\cos\alpha \quad (3)$$

$$F_g = mg\sin\alpha \quad (4)$$

where η_m, i_0, r_w and T_q represent the transmission efficiency, transmission ratio, rolling radius of the wheel, and the motor torque, respectively. C_d, A, ρ and v represent the aerodynamic drag coefficient, frontal area, air density, and the vehicle speed. f represents the coefficient of rolling resistance, which of the highway is usually 0.012.

Integrating Equations (1)–(4), the longitudinal dynamics model of one vehicle can be obtained, shown as follows:

$$m\dot{v}(t) = F_T - F_w - F_f - F_g$$
$$= \frac{4i_0\eta_m}{r_w}T_q(t) - \frac{1}{2}C_d A \rho v^2(t) - fmg\cos\alpha - mg\sin\alpha. \quad (5)$$

Dynamic characteristics between vehicles of a heterogeneous platoon are different. The dynamic model of a heterogeneous platoon is given as follows:

$$\begin{cases} \dot{S}_i(t) = v_i(t) \\ \dot{v}_i(t) = \frac{4T_{q,i}(t)i_{0,i}\eta_{m,i}}{m_i r_{w,i}} - \frac{C_D(d_i)A_i\rho}{2m_i}v_i(t)^2 - g\sin\alpha - fg\cos\alpha, i \in N \\ \tau_i \dot{T}_{q,i}(t) + T_{q,i}(t) = u_i(t) \end{cases} \quad (6)$$

where $S_i(t)$, τ_i and $u_i(t)$ represent the position, delay coefficient of driving system, and the expected torque for vehicle i.

In addition to the road slope, the aerodynamics is taken into account when establishing the dynamic model. Reference [34] revealed that a vehicle's air resistance varied with the distance between vehicles. In the existing research, the aerodynamic drag coefficient is usually a constant, which is inconsistent with the aerodynamics characteristics. In this paper, the mathematical formula between aerodynamic drag coefficient and the vehicle spacing is established, given as follows:

$$C_D(d_i) = C_{D,i}^0 (1 - \frac{a_{lsq}}{b_{lsq} + d_i}), \quad (7)$$

where $C_{D,i}^0$ is the nominal air drag coefficient for a single vehicle, a_{lsq} and b_{lsq} are the empirical coefficients [35], and d_i refers to the distance between the ego vehicle and the preceding one. According to Formula (7), the relationship between the air drag coefficient and the spacing is shown in Figure 3. As shown in Figure 3, the air drag coefficient is greatly affected by the distance between vehicles, when the distance is within 50 m.

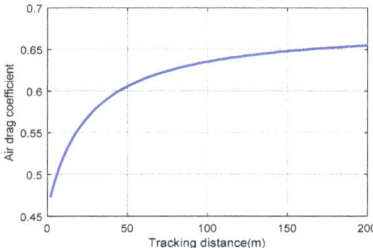

Figure 3. Relationship between air drag coefficient and the spacing.

Equations (6) and (7) form the dynamic model of the heterogeneous platoon, which possesses advantages as follows:

(1) Different properties of each vehicle is presented, such as, η_m, i_0, r_w, and other parameters of each vehicle, can be different.

(2) Road slope and aerodynamics are considered, and the mathematical relationship between air resistance and vehicle spacing is taken into account as well.

3. Cooperative Multi-Objective Control Strategy Based on the DNMPC Method

In this section, a cooperative multi-objective control strategy of heterogeneous platoons based on DNMPC method is presented. DNMPC is the improvement based on MPC, whose important advantage is that multi-objective collaboration can be achieved. Further considering dynamic differences in heterogeneous platoons, the DNMPC method is presented based on MPC. DNMPC controllers are designed for the leader and the followers, respectively and cooperatively.

First, a sub-objective function is designed for each performance. Then, multi-objective function and constraints are established. Finally, for the entire control system of the heterogeneous platoon, stability analysis is conducted based on Lyapunov theory.

3.1. Multi-Objective DNMPC Controller of the Leader

3.1.1. Sub-Objective Function for Energy Saving

The energy-saving objective function $J_1(k|t)$ is expressed as follows:

$$J_1(k|t) = ||W_1 P_1(k|t) \cdot \Delta t||_2, \tag{8}$$

where W_1 represents the weight coefficient of the energy consumption for the leader, and Δt is a time step. $P_1(k|t)$ represents the motor power, and the energy consumption during the predicted time domain is calculated by accumulating the energy power of the motor for N_p time steps.

The motor power of one vehicle i, that is $P_i(k|t)$, can be calculated separately according to the braking and driving conditions, given by Equation (9). $T_{q,i}$, $r_{w,i}$, $i_{g,i}$, η_d, η_b denote the motor torque, rolling radius of the wheel, transmission ratio, driving efficiency and braking efficiency of the motor for vehicle i.

$$P_i(k|t) = \begin{cases} \frac{4T_{q,i}(k|t)v_i(k|t)i_{g,i}}{r_{w,i}\eta_d}, & T_{q,i}(k|t) \geq 0 \\ \frac{4T_{q,i}(k|t)v_i(k|t)i_{g,i}}{r_{w,i}}\eta_b, & T_{q,i}(k|t) < 0 \end{cases} \tag{9}$$

3.1.2. Sub-Objective Function for Stability and Passenger Comfort

For the leading vehicle, its speed should keep as constant as possible in order to ensure the platoon stability and passenger comfort. Thus the stability and passenger comfort objective function $J_2(k|t)$ is expressed as follows:

$$J_2(k|t) = ||R_1(u_1^p(k|t) - u_0(v_1^p(k|t)))||_2, \tag{10}$$

where R_1 represents the weight coefficient, $u_1^p(k|t)$ represents the expected torque of the leading vehicle, and $u_0(v_1^p(k|t))$ is the torque when the vehicle is driving at a constant speed, which is given as Equation (11). In order to improve comfort, the rate of torque change should be kept as low as possible.

$$u_0(v_i^p(N_p|t)) = \frac{r_{w,i}}{4i_{0,i}\eta_{m,i}}(\tfrac{1}{2}C_{D,i}A_i\rho v_i^p(N_p|t)^2 + m_i g f \cos\alpha + m_i g \sin\alpha), i = 1,\ldots,N \tag{11}$$

3.1.3. Multi-Objective Function and Constraints of the Leader

Considering stability, passenger comfort and energy saving targets, the objective function and constraint for the leader's DNMPC controller is designed, shown as follows:

$$\begin{aligned}
\min J^1(t) &= \sum_{k=0}^{N_p-1}(J_1(k|t) + J_2(k|t)) \\
s.t. \quad & v_{\min} \le v_1^p(k|t) \le v_{\max} \\
& T_{\min} \le u_1^*(k|t) \le T_{\max} \\
& v_1^p(N_p|t) = v_{eco} \\
& T_{q,1}^p(N_p|t) = u_0(v_1^p(N_p|t))
\end{aligned} \tag{12}$$

where $J^1(t)$ represents the comprehensive objective function for the leading vehicle, N_p is the quantity of time steps during a predictive time domain, $v_{\min}$ is the minimum speed for a vehicle on the highway, $v_{\max}$ is the maximum speed, $T_{\min}$ is the minimum torque for the motor, $T_{\max}$ is the maximum torque, v_{eco} is the vehicle's economic speed set by the experience, and $u_1^*(k|t)$ is the optimal control sequence to be solved.

3.2. Multi-Objective DNMPC Controller of the Followers

3.2.1. Sub-Objective Function for Vehicle Tracking Performance

The vehicle tracking performance of the followers represents the driving safety of a platoon, and, meanwhile, has a significant impact on the platoon's stability. In this study, according to the selected PFL communication topology, the tracking performance is described by the tracking error between the ego vehicle and the leader, and then between the ego vehicle and the preceding one.

As shown in Figure 1, y_i refers to the state information of vehicle i. The real state of the ego vehicle i is expressed as Equation (13). The desired state of vehicle i is calculated according to the state of the leader, expressed by Equation (14). The desired state of vehicle i calculated according to the preceding vehicle $i-1$ is expressed as Equation (15).

$$y_i^p = [S_i^p \quad v_i^p \quad T_{q,i}^p]^T \tag{13}$$

$$y_{i,des} = [S_1^a - (i-1)d \quad v_1^a \quad T_{q,1}^a]^T \tag{14}$$

$$y_{i,i-1,des} = [S_{i-1}^a - d \quad v_{i-1}^a \quad T_{q,i-1}^a]^T \tag{15}$$

As shown in Equations (13)–(15), the vehicle state set is composed of the position S, the speed v, and the torque T_q. Superscript p denotes that this state is obtained by in-vehicle sensors, and a denotes that the state is obtained by V2V communication. The state may vary due to the communication delay. d denotes the desired spacing between vehicles. $y_{i,des}$ and $y_{i,i-1,des}$ represent the desired state set of vehicle i calculated according to the leader, and the preceding vehicle, respectively.

Then, the tracking objective function for vehicle i is expressed as Equation (16), where Q_i and G_i are the weight coefficients.

$$J_{1,i}(k|t) = \left\|Q_i(y_{i,des}(k|t) - y_i^p(k|t))\right\|_2 \\ + \left\|G_i(y_{i,i-1,des}(k|t) - y_i^p(k|t))\right\|_2 \quad (16)$$

3.2.2. Sub-Objective Function for Energy Saving

Similar to the energy-saving sub-objective function for the leader, that for the following vehicle i is expressed as follows:

$$J_{2,i}(k|t) = \|W_i P_i(k|t) \cdot \Delta t\|_2, \quad (17)$$

where W_i represents the weight coefficient. The calculation method of the vehicle's energy consumption is the same as that of the leader, described as Equation (9).

3.2.3. Sub-Objective Function for Passenger Comfort

Similar to the passenger comfort sub-objective function for the leader, that for the following vehicle i is expressed as follows:

$$J_{3,i}(k|t) = \|R_i(u_i^p(k|t) - u_0(v_i^p(k|t)))\|_2, \quad (18)$$

where R_i, $u_i^p(k|t)$, and $u_0(v_i^p(k|t))$ represent the weight coefficient, the expected torque of vehicle i, and the torque when the vehicle is driving at a constant speed, respectively. The calculation of $u_0(v_i^p(k|t))$ is the same as that of the leader, expressed as Equation (11).

3.2.4. Sub-Objective Function for Communication Stability

In order to further improve the stability performance of the platoon, the accuracy of information transmission should be ensured. For this, the communication stability sub-objective function is designed, given as follows:

$$J_{4,i}(k|t) = \left\|F_i((y_i^p(k|t) - y_i^a(k|t)))\right\|_2, \quad (19)$$

where F_i is the weight coefficient, $y_i^p(k|t)$ is the expected state set of vehicle i, and $y_i^a(k|t)$ is the state set sent to other vehicles of the platoon by V2V communication.

3.2.5. Multi-Objective Function and Constraints of the Followers

Taking all these targets into consideration at the same time, the objective function and constraints for the follower's DNMPC controller is designed, shown as follows:

$$\min J^i(t) = \sum_{k=0}^{N_p-1} (J_{1,i}(k|t) + J_{2,i}(k|t) + J_{3,i}(k|t) + J_{4,i}(k|t)) \\ s.t. \quad v_{\min} \leq v_i^p(k|t) \leq v_{\max} \\ T_{\min} \leq u_i^*(k|t) \leq T_{\max} \\ v_i^p(N_p|t) = v_1^p(N_p|t) \\ S_i^p(N_p|t) = S_1^p(N_p|t) - (i-1)d \\ T_{q,i}^p(N_p|t) = u_0(v_i^p(N_p|t)) \quad (20)$$

where $J^i(t)$ represents the objective function for the following vehicle i ($i = 2, \ldots, n$). The terminal constraints are designed to ensure that the vehicle state could be the desired one calculated according to the state of the leader.

3.3. Stability Analysis Based on Lyapunov Theory

The stability of the proposed control system is analyzed based on the Lyapunov theory. The control system can be expressed as follows:

$$x(t) = f(x(t), u^*(t)). \tag{21}$$

Assume that $x = 0$ is a balance point. Based on the framework of Lyapunov theory, the stability is defined as follows:

Definition 1. *For any $\epsilon > 0$, there exists $\delta(\epsilon) > 0$, satisfying $||x(0)|| < \delta(\epsilon) \Rightarrow ||x(t)|| < \epsilon, \forall t \geq 0$. It is controllable and stable near the initial point $x = 0$.*

Definition 2. *If the closed loop system is stable at the balance point $x = 0$, and there exists δ that satisfies $||x(0)|| < \delta \Rightarrow \lim_{t \to \infty} x(t) \to 0$, the closed loop system is asymptotically stable nearby the balance point.*

At random moment t, the comprehensive multi-objective function for the vehicle i's controller is shown as follows:

$$J^*_{i,\Sigma}(t) = \sum_{i=1}^{N} J^*_i(x_i(t), u^*_i(\cdot|t)) \tag{22}$$

where i represents the number of the vehicle, and N represents the quantity of the vehicles in the platoon. At the moment t, the cost function for vehicle i is given as follows:

$$J^*_{i,\Sigma}(x(t)) = \sum_{k=1}^{N_p} \begin{array}{l} L_i(x^*_i(k|t), u^*_i(k|t), x^a_i(k|t), x^a_j(k|t), x^a_1(k|t)) \\ + \left|\left| Q_i(y_{i,des}(k|t) - y^p_i(k|t)) \right|\right|_2 \\ + \left|\left| G_i(y_{i,i-1,des}(k|t) - y^p_i(k|t)) \right|\right|_2 \\ + \left|\left| W_i P_i(k|t) \cdot \Delta t \right|\right|_2 + \left|\left| R_i(u_i{}^p(k|t) - u_0(v^p_i(k|t))) \right|\right|_2 \\ + \left|\left| F_i((y^p_i(k|t) - y^a_i(k|t))) \right|\right|_2 \end{array} \tag{23}$$

At the moment $t + 1$, the value to be optimized is given as follows:

$$\begin{array}{l} J^*_{i,\Sigma}(t+1) \leq \\ \quad L_i(x^*_i(\cdot|t+1), u^*_i(\cdot|t+1), x^a_i(\cdot|t+1), x^a_j(\cdot|t+1), x^a_1(\cdot|t+1)) \\ = \sum_{k=0}^{N_p-1} \begin{array}{l} l_i(x^*_i(k|t+1), u^*_i(k|t+1), \\ x^a_i(k|t+1), x^a_j(k|t+1), x^a_1(k|t+1)) \end{array} \end{array} \tag{24}$$

then,

$$J_{i,\Sigma}^*(t+1) - J_{i,\Sigma}^*(t) \leq$$
$$-\sum_{k=0}^{N_p-1} L_i(x_i^*(k|t), u_i^*(k|t), x_i^a(k|t), x_j^a(k|t), x_1^a(k|t))$$
$$+\sum_{k=1}^{N_p-1} L_i(x_i^*(k|t), u_i^*(k|t), x_i^*(k|t), x_j^*(k|t), x_1^*(k|t)) \quad (25)$$
$$= -l_i(x_i^*(0|t), u_i^*(0|t), x_i^a(1|t), x_j^a(1|t), x_1^a(1|t))$$
$$+\sum_{k=1}^{N_p-1} \{[l_i(x_i^*(k|t), u_i^*(k|t), x_i^*(k|t), x_j^*(k|t), x_1^*(k|t)]$$
$$-l_i(x_i^*(k|t), u_i^*(k|t), x_i^a(k|t), x_j^a(k|t), x_1^a(k|t))\}$$

Analyzing Equation (25), the formula could be obtained, as follows:

$$l_i(x_i^*(k|t), u_i^*(k|t), x_i^*(k|t), x_j^*(k|t), x_1^*(k|t))$$
$$-l_i(x_i^*(k|t), u_i^*(k|t), x_i^a(k|t), x_j^a(k|t), x_1^a(k|t)) \quad (26)$$
$$= \sum_{i=1}^{N} \begin{Bmatrix} ||G_i(y_j^*(k|t) - y_i^*(k|t))||_2 - ||G_i(y_j^a(k|t) - y_i^*(k|t))||_2 \\ -||F_i(y_i^*(k|t) - y_i^a(k|t))||_2 \end{Bmatrix}$$

According to the norm triangle inequality, Equation (26) could be expressed as follows:

$$\sum_{i=1}^{N} \begin{Bmatrix} ||G_i(y_j^*(k|t) - y_i^*(k|t))||_2 - ||G_i(y_j^a(k|t) - y_i^*(k|t))||_2 \\ -||F_i(y_i^*(k|t) - y_i^a(k|t))||_2 \end{Bmatrix} \quad (27)$$
$$\leq \sum_{i=1}^{N} ||G_i(y_j^*(k|t) - y_j^a(k|t))||_2 - ||F_i(y_i^*(k|t) - y_i^a(k|t))||_2$$

One single step iteration of each controller is given as follows:

$$J_\Sigma^*(x(t+1)) - J_\Sigma^*(x(t))$$
$$\leq -\sum_{i=1}^{N} L_i(x_i^*(1|t), u_i^*(0|t), x_i^a(1|t), x_j^a(1|t), x_1^a(1|t)) + \sum_{k=1}^{N_p-1} \varepsilon_\Sigma(k) \quad (28)$$

where,

$$\varepsilon_\Sigma(k) = \sum_{i=1}^{N} [\sum_j ||G_i(y_j(k|t) - y_i^p(k|t))||_2 - ||F_i(y_i^p(k|t) - y_i^a(k|t))||_2] \quad (29)$$

Only if $\sum_{k=1}^{N_p-1} \varepsilon_\Sigma(k) \leq 0$ can the stability of the platoons' control system can be achieved. In the formula, G_i and F_i are the weight coefficients, set by the designers. Therefore, as long as artificially set coefficients satisfy $\varepsilon_\Sigma(k) \leq 0$, the asymptotic stability of the platoon's control system can be guaranteed based on the Lyapunov theory.

4. NSGA-II-Based Weight Coefficient Optimization

The empirical method is commonly utilized to determine the weight coefficient in the existing research. In this study, the NSGA-II-based weight coefficient optimization method is presented, to obtain the optimal weight coefficient set for each following vehicle. This proposed method takes into account the differences in dynamic characteristics between vehicles, and is able to effectively improve the multi-objective integrated performance of the heterogeneous platoon.

For each follower of a heterogeneous platoon, the control block diagram with the NSGA-II-based weight coefficient optimization method is shown in Figure 4.

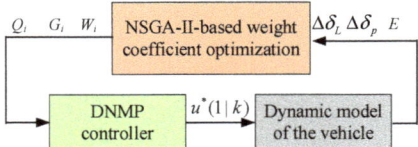

Figure 4. Control block diagram with the NSGA-II-based weight coefficient optimization method.

As shown in Figure 4, the weight coefficient optimization calculation is executed offline. After one complete control cycle, this optimization calculation is performed. $\Delta\delta_L$ refers to the root mean square of the tracking error between the ego vehicle and the leading vehicle, $\Delta\delta_p$ refers to the root mean square of the tracking error with the preceding vehicle, and E represents the energy consumption of the ego vehicle. Q_i, G_i, and W_i are weight coefficients of the multi-objective function to be optimized. For the weight coefficient optimization module, the objective function is designed as follows:

$$\min L = [\Delta\delta_L(X) \quad \Delta\delta_P(X) \quad E(X)], \tag{30}$$

where X represents the state variable set at any moment through the control cycle.

The optimization solution for the weight coefficients is carried out based on the function shown as Equation (30). The optimization solution process of genetic algorithm (GA) includes selection, crossover and mutation. On the basis of classic GA, the NSGA-II algorithm introduces an elite strategy to further expand the sampling space, which is able to prevent the loss of the optimal solution during the update of the population. The specific solution can be solved simply by using MATLAB, and therefore the solution process will not be described.

5. Simulation and Analysis

In order to verify the effectiveness of the proposed method, a simulation platform is developed, and comparative experiments are carried out. The approach for comparison is the classic cruise control method. Comparison simulation tests have been conducted on the road with designed slope curve, and the actual highway with varying slopes, separately. Moreover, a real-road experiment is conducted to verify the effectiveness and real-time computational performance in real applications.

5.1. Simulation Platform and Simulation Setting

Based on Matlab/Simulink, the dynamic model, the DNMPC controller for each vehicle, the cooperative multi-objective control algorithm, and the off-line weight coefficient optimization algorithm were built for a heterogeneous platoon, which consisted of five trucks. Parameters of the driving road and vehicles were set based on PreScan.

The parameters of the five trucks were designed according to the actual vehicle's parameters of the FAW Jiefang vehicles. Two types of vehicles with different dynamic characteristics were chosen to form the platoon, as shown in Table 2.

Table 2. Dynamic parameters of two types of vehicles.

No.	Mass	Rolling Radius of the Wheel	Frontal Area of the Vehicle
1	3900 kg	0.364 m	2.4 m^2
2	6100 kg	0.497 m	4.8 m^2

For the simulation tests on the road with designed slope curve and tests on the actual highway with varying slopes, the simulation settings are exactly the same. The initial speed of each vehicle is 22 m/s, and the desired speed is 23.5 m/s, which is the average economic-speed on the highway for this platoon. The initial spacing is just the desired one, which is 15 m.

In order to purely verify the effectiveness of the multi-objective control method, in the comparative tests on the two types of roads, the weight coefficients are set as empirical values, according to the traditional way. In this case, the comparison results show completely the differences between these two control methods, without the impact of weight coefficient optimization. Then, the effectiveness of the NSGA-II-based weight coefficient optimization algorithm is verified and comparative test is described in detail in Section 5.2.3.

5.2. Simulation Result and Discussion

5.2.1. Test on the Road with Designed Slope Curve

The comparative simulation test is carried out on the road with designed slope curve for the heterogeneous platoon with five trucks. The road is designed as shown in Figure 5. According to the standard of the highway, the slope range is set as $(-0.066, 0.066)$ rad.

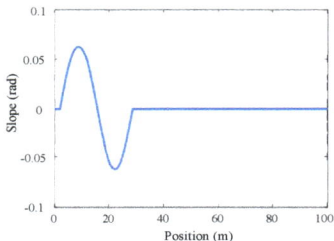

Figure 5. Slope curve of the designed road.

As shown in Table 2, there are two types of vehicles with different masses in the platoon. The performance of the platoon may vary greatly with different mass distributions. In this paper, three platoons with different mass distributions have been tested separately, and their vehicle tracking and energy saving performances have been analyzed, as shown in Table 3.

Table 3. Tracking and energy-saving performances of platoons with different mass distributions.

Mass Distribution	Performances	Speed Tracking Error (m/s)	Distance Tracking Error (m)	Energy Consuming (kW·h)
6100, 6100, 6100, 3900, 3900		0.1087	0.3164	2.1364
3900, 3900, 6100, 6100, 6100		0.1136	0.3348	2.0421
6100, 3900, 6100, 3900, 6100		0.1246	0.3442	2.0267
3900, 3900, 3900, 3900, 3900		0.0419	0.0816	1.5269

It is obvious from the test results that the control performance of homogeneous platoon is better than that of heterogeneous platoon. It also confirms a consensus that heterogeneity of vehicle dynamics makes platooning control more difficult.

Different types of heterogeneous platoons are tested, as shown in Table 3. Speed tracking error and distance tracking error are typical indicators for tracking/safety performance of platooning control, representing the deviation between actual speed/spacing and the expected one. For platoon 3, in which two types of vehicles are arranged in alternating order, every two adjacent vehicles affect each other, so vehicle tracking performance of this platoon is the worst. With the alternating order, the vehicle with a larger frontal area could withstand wind resistance for the following vehicle, and energy consuming of the following one could be effectively reduced. Therefore, energy saving performance of platoon 3 is the best, as shown in Table 3.

The mass distribution of platoon 1 is the most popular, so platoon 1 is selected in this paper to make the comparative analysis between the proposed DNMPC-based multi-objective control method and the classic cruise control method. For the test on the road with designed slope curve, vehicle speed, speed tracking error, distance tracking error, and energy consumption are shown in Figure 6.

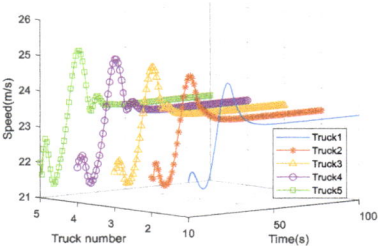

(**a**) Speed curve of each vehicle with the proposed method

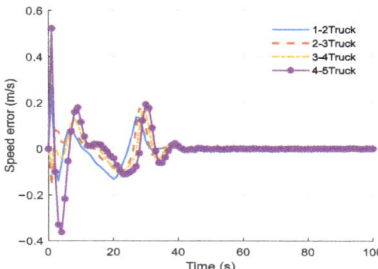

(**b**) Speed tracking error with the proposed method

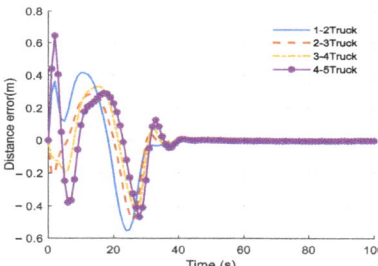

(**c**) Distance tracking error with the proposed method

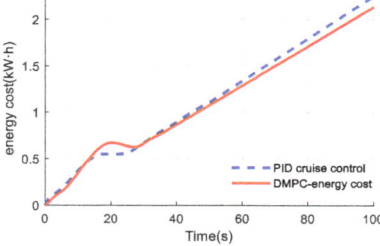

(**d**) Comparison result of energy consumption

Figure 6. Test results of the heterogeneous platoon driving on the designed road.

According to Figure 6, several points could be drawn, shown as follows.

(1) As shown in Figure 6b, when driving on a sloped road, the proposed DNMPC-based cooperative multi-objective control method can ensure that the tracking error fluctuates in a small range, and the platoon stability could be quickly achieved.

(2) As shown in Figure 6a, the vehicles accelerate a little earlier before going uphill, in order to avoid sudden acceleration when reaching the uphill. During the climbing process, vehicles reduce the speed to ensure sufficient torque. During the downhill process, motors of vehicles do not generate torque, and in the meanwhile, the energy is recovered. As the red line shows in Figure 6d, the energy consumption of the platoon decreases during downhill due to the energy recovery. Thus, it can be seen that the proposed DNMPC-based cooperative multi-objective control method takes into account the impact of road slope on the energy consumption, and calculates an optimized speed curve according to the road slope.

(3) The detailed comparison results of the simulation test on the designed road are shown in Table 4. As can be observed from Table 4, compared with the classic cruise control method, the proposed DNMPC-based multi-objective control method can effectively reduce energy consumption by 5.14%, while maintaining a good vehicle tracking performance.

Table 4. Comparison results of the heterogeneous platoon on the designed road with different control methods.

Performances \ Control Method	The Proposed DNMPC-Based Multi-Objective Control Method	The Cruise Control Method
Average speed tracking error (m/s)	0.1087	0.5103
Average distance tracking error (m)	0.3164	0.3157
Total energy consumption (kW·h)	2.1364	2.2523

5.2.2. Test on the Actual Highway with Varying Slopes

In order to further verify the effectiveness of the proposed multi-objective control method, an actual highway is chosen, which is a road section of the highway from Beijing to Tianjin. The slope of the chosen road section is shown as Figure 7, and simulation tests haven been carried out. In order to clearly show the impact of road slope on the test results, a space-time conversion is made and therefore the horizontal axis in Figure 7 is time.

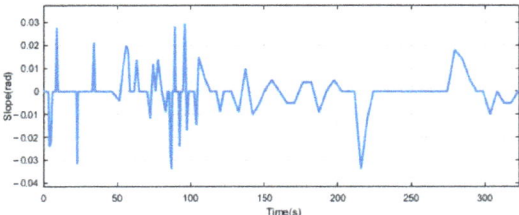

Figure 7. Road slope of the chosen highway section.

Still taking platoon 1 in Table 3 as an example, analyze the platoon's vehicle tracking performance and the energy saving performance, as shown in Figure 8.

The platoon adjusted its speed from 22 m/s to the economic speed 23.5 m/s during the initial 10 s, and then drove at a constant speed of 23.5 m/s. As shown in Figure 8a,b, when driving at a constant speed, both the speed tracking error and distance tracking error can be kept within a quite small range. Even when the platoon adjusted its speed, the proposed DNMPC-based cooperative multi-objective control method could ensure that the tracking error fluctuated in a small range, and the platoon stability could be quickly achieved.

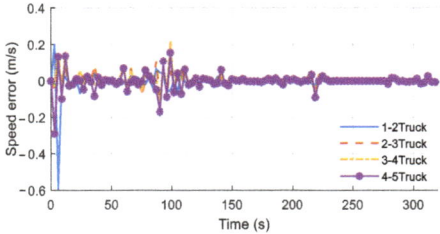

(**a**) Speed tracking error with the proposed method

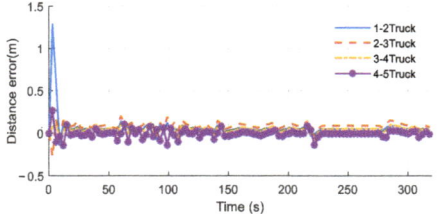

(**b**) Distance tracking error with the proposed method

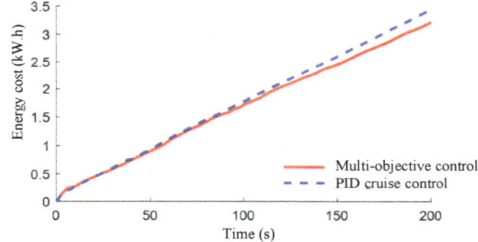

(**c**) Comparison result of energy consumption

Figure 8. Test results of the heterogeneous platoon driving on the actual highway with varying slopes.

The detailed comparison of the results of the simulation test on the actual highway with varying slopes are shown in Table 5. As shown in Figure 8c and Table 5, compared with the cruise control method, the proposed multi-objective control method shows better energy saving performance and vehicle tracking performance. The energy consumption can be saved by 5.66%, while reducing vehicle tracking error.

Table 5. Comparison of the results of the heterogeneous platoon on the actual sloped road with different control method.

Performances	The Proposed DNMPC-Based Multi-Objective Control Method	The Cruise Control Method
Average speed tracking error (m/s)	0.1203	0.2764
Average distance tracking error (m)	0.2810	0.2908
Total energy consumption (kW·h)	3.2785	3.4752

5.2.3. Test of NSGA-II-Based Weight Coefficient Optimization Method

In order to verify the effectiveness of the proposed weight coefficient optimization method, the comparative simulation test is carried out.

According to reference [23], the weight coefficients are designed with the empirical method, as shown in Table 6. In addition, the optimal weight coefficients are calculated for each follower with the proposed NSGA-II-based optimization method, as described in

Section 4. With different weight coefficients, the performances of the heterogeneous platoon based on the multi-objective control method are shown in Figure 9. The detailed comparison results are shown in Table 7. As shown in Figure 9 and Table 7, with the proposed NSGA-II-based weight coefficient optimization method, the vehicle tracking performance and energy saving performance of the platoon can be improved simultaneously.

Table 6. Weight coefficients with the empirical method and the optimization method.

No.	Weight Coefficients with the Empirical Method	Weight Coefficients with the Optimization Method
1	$Q_1 = 5, G_1 = 5, W_1 = 5$	/
2	$Q_2 = 5, G_2 = 5, W_2 = 5$	$Q_2 = 3.2102, G_2 = 1.8589, W_2 = 4.3012$
3	$Q_3 = 5, G_3 = 5, W_3 = 5$	$Q_3 = 0.4688, G_3 = 5.8102, W_3 = 1.7082$
4	$Q_4 = 5, G_4 = 5, W_4 = 5$	$Q_4 = 0.1540, G_4 = 3.7788, W_4 = 1.2393$
5	$Q_5 = 5, G_5 = 5, W_5 = 5$	$Q_5 = 0.5830, G_5 = 1.8529, W_5 = 22.2115$

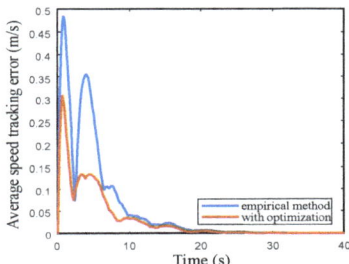

(**a**) Average speed tracking error of the platoon

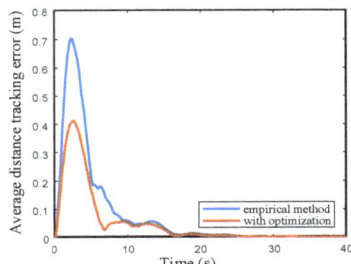

(**b**) Average distance tracking error of the platoon

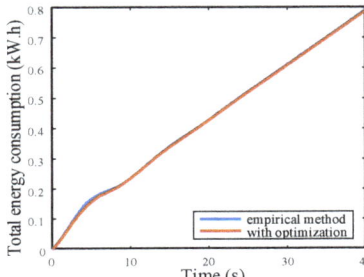

(**c**) Total energy consumption of the platoon

Figure 9. Test results of the heterogeneous platoon with different weight coefficients.

Table 7. Comparison results of the heterogeneous platoon with different weight coefficients.

Performances	The Typical Empirical Method	The Proposed Optimization Method	Percentage of the Improvement
Average speed tracking error (m/s)	0.2272	0.1234	45.7%
Average distance tracking error (m)	0.3226	0.1996	38.1%
Total energy consumption (kW·h)	0.7903	0.7884	0.24%

5.3. Real Road Experiment Based on Micro-Vehicle Platoon

In order to verify the effectiveness and real-time performance of the proposed control system, a real-road experiment is conducted based on three micro-vehicles, which are manufactured by JROBOT, as shown in Figure 10. Vehicle 1 is a wheeled one, WARTHOG□, which acts as the leader in the platoon, and vehicle 2 and 3, Komodo, are the followers.

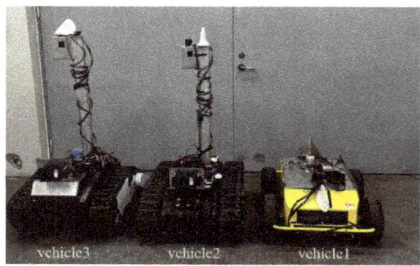

Figure 10. Three micro-vehicles for the experiment.

This experiment aims to verify the real-time computational performance of the proposed control system, and therefore an ordinary vehicle control unit (VCU) is chosen as the core controller, as shown in Figure 11a. The test field consists of a straight section and curved section, and the snapshot of road experiment is shown in Figure 11b.

(**a**) VCU   (**b**) Snapshot of the road experiment

Figure 11. Photos of the real-road experiment.

The speed trajectories of three vehicles, and the tracking error of two followers, are shown in Figure 12. The blue line represents vehicle 1, the leader, the orange dashed line for vehicle 2, and the green dotted line for vehicle 3. The platoon entered the curved section at about 28 s, so the speed of vehicle 1 decreased suddenly (blue line of Figure 12a), and speed tracking error of two followers increased (Figure 12b) but soon was regulated to within 0.5 m/s. During the whole process, the platoon was able to drive safely and stably, speed tracking error was controlled within ±0.8 m/s, and distance tracking error was controlled within ±1 m.

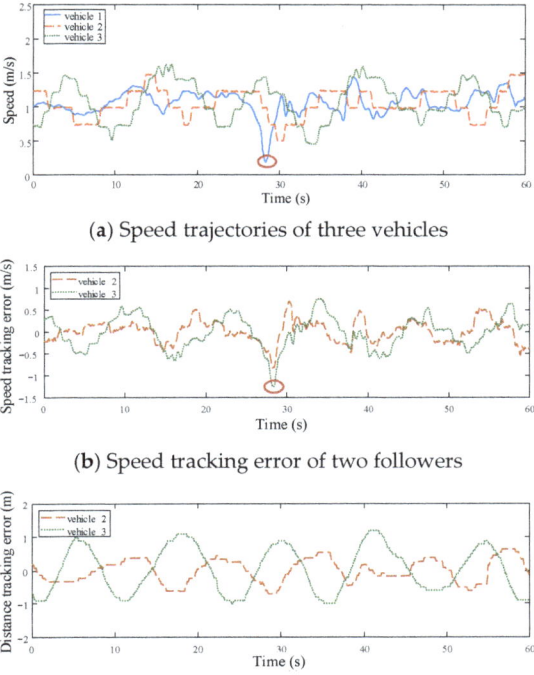

(a) Speed trajectories of three vehicles

(b) Speed tracking error of two followers

(c) Distance tracking error of two followers

Figure 12. Results of the real-road experiment.

The experiment verifies that the proposed control method can work on the VCUs of micro-vehicles, and ensure the stability of the platoon. Thus, the real-time computational requirements can be satisfied in real applications.

6. Conclusions

Aiming to improve the overall performance of a heterogeneous platoon on the highway, this paper presents a cooperative multi-objective control system, which takes four major objectives into consideration, as well as the road slope. The following conclusions can be drawn:

(1) A two-layer architecture of the multi-objective control system for heterogeneous platoons is presented. For the dynamic layer, a nonlinear model of a heterogeneous platoon is established, depicting various dynamic characteristics of vehicles and the influence of road slope and wind resistance. For the control layer, rich information is provided to distributed controllers for the calculation of the optimal control variables. The proposed architecture is the basic of multi-objective control of heterogeneous platoons.

(2) A cooperative multi-objective control strategy based on the DNMPC method is proposed, and controllers for the leader and followers are designed cooperatively. Comprehensive objective functions with multiple targets are built up, achieving integrated optimization of safety, stability, energy saving, and passenger comfort. Through comparative simulation tests on the highway with slopes, it is verified that, compared with the classic cruise control method of vehicle platoons, the proposed approach can improve the fuel economy by more than 5% and reduce tracking error simultaneously, on the premise of ensuring safety and passenger comfort.

(3) The NSGA-II-based weight coefficient optimization method is presented, to obtain the optimal weight coefficient set for each vehicle. Through comparative simulation tests,

it is shown that, compared with the commonly used empirical method, multi-objective collaborative optimization capability of the heterogeneous platoon can be further improved.

(4) In the simulation tests, three types of heterogeneous platoons with different structural parameters have been tested, and the performances have been analyzed.

(5) The proposed control system was developed and equipped on three micro-vehicles. Real-road experiments show that the proposed control system can effectively work, and real-time computational requirements can be satisfied in real applications.

The quality of information transmission between controllers will greatly affect the performances of platooning control. There is an assumption in this study, which is that a V2V (vehicle-vehicle) communication network is ideal. We will further study the platooning control method with non-ideal communication in the future.

Author Contributions: Conceptualization, W.K. and Y.L.; methodology, Y.L.; software, X.W.; validation, W.K., X.W. and Y.L.; writing—original draft preparation, W.K. and T.C.; writing—review and editing, F.J. All authors have read and agreed to the published version of the manuscript.

Funding: This research was funded by National Natural Science Foundation of China grant number [52002209], and the State Key Laboratory of Automotive Safety and Energy grant number [KFY2210]. And the APC was funded by [KFY2210].

Institutional Review Board Statement: Not applicable.

Informed Consent Statement: Not applicable.

Data Availability Statement: Not applicable.

Conflicts of Interest: The authors declare no conflict of interest.

References

1. Shladover, S.E.; Desoer, C.A.; Hedrick, J.K.; Tomizuka, M.; Walrand, J.; Zhang, W.-B.; McMahon, D.H.; Peng, H.; Sheikholeslam, S.; McKeown, N. Automated vehicle control developments in the PATH program. *IEEE Trans. Veh. Technol.* **1991**, *40*, 114–130. [CrossRef]
2. Shladover, S.E. PATH at 20-history and major milestones. *IEEE Trans. Intell. Transp. Syst.* **2007**, *8*, 584–592. [CrossRef]
3. Liu, Y.; Yao, D.; Li, H.; Lu, R. Distributed cooperative compound tracking control for a platoon of vehicles with adaptive NN. *IEEE Trans. Cybern.* **2022**, *52*, 7039–7048. [CrossRef]
4. Guo, G.; Dandan, L. Adaptive sliding mode control of vehicular platoons with prescribed tracking performance. *IEEE Trans. Veh. Technol.* **2019**, *68*, 7511–7520. [CrossRef]
5. Guo, G.; Wang, Q. Fuel-efficient en route speed planning and tracking control of truck platoons. *IEEE Trans. Intell. Transp. Syst.* **2019**, *20*, 1–13. [CrossRef]
6. Peter, A.C. Stable control of vehicle convoys for safety and comfort. *IEEE Trans. Autom. Control* **2007**, *52*, 526–531.
7. Zuo, L.; Wang, P.; Yan, M.; Zhu, X. Platoon tracking control with road-friction based spacing policy for nonlinear vehicles. *IEEE Trans. Intell. Transp. Syst.* **2022**, *23*, 20810–20819. [CrossRef]
8. Besselink, B.; Johansson, K.H. String Stability and a Delay-Based Spacing Policy for Vehicle Platoons Subject to Disturbances. *IEEE Trans. Autom. Control* **2017**, *62*, 4376–4391. [CrossRef]
9. Zheng, Y.; Li, S.E.; Li, K.; Wang, L.-Y. Stability Margin Improvement of Vehicular Platoon Considering Undirected Topology and Asymmetric Control. *IEEE Trans. Control Syst. Technol.* **2016**, *24*, 1253–1265. [CrossRef]
10. Zheng, Y.; Li, S.E.; Wang, J.; Cao, D.; Li, K. Stability and Scalability of Homogeneous Vehicular Platoon: Study on the Influence of Information Flow Topologies. *IEEE Trans. Intell. Transp. Syst.* **2016**, *17*, 14–26. [CrossRef]
11. Alam, A.A.; Gattami, A.; Johansson, K.H. An experimental study on the fuel reduction potential of heavy duty vehicle platooning. In Proceedings of the 13th International IEEE Conference on Intelligent Transportation Systems, Madeira, Portugal, 19–22 September 2010; pp. 306–311.
12. Dey, K.C.; Yan, L.; Wang, X.; Wang, Y.; Shen, H.; Chowdhury, M.; Yu, L.; Qiu, C.; Soundararaj, V. A Review of Communication, Driver Characteristics, and Controls Aspects of Cooperative Adaptive Cruise Control (CACC). *IEEE Trans. Intell. Transp. Syst.* **2016**, *17*, 491–509. [CrossRef]
13. Chiedu, N.M.; Keyvan, H.Z. Energy-based analysis of string stability in vehicle platoons. *IEEE Trans. Veh. Technol.* **2022**, *71*, 5915–5929.
14. Rakkesh, S.T.; Weerasinghe, A.R.; Ranasinghe, R.A.C. An intelligent highway traffic model using cooperative vehicle platooning techniques. In Proceedings of the Moratuwa Engineering Research Conference (MERCon), Moratuwa, Sri Lanka, 29–31 May 2017; pp. 170–175.
15. Zegers, J.C.; Semsar-Kazerooni, E.; Fusco, M.; Ploeg, J. A multi-layer control approach to truck platooning: Platoon cohesion subject to dynamical limitations. In Proceedings of the IEEE International Conference on Models and Technologies for Intelligent Transportation Systems (MT-ITS), Naples, Italy, 26–28 June 2017; pp. 128–133.

16. Chehardoli, H.; Ghasemi, A. Adaptive Centralized/Decentralized Control and Identification of 1-D Heterogeneous Vehicular Platoons Based on Constant Time Headway Policy. *IEEE Trans. Intell. Transp. Syst.* **2018**, *19*, 3376–3386. [CrossRef]
17. He, Z.C.; Kang, H.; Li, E.; Zhou, E.L.; Cheng, H.T.; Huang, Y.Y. Coordinated control of heterogeneous vehicle platoon stability and energy-saving control strategies. *Phys. A Stat. Mech. Its Appl.* **2022**, *606*, 128155. [CrossRef]
18. Chehardoli, H.; Homaeinezhad, M.R. Stable control of a heterogeneous platoon of vehicles with switched interaction topology, time-varying communication delay and lag of actuator. *Proc. Inst. Mech. Eng. Part C J. Mech. Eng. Sci.* **2017**, *231*, 4197–4208. [CrossRef]
19. Harfouch, Y.A.; Yuan, S.; Baldi, S. An Adaptive Switched Control Approach to Heterogeneous Platooning with Intervehicle Communication Losses. *IEEE Trans. Control Netw. Syst.* **2018**, *5*, 1434–1444. [CrossRef]
20. Hu, J.; Bhowmick, P.; Arvin, F.; Lanzon, A.; Lennox, B. Cooperative control of heterogeneous connected vehicle platoons: An adaptive leader-following approach. *IEEE Robot. Autom. Lett.* **2020**, *5*, 977–984. [CrossRef]
21. Guo, X.G.; Wang, J.L.; Liao, F.; Teo, R.S.H. Sting stability of heterogeneous leader-following vehicle platoons based on constant spacing policy. In Proceedings of the 2016 IEEE Vehicles Symposium (IV), Gothenburg, Sweden, 19–22 June 2016; pp. 761–766.
22. Xu, L.; Zhuang, W.; Yin, G.; Bian, C.; Wu, H. Modeling and robust control of heterogeneous vehicle platoons on curved roads subject to disturbances and delays. *IEEE Trans. Veh. Technol.* **2019**, *68*, 11551–11564. [CrossRef]
23. Zheng, Y.; Li, S.E.; Li, K.; Borrelli, F.; Hedrick, J.K. Distributed Model Predictive Control for Heterogeneous Vehicle Platoons Under Unidirectional Topologies. *IEEE Trans. Control Syst. Technol.* **2017**, *25*, 899–910. [CrossRef]
24. Li, S.E.; Qin, X.; Zheng, Y.; Wang, J.; Li, K.; Zhang, H. Distributed platoon control under topologies with complex eigenvalues: Stability analysis and controller synthesis. *IEEE Trans. Control Syst. Technol.* **2019**, *27*, 206–220. [CrossRef]
25. Ebrahim, H.M.; Dominy, R.G.; Leung, P.S. Evaluation of vehicle platooning aerodynamics using bluff body wake generators and CFD. In Proceedings of the International Conference for Students on Applied Engineering (ICSAE), Newcastle upon Tyne, UK, 20–21 October 2016; pp. 218–223.
26. Fu, L.; He, B.; Wu, Y.; Hu, X.; Lai, C. The influence of inter-vehicle distance on aerodynamic characteristics of vehicle platoon. *Automot. Eng.* **2007**, *29*, 365–368.
27. Norrby, D. A CFD Study of the Aerodynamic Effects of Platooning Trucks. Master's Thesis, KTH Royal Institute Technology, Stockholm, Sweden, 2014.
28. Caltagirone, L.; Torabi, S.; Wahde, M. Truck Platooning Based on Lead Vehicle Speed Profile Optimization and Artificial Physics. In Proceedings of the IEEE 18th International Conference on Intelligent Transportation Systems, Gran Canaria, Spain, 15–18 September 2015; pp. 394–399.
29. Turri, V.; Besselink, B.; Johansson, K.H. Cooperative look-ahead control for fuel-efficient and safe heavy-duty vehicle platooning. *IEEE Trans. Control Syst. Technol.* **2017**, *25*, 12–28. [CrossRef]
30. Alam, A.; Besselink, B.; Turri, V.; MåRtensson, J.; Johansson, K.H. Heavy-Duty Vehicle Platooning for Sustainable Freight Transportation: A Cooperative Method to Enhance Safety and Efficiency. *IEEE Control Syst. Mag.* **2015**, *35*, 34–56.
31. Zhang, S.; Luo, Y.; Li, K.; Li, V. Real-Time Energy-Efficient Control for Fully Electric Vehicles Based on Explicit Model Predictive Control Method. *IEEE Trans. Veh. Technol.* **2018**, *67*, 4693–4701. [CrossRef]
32. Turri, V.; Besselink, B.; Johansson, K.H. Gear management for fuel-efficient heavy-duty vehicle platooning. In Proceedings of the IEEE 55th Conference on Decision and Control (CDC), Las Vegas, NV, USA, 12–14 December 2016; pp. 1687–1694.
33. Zhai, C.; Liu, Y.; Luo, F. A switched control strategy of heterogeneous vehicle platoon for multiple objectives with state constraints. *IEEE Trans. Intell. Transp. Syst.* **2019**, *20*, 1883–1896. [CrossRef]
34. He, B. Research on Automotive Aerodynamic Characteristics of Platoon. Ph.D. Thesis, Jilin University, Changchun, China, 2009.
35. Hucho, W.-H. Aerodynamics of Road Vehicles. *Annu. Rev. Fluid Mech.* **1993**, *25*, 485–537. [CrossRef]

MDPI
St. Alban-Anlage 66
4052 Basel
Switzerland
www.mdpi.com

Symmetry Editorial Office
E-mail: symmetry@mdpi.com
www.mdpi.com/journal/symmetry

Disclaimer/Publisher's Note: The statements, opinions and data contained in all publications are solely those of the individual author(s) and contributor(s) and not of MDPI and/or the editor(s). MDPI and/or the editor(s) disclaim responsibility for any injury to people or property resulting from any ideas, methods, instructions or products referred to in the content.

www.ingramcontent.com/pod-product-compliance
Lightning Source LLC
LaVergne TN
LVHW070633100526
838202LV00012B/798